Keeping a Fing

Rebecca C. Lubot

Keeping a Finger on the Button

Presidential Continuity and the Nuclear Age

Rebecca C. Lubot
Lubot Strategies
Montclair, NJ, USA

ISBN 978-3-032-02477-0   ISBN 978-3-032-02478-7   (eBook)
https://doi.org/10.1007/978-3-032-02478-7

© The Editor(s) (if applicable) and The Author(s), under exclusive license to Springer Nature Switzerland AG 2025

This work is subject to copyright. All rights are solely and exclusively licensed by the Publisher, whether the whole or part of the material is concerned, specifically the rights of translation, reprinting, reuse of illustrations, recitation, broadcasting, reproduction on microfilms or in any other physical way, and transmission or information storage and retrieval, electronic adaptation, computer software, or by similar or dissimilar methodology now known or hereafter developed.
The use of general descriptive names, registered names, trademarks, service marks, etc. in this publication does not imply, even in the absence of a specific statement, that such names are exempt from the relevant protective laws and regulations and therefore free for general use.
The publisher, the authors and the editors are safe to assume that the advice and information in this book are believed to be true and accurate at the date of publication. Neither the publisher nor the authors or the editors give a warranty, expressed or implied, with respect to the material contained herein or for any errors or omissions that may have been made. The publisher remains neutral with regard to jurisdictional claims in published maps and institutional affiliations.

Cover image: iStock, Romolo Tavani

This Palgrave Macmillan imprint is published by the registered company Springer Nature Switzerland AG
The registered company address is: Gewerbestrasse 11, 6330 Cham, Switzerland

If disposing of this product, please recycle the paper.

While the light in the White House may flicker, it never goes out.
—*Jack Valenti.*[1]

---

[1] Jack Valenti, "The Unforgettable Afternoon," *The New York Times*, November 22, 1998, w17. As quoted in Steven M. Gillon, *The Kennedy Assassination: 24 Hours After Lyndon B. Johnson's Pivotal First Day as President* (New York: Basic Books, 2009), 142.

In memory of Dr. Eric S. Lubot
For Emerson, Harris, and Marisol

Acknowledgments

My dad was my soccer coach when I was a girl. On Saturday mornings when we drove through the mountains in Ringwood, New Jersey, and passed the reservoir to the field where the game would take place, he suggested that I envision myself making a successful play or scoring a goal. When I worked on this book, I envisioned writing my acknowledgments. I am elated to be articulating my gratitude to those who helped me reach this goal.

My Ph.D. dissertation manuscript became the basis for this book. I had the privilege of working with an eminent committee: David Greenberg, Richard McCormick, Jackson Lears, Paul Clemens, and Ross Baker. David read numerous drafts and both David and Dick opened doors for me. Don Ritchie and Katherine Scott allowed me to research the files of the US Senate Historian's office, having hosted David and Ross in the past. But I also reached out to many individuals on my own and always found them accessible and interested in the topic. I contacted historians Steve Gillon and Garrett Graff, the latter of whom allowed me to read the parts of his fascinating *Raven Rock* manuscript having to do with the Twenty-Fifth Amendment prior to its publication. Cultural historians Bob Mann and Allan Winkler gave me encouragement, and I relied on the knowledge I gleaned from their work.

Former Colorado State Senator John Bermingham and I had an interesting conversation about his experiences with nuclear anxiety at the end of WWII when he served in the Pacific. Also from the government sector, several of Senator Birch Bayh's former staff members agreed to talk with me including Bob Keefe, Eve Lubalin, and Darry Sragow. Former Bayh staff member and biographer Bob Blaemire allowed me to view the videos of interviews he conducted. Bob helped connect me to Senator Bayh and his wife, Kitty. Speaking with the architect of the amendment early in the process gave me hope that my hypothesis was correct. As a historian, it was a thrill to talk with the senator—whom I found personable and witty—and to touch a part of history in this way.

Dean Emeritus of Fordham University Law School John Feerick was integral to the amendment's drafting and ratification process as well. I am grateful for his generosity in speaking with me often and allowing me access to his personal files in Larchmont, New York. He invited me to participate in panels on presidential continuity at Fordham University Law School, and the *Fordham Law Review* published my work. Through my panel participation, I connected with Roy Brownell, Joel Goldstein, Rose McDermott, and John Rogan. Rose shared advice, Joel provided suggestions and edits on an earlier version of this manuscript, and Reb provided invaluable comments on my Conclusion.

I am thankful to the librarians, archivists, and administrators that have assisted me during this journey. Tom Eisinger and Alison Trulock at the National Archives and Records Administration in Washington, DC., and Allen Fisher and Liza Talbot at the Lyndon Baines Johnson Library were not only knowledgeable but welcoming. I also am thankful to Karen Abramson and Michael Desmond, archivists of the Robert F. Kennedy papers at the John F. Kennedy Library and Museum; Lori Birrell and Alan Unsworth at the Kenneth B. Keating papers, University of Rochester; Robert Garcia in the Office of Legislative Legal Services at the Colorado State Capitol; Ken Ritchie, law librarian at the New Jersey State Library; Richard Collins at the American Bar Association; and Kate Cruikshank and Sara Marie Stefani, archivists of the Senator Birch Bayh Senatorial Papers at Indiana University. At Rutgers University, I am thankful to the librarians, as well as Dawn Ruskai and Candace Walcott-Shepherd in New Brunswick and Christina Strasburger in Newark.

I am grateful to Rutgers Professors Warren Kimball and Clement Price, Boston University Professors Robert Dallek, Michael Corgan, and Mark Silverstein, and London School of Economics Professor Steven Casey. I would also like to mention teachers that were formative to my early learning: Mrs. Verwer, Mrs. Hanvey, Mr. Reiner, Mr. Ruzyam, and Mrs. Kohmuench. My most recent teacher, my writing coach, El Glasberg, improved my writing immeasurably. My editor, Christian Winting, knowledgeably instructed me throughout the publication process.

Last but not least, I would like to thank members of my family: Harold and Rose Bavley, Howard and Ruth Lubot, and Henry and Helene DiCarlo. Uncle Henry read my entire dissertation manuscript as did my brother, Steve, who is a fount of knowledge—a Renaissance man like my dad. I would also like to thank my mother, who typed the entirety of my dad's doctoral dissertation in the 1970s. I am grateful to my husband, Alex, for his support and love. I admire his work ethic and his concomitant ability to inject fun into our lives as I wrote about such a serious topic. This book is in memory of my dad, Dr. Eric S. Lubot, and dedicated to my children Emerson, Harris, and Marisol. I hope they will strive to meet their goals. Reach for the stars.

Contents

1. Introduction: An Amendment at the Crossroads of Nuclear Power and Presidential Fallibility 1
2. Time Quickens: The History of Sudden Successions and Succession Solutions Prior to the Twenty-Fifth Amendment 15
3. The Nuclear Paradox: Power, Fallibility, and the Twenty-Fifth Amendment 47
4. Ingraining Anxiety: Ratifying the Twenty-Fifth Amendment in the Nuclear Age 91
5. "A *Dr. Strangelove* Situation": The Twenty-Fifth Amendment in Practice 147
6. "The [Doomsday] Clock Ticks": The Twenty-Fifth Amendment on the Precipice 199
7. Conclusion: The Next Stages—Nuclear Anxiety and the Amendment 269

Index 309

Abbreviations

CJ	Senate Committee on the Judiciary
Cong	Congress
H.	House bill
H. Res.	House of Representatives Resolution
H.J. Res.	House Resolution
LBJL	Lyndon Baines Johnson Presidential Library
NA	National Archives and Records Administration
NSF	National Science Foundation
PI ABA	Presidential Inability, American Bar Association
PI Hearings	Presidential Inability Hearings
S.	Senate bill
S. Res.	Senate Resolution
SCA	Senate Committee on the Judiciary, Subcommittee on Constitutional Amendments
S.J. Res.	Senate Joint Resolution

CHAPTER 1

Introduction: An Amendment at the Crossroads of Nuclear Power and Presidential Fallibility

On October 22, 1962, President John F. Kennedy imposed a naval quarantine of Cuba, just days after discovering Soviet nuclear missile sites on the island. Later that evening, the president declared in a nationally televised speech that the build-up on the island, just ninety miles off the coast of Florida, was "deliberate, provocative, and unjustified." He insisted the United States must respond "if our courage and our commitments are ever again to be trusted by either friend or foe." As a result, marines were sent to reinforce the US naval base at Guantanamo, troops were moved south, 180 warships sent to patrol the Caribbean, and B-52 bombers loaded with nuclear missiles were airborne, awaiting the president's command.[1]

Birch Bayh, a young US Senate candidate from Terre Haute, Indiana, watched intently as he considered how the news would affect his campaign against the Republican incumbent Homer E. Capehart, who had held the seat since 1945. The election was only a few weeks away. President Kennedy had campaigned at Indiana's Weir Cook Airport for Bayh just three days before he was briefed about the missiles in Cuba.[2] Initially, prospects for Bayh and others on the Democratic ticket seemed bleak. In fact, as the crisis became unbearably tense and the nation seemed uncertain about its young leader's judgment, Capehart became so sure of his reelection that he returned to his farm and business interests. On

October 28, 1962, after a tense two weeks, the Soviets began dismantling their missiles in Cuba. The two superpowers had cut a deal: Kennedy agreed to quietly remove missiles from Turkey, though no quid pro quo would be acknowledged.[3] Nuclear war had been avoided. In the eyes of the American public, Kennedy had succeeded in forcing Soviet leader Nikita Khrushchev to stand down. The nation, and the world, breathed a collective sigh of relief.

Bayh sought to capitalize on the president's new-found popularity. His campaign took out full-page advertisements that read: "Stand behind the president, vote for Bayh."[4] Two weeks later, Bayh defeated Capehart by ten thousand votes statewide (an average of only two votes per precinct) in what some saw as a referendum on Kennedy's handling of the crisis.[5] Bayh's upset victory over a longtime incumbent apparently did not sink in right away. During one of the first roll call votes in the Senate in January 1963, the clerk called Capehart's name, although he was no longer a member.[6] As a very junior member of a body that prized seniority, Bayh had little power to influence policy or debates in the Senate in 1963. But Bayh's fortune took a turn for the better when a senior member, Estes Kefauver of Tennessee, died of a heart attack and Bayh stepped into the chairmanship of the Judiciary Subcommittee on Constitutional Amendments left vacant by his colleague's death.

Beyond his party allegiances to the president, Bayh was impressed by Kennedy. He was a young man who had prevented a nuclear crisis from erupting. But he was suddenly lost when, on November 22, 1963, Kennedy was assassinated in Dallas, Texas. Bayh saw a problem: the prospect of a nuclear exchange without a clear plan of succession should the president die or become disabled during, or because of, the exchange. Less than two weeks after Kennedy's assassination, the freshman senator drafted language for a constitutional amendment that sought to address the need for presidential continuity in the nuclear age.

Because the president wielded the power of the bomb, he literally had the power of life and death, something that never could have been imagined by the framers of the Constitution. Asked years later if the Cuban missile crisis and nuclear anxiety—defined here as real and legitimate fear of nuclear war and its consequences[7]—was in the back of his mind as he began work on what became the Twenty-Fifth Amendment, Bayh replied, "I think it was impossible for it not to be on the *forefront*, not the back of [my] mind." The Cuban missile crisis "was very much a reason" for the amendment, the author said.[8] Bayh perceived that the framers had not anticipated the effects of nuclear weaponry on the presidency, and this coupled with the fallibility of any individual president led him to conceive of the necessity for a constitutional amendment to address succession and inability issues. During the 179 years from the ratification of the Constitution until the ratification of the Twenty-Fifth Amendment, eight presidential and sixteen vice presidential unplanned transitions took place without the Constitution being changed to deal with such challenges. At the time of Kennedy's assassination, no explicit legal mechanism for transferring presidential powers had the president been left incapacitated existed nor did a formal method to appoint a new vice president in the case of the president's death or removal from office. Questions of presidential succession and how a president might transfer power in the case of incapacitation were on the public's mind, and, in 1963, took on additional urgency in the shadow of the Cuban missile crisis.[9] The problem of succession also raised questions of who should succeed to the vice presidency if the vice president became the president, as well as to the precise definition of "inability."

The Twenty-Fifth Amendment, which was ultimately ratified on February 10, 1967, in the wake of the Kennedy assassination and a period of great anxiety about nuclear weapons, addressed many of these questions. Section 1 specifically clarifies that the vice president will succeed to the presidency, should a presidential vacancy exist. Section 2 says that the president will nominate a successor if a vacancy in the vice presidency occurs. Section 3 states that when the president transmits a written declaration to the president pro tempore of the Senate and the speaker of the House that he is unable to discharge his duties, the vice president will assume presidential responsibilities as "acting president" temporarily. This section allows the president to determine when he is able to return to his duties. Section 4 states that whenever the vice president and a majority of the Cabinet, or another body that Congress creates by law, decide the president is incapacitated, the vice president will assume presidential powers until the president submits a communication to the contrary. It details the procedures in the event that the vice president and the majority of the Cabinet disagree with the president's declaration that he is again able to resume the duties of the office.[10] The Twenty-Fifth Amendment was an attempt to avoid the development of a confused process in which decisions were left unmade or made by a person whose qualifications were not necessarily agreed upon.

Bayh's insight as a member of a political body that recognized the need for presidential continuity due to this new method of warfare was echoed in American culture more generally.[11] Linking human fallibility to the era of nuclear destruction, *The New York Times* columnist James Reston asked on December 2, 1963:

> Has the Congress prepared the presidency adequately for the possibilities of a violent age? Is the rule of presidential succession satisfactory for these days of human madness and scientific destruction? Or do not the men in line for the presidency—all of them, not just one or two—have to be selected and instructed much more carefully than in the past?[12]

In film, fiction, and the popular imagination, it had become common to envision various crisis scenarios of this sort. The movie *Fail-Safe*, timed for release just prior to the 1964 presidential election, depicted a US president and Soviet premier collaborating to prevent a nuclear war after a mistake due to electrical malfunction sends American planes to drop nuclear missiles on Moscow. Also released in 1964, the black comedy by Stanley Kubrick called *Dr. Strangelove or How I Stopped Worrying and Learned to Love the Bomb*, is a now-classic film about a US president who, in order to avoid nuclear Armageddon, volunteers to launch a nuclear strike on New York after an insane US general launches one on Moscow.[13] The film ends abruptly with nuclear explosions. In the world of science fiction, author Isaac Asimov noted that writers could no longer submit manuscripts with nuclear themes to publishers because the market became so saturated.[14] Authors, such as Tim O'Brien (*The Things They Carried*), a member of the 23rd Infantry Division in Vietnam, wrote about not only combat but nuclear anxiety from a soldier's perspective.[15]

Wars had been fought in the past resulting in great numbers of casualties, but the potential for mankind to come to an end because of the actions of just one individual, the president, was now, for the first time, a very real possibility. Ironically, man's most advanced scientific development could send the world back to the stone age. The last presidential inability prior to the nuclear age, that of Woodrow Wilson (who had suffered a stroke), occurred just after the First World War. Article II of the Constitution gives most foreign policy powers to the president. But even though foreign policy decisions came to a standstill during Wilson's inability, the war had occurred half a world away and many Americans believed, for geopolitical reasons, that the United States was impregnable.

In an age of nuclear missiles, however, the president might be forced to decide the fate of millions in a matter of mere minutes. This time element made passage of the amendment urgent. And even if total annihilation did not occur, a nuclear attack could suddenly destabilize the American government; structural and procedural safeguards were needed to guard against that possibility.

Bayh's eagerness to develop a constitutional succession plan reflected the widespread belief that the American public and its government could no longer tolerate a potential absence at the helm during this era of nuclear apprehension. Nor could it afford a suddenly incapacitated, or insane president with his finger on the nuclear trigger—an image increasingly common in cultural representation. When Bayh telephoned his wife to confirm the news of Kennedy's assassination, she told him of the "frightening early reports surrounding the assassination.… There had been rumors of evidence that all top government leaders were in danger."[16] Many Cabinet members were on a plane over the Pacific when they heard the news that the president had been shot.[17] And rumors swirled about some larger conspiracy against the American government, fostered in part by the Central Intelligence Agency's failure to locate Soviet leader Nikita Khrushchev for more than twenty-four hours after the assassination.[18] Hanging up the phone, Bayh realized that "at this moment, the United States had no vice president, and to make matters worse there was absolutely *no way* [italics Bayh's] to fill the vacancy in that office."[19] In early December 1963, Bayh assembled his team, which soon included members of the American Bar Association, and got to work on a solution to the succession and inability issues plaguing the nation.

It is clear in *One Heartbeat Away: Presidential Inability and Succession*—Bayh's story of the amendment's ratification—that the proximate catalyst for the draft amendment he introduced on December 12, 1963, was the Kennedy assassination.[20] But considering global developments around the nuclear bomb provides a fuller account of why the amendment was conceived at that time and in the specific form it would take. The amendment's journey through Congress was long and tortuous, and those who testified in favor in subcommittee hearings or expressed their support on the floor of the House and Senate, like the author of the amendment himself, often invoked the specter of nuclear war. Some senators wanted additional language written into the amendment to prepare the presidency for nuclear attack, while others wanted the amendment to be as plain as possible.[21] Throughout the course of passage, congressmembers employed phrases such as "the possibility of cataclysm"[22] and warned that the president's finger rested on the nuclear button.[23] President Lyndon Johnson himself urged ratification of the succession and inability amendment to avert "the potential for paralysis"[24] of the executive branch and promised the passage of the amendment would "allay the future anxiety"[25] of not just Americans, but people around the world. When the amendment reached the states for ratification, state legislators asked "Is there any reason why the succession law could not be amended to cover an atomic holocaust?" and "How would the government get started again?"[26] Whether these lawmakers were for or against the addition of specific language in the amendment that would prepare the country for a sudden presidential transition during a nuclear war, almost every last one was in agreement that a permanent solution was needed immediately to solve the succession and inability issue. Bayh was correct in asserting that this was the time to pass such legislation.

Formulation of the amendment and its passage reflected the complex anxieties of the times about shifts in warfare, the role of soldiers and legislators, and especially the role of the president. Senator Sam Ervin of North Carolina stated the Twenty-Fifth Amendment was the most complicated piece of legislation Congress had attempted to pass since he had been elected in 1954. "We had more cooks with more zeal concerned with preparing this 'broth' than any piece of proposed legislation I have ever seen in the time I have been in the Senate," he said.[27] Constitutional law expert and historian David Kyvig, in his book *Explicit and Authentic Acts: Amending the US Constitution, 1776–1995*, wrote it was "the longest and most technical of all the amendments."[28] While Kyvig's claim that the Twenty-Fifth was the "longest" amendment is incorrect—the Fourteenth has a greater word count—the latter part of his statement pointing to the complexity of the Twenty-Fifth rings true.

It is commonly argued, as Garry Wills has in *Bomb Power: The Modern Presidency and The National Security State*, that the development of nuclear weapons "fostered an anxiety of continuing crisis" that has "altered [America's] subsequent history down to its deepest constitutional roots."[29] Yet despite the importance of the Twenty-Fifth Amendment and its emergence from a Cold War culture fraught with anxiety over nuclear war, the history of the amendment's ratification has not been examined through this lens. Applying this filter allows for a deeper understanding of the US Constitution as a living document reflecting the exigencies of the age, as the framers originally intended. Conversely, no historian has sought to shed light on the Cold War through a constitutional amendment. This book strives to provide a new way of looking at the Twenty-Fifth Amendment, the Constitution, and the political and cultural mood of the era.

The argument unfolds over five chapters and a conclusion. *Chapter 2: Time Quickens: The History of Sudden Succession and Succession Solutions Prior to the Twenty-Fifth Amendment* provides a brief discussion of the framers' view of succession and inability issues, as well as the historiography of both statutory laws and constitutional amendments dealing with those issues. The chapter also outlines the history of sudden presidential transitions and inabilities, and the solutions offered in their wake. When focusing on the Franklin D. Roosevelt/Harry S. Truman transition, which sets the stage of nuclear anxiety at the beginning of the era, what becomes clear is that with the destructive power of the bomb came a concomitant increase in presidential power and interest in the line of succession. Thus, Truman and Eisenhower worked more diligently toward succession and inability solutions than had their predecessors. The 1947 Presidential Succession Act and the Dwight D. Eisenhower/Richard M. Nixon letter agreement—key precursors to the Twenty-Fifth Amendment—were the results of their efforts.

The political and cultural mood of nuclear anxiety in the period between the first uses of nuclear weapons in 1945, through the amendment's ratification in 1967, is the topic of *Chapter 3: The Nuclear Paradox: Power, Fallibility, and the Twenty-Fifth Amendment*. The omnipresent and growing fear of nuclear Armageddon reached a peak in the early 1960s in a series of confrontations between the two superpowers. Fear of nuclear attack contributed to a strong desire for stability at the top echelon of government at all times, leading to Continuity of Government plans. The anxieties about continuity of government were a symptom of the paradox of presidential power being linked to an era of nuclear power. Eisenhower's illnesses and John F. Kennedy's sudden death pointed to the contradiction that the president—who wielded the almost superhuman power to potentially bring an end to mankind—was human and, therefore, mortal. In discussing how representations of nuclear anxiety run through, and often intersect in, pop culture and politics, this chapter provides a fuller account of why the amendment developed at this time.

Chapter 4: Ingraining Anxiety: Ratifying the Twenty-Fifth Amendment in the Nuclear Age analyzes the Twenty-Fifth Amendment's ratification process through the lens of nuclear anxiety. Traditional histories of the amendment argue that Kennedy's assassination was both the proximate and prime factor in the development of the amendment, but because they do not consider the omnipresence of nuclear anxiety, such assessments remain incomplete. Witnesses' testimony and congressmembers' debate during congressional hearings, backroom conversations and negotiations, and state legislators' concerns suggest nuclear anxiety played a role in every stage of the process from its drafting, through debate and passage in both houses, and ratification in the states. However, the role of anxiety—an amorphous concept—was complicated. While nuclear anxiety pushed the process forward overall, it also led to debate in both houses of Congress over language, amount of detail, and time limits. For a richer understanding of the reasons behind the Twenty-Fifth Amendment's ratification, this chapter argues that nuclear anxiety must be taken more fully into account.

Chapter 5: "A Dr. Strangelove Situation": The Twenty-Fifth Amendment in Practice builds on the implications of the amendment's being ingrained in the Constitution. February 1967, when the amendment was written into the Constitution, signaled a new chapter in the Constitution's history. The Twenty-Fifth Amendment was invoked just seven times between 1967 and 2025. During the first three invocations—all involving Section 1 and 2 of the amendment—successful unplanned transitions occurred. But these initial invocations reveal complicating gaps and vagaries in the amendment. Any history that traces the times the amendment was invoked also must consider the times it might have been invoked but was not. Sections 3 of the amendment, invoked only four times between 1967 and 2025, was designed to leave the decisions both to surrender and then to retake power in the president's own hands. In this chapter, examination of the amendment in periods of heightened nuclear anxiety during the presidential administrations of Richard Nixon, Ronald Reagan, and George W. Bush reveals that, at times, Section 3 was avoided when it arguably should have been invoked. Presidents, in trying to present an image of strength and good health, have not given up power willingly. Section 4 of the amendment has never been invoked due to these same political concerns. Thus, while nuclear anxiety worked to produce the amendment, it was a factor in suppressing invocation of the amendment in practice. Presidents have even taken it upon themselves to find solutions to the succession and inability issue, sometimes stretching the flexible boundaries of the Constitution itself.

Chapter 6 *"The [Doomsday] Clock Ticks": The Twenty-Fifth Amendment on the Precipice* follows the amendment into the present. As soon as Donald Trump was sworn in as the forty-fifth president, questions of unfitness and calls to remove the president swirled through mainstream media. Talk of invoking Section 4 of the amendment occurred at the highest levels of government. Due to concerns about mental acuity, physical frailty, and age, such calls continued during Joseph Biden's presidency. The resurgence of nuclear anxiety in politics and culture mirrored building tensions across the world. The framers of the amendment had assumed that decision-makers shared a common mindset that placed allegiance to the country above personal gain. While some have acted on behalf of the common good, promising to block the "unlawful" use of nuclear weapons, the persistent number of misunderstandings around the intent and mechanics of the amendment along with the prioritization of the retention of power suggest that the pattern of concern discussed in Chapter 5 will continue.

"We needed a plan," said Bayh. "We had to make sure there was always somebody who had his finger on the button."[30] Now, as the world hovers on the brink of World War III, *Keeping a Finger on the Button: Presidential Continuity and the Nuclear Age* provides a history of the Twenty-Fifth Amendment's creation, language, ratification process, and aftereffects through the lens of Cold War nuclear anxiety, a presidential assassination transition, and the political realities of a democracy in crisis.

Notes

1. "Spinning Out of Control: The Cuban Missile Crisis," *American Foreign Relations: A History* Volume 2 Since 1865, Seventh Edition, Thomas G. Paterson, J. Garry Clifford, Shane J. Maddock, Deborah Kisatsky, and Kenneth J. Hagan (Boston, MA: Wadsworth, Cengage Learning, 2010), 341.
2. John F. Kennedy spent an hour at the airport campaigning for Democratic candidates on October 13, 1962. He was briefed about the presence of the missiles in Cuba on October 16. Dawn Mitchell, "Indiana Reaction to the Assassination of Pres. John F. Kennedy," *IndyStar* (November 22, 2016). http://www.indystar.com/story/news/history/retroindy/2016/11/22/john-kennedy-assassination-jfk/94271142/.

3. Premier Khrushchev ultimately ordered Soviet vessels to turn around. The military and diplomatic resolution to the crisis is detailed in Chapter 3. For a recent history of the Cuban missile crisis that reveals the Cuban-for-Turkish missile deal see, for example: Sheldon M. Stern, *The Cuban Missile Crisis in American Memory: Myth Versus Reality* (Stanford, CA: Stanford University Press, 2012).
4. Bayh recalls spending about $465,000 on the 1962 campaign. Birch Bayh, Interviews with Bob Blaemire, 2012. Though seats were lost in the House, Democrats still retained a majority of 259–176. They gained four seats in the Senate, one of which was Bayh's. This number was reduced to a gain of only three seats by the start of the next Congress when Democratic Senator Dennis Chavez of New Mexico, who was not up for reelection, died on November 18, and was replaced by Republican Senator Edwin L. Mechem.
5. See traditional histories of the Cuban missile crisis such as: Robert F. Kennedy, *Thirteen Days: A Memoir of the Cuban Missile Crisis* (New York: W.W. Norton & Co., 1969). Arthur M. Schlesinger, Jr., *A Thousand Days: John F. Kennedy in the White House* (Boston, MA: Houghton Mifflin Company, 1965).
6. "Senator Birch Bayh Finds Victory over Capehart Is Quickly Undone," *The New York Times* (January 14, 1963), 4.
7. Tom W. Smith, "Nuclear Anxiety," *Public Opinion Quarterly,* Issue 52, 1988, 557.
8. Birch Bayh, Interview with Author, November 11, 2014. This definition of nuclear anxiety can be found in: Tom W. Smith, "A Report: Nuclear Anxiety," *The Public Opinion Quarterly* Volume 52, Number 4 (1988), 557–75. http://www.jstor.org.proxy.libraries.rutgers.edu/stable/2749262.
9. John D. Feerick, *The Twenty-Fifth Amendment: Its Complete History and Applications. Fordham University Press* (New York: 1992), 10–11. As quoted in *The Presidency: Preserving Our Institutions: The Second Report of the Continuity of Government Commission: Presidential Succession* (Washington, DC: Continuity of Government Commission, June 2009), 35. Both President Dwight D. Eisenhower and future President Lyndon B. Johnson suffered heart attacks in 1955.
10. The exact text of the Twenty-Fifth Amendment appears in Chapter 4.

11. Much of the body of literature on anxiety around the bomb can be found outside the discipline of history. See, for example: Colin S. Gray, "Nuclear Strategy: The Case for a Theory of Victory," In *Strategy and Nuclear Deterrence*, edited by Steven E. Miller (Princeton, NJ: Princeton University Press, 1984), 23–56. http://www.jstor.org.proxy.libraries.rutgers.edu/stable/j.ctt7zvv5x.6. Patricia A Gwartney-Gibbs and Denise H. Lach, "Sex Differences in Attitudes toward Nuclear War," *Journal of Peace Research* 28, Number 2 (1991), 161–74. http://www.jstor.org.proxy.libraries.rutgers.edu/stable/424386. Tom W. Smith, "A Report: Nuclear Anxiety," *The Public Opinion Quarterly* Volume 52, Number 4 (1988), 557–75. http://www.jstor.org.proxy.libraries.rutgers.edu/stable/2749262. Robert T. Schatz and Susan T. Fiske. "International Reactions to the Threat of Nuclear War: The Rise and Fall of Concern in the Eighties." [Political Psychology 13, no. 1 (1992): 1–29. Robert W. Tucker, "The Nuclear Debate," Foreign Affairs Volume 63, Number 1 (1984), 1–32.
12. Birch Bayh, *One Heartbeat Away: Presidential Inability and Succession* (New York: The Bobbs-Merrill Company, Inc., 1968), 10.
13. *Dr. Strangelove or: How I Learned to Stop Worrying and Love the Bomb* (Columbia Pictures, 1964).
14. Allan M. Winkler, *Life Under a Cloud: American Anxiety About the Atom* (New York: Oxford University Press, 1993), 7.
15. Tim O'Brien, *The Things They Carried* (New York: Houghton Mifflin, 1990).
16. Birch Bayh, *One Heartbeat Away*, 4.
17. The plane's passenger list included: Secretary of State Dean Rusk, Treasury Secretary C. Douglas Dillon, Interior Secretary Stewart Udall, Agriculture Secretary Orville Freeman, Labor Secretary Willard Wirtz, as well as Treasury Undersecretary Henry Fowler and Council of Economic Advisors Chairman Walter Heller, other officials, and their spouses. They were travelling to an annual meeting of US and Japanese Cabinet members. See Secretary Willard Wirtz's memoir: Willard Wirtz, *In the Review Mirror* (Beloit, WI: Beloit College Press, 2008).
18. Richelson, Jeffrey T. "CIA Reactions to JFK Assassination Included Fear of Possible Soviet Strike against US." *Studies in Intelligence: New Articles from the CIA's In-house Journal*,

National Security Archive No. 493, (Updated November 20, 2014), 3.
19. Birch Bayh, *One Heartbeat Away*, 6.
20. Birch Bayh's *One Heartbeat Away* can be downloaded here: https://ir.lawnet.fordham.edu/twentyfifth_amendment_books/1/.
21. Senator Robert F. Kennedy (D-NY), the slain president's brother, wanted more specifics written into the amendment, while another powerful senator, Everett Dirksen (R-IL), argued for a much simpler version that would have simply enabled Congress to act in cases of presidential succession and inability.
22. "Statement of Senator James B. Pearson, 31–160 018," NA, CJ, SCA, Box 8, Folder "88th Congress, PI- Hearings- Report- Mock-Up, 1–22, 1964."
23. Hearings Before the Committee on the Judiciary Eighty-Ninth Congress, First Session on Miscellaneous Proposals Relating to Presidential Inability. February 9, 10, 16, and 17, 1965, 2. https://babel.hathitrust.org/cgi/pt?id=ucl.$b654933;view=1up;seq=5.
24. "For Release on Delivery to the Senate," Box 3. Office Files of Bill Moyers: Special Message on Office of the President. LBJL.
25. *Congressional Record*, Vol. 111, Part II. 89th Congress, 1st Session, 1460. http://heinonline.org.proxy.libraries.rutgers.edu/HOL/Page?handle=hein.congrec/cr1110002&id=1&size=2&collection=congrec&index=congrec/creu.
26. These quotes are attributed to Senator John Bermingham of Colorado, whom the author interviewed on February 2, 2015. See Chapter 4. Is there any reason: "Letter to Mr. H. Michael Spence from John R. Bermingham, August 26, 1965," NA, CJ, SCA, Box 6, Folder, "PI ABA Junior Bar Conference 3 of 4, Dale Tooley File 1965 Jun-Dec." How will the government: "Letter to American Bar Association from John R. Bermingham, August 10, 1965," NA, CJ, SCA, Box 6, Folder, "PI ABA Junior Bar Conference 3 of 4, Dale Tooley File 1965 Jun–Dec."
27. Birch Bayh, *One Heartbeat Away: Presidential Inability and Succession*, 330.
28. David E. Kyvig, *Explicit and Authentic Acts: Amending the US Constitution, 1776–1995* (Lawrence, Kansas: University Press of Kansas, 1996), 362.

29. Wills views the advent of nuclear weapons, and the president's power to order a nuclear attack, as crucial to the emergence of the National Security State and the ensuing burgeoning of executive power. The secret Manhattan Project he calls "the seed of all the growing powers that followed." Ever since, he contends, the bomb has driven the steady expansion of presidential power. Certainly, if a president has the Zeus-like capacity to destroy entire nations and snuff out millions of lives instantaneously, all other powers are trivialized in comparison. When the 1946 Atomic Energy Act granted this cosmic authority solely to the president, Wills writes, "the nature of the presidency was irrevocably altered," leading to a vast expansion of executive power in all directions, including a sprawling security apparatus to protect nuclear secrets. Garry Wills, *Bomb Power: The Modern Presidency and the National Security State* (New York: The Penguin Press, 2010), 1.
30. Birch Bayh, Interview with Author, November 11, 2014.

CHAPTER 2

Time Quickens: The History of Sudden Successions and Succession Solutions Prior to the Twenty-Fifth Amendment

The drafters of the US Constitution sought to envision all kinds of eventualities that might confront their new nation, but even among as gifted a group of statesmen as gathered in Philadelphia in 1787, certain potential problems went unaddressed. Prior to the ratification of the Twenty-Fifth Amendment, the Constitution did not designate which officers were in the line of presidential succession past the vice president, did not offer direction on cases of presidential inability, and left numerous related questions unanswered. To allow for a better understanding of why it took until the nuclear age to develop and ratify an amendment giving more clarity to these issues, this chapter examines the history of previous sudden succession transitions and solutions. Eight presidents have died while in office: William Henry Harrison, Zachary Taylor, Abraham Lincoln, James Garfield, William McKinley, Warren Harding, Franklin Roosevelt, and John Kennedy. Additionally, significant presidential inabilities occurred during the terms of Garfield, Grover Cleveland, Woodrow Wilson, and Dwight Eisenhower. In the cases of presidential deaths, succession was clear—in accordance with Article II, Section I of the Constitution, the vice president became president. The vice presidency remained vacant because no constitutional mechanism to nominate a new vice president existed. In the case of presidents who were incapacitated for medical reasons, no provisions were in place allowing for the temporary transfer of power to the vice president. The Constitution was silent on these issues.

© The Author(s), under exclusive license to Springer Nature Switzerland AG 2025
R. C. Lubot, *Keeping a Finger on the Button*,
https://doi.org/10.1007/978-3-032-02478-7_2

Prior to Kennedy's assassination, discussion of issues regarding presidential succession and incapacity reveal an almost naïve mindset about their import. The Constitution's silence on succession and inability remained unaddressed, despite the relative frequency of presidential deaths in the nineteenth century—four presidents died in office between 1841 and 1881, two by assassination—and the illnesses that left Cleveland and Wilson incapacitated. This was a mindset the nation could no longer afford after it entered the nuclear age.

The founders certainly were aware that presidents could die in office or resign. For that reason, they included the succession mechanism in Article II of the Constitution designating the vice president as a successor should the president die, resign or prove to be unable "to discharge the powers and duties" of the presidency. It gave Congress the power to pass a law to provide for succession should both the presidency and vice presidency become vacant. That "officer shall then act as president ... until the disability be removed, or a president shall be elected."[1]

Why were the succession and inability issues not settled more conclusively when the Constitution was adopted? One logical conclusion is that the founders did not consider the issue to be critical to a system in which Congress, not the executive, was thought to be paramount. The presidency, after all, was relegated to Article II of the Constitution, after the section dealing with the houses of Congress. Article I promised that all members of the House of Representatives would be elected directly by the people. The notion that the president's successor should be democratically chosen would create tension when deciding whether the Cabinet or Congress was next in line for succession during debate of every major change in succession law from that point forward.[2]

One of the few references to succession during the Constitutional Convention was made by Alexander Hamilton. In the so-called British Plan that he proposed, Hamilton suggested that the chief executive be replaced by the president of the Senate until a successor was appointed: "On the death, resignation or removal of the governor his authorities to be exercised by the president of the Senate till a successor be appointed."[3] Rather than a fixed line of succession, the president of the Senate would take over the governor's duties until an election replaced the chief executive or the Senate appointed a new one. This was not what Article II ultimately dictated. Hamilton's idea that the executive be appointed for life (just as the British monarch rules for life) during "good behavior" was not incorporated into the Constitution either.

Other delegates had ideas of their own about the nature of the presidency and how succession should be handled. Two of these plans were proposed on the same day, May 29, 1787: the Virginia Plan, which the state's governor, Edmund Randolph, put forward; and the Pinckney Plan, which was the work of South Carolina Governor Charles Pinckney. Under both plans, the legislative branch would be given the responsibility of appointing a new president.

The Constitution, while not focused on the chief executive, says even less about the vice president. The vice president was simply the person who obtained the next-greatest number of votes in the Electoral College and, as the president of the US Senate, cast tie-breaking votes.[4] It was after the tie (which took thirty-six votes to break) between Thomas Jefferson and Aaron Burr in 1800 that the Twelfth Amendment was ratified in 1804, not just as a means to eliminate future ties but also to facilitate the election of a president and vice president of the same political party (an important point of consideration as the Twenty-Fifth was debated). Ratified in 1804, the Twelfth Amendment provided that in the case of death, resignation, or inability the vice president shall act as president: "And if the House of Representatives shall not choose a president whenever the right of choice shall devolve upon them, before the fourth day of March next following, then the vice president shall act as president, as in the case of the death or other constitutional disability of the president."[5] This statement was in line with the intent of Article II Section I Clause 6: In the case of the death, resignation, or inability to discharge the duties of the office of the presidency, they would devolve on the vice president.

All matters related to the president and succession not explicitly written under Article II were left for Congress to determine in the absence of a president and vice president. Congress began debating what officers should fill in presidential and vice presidential vacancies on December 21, 1790.[6] On January 13, 1791, for example, the chief justice of the Supreme Court, president pro tem of the senate, and secretary of state were all considered as potential successors to the presidency. In the end, the First Congress did not reach any conclusions. The issue was again considered in the Second Congress in November 1791.[7] Because the Senate met in closed sessions until 1794, little is known about the chamber's debates, but the bill called for the president and vice president to be succeeded by the president pro tempore of the Senate and the speaker of the House. Records of the House debate, however, show that the

Congress considered different officers to fill presidential and vice presidential vacancies, including the senior associate justice of the Supreme Court and the secretary of state. The secretary of state was chosen. However, the Senate rejected the House's version on February 20, 1792, and reinserted the two congressional officers. The Senate seems to have rejected the secretary of state for political reasons; Federalists dominated the Senate, and they did not want to see Secretary of State Thomas Jefferson, leader of the rival Democratic-Republican faction, in the line of succession.[8] The bill became law on March 1, 1792. This law remained unchanged for ninety-four years.[9]

For the first fifty-two years, America's presidents remained healthy enough to discharge the duties of the office, but questions loomed. In *The Twenty-Fifth Amendment: Its Complete History and Earliest Applications*, John D. Feerick, who as chair of the Junior Bar Conference of the American Bar Association provided much of the legal and historical context for the amendment, presented the early efforts to solve the inability question. Feerick's work enables the reader to glean a sense of the complexity of the questions lawmakers were grappling with—if the vice president succeeded to the presidency, was he legally president or just in practice? Who decided when the president was incapacitated, and, if relevant, when that incapacitation had ended? If the vice president succeeded to the presidency, how would a new vice president be chosen?[10]

The first sudden presidential succession took place in 1841, when William Henry Harrison became ill with pneumonia after delivering an overly long inaugural address on an inclement March day in Washington. He died a month later, and John Tyler became the first vice president to succeed to the presidency. But opposition leaders in Congress, including John Quincy Adams, initially did not accept Tyler as a legitimate president. Adams, a congressman who had the unique distinction of having been president, argued that Tyler should hold the title of "Acting President" or should remain vice president in name while discharging the duties of the office of the president. Although the Cabinet, followed by the Senate and House, approved Tyler's accession, Tyler's enemies sneeringly referred to him as "His Accidency." In a special session, the Twenty-Seventh Congress passed the Wise Resolution.[11] It confirmed that Tyler would not only be performing the duties of the president, but would be called "President" and would receive the president's salary. The concept that the vice president would fulfill the role as president in its entirety and not merely as "Acting President" would be called the "Tyler

Precedent." Without issue, the Tyler precedent was followed twice in the next forty years, first by Vice President Millard Fillmore when President Zachary Taylor died on July 9, 1850, having contracted a fatal intestinal disorder from eating bad cherries at a July 4 ceremony, and second by Andrew Johnson following Abraham Lincoln's assassination on April 15, 1865.

The first of these two sudden successions took place relatively swiftly and smoothly. Vice President Millard Fillmore was aware of Taylor's illness and immediately upon Taylor's death the Cabinet began addressing Fillmore as "The President of the United States."[12] He was sworn in at noon on July 10, 1850. The members of the Cabinet then tendered their resignations, which the new president accepted. He replaced them with individuals he felt would act as salves against the growing sentiment of sectionalism. The sectionalism reached a breaking point after Lincoln's election during the secessionist winter of 1860–1861 (when the states of South Carolina, Mississippi, Florida, Georgia, Alabama, Louisiana, and Texas seceded from the Union).

As Lincoln's name did not appear on the ballot in ten southern states, Confederates made the argument that he did not represent all Americans; however, Lincoln's murder remains pertinent to the succession question because it was part of a larger plot to kill others in the line of succession. A group of four Confederate sympathizers intended to kill the president at Ford's Theatre as well as Vice President Andrew Johnson at Kirkwood House and Secretary of State William Henry Seward at his home on April 14, 1865. Already bedridden due to an accident, Seward was stabbed several times but recovered. (Initial reports suggested he, too, had died and a conspiracy to assassinate many top government officials was suspected. In his papers, Treasury Secretary Salmon P. Chase stated that callers to his home told him that Seward had been assassinated and additional security had been placed around "all the prominent officials under the apprehension that the plot had a wide range."[13]) The man charged with the task of murdering Johnson, George Atzerodt, changed his mind when seated at the bar of the Kirkwood House and fled to Maryland. Johnson remained unharmed.[14]

Less than three hours after Lincoln died on April 15, 1865, Johnson was sworn in as the seventeenth president of the United States. But during his presidency he warred with Republicans in Congress (he was a Democrat), and the House of Representatives impeached him in 1868. The Senate ultimately acquitted Johnson by just one vote, with senators very much aware that succeeding him would have been a political opponent, Radical Republican Senate president pro tempore Benjamin J. Wade, who had voted to convict Johnson of high crimes and misdemeanors. After this acquittal, Johnson noted the obvious problems with placing the president pro tempore in the line of succession because he would therefore be "interested in producing a vacancy."[15]

These events did prompt some reconsideration of the line of succession. The 1792 Act dictated that members of Congress were next in line of succession after the vice president, but after Lincoln's assassination and Johnson's impeachment, Johnson himself called for changing the line of succession to Cabinet members to prevent Congress from using its impeachment powers to position one of its own members in the presidency. Congress chose not to act on the matter and the issue of succession blended into the background while the nation focused on Reconstruction efforts to heal the wounds inflicted by the Civil War.

Twelve years later, however, the nation faced another crisis of succession brought about by an assassin's bullet—this time the shooting of James Garfield on July 2, 1881, as he walked to a rail station in Washington, DC, in the company, among others, of his secretary of war, Robert Todd Lincoln, the murdered president's son. The attack on Garfield, who had been sworn in only four months earlier, not only raised the issue of succession but also the issue of incapacitation, as Garfield clung to life for eighty days following the shooting. A wave of shock and horror passed over the American people, most of whom had fresh memories of Lincoln's murder. "The astonishment following the startling announcement deepened into unbelief," read *The New York Times*, "and the people seemed paralyzed with the horror of the moment."[16]

Vice President Chester A. Arthur's hesitancy to assume the presidency during the months when Garfield lay dying was freighted with political considerations. The Republican Party was fractured. Arthur was a member of the party's Stalwart wing that opposed President Hayes' Reconstruction policy. (The Stalwarts named their opponents within the Party the "Half Breeds," suggesting they were not fully Republican.[17]) Arthur's nomination as vice president was meant as a peace offering from the Half Breeds who supported Garfield.

The man who shot Garfield, Charles J. Guiteau, was apprehended carrying a letter addressed to the White House in his pocket. The letter read "I did it and will go to jail for it. I am a Stalwart, and Arthur will be president."[18] Although no one seriously believed Arthur was part of the plot, the Stalwart wing of the party stood to gain from Garfield's assassination. Garfield's only official act during his eighty days of agonized incapacitation was the signing of an extradition paper. His doctors prevented him from performing any kind of work. Secretary of State James A. Blaine, a Half Breed like Garfield, prepared a paper on presidential disability in August 1881, arguing that since no provisions for succession existed, Arthur should assume the presidency. Fearful of being labeled a usurper, Arthur made it clear that he would do no such thing. When Garfield's condition deteriorated at the end of August, *The New York Times* reported that he had no intention of going to Washington.[19] He succeeded to the presidency only after Garfield died on September 19, 1881, in New Jersey.

In the interim, the Cabinet tried to execute Garfield's duties, but they could not, by law, complete most of them; foreign affairs were utterly neglected, for example. Arthur continued to express concern over the succession process in messages to Congress after he became president. When Arthur assumed the presidency, the offices of vice president, president pro tempore of the Senate, and speaker of the House were vacant.

Garfield's incapacitation and death raised key questions about the Presidential Succession Act of 1792. What if Arthur died?[20] The leadership in Congress was in flux. In one of his first acts as president, Arthur convened a special session of the Senate on October 10, 1881, to elect a new president pro tempore. But even this routine procedure was complicated. Three vacancies in the Senate had been filled by Republicans who were supposed to be sworn in by the president pro tem. Without those Republicans, the Senate was in Democratic hands and would elect one of their own as president pro tem. With them, the Senate was evenly divided. Republicans submitted a resolution that would have allowed the new senators to be sworn in before a new president pro tem was elected. The resolution was defeated; a Democrat, Thomas F. Bayard, was chosen as president pro tem and so was next in line should Arthur die in office. The new Republicans were sworn in on October 12, 1881. The following day, an independent senator, David Davis of Illinois, unseated Bayard as president pro tem. Speaker of the House, the position of next in line to the presidency after the president pro tem, remained vacant until December because the House was not scheduled to convene. A Republican speaker of the House (Warren Keifer of Ohio) was elected on December 5, 1881, more than two months after Garfield's passing.

The other questions (which remained unanswered) were posed by Arthur himself in messages to Congress starting in 1881. What was meant by "inability"—was it physical or mental? Did the duration and the extent of the inability matter? What expert, or group of experts, would determine whether the president was disabled? Who would choose these experts? Did the president have a say in whether he was disabled and when his disability came to an end? If the vice president did succeed to the office, how long would his term last? Would the president, once his inability ended, be allowed to resume his duties as president? Could the vice president then return to his vice presidential responsibilities?[21]

Just four years later, the vice presidency was again vacant under President Grover Cleveland, when Vice President Thomas Hendricks died in office. Anxiety over Hendricks' death in 1885, after less than a year in office, renewed the focus on succession law. Cleveland had grown close to Hendricks and had given him more responsibilities than previous vice presidents. Cleveland's first message to Congress on December 8, 1885, cited the public's anxiety over the vice president's death and other vacancies in the line of succession as reasons to make changes to the law. He stated:

> The present condition of the law relating to the succession to the presidency in the event of the death, disability, or removal of both the president and vice president is such as to require immediate amendment. The subject has repeatedly been considered by Congress, but no result has been reached. The recent lamentable death of the vice president and vacancies at the same time in all other offices the incumbents of which might immediately exercise the functions of the presidential office, have caused public anxiety and a just demand that a recurrence of such a condition of affairs should not be permitted.[22]

Cleveland's message prodded Massachusetts Senator George Frisbie Hoar to reintroduce a bill (S. 471) that substituted Cabinet officers for the Senate president pro tempore and the speaker of the House in the line of succession. Hoar began his plea to fellow Senators by charging that the "present arrangement is bad" as it was adopted because of the "jealousy entertained toward Mr. Jefferson by the leading Federalists of the first [presidential] administration." He then argued that the Senate president was not the appropriate official to assume the presidency because "he is not elected with reference to his fitness for executive functions," but rather "he is chosen for his capacity as legislator and debater." Hoar pointed out that, because the pro tem "ha[d] little or no executive experience," with just one exception, no president pro tem had run for president.[23]

In addition to changing the order of succession, the 1886 Act also provided for presidential inability. The officer next in line would act as president until the disability of the president or vice president was removed or a new president was elected. Although no time frame was set for a presidential election, the act set a time frame of twenty days for Congress to meet should it be in recess at the time of the president's death, resignation, removal, or inability (as it had been when Garfield died). The Act of 1886 was unique in that it finally addressed inability.

Ironically, though, when the moment came to apply the 1886 law, the president—Cleveland—chose to ignore it in an attempt to address the nation's worst economic crisis to date. Suffering from oral cancer, Cleveland underwent an operation to remove part of his jaw onboard a friend's yacht, the *Oneida*, during the summer of 1893, the first year of his second nonconsecutive term. The operation required that he be completely anesthetized. His jaw was replaced by a false one at his summer home in Buzzard's Bay, Massachusetts. He took a second cruise on the *Oneida* to undergo further surgery for the removal of additional tissue. Rather than make the news public and provide for someone to assume his presidential duties while he was unconscious, Cleveland chose to swear his doctors to secrecy. He believed his influence would swing a congressional vote to repeal the Sherman Silver Purchase Act of 1890, an act that he blamed for causing the financial depression. President Cleveland called Congress into special session on June 30. When Congress convened on August 8, he addressed the "existence of an alarming and extraordinary business situation involving the welfare and prosperity of all our people" that had caused him to call the extra session "to the end that… present evils might be mitigated and dangers threatening the future might be averted." He emphasized that "every day's delay in removing one of the plain and principal causes of the present state of things, enlarges the mischief already done and increases the responsibility of the government for its existence."[24] Because the doctors' work was successful, Cleveland's artificial jaw allowed him to speak clearly (not that most Americans would have noticed in this era before mass broadcasts). The president's call to convene Congress and the start of the special session served as bookends to his surgery. Historians such as Allan Nevins credit Cleveland's presence for the repeal of the Sherman Anti-Trust Act.[25] But Cleveland's actions did nothing to provide a solution to the question of presidential disability.

The issue persisted. William McKinley's vice president, Garrett Hobart, died in 1899, and the office remained vacant until McKinley and his new running mate, Theodore Roosevelt, were sworn in for McKinley's second term on March 4, 1901. Six months later, on September 6, McKinley was shot in Buffalo, New York. He lingered for eight days, and at times appeared to be improving. Roosevelt left for a planned vacation in the Adirondack Mountains three days later. But McKinley soon took a turn for the worse—gangrene was poisoning his body—and Roosevelt was summoned to return from his vacation. The president died on September 14 while Roosevelt was en route by train. He was sworn in as president when he arrived in Buffalo. He requested McKinley's Cabinet members to remain at their posts to help him as he sought to reassure the nation and provide a semblance of continuity. McKinley was the third president to be murdered in less than forty years. Many Americans, then, had living memories of three presidential assassinations, two of which (Garfield and McKinley) led to a prolonged period of presidential disability before the victims died. In that same period, three vice presidents had died, leaving the office vacant.

During Roosevelt's term, the president led the federal government in embracing the new activism of the Progressive Era and Washington continued to claim its place on the world stage—Roosevelt won a Nobel Peace Prize for brokering an end to the Russo-Japanese war in 1905. Under Roosevelt, the president did not merely preside, he acted. As biographer John Milton Cooper, Jr., remarked "from the beginning, Roosevelt differed in his energy and his imaginative grasp from others who sought to uphold the existing order in the United States."[26] When Roosevelt handed over the presidency to his friend and protégé William Howard Taft on March 4, 1909, it was a different institution than that which Roosevelt himself inherited upon McKinley's death. As President Woodrow Wilson would later say of Roosevelt, whom he called "an aggressive leader" that had "made Congress follow him," Roosevelt had shown "it was not necessary to amend the Constitution to bring about a closer relationship between its elected branches; rather, the task was to use the existing powers of the executive more fully."[27]

Under Wilson, who succeeded Taft in 1913, the president's powers and influence on the world stage continued to grow, culminating in his outsized role as the conscience of the Allied powers in the aftermath of

World War I. According to economist John Maynard Keynes, who was part of the peace delegation, Wilson, the first sitting president to venture beyond the territorial United States, "enjoyed prestige and moral influence throughout the world unequaled in history."[28] Wilson was a key player in negotiating the Treaty of Versailles, and it was he who advocated for the founding of what became the League of Nations. But many Americans, some disillusioned by war, others seeing political advantage, opposed American membership in the League. Wilson, nearing the end of his second term, embarked on a nationwide tour to drum up support for the Treaty and the League. During this critical time, on September 26, 1919, Wilson suffered a severe stroke at age sixty-two and was incapacitated. Through his personal physician, Dr. Cary T. Grayson, the White House attempted to manage the perceptions of the president's ability. *The New York Times* first reported that Dr. Grayson had suggested that the president end his tour and return to the White House rather than "a health resort." Initially, the fact that he was returning home rather than to a hospital was enough proof for the press to believe that the inability would be brief; *The Times* declared it was "sufficient indication that the present indisposition is in no way threatening, and that in a few days it will probably have disappeared."[29] Yet in more news on the president's condition the next day, the paper noted that he was not conducting official business (in favor of rest). He was "forbidden to discuss the Treaty struggle."[30] The doctor updated *The Times* on October 6, calling Wilson's condition "encouraging." The October 6 article also reported that Secretary of State Robert Lansing had called the Cabinet together that morning to discuss the president's illness and that the president's private secretary, Joseph Tumulty, had denied the rumor that Vice President Thomas R. Marshall might be requested to take over the president's powers and duties.[31]

Vice President Marshall opted not to fight for the presidency. Instead, Woodrow Wilson's wife, Edith Bolling Wilson, and Dr. Grayson, ran the government in Wilson's name, controlling and curtailing access to the president. Nicknamed "the Presidentress," the First Lady was quoted stating she did not make decisions in the realm of public affairs, but she did decide "what was important and what was not."[32] By acting as his steward, she believed she was furthering his wishes by helping him retain the powers and duties of the presidency.[33] Further, by restricting Wilson's contact with others, Mrs. Wilson and Grayson were "following the medical thinking of the time about treating stroke patients," according to Cooper. But speculation in newspapers across the country suggested Wilson was too ill to carry out his presidential responsibilities. On October 12, for example, *The New York Times* published a letter to a constituent from Senator George H. Moses of New Hampshire revealing the Senator's opinion that even if Wilson did live "he [would] not be any material force or factor in anything."[34] Though some Americans were publicly calling for action, Grayson continued to argue that no legal matters were pressing.[35]

Wilson's inability launched debates in Congress, mainly about how to, and who would, determine whether an inability existed. Even before Wilson's major stroke, in the summer of 1919 when the president attempted to lobby senators to support the treaty, it had become "discernable to others" that the president was experiencing "mental decline."[36] Now, separate proposals included allowing the Supreme Court and secretary of state to make the disability determination. Hearings were held in the House Judiciary Committee, but no further action was taken. The Republican-led Congress did not act against Wilson, a Democrat, for fear of both Democratic reprisals and voter backlash. It was to their political advantage to have the inactive Wilson in office. Tumulty wrote to Mrs. Wilson in mid-December listing at least a dozen items that required the president's immediate action, but the White House continued to be "awash in denial," and the "opacity" around the president's illness led to rumors that increased in both negativity and number.[37] As Cooper stated, "Not surprisingly, the one person who does not seem to have contemplated [resigning] was Wilson himself."[38] President Wilson did not want to give up his powers.

The period of presidential inability ended with the inauguration of Wilson's Republican successor, Warren Harding, in 1921. The tensions of wartime, combined with Wilson's inability and failure to secure the League of Nations, paved the way for what Harding famously called a "return to normalcy." But if Harding returned the nation to a more tranquil, less anxious age, the eternal problem of presidential succession remained acute. On August 2, 1923, Harding died in office at the age of fifty-seven after an extensive speaking tour. He suffered from heart trouble—a heart dilation was misdiagnosed as acute indigestion. Vacationing in Vermont, the vice president, Calvin Coolidge, was sworn in as president by his father, a notary public. To soothe the nation's qualms, the new president immediately began addressing the public via radio and holding press conferences twice a week. By the time Congress reconvened in December 1923, Coolidge had already been serving as commander-in-chief for a third of a year and had quelled anxiety over the Teapot Dome scandal, which implicated Harding's secretary of the interior, Albert Fall.

The next major reconsideration of succession rules occurred during the Great Depression and the long winter of 1932–1933 when the Twentieth Amendment, moving the president's inauguration from March 4 to January 20, was ratified on January 23, 1933. The intention of the amendment was to put an end to lame duck Congresses and presidents.[39] Until that point, new members of Congress would have to wait thirteen months before being sworn in and those that had been voted out were without mandates to act. In addition to shortening the interregnum between old and new administrations, the amendment provided a plan should the president-elect die before inauguration day.[40] The amendment could have been tested just three weeks after it was ratified had bullets struck their mark; President-elect Franklin Roosevelt was fired on during a visit to Florida—the bullets missed FDR, but mortally wounded Chicago Mayor Anton Cermak, who was standing near Roosevelt's car. The public's response to the fact that Roosevelt survived a close call was positive, strengthening the president-elect's image at a time when the country's economy was in a disastrous condition. *The Washington Post* reported that "the whole affair brought a tremendous response from the American public" as evidenced by the number of encouraging telegrams the president-elect had received.[41] More generally, the amendment authorized Congress to legislate on matters of presidential transitions.

The final sudden presidential succession before the nuclear age took place on April 12, 1945, when Franklin Roosevelt died in Warm Springs, Georgia, of a cerebral hemorrhage. Roosevelt's death shocked the nation, and while it abruptly transformed Harry Truman from a relatively unknown and brand-new vice president to a wartime president, the transition may not have taken the new president completely by surprise. After hearing an unsubstantiated rumor in February 1945 that the president had died at sea onboard the USS *Quincy* (en route to Washington from the Yalta Conference), Truman wrote in his *Memoirs* that he was "shocked" by Roosevelt's haggard appearance and evident weakness upon his return to the Capitol.[42] Roosevelt's deterioration in 1944 and early 1945 was evident to most people who were close to him.[43] He looked frail and had lost weight; his hands shook during his brief 550-word inaugural address on January 20, 1945.[44]

Truman was on Capitol Hill when House Speaker Sam Rayburn told him the president's press secretary, Steve Early, had telephoned that the vice president was wanted at the White House. The matter seemed urgent as Early had told him to enter through the main Pennsylvania Avenue entrance, rather than the east entrance he went through for private meetings with the president.[45] Truman ran through the Capitol's basement back to his office to get his hat, and then, with his driver, fought his way through rush hour traffic to the White House, without any Secret Service protection. When he arrived in the private quarters of the White House, First Lady Eleanor Roosevelt informed him that the president was dead.[46]

Within two hours and twenty-four minutes of FDR's death, Truman was sworn in and, shortly thereafter, told of the development of a new explosive device of unprecedented power. The nation's leaders gathered in the Cabinet room of the White House—including Secretary of State Edward Stettinius (now next in line of succession), Speaker of the House Sam Rayburn, and House Majority Leader John McCormack—in a show of support, to keep the gears grinding on the wheels of democracy. After the swearing-in ceremony, Truman met with the Cabinet. Secretary of War Henry Lewis Stimson, the most senior member, stayed behind to inform the new president they would need to discuss an urgent matter: the top-secret Manhattan Project. Roosevelt had not taken his vice president into his confidence about the Manhattan Project, in part because it would have been atypical for the vice president to enjoy the president's confidence on top-secret national security matters in the early 1940s. Roosevelt also did not reveal the existence of the atomic bomb because, although he knew his health was failing, "like virtually all his predecessors... he didn't care to be reminded of the hovering Reaper."[47]

On the opening day of the United Nations Conference, the twelfth day of his presidency, Truman was briefed by Stimsonon the development of the atomic bomb.[48] Stimson purposefully designed the memo to be alarmist. Rather than a focus on ending the war, it contained phrases such as "modern civilization might be completely destroyed" because of the existence of the bomb.[49] Nuclear anxiety was evident within the administration.

The nuclear question and presidential succession were very much on Truman's mind during the tumultuous events following his sudden ascension to the presidency. Truman wrote in his *Memoirs* that he "already had in mind the idea of recommending to Congress a change in the order of succession in case the vice president, as well as the president, were to die in office," but that "legislation" would "take time."[50] On April 16, Truman's first message to Congress centered only on his vow to continue Roosevelt's policies. It was well received by Congress (and a radio audience of more than sixteen million). An opinion piece in *The Wall Street Journal* concluded, "At least we have manifested to all the world, friends and enemies alike, that our national foundations are still sound at bottom."[51] Senator Claude Pepper of Florida told *The New York Times* that Truman was a "worthy heir to President Roosevelt in both foreign and domestic policy,"[52] and Majority Leader McCormack said assuredly that the new president was "well equipped to steer the ship of state."[53]

Government officials interviewed by the press had high hopes for the new president, but when world leaders heard the news about Roosevelt, some questioned Truman's leadership capabilities and whether the transition would be a success. Supporters in Congress made statements to the media suggesting that Truman, a former senator, was one of them and would ensure the nation's stability. For example, Senator Robert F. Wagner of New York announced that although the nation was in mourning, America "pledges its loyalty to our new leader who grasps the torch of our destiny and holds it unafraid."[54,55] Yet, General Dwight D. Eisenhower, the supreme commander of Allied forces in Europe, was "depressed" at the prospect of a Truman presidency as the war neared its conclusion.[56] And Churchill, years later, would apologize for his first thoughts on Truman's succession. He "confessed" that at Potsdam he held Truman "in very low regard," that he "loathed" Truman succeeding Roosevelt, but that he had "misjudged [Truman] badly." He then credited Truman "more than any other man," as having "saved Western civilization."[57] Ultimately, the transition from Roosevelt to Truman was reminiscent of the abrupt change from Lincoln to Johnson. In both cases the deceased president had led the nation through uncertain, difficult times with positive results.

Roosevelt's death brought attention yet again to the troubling succession question. One issue was the matter of who would be next in line of succession. The office of the vice president was vacant and next in line was Secretary of State Stettinius, who did not think much of the new president.[58] Truman thought that neither Stettinius, nor James F. Byrnes whom Truman chose to replace Stettinius, should have been next in the line of succession.[59] In fact, Truman believed that it was undemocratic for Cabinet secretaries to be placed directly behind the vice president in the line of succession (as had been the case since 1886) because the public does not have a say in Cabinet appointments.

On June 19, 1945, Truman delivered a "Special Message to Congress on Succession to the Presidency," recommending that Congress legislate on the succession issue. Truman stated that he agreed with the provisions of the 1792 Presidential Succession Act that placed the Senate president pro tempore and the speaker of the House next in line to the presidency after the vice president. He pointed out that no federal officer was elected by the entire electorate besides the president and vice president. The speaker of the House, who was elected by the voters in his district and chosen to preside over the House by a vote of all the representatives of the country, would be the closest replacement. He therefore recommended reversing the order of the 1792 Act to make the speaker third, ahead of the president pro tem.

The US Senate Historical Office suggested that an "institutional factor" may have influenced his decision to place the speaker ahead of the president pro tempore. By the time Truman was considering succession issues, the position of president pro tempore had become mostly ceremonial, with no real role in passing legislation or exerting leadership in the chamber. The majority leader had become a more apt parallel to the speaker of the House.[60] However, the position of Senate majority leader was created by the parties, as opposed to the president pro tempore which is a constitutionally created position. The US Senate Historical Office added to its assessment that "it is likely that specific personalities also played a role in Truman's thinking."[61] The Historical Office was alluding to Truman's good friend and confidante, Sam Rayburn, the speaker of the House, whom Truman may have wished to see next in line to the presidency.[62]

In the "Special Message to Congress," Truman, in addition to recommending that the speaker be third in the line of succession, also said that he was uncomfortable with the idea that the president could chose his successor. He stated, "by reason of the tragic death of the late president, it now lies within my power to nominate the person who would be my immediate successor in the event of my own death or inability to act. I do not believe that in a democracy this power should rest with the chief executive."[63] In the interim, however, he believed it was his "duty" to choose a secretary of state "with the proper qualifications" should Truman himself die in office.[64] Shortly after the president's message to the 79th Congress, on June 29, 1945, a bill (H.R. 3587), providing for the line of succession in the order the president had suggested passed the House. But it failed in the Senate. Opponents argued that the speaker of the House and Senate president pro tempore were not "officers" of the government within the parameters of Article II, Section I, Clause 6 of the Constitution.[65]

On February 5, 1947, Truman sent a message to the 80th Congress, reaffirming his message of June 19, 1945, and insisting Congress act immediately on the succession issue.[66] Acting Attorney General Douglas W. MacGregor submitted a letter to the *Congressional Record*, which attested to the constitutionality of the president's proposed succession plan. In the letter, he argued Article II, Section I referred to members not just of the executive, but of the legislative and judicial branches as well.[67] Further support for their legitimacy as "officers" included the fact that many of the framers of the Constitution were among the legislators who passed the 1792 Act which designated the Senate president pro tem and the speaker as "officers" next in the line of succession.[68] The House Judiciary Committee agreed with the Attorney General's findings. Meanwhile, the Senate passed S. 564 on June 27, 1947. These developments paved the way forward.[69]

On July 18, 1947, Truman signed the Presidential Succession Act of 1947, clarifying the line of succession beyond the vice president by amending the 1886 act—the last action on the succession issue—to make the speaker of the House third, and the president pro tempore of the Senate fourth.[70] Putting two congressional leaders next in the line of succession revived potential problems that the presidency might switch political parties midterm. But that concern did not bother Truman, who was focused on the fact that the Cabinet was appointed by the president, not elected by the people.[71] The president successfully pushed Congress to adopt his succession proposals even after the 1946 midterm elections, when Republicans took control of both houses of Congress, meaning that under the legislation, Republican Speaker Joseph W. Martin of Massachusetts would be next in line if Truman died.[72] (The measure passed 50–35, with all but three Democrats voting as a bloc against the legislation.)

The 1947 Presidential Succession Act established the line of succession after the vice president, but did not cover inability. The succession and inability issue returned in 1955 when President Dwight Eisenhower suffered a heart attack during a working vacation at his in-laws' house in Denver, Colorado. Vice President Richard M. Nixon unofficially took on some presidential duties while Eisenhower found respite first in Denver, then at his farm in Gettysburg, and finally at the Truman Little White House in Key West. The president recovered, but he suffered from health scares on two more occasions (an operation to relieve ileitis on June 9, 1956, and a stroke on November 25, 1957) that revived the issue. On the eve of the president's sixty-sixth birthday (October 14, 1956), *New York Times* columnist Harrison E. Salisbury noted that Democratic Nominee Adlai Stevenson had referred to Eisenhower as "the aging president" and suggested Richard Nixon likely would succeed him before his term had ended.[73]

The president's birthday coincided with a statement by Dr. Lawrence H. Snyder of the American Association for the Advancement of Science that "continuance of hydrogen tests could lead to nuclear war or 'universal death,'" giving Salisbury the opportunity to add in the same article that the Democratic Nominee "regard[ed] the question of the hydrogen bomb as perhaps the gravest that confronts mankind."[74] Another *New York Times* contributor Robert McKinney, also observed that Americans were tying presidential transitions to the bomb stating, "one of the strangest of the startling developments during the presidential campaign was the American public's being asked to give judgment on national atomic policies."[75] Into the fall, Democrats tried to use Eisenhower's health—and Nixon's possible ascent to the White House, where he would have his finger on the nuclear button—as a campaign issue.

That year, Eisenhower directed Attorney General Herbert Brownell, Jr., to draft a plan to deal with a temporary presidential inability. In January 1957, after the election, work began again, and after seeking the advice of the Cabinet as well as individuals outside of Washington, Brownell proposed a constitutional amendment. The proposed amendment had four sections. The first stated that if the president were to be removed from office, die or resign, the vice president would take over the president's duties until the president's term had expired. The second said that the president would declare any inability in writing, at which time the vice president would take over the president's duties as "Acting President." The third allowed the vice president to solicit the approval of a majority of the heads of executive departments who were members of the Cabinet if he felt the president was disabled but the president had not declared his own inability in writing. The last gave the president the power to declare when his inability had ended.[76]

Originally, Brownell's proposal was to be sent to Congress alongside a special message from the president urging its passage. But Rayburn cautioned that, if word were to spread to the American public that the president wanted Congress to consider an amendment, the people might become alarmed about his life expectancy. Instead, Brownell testified before a House Judiciary Special Subcommittee on the Study of Presidential Inability. The subcommittee held hearings considering several joint resolutions.[77] The sticking point was a section allowing the president himself to declare when his inability had ended. One of the sharpest critics of Brownell's proposal, Republican Representative Kenneth Keating of New York, suggested a ten-member inability commission to make the determination of presidential inability, while House Judiciary Chairman Emanuel Celler, a New York Democrat, wanted to leave the matter for the vice president and president alone to decide.[78] Former Presidents Hoover and Truman both weighed in. Hoover argued that the Cabinet should decide whether a president was disabled.[79] Truman, in a letter to *The New York Times*, proposed a seven-member commission composed of members of all three branches of government. This commission would choose a panel of medical experts "drawn from the top medical schools of the nation." If the medical board determined that the president was incapacitated, and a two-thirds majority of both houses of Congress agreed with the experts' findings, the president would be replaced by the vice president for the remainder of the president's term. Notably, even if the president experienced a complete recovery from his illness, he would not, according to the former president's proposal, be allowed to resume his duties.[80]

During these hearings, the fear of an atomic attack was openly voiced. Democratic Senator John J. Sparkman of Alabama testified on the heightened importance of planning for possible presidential inability or sudden transitions (in both the executive and legislative branches) in case of disaster such as atomic attack. Celler prodded Starkman: "In this atomic age nobody knows what might happen."[81] Sparkman responded, "I have in mind where, Mr. Chairman, the possibility of an atomic attack on the Capitol for instance where it would not be feasible to make the [inability] determination here but perhaps in some other part of the country." At this point, Keating joined the questioning, stating that "for quite a time" he "had in mind" legislation that would reference an "atomic attack wiping out one-third of the Congress." He suggested Congress "put [its] own house in order" by providing for a congressional succession plan before considering the president's inability. Sparkman admitted that he "shudder[ed] at the optimism in thinking of just one-third of the Congress being destroyed." He then said, "I might remark, rather facetiously, that I notice in the program for vacating the Capitol that the Congress is to be left here." Keating retorted, "Yes, we are expendable." Sparkman then replied,

> I have seen, and I am sure members of this committee have seen, the time when one single well- placed bomb could virtually wipe out the government. I have seen both houses of Congress, the chief executive and all of the Supreme Court and all of the Cabinet members together at one time.... I think all these matters ought to be considered, and it is high time that we were making some decision.

Despite it being "high time," the subcommittee did not reach an agreement.

After Eisenhower's stroke in 1957, Estes Kefauver, now chair of the Senate Judiciary Subcommittee on Constitutional Amendments, reintroduced Brownell's proposal with new language that would provide a means to address a situation in which a disagreement occurred between the president and vice president as to whether the president was incapacitated. Brownell expressed his "great appreciation" that the subcommittee was "seriously considering" his proposal "as a part of realizing we are in an atomic age."[82] Under the specter of the arms race, Eisenhower and Nixon signed a letter agreement, which was released to the public on March 3, 1958.[83] In the letter, the president and vice president agreed that the vice president would assume presidential powers in the event the president declared himself unable to perform his duties.[84] If the president was not in a position to declare himself unable to perform his duties, the vice president, after consulting with whomever he deemed appropriate, would make the determination of inability.[85] As with the Brownell proposal, the president would determine when the inability had ended, and his powers would be immediately restored.[86] (These are often referred to as "the letter agreements.") Notably, the consensus between the administration, members of the subcommittee, and expert witnesses seemed to be that there was a need for an amendment to solve the inability issue.[87]

Brownell's article, "Presidential Disability: The Need for a Constitutional Amendment," in the December 1958 edition of *The Yale Law Journal* underscored the importance of the fact that America had entered the atomic age. "The realization has grown among thoughtful people that our very survival in this age may rest on the capacity of the nation's chief executive to make swift and unquestioned decisions in an emergency," it began. "Now that the issue is so forcefully upon us, with our future existence possibly depending on the forethought that we exercise in resolving it, failure to take proper steps to answer promptly the constitutional question would be the height of irresponsibility."[88]

Others, too, were weighing nuclear peril heavily, such as lawyer Richard H. Hansen who wrote *The Year We Had No President*. In this scholarly work dedicated to President Eisenhower "the first president to take positive action on presidential disability," Hansen detailed Brownell's proposed amendment as well as the history of past presidential inabilities for a collegiate audience. In a foreword to the book, Kefauver argued that "the demands of the nuclear age upon the office of president require that the discharge of its duties never be in suspension or uncertainty."[89] From his position in Congress, Kefauver would continue to pursue succession and inability legislation.

Presidents Truman and Eisenhower both pushed for new succession and inability law with more purpose than their predecessors. The new emphasis on these laws during the Truman and Eisenhower eras by members of Congress and scholars, and particularly by the presidents themselves, reflects the nuclear anxiety of the age. As the 1960s arrived, the incandescent tensions peaked—the political rhetoric of Cold War leaders became more bellicose, the arms race ensued, and the superpowers threatened proxy wars in all corners of the globe, some of which had the potential to become nuclear. As the world appeared less stable, the need for a strong, competent leader at the helm increased. Congress began in earnest to find a more permanent solution to presidential succession and inability issues.

US Senator Birch Bayh with President John F. Kennedy, 1962.[90]

Notes

1. The Constitution of the United States. Articles I and II.
2. Akhil Reed Amar, *America's Constitution: A Biography* (New York: Random House, 2005), 15, 151, 447–53.
3. While the plan was well-received, it was not seriously considered because it was too similar to the British form of government. "The British Plan," *The US Constitution*, http://www.usconstitution.net/plan_brit.html#f5.
4. Article I, Section 3 provided that the vice president would preside over the Senate but allowed senators to elect a temporary chair in his absence. Akhil Reed Amar, *America's Constitution*, 170 fn. "Pro tempore" is Latin for "of the time."
5. "From John Adams in 1789 to Richard Nixon in the 1950s, presiding over the Senate was the chief function of vice presidents, who had an office in the Capitol, received their staff support and

office expenses through the legislative appropriations, and rarely were invited to participate in cabinet meetings or other executive activities." "President Pro Tempore," *Senate Historical Office* (United State Senate), http://www.senate.gov/artandhistory/history/common/briefing/President_Pro_Tempore.htm.
6. "Vacancy in the Presidency," *Annals of Congress*, House of Representatives, 1st Congress, 3rd Session (Library of Congress), 1911–15. For a literature on the history of succession see, for example: Philip Abbott, *Accidental Presidents: Death, Assassination, Resignation, and Democratic Succession* (New York: Palgrave Macmillan, 2008). Wilfred E. Binkley, *The Man in the White House: His Powers and Duties* (Baltimore, MD: The Johns Hopkins Press, 1958), 262–287. Edward S. Corwin, The President: Office and Powers, 1787–1984, 5th edition (New York: New York University Press, 1984). Richard H. Hansen, *The Year We Had No President* (Lincoln, NE: University of Nebraska Press, 1962). Laurin L. Henry, *Presidential Transitions* (Washington, DC: The Brookings Institution, 1960). Rose McDermott, *Presidential Leadership, Illness, and Decision-Making* (New York: Cambridge University Press, 2008). Ruth Silva, *Presidential Succession* (New York: Greenwood Press, 1968).
7. This bill entitled "An act relative to the election of a president and vice president of the United States, and declaring the officer who shall act as president in the case of vacancies in the offices both of president and vice president," passed the Senate and was sent to the House. "Proceedings and Debates of the House of Representatives of the United States," *Annals of Congress*, House of Representatives, 2nd Congress, 1st Session (Library of Congress). http://memory.loc.gov/cgi-bin/ampage?collId=llac&fileName=003/llac003.db&recNum=68.
8. Political factions hardened as Hamilton and Jefferson, both members of President Washington's Cabinet, disagreed over issues such as a national bank. Federalists (Hamilton) split from Democratic-Republicans (Jefferson) in the 1790s. After the failed Hartford Convention, the conclusion of the War of 1812 brought with it the end of the Federalist Party. At that point, the Federalists were no longer a national force and, throwing their weight behind policies previously supported by the Federalists (such as federal support for national infrastructure), the Democratic-Republicans

began "out-Federalizing" the Federalists. The House voted on the Senate's changes the next day, approving the congressional line of succession by a vote of 31-24.
9. The law that changed after the death of James A. Garfield made Chester A. Arthur president in September 1881, as described in this chapter.
10. John D. Feerick, *The Twenty-Fifth Amendment: Its Complete History and Earliest Applications* (New York: Fordham University Press, 1976).
11. Named after Representative Henry A. Wise of Virginia who introduced the legislation.
12. John D. Feerick, *From Failing Hands: The Story of Presidential Succession* (New York: Fordham University Press, 1965), 162.
13. Salmon P. Chase and John Niven, "April 14, 1865," *The Salmon P. Chase Papers*. Vol. 1 (Kent, Ohio: Kent State University Press, 1993), Samuel Chase, 528–29.
14. For an example of initial reports of Seward's death, see *The Alabama Beacon*. "Glorious News. Lincoln and Seward Assassinated!" *The Alabama Beacon* (April 21, 1865). http://rememberinglincoln.fords.org/node/192. Chase quote: Doris Kearns Goodwin, *Team of Rivals: The Political Genius of Abraham Lincoln* (New York: Simon & Schuster, 2005), 738. Ford's Theatre holds several primary sources related to Lincoln's assassination and its aftermath. See "Lincoln's Assassination," https://www.fords.org/lincolns-assassination/.
15. "President Pro Tempore," *Senate Historical Office* (United State Senate), http://www.senate.gov/artandhistory/history/common/briefing/President_Pro_Tempore.htm.
16. "A Great Nation in Grief: President Garfield Shot by an Assassin," *The New York Times* (July 3, 1881).
17. The Stalwarts opposed the Half Breeds' embrace of civil service reform, among other issues.
18. "A Great Nation in Grief: President Garfield Shot by an Assassin," *The New York Times* (July 3, 1881).
19. "Anxiety Dispelling Hope: The President in a Very Critical Condition," *The New York Times* (August 26, 1881).
20. Unknown to anyone at the time, and buried in a *New York Times* tribute to Arthur upon his death in 1886, was the fact that Arthur had prepared for the eventuality of his death prior to the convening

of the October 10 session by writing a proclamation calling the Senate into special session to elect a president pro tem. He placed the document in a sealed envelope addressed to the "President in Washington." If he, too, died before the Senate met in special session, a mechanism would exist to choose a successor. "Voice to Sorrow," *The New York Times* (November 21, 1886).
21. Chester A. Arthur, "First Annual Message (December 6, 1881)," Transcript. Miller Center (University of VA), http://millercenter.org/president/arthur/speeches/speech-3560.
22. Grover Cleveland, "First Annual Message (December 8, 1885)," Transcript. Miller Center (University of VA), http://millercenter.org/president/cleveland/speeches/speech-3755.
23. The exception Hoar was referring to was Lewis Cass, who served as secretary of war under President Andrew Jackson and secretary of state under President James Buchanan. The Democrats ran Cass in 1848, but he lost to Zachary Taylor. Hoar elided mention of John Tyler, the only Senate president pro tempore (March 1835) to become president. US Congressional Documents Volume 17, 49th Congress Special and 1st Session, 180-82.
24. "Grover Cleveland Special Session Message, August 8, 1893," *The American Presidency Project*. http://www.presidency.ucsb.edu/ws/index.php?pid=70711.
25. Allan Nevins, *Grover Cleveland: A Study in Courage*, Volumes I and II, Fifth Edition (New York: Dodd, Mead & Company, 1933).
26. John Milton Cooper, Jr., *The Warrior and the Priest: Woodrow Wilson and Theodore Roosevelt* (Cambridge, MA: The Belknap Press of Harvard University Press, 1983), 33.
27. Sidney M. Milkis and Michael Nelson, *The American Presidency: Origins and Development*, 1776–1993, Second Edition (Washington, DC: CQ Press, 1994), 238.
28. John Maynard Keynes, *The Economic Consequences of the Peace* (New York: Penguin Books, 1995), 38.
29. "The President's Illness," *The New York Times* (September 27, 1919).
30. "Wilson Returns to Washington Worn and Shaken," *The New York Times* (September 28, 1919).
31. "Cabinet Meets, Lansing Presiding," *The New York Times* (October 6, 1919).

32. Feerick, *From Failing Hands*, 162. The public was unaware of the fact that Edith Bolling had at least some prior knowledge of world affairs. Wilson's courtship of her included allowing her to read important policy statements. For more on her introduction to confidential papers, see Cooper, Jr., *The Warrior and the Priest*, 294.
33. John Milton Cooper, Jr., in *Woodrow Wilson: A Biography* argues that it was not the fact that staying on as president would help him recover, which had been the prevailing school of thought. Cooper, Jr., *Woodrow Wilson*, 536.
34. "Reports Wilson Suffered Shock: New Hampshire Senator Expresses Pessimistic Opinion," *The New York Times* (October 12, 1919).
35. Complicating the inability issue, one of Wilson's doctors, neurologist Francis X. Dercum of Philadelphia, suggested resigning the presidency would remove Wilson's desire to live, thereby killing him. Feerick, *From Failing Hands*, 173.
36. Berg, *Wilson*, 616.
37. Berg, *Wilson*, 657, 662.
38. Cooper continues, "Just a few times during the rest of his presidency would he mention resigning, and those would be months after he suffered the stroke and had begun to recover" Cooper, Jr., *Woodrow Wilson*, 535.
39. David E. Kyvig, *Explicit and Authentic Acts: Amending the US Constitution, 1776–1995* (University Press of Kansas), 274.
40. Section 3 of the Twentieth Amendment states that the vice president elect becomes president if the president elect dies during the interregnum. For the full text of the Twentieth Amendment see The Constitution of the United States. Twentieth Amendment.
41. "Roosevelt Describes Attempt on His Life," *The Washington Post* (February 17, 1933).
42. Harry S. Truman, *Memoirs: Year of Decisions*, Volume 1 (Garden City, NY: Doubleday & Company, 1955), 2. In his article of June 24, 1957, Truman later elaborated on this point, stating that until Roosevelt's return from Yalta, he thought presidential incapacitation was "an academic problem in history." Harry S. Truman, "Truman Proposes Disability Panel, *The New York Times* (June 24, 1957).

43. Cardiologist Howard Bruenn diagnosed Roosevelt with congestive heart failure because of chronic high blood pressure in March 1944. See Joseph Lelyveld, *His Final Battle: The Last Months of Franklin Roosevelt* (New York: Alfred A. Knopf, 2016), 308.
44. Franklin Roosevelt's 1945 inaugural address was the second shortest in history, second only to George Washington's 130-word second inaugural. Truman was only with Roosevelt a few times between his nomination and the election, but when lunching together in August 1944, Truman could not help noticing the president's frailty: "his hand trembled so much when he tried to pour cream into his coffee that most of it spilled into a saucer." On March 1, 1945, FDR delivered his last speech to Congress. "Attentive onlookers" noticed that he lost his place in the text, filled in with unscripted text, and repeated himself. Lelyveld, *His Final Battle*, 200, 298. For someone so experienced in delivering public speeches, this was indicative not of nervousness, but of mental confusion.
45. According to Joseph Lelyveld, House Speaker Sam Rayburn said "Truman knew exactly what to expect." Truman had muttered "Jesus Christ and General Jackson," upon hanging up the phone with Early. As quoted in See Lelyveld, *His Final Battle*, 331.
46. It took him a moment to compose himself before replying "Is there anything I can do for you?" She responded, "Is there anything we can do for you? For you are the one in trouble now." Truman, *Memoirs*, 5.
47. The vice president was given a statutory national security role with the establishment of the National Security Council in 1947. President Jimmy Carter increased the responsibilities of the vice president and gave him an office in the West Wing in the late 1970s. Lelyveld, *His Final Battle*, 332.
48. "Henry Stimson to Harry S. Truman," April 24, 1945. *Harry S. Truman Library and Museum*. https://www.trumanlibrary.gov/sites/default/files/BombDecision_Handouts.pdf.
49. David McCullough, *Truman* (New York: Simon & Schuster, 1992), 289, 376, and 378.
50. Truman, *Memoirs: Year of Decisions*, 23.
51. Thomas F. Woodlock, "Thinking it Over," *The Wall Street Journal* (April 25, 1945).

52. "Congress Acclaim Won by Truman," *The New York Times* (April 17, 1945).
53. William T. Peacock, "Truman Goes to Hill, Wins Unanimous Pledge of Aid," *The Washington Post*, April 14, 1945.
54. *The New York Times* wrote "those who have long associated with the president pay great tribute to his sincerity and honesty of purpose." Lewis Wood, "Turn to Right Seen: New President's Friends Say Legislative Branch Will Have Large Role," *The New York Times*, April 13, 1945, https://www.nytimes.com/1945/04/14/archives/turn-to-right-seen-new-presidents-friends-say-legislative-branch.html.Supporters in Congress: C.P. Trussell, "Congress to Hear Truman Monday," *The New York Times*, April 14, 1945, https://www.nytimes.com/1945/04/14/archives/congress-to-hear-truman-monday-he-talks-with-leaders-at-capitol.html.
55. C.P. Trussell, "Congress to Hear Truman Monday," *The New York Times*, April 14, 1945, https://www.nytimes.com/1945/04/14/archives/congress-to-hear-truman-monday-he-talks-with-leaders-at-capitol.html.
56. McCullough, *Truman*, 349.
57. The fact that Truman's accession was a good omen in the eyes of the Nazis illustrates that the enemy believed Roosevelt was a more formidable opponent. The news of Roosevelt's death broke in Germany on Friday the 13th: Nazi propaganda minister Joseph Goebbels called Fuehrer Adolf Hitler personally to tell him, "it was a turning point written in the stars." British Foreign Secretary Anthony Eden telegraphed Prime Minister Winston Churchill that Truman seemed "honest and friendly." Nazis: McCullough, *Truman*, 345. Winston, Churchill, *The Second World War*. Vol. VI: *Triumph and Tragedy* (London: Penguin Books, 2005), 484. Low regard: "The Presidency: The World of Harry Truman," *Time*, January 7, 1973, http://content.time.com/time/magazine/article/0,9171,910501,00.html.
58. Truman's association with Tom Pendergast's political machine in Kansas City, Missouri did not recommend him to Washington denizens. Stettinius regarded the new president as little more than a small-town hack. He saw the transition from Roosevelt to Truman as similar to that of Woodrow Wilson giving way to Warren

Harding in 1921, with "cheap courthouse politicians taking over." McCullough, *Truman*, 349.
59. Truman decided to replace Stettinius with James F. Byrnes, a former US Supreme Court justice and US senator from South Carolina, as soon as Stettinius' work was done at the United Nations Conference in San Francisco. Four people held the position of secretary of state during Truman's presidency: Edward R. Stettinius (November 1944) April 1945–June 1945), James F. Byrnes (July 1945–January 1947), George C. Marshall (January 1947–January 1949), and Dean Acheson (January 1949–January 1953).
60. "President Pro Tempore," *Senate Historical Office* (United State Senate), http://www.senate.gov/artandhistory/history/common/briefing/President_Pro_Tempore.htm.
61. "President Pro Tempore," *Senate Historical Office* (United State Senate), http://www.senate.gov/artandhistory/history/common/briefing/President_Pro_Tempore.htm.
62. McCullough, *Truman*, 357.
63. "Special Message to Congress on Succession to the Presidency," (June 19, 1945), Truman Presidential Library. https://www.trumanlibrary.gov/library/public-papers/22/letter-president-senate-and-speaker-house-succession-presidency.
64. Truman, *Memoirs*, 23.
65. They cited the 1798 Senate impeachment case against Senator William Blount of Tennessee who had argued that his commission was from the state of Tennessee, not the federal government, and he was therefore not a "civil officer of the United States." The Senate had agreed with Blount and dismissed the articles of impeachment. Supporters of the succession bill pointed to a 1916 Supreme Court case, Lamar v. US, which held that members of Congress were "civil officers" within Article II, Section IV.
66. Truman's speech was reprinted in June 1947. "House of Representatives—Thursday, July 10, 1947," Volume 93, 80th Congress, 1st Session, *Congressional Record* 8618 (1947), 8620–21.
67. MacGregor also argued that the Blount case was not applicable.
68. "House of Representatives—Friday, June 27, 1947," Volume 93, 80th Congress, 1st Session, *Congressional Record* (1947), 7768–70.

69. The bill passed: "provid[ed] for the performance of the duties of the office of president in case of the removal, resignation, death, or inability both of the president and vice president" (July 9, 1947). Serial Set Vol. No. 11121, Session Vol. No. 4. 80th Congress, 1st Session. H. Rpt. 817.
70. 3 United States Code, Section 19 (2012).
71. In a June 19, 1945 statement to Congress, President Truman wrote, "[T]he office of the President should be filled by an elective officer.... I believe that the Speaker is the official in the Federal Government whose selection, next to that of the President and Vice President, can be most accurately said to stem from the people themselves." House of Representatives, Report Number 79-289, 1–2.
72. All of Truman's proposals, except a special election, were incorporated in the bill passed in 1947. Among those voting in favor were Representative Lyndon B. Johnson of Texas and Representative John W. McCormack of Massachusetts. Feerick, *From Failing Hands*, 208.
73. Harrison H. Salisbury, "Stevenson Makes Eisenhower's Age a Campaign Issue," *The New York Times* (October 14, 1956).
74. Salisbury, "Stevenson Makes Eisenhower's Age a Campaign Issue."
75. Robert McKinney, "Peaceful Atoms to Stop War," *The New York Times* (December 9, 1956).
76. See, for example: "Dwight D. Eisenhower, 42- The President's News Conference, March 5, 1958," *The American Presidency Project*. http://www.presidency.ucsb.edu/ws/index.php?pid=11315.
77. These House Resolutions are only discernable in the hearing report by the letters "A," "B," "C," "D," and "E." "Presidential Inability," *Hearings Before Special Subcommittee to Study Presidential Inability of the Committee on the Judiciary House of Representatives Eighty-Fourth Congress Second Session on Problem of Presidential Inability April 11 and 12, 1956*, Serial No. 20 (Washington: United States Government Printing Office, 1956).
78. "Presidential Inability," *Hearings Before Special Subcommittee to Study Presidential Inability of the Committee on the Judiciary House of Representatives Eighty-Fourth Congress Second Session on Problem of Presidential Inability April 11 and 12, 1956*, Serial No. 20 (Washington: United States Government Printing Office, 1956).

79. "President's Duties." In *CQ Almanac* 1956, 12th ed., 08-590-08-591. Washington, DC: Congressional Quarterly, 1957.
80. Harry S. Truman, "Truman Proposes Disability Panel, *The New York Times* (June 24, 1957).
81. "Presidential Inability," *Hearings Before Special Subcommittee to Study Presidential Inability of the Committee on the Judiciary House of Representatives Eighty-Fourth Congress Second Session on Problem of Presidential Inability* April 11 and 12, 1956, Serial No. 20 (Washington: United States Government Printing Office, 1956).
82. Brownell made this statement on April 1, 1957, during another Special Subcommittee on Presidential Inability Hearing. This sense of urgency allowed a resolution similar to Brownell's proposal to pass the subcommittee; yet it did not make it to a full floor vote. "Presidential Inability," *Hearing Before the Special Subcommittee on Study of Presidential Inability of the Committee on the Judiciary House of Representatives Eighty-Fifth Congress First Session on Problem of Presidential Inability* April 1, 1956 Serial No. 3 (Washington: United States Government Printing Office, 195).
83. "Agreement Between the President and the Vice President as to Procedures in the Event of Presidential Disability," *Public Papers* 196, March 3, 1958.
84. "Agreement Between the President and the Vice President as to Procedures."
85. "Agreement Between the President and the Vice President as to Procedures."
86. "Agreement Between the President and the Vice President as to Procedures."
87. The author agrees with John Feerick's assessment. See Feerick, *The Twenty-Fifth Amendment*, 55.
88. Herbert Brownell, Jr., "Presidential Disability: The Need for a Constitutional Amendment," Vol. 68. No. 2. *The Yale Law Journal* (December 1958), 1.
89. Hansen was among those who testified in 1963, prior to President Kennedy's assassination, in favor of a succession and inability amendment. See the footnotes for Chapter 4. Richard H. Hansen, *The Year We Had No President*, (Lincoln, NE: University of Nebraska Press, 1962), vii.

90. Bayh with President John F. Kennedy (84-1074), July 1962, Photograph Collection, Birch Bayh Senatorial Papers, Modern Political Papers Collection, Indiana University Libraries, Bloomington, Indiana.

CHAPTER 3

The Nuclear Paradox: Power, Fallibility, and the Twenty-Fifth Amendment

From the nation's founding until the 1950s, questions of presidential succession had frequently tapped into deep-seated anxieties about the durability of democratic government, specifically whether it could withstand the threats posed by disruptive, unplanned changes to the nation's highest office. Following the United States' use of atomic bombs against Japan at the end of World War II, however, those anxieties took on a new gravity. "Merely by existing [nuclear weapons] have already set off chain reactions throughout American society and within every one of its institutions,"[1] stated the *Bulletin of the Atomic Scientists*. The *Bulletin* recognized that nuclear anxiety had become a staple of American popular and political culture overnight, but that it was difficult to quantify. In response, they designed the Doomsday Clock in 1945 as a gauge of how close mankind is to destroying itself, with midnight being the apocalypse.[2] The president had the Zeus-like power to destroy entire nations and snuff out millions of lives with the press of a button in an instant; all other powers were trivial by comparison.[3] The 1946 Atomic Energy Act granted this cosmic authority solely to the president.[4]

After the development of more powerful bombs by both superpowers and a method to deliver them, with the launch of Sputnik in 1957, nuclear anxiety had begun to spur government officials in both Congress and the Eisenhower administration to find a solution to the presidential succession and inability problem that had been elusive since the Constitution's ratification. The fear of a nuclear attack became a pervasive undercurrent in American politics and culture, evident in presidential speeches and political advertisements, as well as in popular films, books, and songs. Public discourse was filled with concern for the need for a competent leader in control of the nuclear button. Finding a solution to the centuries-old problem was becoming a necessity.

Nuclear anxiety flourished even more intensely after the assassination of John F. Kennedy in 1963, and the specter of a nation without firm leadership during a time of nuclear crisis ultimately provided the impetus to resolve the issue. The Cold War, specifically the decade from 1961–1971, saw more total amendments debated than any era since the nation's founding.[5] What the historian David Kyvig called the "extraordinary eruption of Article V activity"[6] suggests that leaders recognized that the world was changing radically and quickly. The Constitution needed to account for those changes. The destructive power of the bomb meant that these leaders now were required to make decisions that would affect the world on an order of magnitude greater than any previously seen.

The nuclear issue set the sudden transition from John F. Kennedy to Lyndon Johnson apart from other unexpected presidential successions in the past. Although seven other presidents had died in office, Kennedy was the first to die instantaneously, fatally wounded by an assassin's bullet.[7] Garfield clung to life for eighty days, Lincoln survived overnight, and McKinley remained alive for five days. But Kennedy's immediate death—coupled with Johnson's presence in the same motorcade where JFK was shot, rendering him potentially vulnerable as well—highlighted the long-standing concern that the passage of power to the vice president might not always run smoothly. The presidential assassination had resulted in a sudden transfer of power to a vice president whose own health was subject to question.

For this reason, traditional histories, such as that of Kyvig, have argued that the Twenty-Fifth Amendment, though a product of "long-standing concerns about presidential disability and succession," was most immediately "a reaction to the assassination of President John F. Kennedy."[8] Media reports, accounts of interactions among decision-makers, and intergovernmental correspondence reveal the varied but often interconnected fears relating to concerns stemming from Kennedy's murder: fantasies that the assassination was part of a wider conspiracy, perhaps waged by Soviet or ultra-right-wing groups; a dislike of Johnson, leading to depictions of him as a usurper; and doubts about Johnson's capabilities to lead.

As most historians have noted, these disparate anxieties, tensions, and worries suggest Bayh drafted the Twenty-Fifth Amendment largely in response to Kennedy's assassination. Yet the assassination does not fully explain the amendment's sinuous journey through Congress and its ratification in 1967, more than three years after Kennedy's death. For a more complete account, the climate of nuclear anxiety evident in culture and politics must be factored into the ratification of the Twenty-Fifth Amendment. The development of increasingly powerful weapons heightened tensions between the superpowers while political rhetoric fed off, and contributed to, nuclear anxiety. Civil defense planning emerged as a buffer against those fears. Amid the growing nuclear anxiety, Eisenhower's illnesses and Kennedy's sudden death exposed the paradox that the president was at once both powerful and fallible. In response, continuity of operations plans and the Eisenhower/Nixon and Kennedy/Johnson letter agreements provide evidence that presidents were working to ensure the line of presidential succession against the threat of a disruption at the highest levels of government leadership. These factors taken in the context of an overriding nuclear anxiety would eventually result in ratification of the Twenty-Fifth Amendment.

* * *

In 1945, the first superficial cultural representations of Hiroshima and Nagasaki such as the new "atomic cocktail" made of Pernod and gin appeared to celebrate America's victory in the Pacific[9]—yet even these festive representations of US power demonstrated that the awesome power of the bomb, once detonated, was never far from Americans' thoughts. Any lightheartedness on the topic soon gave way, as one sociologist wrote at the time, to an intrinsic, paralyzing anxiety.[10] The first images of the destruction caused by the bomb were grainy photographs in *Life* magazine on August 20, 1945.[11] But the sense of foreboding was implanted in the nation's psyche by John Hersey's gruesome account of the human suffering published in the August 31, 1946 issue of *The New Yorker*.[12] Hersey's articles were developed into a bestselling book, *Hiroshima*, and depicted scenes too horrible to imagine such as dress fabric motifs permanently imprinted onto women's bodies and the burned skin of children hanging from their faces.[13] The destructive possibilities of this new weapon were immediately portrayed on film for a popular audience. That year, for example, the Truman White House officially approved the script of a Metro-Goldwyn Mayer (MGM) studios production depicting the bombing of Japan. The title, *The Beginning or the End*, was provided by the president himself in an early interview.[14] "Make your film, gentlemen, and put this message into your picture—tell the men and women of the world that they are at the beginning, or the end," Truman said.[15] It was meant to suggest that the world was at a tipping point because of the harnessing of atomic energy.

Nuclear anxiety below the surface was sometimes belied by Americans' attempt to give the appearance of living an ordinary life.[16] Post-World War II Levittowns and Sloan Wilson's 1955 book, *Man in the Grey Flannel Suit*,[17] made into a movie in 1956, neatly summarize the decade as one of consensus and conformity. Yet, this disconnect was captured at the end of the decade, when *Life* added an element of levity to the topic of nuclear anxiety by publishing an article on newlyweds who decided to spend their honeymoon in their new bomb shelter.[18] With perils awaiting at every turn and strict conformity enforced in the workplace, the new suburban home was designed to be a place where a male breadwinner could relax and, if possible, put aside the anxieties of the age, including the ever-present fear of the bomb.

But the popularity of nuclear doomsday plots demonstrated that Americans were not successful in their attempts to put aside their deep-seated nuclear anxiety. Science fiction author Isaac Asimov noted that nuclear doomsday plots became so numerous by this time that editors began to refuse manuscripts without so much as a glance.[19] Authors were not just giving voice to their nuclear anxiety but living it. Tim O'Brien, author of the Vietnam war novel *The Things They Carried*, revealed that CONELRAD tests (Control of Electromagnetic Radiation, a form of emergency radio broadcasting devised during the Truman administration that produced a tone for fifteen seconds) struck such a chord of fear in him as a child that in 1958 he converted his ping-pong table into a fallout shelter.[20] Todd Gitlin, social scientist, activist, and author of *The Sixties: Years of Hope, Days of Rage*, pointed out that he grew up among the first generation of Americans "to fear not only war but the end of days." He added:

> Under the desks and crouched in hallways, terrors were ignited, existentialists were made. Whether or not we believed that hiding under a school

desk or in a hallway was really going to protect us from the furies of an atomic blast, we could never quite take for granted that the world we had been born into was destined to endure.[21]

As the bombs tested became more powerful, and the tests themselves more numerous, Gitlin's existential crisis was reflected in films about the fear of fallout, not just a direct hit. Nevil Shute romanticized what nuclear war and fallout might do to relationships between men and women in the 1957 novel *On the Beach*. Shute imagined a post-apocalyptic world only a few years into the future, and it (and the 1959 film adaptation) ended with the complete destruction of mankind.[22] Films such as *Godzilla: King of the Monsters!* (1956), *The Amazing Colossal Man* (1957), the *4-D Man* (1959 and 1963) all treated the concept of atomic-mutation monsters, individual isolation, and the unsuccessful search for meaning.[23] Song lyrics also contained this theme. In May 1963, Bob Dylan released his song "A Hard Rain's a-Gonna Fall."[24] Although Dylan has said it was not his intention, his fan base associated the lyrics with the fear of nuclear fallout.[25]

Between 1961 and 1964, what seemed like an endless stream of works captured the nation's anxiety that events would spiral out of control toward a nuclear apocalypse. The 1961 novel *The Bedford Incident* depicted a naval game between the destroyer USS *Bedford* and a Soviet submarine that ended with the accidental torpedoing of the Soviet sub, and a nuclear explosion.[26] In 1961, a Hollywood hit, *Voyage to the Bottom of the Sea*, emphasized "nuclear retribution as the expression of God's displeasure."[27] The movie featured deranged leaders who battled with the question of accepting the inevitability of nuclear war.

After the sudden Kennedy—Johnson transition, films continued to focus on the terror of uncontrollable events but centered even more closely on the human weakness behind the power of the bomb. Fletcher Knebel and Charles W. Bailey II's novel *Seven Days in May*, written during the early days of Kennedy's presidency, was adapted by Rod Serling into a screenplay in 1964, and was nominated for a Writer's Guild of America Award for Best Written American Drama. The political thriller featured a plot to overthrow a president who had pushed an unpopular nuclear disarmament treaty through the Senate. The military leaders who planned the coup were convinced the Soviets would launch a first strike; stoking Americans' feelings, in both the film and reality, that the Soviets could not be trusted. Also focused on US–USSR relations, *Fail-Safe* portrayed a fictional American president and Soviet premier attempting to reach an equitable solution after a technological error leads American planes to be sent to drop nuclear bombs on Moscow. Bill Moyers, a key developer of Johnson's 1964 presidential campaign message, persuaded the producers of *Fail-Safe* to release the film in October 1964, just prior to the presidential election, with the intention of employing this fear to swing the vote in Johnson's favor.[28] The film served to remind those who watched of the ever-present danger of nuclear warfare and perhaps subconsciously served as a connection between the movies and the political campaign ads on television that emphasized nuclear anxieties. Although this film did not portray a psychotic president with his hand on the nuclear button—as would have been most ideal for the Johnson campaign—it reminded Americans that even with a responsible president at the helm, events could culminate in nuclear disaster.

That year, the power of the bomb in the hands of a mentally disabled leader was the theme of the Stanley Kubrick's black comedy *Dr. Strangelove or How I Stopped Worrying and Learned to Love the Bomb*. *Dr. Strangelove* is the archetypal movie about a US president who volunteers to launch a nuclear strike on New York after an insane US general launches one on Moscow, to avoid additional nuclear reprisals.[29] The film ends abruptly with nuclear explosions that presumably cause the destruction of both New York and Moscow. The gallows humor may have been entertaining, but it gave Americans a different perspective from which to consider their president's competency, and his nuclear policies.[30] The fact that *Dr. Strangelove* is listed on the National Film Registry of the Library of Congress underscores the plot's enduring cultural significance.[31]

* * *

Pop cultural anxieties regarding the ability of the president who had his finger on the nuclear trigger mirrored political reality when, as early as Eisenhower's first presidential campaign in 1952, Truman expressed the opinion that Eisenhower was unfit to be trusted with the nation's atomic arsenal due to his advanced age. This argument was perhaps not one Truman was in a position to make, given that he was six years older than his eventual successor. But in an October 4, 1952, speech in Oakland, California, Truman called Eisenhower "a sad and pathetic spectacle," whose potential victory was a "danger to national security."[32] The next presidential election, in 1956, was the first during the nuclear age in which a candidate's mental ability was called into question. Democratic presidential candidate Adlai Stevenson, who had lost to Eisenhower in 1952, tied Eisenhower's health issues and Vice President Richard Nixon's mental fitness to increasing anxiety over nuclear war. After charging that Eisenhower's "part-time conduct" as president had produced the "crises in world affairs," Stevenson argued that putting Nixon in charge of the Republican Party (which was "inevitable" due to Eisenhower's "age" and "health") was dangerous.[33] Stevenson questioned the nation: "Do you want this man as commander-in-chief to exercise power over peace and war?" and "Do you want to place the hydrogen bomb in his hands?"[34] *New York Post's* Max Lerner also cited Nixon's mental state as one of a three-pronged set of problems as to why Eisenhower and Nixon should not be reelected. The Soviets' successful detonation of the hydrogen bomb and Eisenhower's health concerns (the ileitis and his most recent heart attack) were the other two.[35] In a nationally televised speech the night before the election, Lerner, one of the nation's most renowned columnists, predicted Eisenhower would not live through a second term and that Nixon would not be a reliable successor because he had neither the competence nor presence of mind required for split-second decision-making in the nuclear age. "I recoil at the prospect of Mr. Nixon as … guardian of the hydrogen bomb," Lerner said.[36] Voters, deciding they did not want to switch teams in the middle of a decade laden with anxiety, reelected Eisenhower.

This ongoing anxiety about presidential inability led Eisenhower and Nixon to sign a letter agreement, released to the public on March 3, 1958, under the specter of the arms race. The agreement provided that in the event of presidential inability, the president would inform the vice president (if possible) and the vice president would serve as Acting President, exercising the powers and duties of the office until the inability had ended. If the president was incapacitated to the point where he could not inform the vice president, the vice president would be empowered to make the call that the president was incapacitated and assume the president's responsibilities. In either case, the president reserved the sole right to determine when his inability had ended and he could reassume presidential powers and responsibilities.

* * *

In addition to concern over Eisenhower's illnesses, the rapid pace of the arms race and the development of ever-more powerful bombs increased Americans' fear that civilization would end abruptly.[37] With the development of the thermonuclear bomb—tested on November 1, 1952, three days prior to Eisenhower's victory—the magnitude of potential destruction changed. This new bomb used the same fission reaction in atomic explosions to start a fusion reaction which could create a blast that was a thousand times more powerful and measured in megatons. The first successful explosion by the United States created a ten-megaton blast. The likelihood that humans would not survive a nuclear war increased, and the magnitude of public anxiety grew to new heights. Despite countless wars throughout history, the underlying, inherent assumption of the continuity of the human race had never been questioned. This assumption began to fade, if not disappear, with the fission bomb and further eroded with the development of the fusion bomb. The continuity of the presidency could suddenly be linked to the continuity of human life.

During the immediate post-war years, only the United States had such weapons; then, in 1949, much to Americans' alarm, the Soviets developed an atomic bomb much sooner than US scientists had predicted. The Doomsday Clock stewards placed the hands at three minutes to midnight. With this development, the possibility for a catastrophic war was no longer an abstraction. Any heightening of tensions between the two former allies could lead inexorably to a nuclear exchange with horrifying consequences for the entire planet. In fact, a 1950 Gallup poll found that most Americans thought the United States was "now actually in WWIII."[38] Further, it was only a matter of time before the Soviets would match the United States by testing a thermonuclear weapon, and that is precisely what happened August 12, 1953. The hands of the Doomsday Clock reached two minutes to midnight.

The sudden increase in the world's nuclear arsenal, and the realization that the superpowers now had the power to destroy the world many times over, changed domestic political rhetoric. Sensing the mood of the country—specifically America's discomfort at the prospect of living "on the brink"—Eisenhower made an effort to convey cohesive leadership at the top, by instructing aides not to attribute any comments to him that might be construed as favoring a nuclear confrontation, or to make any public statements themselves along those lines.[39] That year, Eisenhower delivered a speech that became known as "The Chance for Peace," in which he suggested that weapons and food for the populace were mutually exclusive: "Every gun that is made, every warship launched, every rocket fired signifies, in the final sense, a theft from those who hunger and are not fed," he said.[40] In December 1953, Eisenhower followed up with his more well-known "Atoms for Peace" speech at the United Nations General Assembly. In a draft of the speech, he stated that the potential for nuclear war had caused him, much to his chagrin, to speak an entirely new language: "the language of atomic warfare."[41] The president described the tension as follows: "two atomic colossi are doomed malevolently to eye each other indefinitely across a trembling world." He suggested that no power would be the victor if nuclear warfare erupted.[42] He wished to move from the "dark chamber of horrors into the light."[43] Americans would remember the more popular, and positive, words of the final version delivered on December 8; the president was "determined to solve the fearful atomic dilemma" by ensuring that "the miraculous inventiveness of man would not be dedicated to his death, but consecrated to his life."[44] The speech led to US agreements with thirty-nine nations to develop nuclear energy for peaceful purposes. But tensions remained elevated, especially after the United States detonated a fifteen-megaton thermonuclear weapon, code-named CASTLE BRAVO, killing twenty-six Japanese men aboard the Lucky Dragon trawler that had been downwind of the blast.[45]

These tensions around "the fearful atomic dilemma" persisted through the end of the decade. In October 1957, the Soviets sent Sputnik into orbit. This "inventiveness" heightened anxieties about nuclear conflict and removed America's presumed technological edge. The Soviets' success raised the possibility of an arms race in space—a race in which the Soviets had the upper hand. With powerful rockets, the Soviets could reach US cities with nuclear warheads. Physicist and historian Spencer Weart wrote that the launch of Sputnik was a "turning point" for Americans, the moment when the prospect of possible annihilation struck home. He explained the reason for the alarm: "unstoppable missiles had seemed like something for a remote science fiction future," but now the distant possibility had become very plausible.[46] As the decade drew to a close, events seemed to spiral toward the ultimate catastrophe. These included the Soviet capture of a U-2 plane and its pilot Gary Powers on May 1, 1960, which put a halt to the planned summit talks in Paris scheduled to begin on May 16, and the hope of a nuclear armament agreement there.

* * *

These heightened fears and uncontrollable events resulted in a flurry of civil defense preparedness.[47] The first nationwide civil defense drills were held during the Eisenhower administration. As part of the scenario, twelve million Americans "died" in a mock nuclear attack. The consensus among government officials was that the drill had progressed smoothly.[48] A 1955 National Security Council (NSC) study painted a bleaker image. The study predicted that if a nuclear war should occur three years in the future (1958), total economic collapse would result and two-thirds of Americans would need medical attention.[49] Following another drill, dubbed "Operation Alert Eisenhower," on July 25, 1956, officials again informed the president that all had gone as planned. But Eisenhower reminded his advisors that in the event of a real nuclear attack, the people being evacuated "will be scared, will be hysterical, will be absolutely nuts."[50] The earlier "duck and cover" government propaganda—a memorable slogan that reminded school children to duck under their desks and cover their heads in the event of a nuclear attack—had changed to a strategy of "run like hell," according to the *Bulletin of the Atomic Scientists*.[51] Eisenhower believed that 1956 Federal Highway Act, officially called the "National System of Interstate and Defense Highways," would provide evacuation routes, but even they would become clogged with traffic.

The president's expanded US Strategic Air Command (SAC) played a major role in the civil defense preparations. SAC's planning for nuclear war included going on the offensive once attacked, which almost guaranteed mutually assured destruction (MAD). SAC also advocated for the development of even stronger weapons, such as the Titan II. Tested in 1959, the Titan II intercontinental ballistic missile became part of the Strategic Air Command in 1963. Ten stories tall, it had the explosive power of nine million tons of TNT (the equivalent of 700 Hiroshima bombs).[52]

Together with the development of these advanced nuclear bombs and civilian contingency planning came a new military subspecialty: Continuity of Government (COG) and Continuity of Operations Planning (COOP).[53] Preserving the nation's chain of command and allowing for a semblance of continuity in the event of a nuclear attack clearly were top priorities for the government. That had been true since the Truman administration, when refurbishment of the White House included the addition of a bomb shelter in the basement. The decision to add these tunnels was made early in the Korean conflict, when the possibility that it might erupt into a Third World War seemed very plausible.[54] Truman was told the shelter would withstand a direct hit. Funding in the amount of $868,000 was provided immediately by Congress, no questions asked.[55]

But if those in the line of presidential succession were unreachable, or rendered unfit or found dead, Eisenhower devised both a secret, and an official, plan for presidential continuity. Evidence exists that the Eisenhower administration put in place a plan for private business leaders to become deputized in a national emergency to take over the government, for pay in whatever currency was being used after a nuclear attack.[56] Eisenhower also drew up more official plans for a "National Defense Executive Reserve," in the form of Executive Order 10,660. The Executive Reserve was composed of individuals from both the civilian economy and from government who would be trained to take over positions in the executive branch in the event of an emergency.[57]

* * *

Preparing for a potential nuclear attack was a topic that roused voters' fears during the 1960 presidential campaign. In a campaign speech in September 1960, Kennedy underscored one of the central paradoxes of foreign policy in the nuclear era; to maintain peace, America had to prepare for war.[58] In other words, the government developed larger numbers of nuclear weapons with increasingly greater powers of destruction as deterrents to their usage. And with the increase in power came an increase in anxiety. Further, Kennedy claimed that the Eisenhower administration had allowed the Soviet Union to "far out-produce the United States in nuclear technology" causing a "missile gap."[59] His rhetoric, combined with a carefully crafted image of youth and good health, was just persuasive enough for voters; Kennedy won the presidential election by fewer than 120,000 popular votes.[60]

Nuclear policy was also a main focus of the transitional meetings between the outgoing president and his young successor. Kennedy was visibly disturbed by the Eisenhower policy of massive retaliation during his first nuclear policy briefing by Chairman of the Joint Chiefs General Lyman Lemnitzer.[61] And during their final transition meeting on January 19, 1961, Eisenhower discussed the crucial and quick decision Kennedy might need to make to avert a nuclear war and introduced Kennedy to the man with the nuclear "football." Kennedy would travel in the company of this staff member holding a briefcase with nuclear codes and would carry with him a laminated card that would delineate his choices—to activate missile silos, for example—in the event of a nuclear confrontation.[62]

A smooth, calm transition was paramount, but fears about nuclear apocalypse, already high due to events at the end of the 1950s, continued to rise. Kennedy's rhetoric played a role. He mixed dark language such as a promise to "defend freedom in its hour of maximum danger," with the inspiring language his Inaugural Address became known for among later generations of Americans.[63] And just three days later, the United States came close to a nuclear disaster when a B-52 carrying a nuclear bomb crashed in North Carolina.[64] Similar nuclear near misses proved that nobody, not even the president, had complete control over the bomb, and that a need existed for the government to develop new policies and laws to anticipate every possible contingency.

The concern that Kennedy was a foreign policy neophyte added to Americans' feelings of insecurity. His opponent, Nixon, had raised the issue during the campaign, and just a few months into Kennedy's tenure, the new president was presented with a plan to invade the Bay of Pigs in Cuba that tested his mettle. The CIA told Kennedy the plan had been sanctioned by Eisenhower, who had significantly more experience in foreign affairs. But on April 19, 1961, after three days of fighting, the invaders surrendered. In a memo, the president's brother, Robert Kennedy, wrote that the president "felt very strongly that the Cuba operation had materially affected … his standing as president and the standing of the United States in public opinion. We were going to have a much harder role in providing leadership."[65] Although the fiasco did not end in a nuclear confrontation, it led Kennedy to worry that Americans and other world leaders would question his ability to steer the ship.[66]

Further eroding confidence in his leadership, Kennedy's struggle with foreign leaders continued less than two months later, on June 3 and 4, at a conference in Vienna with Soviet Premier Nikita Khrushchev. At the conference, Khrushchev informed Kennedy that the USSR would sign a treaty with East Germany that would abrogate the post-war agreement allowing US access to West Berlin. When Kennedy expressed his regret in leaving the conference in a manner that conveyed to the world that the two nations were moving closer to war, Khrushchev responded that it was the United States that was threatening to start a world war, not the USSR, and that "It was up to the US to decide whether there will be war or peace." Kennedy replied, "Then, Mr. Chairman, there will be war. It will be a cold winter."[67] Kennedy arrived home extremely shaken with the thought that he might be the president to start a nuclear war.[68]

The public was aware that the threat of nuclear war was building throughout the summer of 1961, particularly over Berlin. A Gallup Poll from 1961 showed that fifty-three percent of Americans believed another world war would occur within five years.[69] Kennedy addressed the American people at 7:00 p.m. on the evening of his return to Washington from Vienna, June 6, 1961, stating the results of the conference negotiations, though frank, were unsuccessful with regard to ending nuclear tests and proliferation.[70] James Reston of *The New York Times* covered the lack of agreement between the superpowers, describing Kennedy's mood as "solemn."[71]

Then, elevating tensions, Khrushchev compared American troops in a divided Berlin to "a bone stuck in the throat"[72] and threatened war if the United States would not retreat from the divided city.[73] On August 13, 1961, with tanks facing each other, East German troops began building a barbed-wire-and-concrete wall that came to symbolize East–West divisions through the remainder of the Cold War.[74] When interviewed on *Meet the Press* in September, Robert Kennedy stated that his brother was prepared to use nuclear weapons "if it came to that."[75] The media continued to report that nuclear anxiety was at a high and America's very survival was at stake. In a series of articles in *The Washington Post*, staff writer John M. Goshko wrote that "scholars of a future civilization may try to reconstruct the story of a nation once known as the United States of America." If the people "perish[ed] in the devastation of nuclear warfare," they might find that the answers "began to take shape during the year 1961," he warned.[76] Ultimately, the president chose not to respond militarily to construction of the wall. The aftermath of the Berlin crisis led Kennedy to employ darker language in his speeches about the potential for a nuclear apocalypse.[77] On September 25, 1961, Kennedy delivered his "Sword of Damocles" speech in front of the United Nations, pointing out that at this critical juncture, the fate of mankind was on his shoulders as well as those of Khrushchev: "The events and decisions of the next ten months may well decide the fate of man for the next ten thousand years."[78] He suggested that humanity was hanging by a thread that could be cut by a nuclear sword of Damocles by "accident, miscalculation, or by madness."[79] Testing fate, the Soviets exploded what is still the most powerful bomb detonated in history, the "Tsar Bomba," (which had a yield of fifty-eight megatons of TNT) just one month after Kennedy's speech.

But it was during the Cuban missile crisis of October 1962 that Americans came closest to facing nuclear catastrophe.[80] Kennedy was not taken completely by surprise when Indiana Senator Homer E. Capehart and others suggested the existence of missiles ninety miles off the coast of Florida.[81] Although the Soviets had never placed missiles in other countries before, not even those bound by the Warsaw Pact, US intelligence agencies had been gathering evidence since the summer.[82] The president went to great lengths to quell public anxiety and keep a sense of calm and order during and after the crisis. He stuck to his official schedule as much as possible; had his advisors pack into one car to get to the White House to avoid notice by the press and public; and requested under the premise of "national security" that *The New York Times* hold a story about the brewing crisis. On the day President Kennedy chose to announce the presence of missiles in Cuba to the American public on television, he kept most of his allies and enemies well informed. Many congressmembers were angered, however, when they heard the news of the president's decision to invoke a quarantine, rather than a military strike, to dismantle the missiles; they felt that Kennedy's decision was too passive. But, as historian Sheldon M. Stern argues in *The Cuban Missile Crisis in American Memory*, the president believed that "nuclear weapons had altered the very meaning of war itself, and everything—anything—had to be done to avert a nuclear apocalypse."[83] On October 27, 1962, the nadir of the crisis, smoke emanated from the Soviet Embassy as the Soviets began burning their archives. This seemed a definitive indicator to many that nuclear war was imminent.

Senator Capehart's opponent in the 1962 general election, Birch Bayh, the eventual author of the Twenty-Fifth Amendment, recalled his, and the nation's, relief when the Soviet ship *Gronzy* turned around at the quarantine line and the crisis came to a peaceful end. Bayh said, "We went through a period of almost a week where we didn't know if we'd be blown up or not. And that was the first sign that the [Soviets] might not go forward on this and they took whatever missiles they had out of there and so those were scary times."[84]

Though nuclear war was averted, conclusions to the Berlin and Cuba events did not make Americans more comfortable about the prospects of nuclear war. "We must recognize that the peace of nuclear terror cannot endure for long," physicist Ralph E. Lapp wrote in the *Bulletin of the*

Atomic Scientists in April 1963. Lapp pointed out that eighteen years had passed since an atomic bomb had been detonated during wartime, but "the tempo of the arms race has intensified greatly during the past two years,' increasing the danger of nuclear war."[85] Slowing the unnerving pace of the clashes between the superpowers seemed to be beyond even the leaders' control.

Ruminating on how close the nation had come to the brink of war and unable to secure a test-ban treaty—both superpowers had detonated nuclear tests in the summer and fall as the missile crisis unfolded[86]—Kennedy worked to restart his relationship with Khrushchev.[87] In a news conference on March 21, 1963, the president gave voice to his fears: "Personally I am haunted by the feeling that by 1970... there may be 10 nuclear powers instead of 4." He warned that as many as twenty-five nuclear powers might exist by the year 1975.[88] Then, on June 10, 1963, Kennedy signaled a shift in his administration's stance toward the Soviet Union. Delivering a speech that was months in the making at an American University commencement ceremony, Kennedy said, "We have no more urgent task" than to talk of peace. Remarkably, he emphasized that for all the differences between West and East, both sides shared a great deal in common. "We all inhabit the same planet. We all breathe the same air," he said. "We all cherish our children's future. And we are all mortal." The president announced that he, Khrushchev, and British Prime Minister Harold Macmillan would begin talks to bring nuclear testing to an end.[89] The speech led up to the signing of the test-ban treaty in Moscow on August 5, 1963.[90]

* * *

Although Kennedy had asked Congress to appropriate two hundred million dollars to build or upgrade fallout shelters and other civil defense measures a year earlier, the Cuban missile crisis also had highlighted how woefully unprepared America was for a first strike, leaving Americans scrambling for security.[91] After the Cuban crisis, *The Washington Post* noted nearly twenty million copies of "The Family Fallout Shelter," a thirty-two-page pamphlet, had been distributed by civil defense officials since its publication two years earlier.[92] In Union County, New Jersey, *The Minuteman* magazine announced a milestone had been reached on December 29, 1964: one million New Jersey shelter spaces had been stocked.[93] On August 3, 1965, just a month after S.J. Res. 1 (the Twenty-Fifth Amendment) passed both houses of Congress, the Director of the Office of Emergency Planning, Buford Ellington, noted in a memo to White House Chief of Staff W. Marvin Watson that he had approved eight thousand brochures, updating the ones that had gone out to the public eighteen months prior.[94] Ellington stated that "ordinarily" this "would not have been worthy of bringing to [the chief of staff's] attention except in view of the general climate."[95]

At the federal level, by the 1960s, the plans for presidential protection were more flexible and sophisticated than they had been in the past. In the event of advanced notice of a nuclear attack, the 2857th Test (Helicopter) Squadron would land on the White House lawn, force their way in to the White House shelter, provide the president with a radiation suit, and evacuate him.[96] Aides who received pink identification cards—such as speechwriter Ted Sorensen and staff member Kenny O'Donnell—would accompany the president to any one of a number of shelters which would serve as command posts.[97] OEP Director Buford Ellington listed instructions for continued communications with those in line for the presidency designed to be printed in small books for "Presidential Successors."[98] The books described the "Central Locator System and the way in which the White House can be reached from points within the United States and abroad,"[99] according to a memo from OEP director Buford Ellington to aide Bill Moyers. This sort of detailed communications planning for a sudden succession was another indication that the anxieties of the nuclear age were forcing the issue of succession.

The possibility that the president of the United States might be incapacitated at a critical moment in the nuclear age haunted President Kennedy. As early as the summer of 1961, with Cuba and Berlin looming as potential triggers for a nuclear exchange, Kennedy had sought guidance from his brother, Robert Kennedy, about how to proceed if he were to become incapacitated. In response, Robert sent a memo on August 10, 1961, noting that the nation and the world were in "an age marked by crisis."[100] He said that he was responding to his brother's request for his opinion "on the construction to be given to the presidential inability clause of the Constitution: Article II, Section I, Clause 6."[101] The Attorney General assured his brother that the letter agreement between Eisenhower and Nixon, drafted by former Attorney General Herbert Brownell, was above board, concluding that the understanding of March 3, 1958, was "in keeping with the Constitution, and that the precedent set by it could appropriately be followed by" the Kennedy administration.[102] Robert Kennedy wrote that he, his immediate predecessors, and "the great majority of scholars," confirmed the constitutionality of the letter agreement—whenever possible, the president should inform the vice president of an inability, if that were not possible, the vice president could determine whether inability exists; and the president alone would determine when that inability was over. The Attorney General's opinion had an impact. That same day, the White House issued a press release announcing that Kennedy and Johnson had "agreed to adhere to the procedures identical to those which former President Eisenhower and Vice President Nixon adopted with regard to any questions of presidential inability."[103] Though they agreed to follow the pattern of their predecessors, the letter agreements did not have the same authority as a constitutional amendment.

That the issue was raised at all suggests just how anxious even the youthful Kennedy was about ensuring the orderly transfer of power during a nuclear age. No president or vice president in US history had come to such a public agreement over the issue of presidential inability before Eisenhower and Nixon.[104] That they publicly acknowledged the possibility of an incapacitated president suggests that the conversation about the need for a clear chain of command had become urgent in the nuclear age, when minutes mattered.

Though sometimes mixed with politics, this planning at, and for, every level of society speaks to an intrinsic desire for a measured transition of power in a time of crisis. And it underscores the fact that the anxiety surrounding the potential use of nuclear weapons was omnipresent. By the time of the Kennedy assassination, the topic of survival was infusing average Americans' day-to-day conversation, even at mundane events like cocktail parties and PTA meetings.[105]

* * *

Amid this heightened anxiety and preparation for the end of times, on November 22, 1963, John Kennedy was assassinated by Lee Harvey Oswald in Dallas, Texas. When Kennedy was pronounced dead in Parkland Hospital at 1:00 p.m. CST, the first sudden transfer of power in the nuclear age began to unfold behind the scenes as the nation, and the world, reacted in horror and disbelief.[106] Complications ensued—more than half of Kennedy's Cabinet was on a plane over the Pacific Ocean, headed to Japan. Rumors circulated that Johnson had been shot or had suffered a heart attack.[107] These were plausible, as Johnson had already experienced a heart attack in 1955 and was part of the motorcade in Dallas in a car behind the one carrying the president.

Kennedy's death highlighted the succession problem that had existed since the nation's founding: No method to appoint a new vice president in the case of a presidential death or resignation existed. But while the dilemma was old, the circumstances were new. The bomb and the anxieties of the nuclear age made this sudden transition entirely different than the others. Nuclear weapons had irrevocably altered the nature of the presidency and underlined the need for a clear line of succession. But the Constitution had no answer for the dilemma of John Kennedy being rushed to the emergency room at Parkland, not yet pronounced dead but clearly unable to carry out his duties.[108]

The Kennedy/Johnson letter agreement of August 10, 1961, was the guiding rule should the president become incapacitated. It stated that in the event of presidential inability, not only would the vice president wish to have the support of the Cabinet, but he must confirm the legality of taking office with the attorney general.[109] LBJ and Robert Kennedy had a poor relationship laced with mistrust.[110] Even before the assassination, issues existed around a temporary transfer of power to Johnson. If his brother were disabled, would RFK try to withhold some of the powers of the presidency from Johnson? Or, even worse, would he govern in his brother's name, as Edith Bolling Wilson and Dr. Carry T. Grayson did when Woodrow Wilson was incapacitated earlier in the century?

Johnson, therefore, refused to leave Parkland Hospital without knowing if President Kennedy was alive or dead. Remarkably, Ken O'Donnell, Johnson's liaison to the president, Roy Kellerman, the head of President Kennedy's security detail, and Shift Supervisor Agent Emory Roberts, all knew the president was dead but failed to inform Johnson.[111] Johnson was forced to make an uncomfortable telephone call to Robert Kennedy, who was all at once the attorney general and the brother of the newly slain president, to suggest that he immediately assume the presidency, in part because the assassination was thought to be part of a larger conspiracy.[112]

Both the public and the CIA worried that Moscow or Havana might have arranged to have Kennedy killed. Through the media, Soviet leadership had quickly issued a bulletin that denied involvement with Oswald and declined responsibility for the president's death, placing it on ultra-right-wing extremists within the United States instead.[113] Yet, general rumors of a conspiracy circulated due to the fact that Oswald was once a Soviet citizen, had attempted to apply for Cuban citizenship, and was a self-avowed Communist sympathizer. These fears were heightened when the CIA failed to locate Khrushchev for forty-eight hours afterwards.[114] According to intelligence expert Jeffrey T. Richelson, the CIA surmised that Khrushchev had either gone to a secure location in anticipation of an American reprisal, or he was preparing an attack on the United States.[115] Through the end of November and beyond, the agency still did not rule out a conspiracy, foreign or domestic.[116] And any foreign involvement in the president's death might have become a casus belli for the United States.[117]

The night of Kennedy's death, the new president was concerned that the assassination had been part of a Communist plot against the United States, and that nuclear war might ensue.[118] "What raced through my mind was that, if they had shot our president, driving down there, who would they shoot next?" he told press aide Bill Moyers in a 1966 phone conversation that was captured by the White House taping system. "And what was going on in Washington? And when would the missiles be comin'?" the president fretted.[119] He knew this uncertainty was not only disconcerting; it was dangerous. In an article entitled "The Problem of the Succession to the Presidency," *New York Times* columnist James Reston noted, "In this day of instantaneous attack, nobody could be quite sure whether the assassination was the end or merely the beginning of the agony."[120] The idea that a third world war might erupt momentarily was a real concern, perhaps even greater than during the Berlin and Cuban crises.

In preparation for the possibility of a nuclear attack, the Joint Chiefs of Staff ordered that the DEFCON levels be raised from DEFCON V (normal readiness posture) to DEFCON IV (increased intelligence watch) at 2:15 p.m. EST.[121] Going one step further, a secret naval message stated that "this [was] the time to be especially on the alert" and ordered precautions consistent with DEFCON III (increased readiness posture) be taken, minus the recall of personnel on leave because it would visibly indicate "heightened tensions."[122] Yet, officials denied raising DEFCON levels so as not to incite panic. They told newspapers such as the *New York Herald Tribune* that "no unusual alert of troops at any point in the world" had occurred.[123]

The goal of calming public and private anxiety over a possible conspiracy, one that might escalate to a nuclear attack, governed Johnson's actions and demeanor during the transition. This was central to Johnson's thought process when he took the oath of office aboard Air Force One. He was not sure whether or not the oath had to be taken before his position as president was official, but he was sure that every vice president who suddenly transitioned to the presidency had done so.[124] Aware of the public mood and that many of Kennedy's aides thought poorly of him,[125] the new president focused on eliminating any ambiguity as to whether or not he was now in charge, desiring to convey a sense of command. In the hours and days after the assassination, all who encountered the new president were treated to a cool, calculating, disciplined Johnson, rather than the tempestuous vice president they had been expecting.[126]

Although official records of whether security for the Speaker of the House John McCormack and the Senate president pro tempore Carl Hayden (those next in line for the presidency) was increased after Kennedy's murder seem to be lost to history,[127] *The New York Times* reported that within minutes after the announcement of Kennedy's death, Secret Service arrived at the Capitol to begin an "around-the-clock guard" of the speaker.[128] At the same time that McCormack heard the Secret Service was on its way to the Hill to protect him, reporters told him that Johnson had been shot, allowing him to come to the conclusion that he might suddenly now be president. According to historian William Manchester, the speaker stood up, swooned, and was still recovering in his chair at the House restaurant when another congressman dispelled the rumor.[129] A few days later, the White House announced the speaker would be kept informed on all matters related to national security and be invited to "those National Security Council and other key decision-making meetings."[130] White House Press Secretary Pierre Salinger stated that the speaker's attendance at meetings "would be in no way inconsistent with his legislative responsibilities,"[131] highlighting the separation of powers concern that would become a key point of debate as Bayh's amendment moved through Congress.

Johnson also contacted Truman and Eisenhower, inviting them to the White House on the day after the assassination to further a sense of continuity. The new president ensured that he was photographed with them to bolster his legitimacy.[132] More importantly, he consulted with them prior to his speech before a joint session of Congress on November 27,

1963. This speech, his first public address as president, is the best example of Johnson's measured manner in the aftermath of Kennedy's murder, demonstrating for the world that he was now in control. The presentation drew attention to the succession issue—the television cameras panned from McCormack to Carl Hayden, ages seventy-one and eighty-six respectively, behind him at the podium. Lee Harvey Oswald's shots put a man with little experience in foreign affairs into the most powerful office in the world, and Truman's Presidential Succession Act of 1947 decreed that the aging men sitting behind Johnson were next in line.

Notably, an early draft of Johnson's speech by Adlai Stevenson emphasized the anxieties facing the nation, specifically the possibility of nuclear war. This draft stated that Kennedy's greatest contribution was that as president, he "match[ed] national power with national restraint at a time in history when our national safety can no longer be secured by competitive pursuit of ever-greater nuclear power."[133] The language in Stevenson's draft was softened in the final version and references to nuclear arms were elided. In its place appeared the more ambiguous line "in an age when there can be… no victors in war… we must be prepared at one and the same time for the confrontation of power and the limitation of power."[134] Johnson's final draft soothed the nation—in part because of the content Johnson chose to leave out.

Although not overtly discussed in the final draft of Johnson's speech, the issue of nuclear weapons surfaced in some of the commentary, married with the idea of continuity. The United Information Agency Research and Reference Service's Daily Report Supplement for the president noted that Moscow observed, "When we speak of the Kennedy line, which the new president is preparing to continue, we refer to what was dominant in that line—that is concern for averting thermonuclear war."[135] On that topic, the Soviet satellite state Czechoslovakia broadcast that it would have preferred to have heard language much closer to Stevenson's earlier draft: something of a reiteration of Kennedy's speech before the U.N. General Assembly. In that speech, Kennedy urged the securing of peaceful cooperation. Prague radio believed it was not a good omen that Johnson did not do the same.[136]

* * *

During this tense time, the Italians weathered a transition of their own.[137] In August 1964, Italian President Antonio Segni suffered a cerebral hemorrhage like Franklin Roosevelt in 1945. Unlike the American president who died of the hemorrhage, Segni slipped into coma, and the Italian Senate President, Cesare Merzagora, took on presidential responsibilities until he recovered. The Vice President of the Senate stepped into Merzagora's office, and had Segni not recovered, a presidential election would have taken place within fifteen days. Birch Bayh's supporters in the fight for succession and inability legislation in the US Congress noted that the Italian president, "as in most European systems," served more of a ceremonial role as head of state, but among other responsibilities, the Italian president was head of the Defense Council. In their memo to Senator Bayh, they compared the orderly succession in Italy with the uncertainty that accompanied presidential incapacities in the United States, remarking that "given the corrupt, volatile, and unstable nature of Italian society and politics ... the Italians have handled their crisis much better than Americans did during the Garfield and Wilson episodes."[138] They judged that "the method of deciding inability, although not stipulated by the Constitution or statute, was handled well."[139] The sudden presidential transition in Italy was a stark reminder that in the precarious nuclear age, a president could become incapacitated at any time. The Italian crisis occurred in the middle of the 1964 US presidential election season, accentuating the need for an able commander-in-chief, a succession plan, and a method of filling a vice presidential vacancy.

Nuclear anxiety played a central role in the 1964 campaign, one in which Johnson was determined to secure a landslide victory to prove his legitimacy. Even after Cecil Stoughton's famous photograph of him taking the oath of office recorded the event for posterity, he complained: "I took an oath. I became president. But for millions of Americans, I was still illegitimate, a naked man with no presidential covering, a pretender to the throne, an illegal usurper."[140] One of the most notable passages in Johnson's acceptance speech at the 1964 Democratic National Convention in Atlantic City, New Jersey, was the assertion, "We cannot act rashly with the nuclear weapons that could destroy us all. The only course is to press with all our mind and all our will to make sure, doubly sure, that these weapons are never really used at all."[141] In fact, the first bullet point of the 1964 Democratic platform pamphlet noted that "at the start of the third decade of the nuclear age," maintaining a nuclear arsenal was of the utmost importance. The goal, the document stated, was to "continue the overwhelming supremacy of [America's] Strategic Nuclear Forces."[142]

Republican presidential nominee Barry Goldwater's loose talk of nuclear weapons during the campaign rattled Americans' nerves.[143] In *The Conscience of a Conservative*, Goldwater argued that the United States was in danger of losing its freedom to the Soviet Union; because of nuclear parity, the war would be won by the Soviet's superior manpower.[144] Further, Goldwater believed, the strategy of the United States "must be primarily offensive in nature"—the US should not be afraid to launch a preemptive nuclear attack on the Soviet Union.[145] In May 1964, Goldwater was quoted saying "I don't want to hit the moon. I want to lob one [presumably a nuclear missile] into the men's room of the Kremlin and make sure I hit it."[146] In July, when accepting the Republican nomination in San Francisco's Cow Palace, Goldwater continued to paint himself as an extremist, famously saying: "I would remind you that extremism in the defense of liberty is no vice. And let me remind you also that moderation in the pursuit of justice is no virtue."[147] Johnson capitalized on these quotes, repeating them on the campaign trail through Election Day.[148]

The Soviets, not surprisingly, replied to this saber rattling with vehemence, elevating fears that nuclear war was on the horizon. During a speech televised to the Soviet people, Khrushchev compared the 1964 Republican National Convention to "the Fascist gatherings" in Nuremburg and suggested that the GOP nominee was a "wild" or "semi-wild" man, though he did not mention Goldwater by name.[149] Khrushchev then told attendees at a conference marking the twentieth anniversary of Poland's communist government that the Soviets should "as the saying goes, clean our weapons and stay on full alert.... If the [Americans] want to unleash war, we must not be caught unprepared."[150] The Soviet leader drew attention to the possibility that if voters chose the wrong candidate, they may have been ticking the box inadvertently on their own death sentences.

Because many Americans regarded the possibility of a nuclear war with the Soviets as the most-critical issue of the election, many political ads played on this fear.[151] Advertising firm Doyle, Dane, and Bernbach created "the Daisy Ad," which stands out as the most famous political ad in American history. Though the sixty-second ad aired only once on NBC on September 7, 1964, it was memorable because it connected the next generation with the horror of a nuclear explosion. The ad featured a little girl picking the petals off a daisy while a countdown proceeded in the background; then, reflected in the pupil of her eye, was the explosion of a nuclear bomb. Goldwater's name was not mentioned. Johnson's voice could be heard in a poignant voiceover espousing a Manichaean view of America's future, or lack thereof, under the next president. These ads, and others like them, did not create the electorate's nuclear anxiety, but they did creatively put that fear to work toward obtaining a Johnson victory.[152]

In January 1965, with Johnson elected in his own right and Humphrey installed as vice president, Senator Bayh began to press forward with succession and inability legislation. Johnson arguably had a more productive first one hundred days in office than Franklin Roosevelt. The Twenty-Fifth Amendment can be considered a piece of this effort. But just after the inauguration, Johnson was taken to Bethesda Medical Center and diagnosed with tracheitis, an irritation of the upper breathing tube that causes a cough and is a symptom of the common cold. Though the president's hospitalization was merely a precaution, it again drew attention to the possibility that a president could become incapacitated, or die suddenly, in the middle of a nuclear-age crisis.[153]

Only halfway through the turbulent 1960s, the nation had already experienced overwhelming anxiety that peaked with the Cuban crisis and Kennedy's assassination. Nuclear anxiety infused the political and cultural atmosphere, affecting both legislators' decisions and their constituents' day-to-day actions. The chronology of nuclear advances and related events directly correlates to the rise in anxiety, as seen in cultural institutions and popular media. This nuclear anxiety permeated political culture, taking concrete form in the construction of bomb shelters and the enactment of civil defense measures. America's leaders were no different from their constituents in that they, too, were afraid of their own end, so they devised shelters in secret locations and developed COG plans. But beyond their own mortality, these leaders were concerned about the continuity of the institution of the presidency itself, and the ultimate continuity of the laws. The Twenty-Fifth Amendment would be their response.

Senate Swearing-In Ceremony, 1963.[154]

Notes

1. Robert Karl Manoff, "The Media: Nuclear Security vs. Democracy," *Bulletin of the Atomic Scientists* (January 1984), 29, as quoted in Paul Boyer, *By the Bomb's Early Light: American Thought and Culture at the Dawn of the Atomic Age* (Chapel Hill: University of North Carolina Press, 1994), xvii.
2. Kennette Benedict, "Doomsday Clockwork," *Bulletin of the Atomic Scientists*, January 26, 2017, https://thebulletin.org/2018/01/doomsday-clockwork/.
3. The Single Integrated Operation Plan allowed for the president to make a split-second decision that would set off a reaction down the chain of command launching one or more nuclear warheads.

Because the president need only to give his assent and the entire plan was set in motion, it seemed as though just the push of a single button would bring the world to an end.
4. Atomic Energy Act of 1946, Public Law Number 79-585, 60 Statute 755.
5. Only the 1860s and 1910s were comparable.
6. David E. Kyvig, *Explicit and Authentic Acts: Amending the US Constitution, 1776–1995* (Lawrence, Kansas: University Press of Kansas, 1996), 349.
7. Steven M. Gillon, *The Kennedy Assassination: 24 Hours after Lyndon B. Johnson's Pivotal First Day as President* (New York: Basic Books, 2009), 357.
8. Kyvig, *Explicit and Authentic Acts*, 357.
9. Allan M. Winkler, *Life Under a Cloud: American Anxiety About the Atom* (New York: Oxford University Press, 1993), 27.
10. William Fielding Ogburn "Sociology and the Atom" as quoted in Paul Boyer, *By the Bomb's Early Light*. William Fielding Ogburn, "Sociology and the Atom," *American Journal of Sociology*, 51 (January 1946), 269. Paul Boyer, *By the Bomb's Early Light: American Thought and Culture at the Dawn of the Atomic Age* (Chapel Hill: University of North Carolina Press, 1994), 12.
11. "War's Ending: Atomic Bomb and Soviet Entry Bring Jap Surrender," *Life* (August 20, 1945), 25–31. https://books.google.com/books?id=hkgEAAAAMBAJ&pg=PA17&source=gbs_toc_r&cad=2#v=onepage&q&f=false.
12. John Hersey, "Hiroshima," *The New Yorker* (August 31, 1946). http://www.newyorker.com/magazine/1946/08/31/hiroshima.
13. John Hersey, *Hiroshima* (New York: Alfred A. Knopf, 1946).
14. Originally scripted as a scientist's attempt to explain the rationale of the bomb, it quickly became patriotic propaganda about Hiroshima. Nagasaki was omitted from the storyline. The jingoism was mixed with misinformation and a typical Hollywood romance.
15. As quoted in Toni Perrine, *Film and the Nuclear Age* (New York: Taylor & Francis, 1998).
16. The tension around the bomb and radioactive fallout soon began revealing itself in cultural outlets throughout the world. Having experienced mass destruction firsthand, the Japanese produced

feature films with nuclear terror as a main theme, such as *Godzilla: King of the Monsters* in 1954. Many popular science fiction and horror films of that year, such as *Them!* and *Creature from the Black Lagoon*, followed suit, depicting mutants or monsters unearthed by the bomb or borne of the radioactive fallout that threatened the continuity of mankind. Robert Jay Lifton and Greg Mitchell, *Hiroshima in America* (New York: Harper Perennial, 1995), 361.

17. Sloan Wilson, *Man in the Grey Flannel Suit* (New York: Da Capo Press, 2002).
18. Anthropologist Margaret Mead similarly suggested that "specially chosen members of society and some newlyweds be rotated between bomb shelters so that society would be preserved in the event of an attack." Honeymoon in bomb shelter: Elaine Tyler May, *Homeward Bound: American Families in the Cold War Era* (New York: Basic Books, Inc., 1988), 3. Margaret Mead: Kenneth D. Rose, *One Nation Underground: The Fallout Shelter in American Culture* (New York: New York University Press, 2001), 13.
19. As quoted in Winkler, *Life Under a Cloud*, 7.
20. Winkler, *Life Under a Cloud*, 127.
21. Todd Gitlin, *The Sixties: Years of Hope, Days of Rage* (New York: Bantam, 1987), 22–23. As quoted in Robert Mann, *Daisy Petals and Mushroom Clouds: LBJ, Barry Goldwater, and the Ad That Changed American Politics* (Baton Rouge, LA: Louisiana State University Press, 2011), 13.
22. *On the Beach* was a bestseller for decades after its publication.
23. In the Americanized 1956 version of the 1954 Japanese release Godzilla, some of the nuclear material was cut to balance the competing concerns that portraying the destruction of Japanese cities might offend American veterans of the Pacific war with the fact that the growing popularity of the atomic-monster genre meant the inclusion of such scenes would generate more revenue. Perrine, *Film and The Nuclear Age*, 92, 137.
24. Recorded in December 1962, he wrote it in the summer, prior to the October missile crisis.
25. Dorian Lynskey, *33 Revolutions Per Minute: A History of Protest Songs, From Billie Holiday to Green Day* (New York: HarperCollins Publishers, 2011), 56.

26. Perrine, *Film and The Nuclear Age*, 138.
27. Perrine, *Film and The Nuclear Age*, 137.
28. Mann, *Daisy Petals and Mushroom Clouds*, 78.
29. Historians such as Garrett Graff argue that Dr. Strangelove was modeled after General Curtis LeMay who retired from the Air Force the following year. Others, such as Robert Weisbrot, suggest that mathematician and physicist Herman Kahn, who wrote *On Thermonuclear War*, was the inspiration for the mad general. See Garrett M. Graff, Raven Rock: *The Story of the US Government's Secret Plan to Save Itself—While the Rest of Us Die* (New York: Simon & Schuster: 2017), 200. Robert Weisbrot, *Maximum Danger: Kennedy, the Missiles, and the Crisis of American Confidence* (Chicago, Ivan R. Dee, 2001), 27.
30. Winkler, *Life Under a Cloud*, 178.
31. "Complete National Film Registry Listing," *Library of Congress*, https://www.loc.gov/item/93518001/. Further, a 1965 British film, *The War Game*, hit home in the US: it won an Academy Award for best documentary in 1966 despite the fact that it was a British work of fiction, not a true American documentary.
32. "Texts of Addresses by the President in San Francisco and Oakland," *The New York Times* (October 5, 1952).
33. Harrison E. Salisbury, "Stevenson Holds President Lacks 'Energy' for Job," *The New York Times* (November 4, 1956). (Note: "crises in world affairs" are Salisbury's words, the rest are Stevenson's.)
34. Salisbury, "Stevenson Holds President Lacks "Energy" for Job."
35. Eisenhower suffered heart attacks, developed Crohn's disease, underwent surgery for a bowel obstruction, and, as his Cabinet was aware, later developed aphasia due to a stroke. See, for example, "Nation Again Weighs Its President's Future," *The New York Times* (June 10, 1956).
36. David Greenberg, *Nixon's Shadow: The History of an Image* (New York: W.W. Norton & Company, 2003), 62.
37. Kyvig, *Explicit and Authentic Acts*, 356.
38. Marc Trachtenberg, *History and Strategy* (Princeton, N.J.: Princeton University Press, 1991), 109. In 1951, *The New York Times* reported that "a representative with access to secret intelligence" stated that the Soviets could bomb "twenty-to-thirty"

American cities "at any time." Another Representative, Democrat Henry M. Jackson of Washington, told the newspaper that the Soviets were "stockpiling atom bombs at an alarming rate" and are trying their best to "surpass the United States in the life-or-death atomic armaments race." See "Soviet Could Atom-Bomb 20 Cities, House Hears," *The New York Times* (October 10, 1951).
39. Matthew Connelly, Matt Fay, Giulia Ferrini, Micki Kaufman, Will Leonard, Harrison Monsky, Ryan Musto, Taunton Paine, Nicholas Standish, and Lydia Walker, "'General, I Have Fought Just as Many Nuclear Wars as You Have': Forecasts, Future Scenarios, and the Politics of Armageddon," Volume 117, Number 5, *The American Historical Review* (Washington, DC: Oxford University Press, December 2012), 1445.
40. "'The Chance for Peace' Address Delivered Before the American Society of Newspaper Editors, April 16th, 1953," Dwight D. Eisenhower Presidential Library, Museum and Boyhood Home. https://www.eisenhowerlibrary.gov/sites/default/files/file/chance_for_peace.pdf.
41. See Draft #5 on November 28, 1953. "Atoms for Peace Draft," C.D. Jackson Papers, Box 30, "Atoms for Peace - Evolution (5)"; NAID #12021574 available at Dwight D. Eisenhower Presidential Library, Museum and Boyhood Home.
42. "Atoms for Peace Draft," C.D. Jackson Papers, Box 30, "Atoms for Peace - Evolution (5)"; NAID.
#12021574] available at Dwight D. Eisenhower Presidential Library, Museum and Boyhood Home.
43. "Atoms for Peace Draft."
44. "Atoms for Peace Speech," Dwight D. Eisenhower Presidential Library, Museum and Boyhood Home. https://www.eisenhowerlibrary.gov/sites/default/files/file/atoms_for_peace.pdf.
45. Graff, *Raven Rock*, 49.
46. See Spencer Weart, *Nuclear Fear: A History of Images* (Cambridge, MA: Harvard University Press, 1988). Eisenhower immediately put B-52 bombers on twenty-four-hour alert. After tensions with the USSR increased with the Berlin crisis, twelve B-52's remained airborne at all times. The Defense Advanced Research Projects Agency (DARPA), created in 1958, was another response to the Sputnik launch.

47. Many wealthier Americans chose to build private bomb shelters, which provided endless commercial possibilities. *Life* magazine began ranking different models, though *Consumers Union* would later publish a report that concluded that "no shelter a consumer could afford to build was 'acceptable'." The private sector also took precautions. For example, Roberts Dairy Company of Omaha, Nebraska, announced a plan to build a bomb shelter for two hundred cows. The Department of Agriculture released a publication called *Bunker-Type Fallout Shelter for Beef Cattle*. Private bomb shelters: Winkler, *Life Under a Cloud*, 129. Cow shelters: Kenneth D. Rose, *One Nation Underground: The Fallout Shelter in American Culture* (New York: New York University Press, 2001), 5.
48. "Almanac: A Mock Nuclear Attack," *CBS News*, June 14, 2015, https://www.cbsnews.com/news/almanac-a-mock-nuclear-attack/.
49. "Diary Entry by the President," January 23, 1956, *Foreign Relations of the United States*, 1955–1957, 187–188.
50. "The Eisenhower Ten: The Expanded Cabinet Meeting on Civil Defense," http://conelrad.com/atomicsecrets/secrets.php?secrets=e18. The fact that Eisenhower held a Cabinet meeting on July 25, 1956 between 2:35 p.m. -3:40 p.m. "following [the] operation alert period" is substantiated by his appointment book, "Presidential Appointment Books," *Dwight D. Eisenhower Presidential Library, Museum and Boyhood Home*, https://www.eisenhowerlibrary.gov/sites/default/files/research/online-documents/presidential-appointment-books/1956/july-1956.pdf.
51. "A Hard Look at Civil Defense," *Bulletin of the Atomic Scientists* 12 (Nov. 1956) 346. As quoted in Winkler, *Life Under a Cloud*, 117. A report entitled "Deterrence and Survival in the Nuclear Age," presented to Eisenhower in late 1957, argued that the government needed to expedite civil defense measures. "'If we fail to act at once," it declared, "the risk, in our opinion, will be unacceptable." Clarfield and Wiecek, *Nuclear America*, 167–168 as quoted in Winkler, *Life Under a Cloud*, 119.
52. The recently declassified SAC Atomic Weapons Requirements for Study for June 1959, produced in June 1956, revealed that SAC pushed for a "60 megaton bomb, the equivalent of over 4,000 Hiroshima atomic bombs." The Report's most

striking revelation was that Soviet civilian targets were detailed: a violation of international law. William, Burr, "US Cold War Nuclear Target Lists Declassified for First Time," National Security Archive Electronic Briefing Book No. 538 (December 22, 2015), http://nsarchive.gwu.edu/nukevault/ebb538-Cold-War-Nuclear-Target-List-Declassified-First-Ever/.
53. Ted Gup, "The Ultimate Congressional Hideaway," *Washington Post Magazine*, May 31, 1992.
54. David McCullough, *Truman* (New York: Simon & Schuster, 1992), 881. Secret Service ushered Vice
    President Dick Cheney into these tunnels during the September 11, 2001 attacks and President Obama had the shelter upgraded during his first term. Graff, *Raven Rock*, 399.
55. Graff, *Raven Rock*, 58. Then the government secretly began building a shelter, "Mount Weather", under the Greenbrier Resort in the Allegheny Mountains of West Virginia that could hold the entire Congress and Supreme Court. During the Eisenhower years, Raven Rock, an alternate Pentagon just over the Pennsylvania border from Maryland, also became operational. See Graff, *Raven Rock*, 52.
56. Reacting to Kennedy's handling of the Bay of Pigs, Eisenhower called in advisors to discuss an extra-legal shadow government should an absence, or perhaps further weakness, at the helm occur. Graff, *Raven Rock*, 92. See also Nancy Gibbs and Michael Duffy, *The President's Club: Inside the World's Most Exclusive Fraternity* (New York: Simon & Schuster, 2013), 139.
57. "To the Honorable Robert F. Kennedy, Attorney General, from Arthur B. Focke, General Counsel, July 14, 1964," LBJL, National Security-Defense (GEN ND 1-1 Non-Military Use of Aircraft 11/22/63), Box 3, Folder "ND 2 Civil Defense 11/22/63-9/23/64).
58. "Speech of John F. Kennedy, Civic Auditorium, Seattle, Washington," (September 6, 1960), John F. Kennedy Presidential Library and Museum. http://www.presidency.ucsb.edu/ws/?pid=25654.
59. "*Milestones: 1961–1968: The Limited Test Ban Treaty, 1963*," Office of the Historian, Department of State. https://history.state.gov/milestones/1961-1968/limited-ban.

60. Kennedy garnered 34,226,731 votes to Richard Nixon's 34,108,157.
61. *An Unfinished Life: John F. Kennedy 1917–1963* (New York: Little, Brown and Company, 2003), 344.
62. Graff, *Raven Rock*, 99.
63. Weisbrot, *Maximum Danger*, 40.
64. A series of "broken arrows"—when thermonuclear bombs were either accidentally detonated or lost—had taken place in the late 1950s. In this case, a faulty (low-voltage ready-safe) switch saved the Eastern seaboard from a bomb that carried a destructive yield greater than that of the bombs that hit Hiroshima and Nagasaki combined. The incident was reported in the press at the time but mention of the fact that the second nuclear bomb "fired three of four arming mechanisms and deployed the parachute designed to slow its descent to optimum blast altitude" was not reported. The National Security Administration continues to declassify information on this event, the latest reveals that their explosive yield was 3.8 megatons. Those dropped on Hiroshima and Nagasaki were .01 and .02 megatons respectively. North Carolina near miss: M. Alex Johnson, "One cheap switch saved US from nuclear catastrophe in 1961, declassified document reveals," *NBC News*, https://www.nbcnews.com/news/us-news/one-cheap-switch-saved-us-nuclear-catastrophe-1961-declassified-document-flna4b11221026. Declassification of near misses: Emma Lacey-Bordeaux, "Declassified report: Two nuclear bombs nearly wiped out North Carolina," *CNN*, June 12, 2014, https://www.cnn.com/2014/06/12/us/north-carolina-nuclear-bomb-drop/index.html.
65. "RFK 6/1/61 memo" as quoted in Michael R. Beschloss, *The Crisis Years: Kennedy and Khrushchev 1960–1963* (New York: Edward Burlingame Books, 1991), 143.
66. See Jim Rasenberger, *The Brilliant Disaster: JFK, Castro, and America's Doomed Invasion of Cuba's Bay of Pigs* (New York: Scribner, 2011).
67. As quoted in Robert Dallek, *An Unfinished Life: John F. Kennedy 1917–1963* (New York: Little, Brown and Company, 2003), 413.
68. Pierre Salinger, *With Kennedy* (Garden City, NY: Doubleday, 1966), 255.

69. This is the highest percentage since the early stages of the Korean War. American Institute of Public. Opinion. *The Gallop* Poll, 1738. As quoted in Rose, *One Nation Underground*, 8.
70. "Kennedy's Address to the Nation on His Talks in Europe," *The New York Times* (June 7, 1961).
71. James Reston, "Vienna Talks End: Meeting Closes with Hard Controversy, Kennedy Solemn," *The New York Times* (June 5, 1961).
72. "The Berlin Wall: Blockade and Crisis," *History.com*, https://www.history.com/articles/berlin-wall.
73. In response, Kennedy declared that West Berlin was crucial to the free world, doubled draft calls, mobilized 150,000 reservists, and increased the defense budget.
74. The East German troops began building at the behest of Walter Ulbright, the Communist leader of East Berlin, under the direction of Khrushchev. Ostensibly, this was to keep Westerners out; in reality, it was to keep East Berliners in. East Berlin was hemorrhaging brain power.
75. Rose, *One Nation Underground*, 8.
76. Josh M. Goshko, "National Survival Linked to Massive Shelter Plan," *The Washington Post* (October 4, 1961).
77. For a discussion on how the wall transformed the Cold War and Kennedy's rhetoric, see Lawrence Freedman, *Kennedy's Wars: Berlin, Cuba, Laos, and Vietnam* (New York: Oxford University Press, 2000), 72–110.
78. "Address by President John F. Kennedy to the UN General Assembly," *Department of State* (September 25, 1961), https://www.jfklibrary.org/learn/about-jfk/historic-speeches/address-to-the-united-nations-general-assembly.
79. The Sword of Damocles is a Greek anecdote linking power with anxiety. Kennedy's speech was reminiscent of Jonathan Edwards' fire and brimstone sermon "Sinners in the Hands of An Angry God" when the minister cried that God holds the sinner over the pit of hell, dangling above a cauldron like a spider by a single thread. "Address by President John F. Kennedy to the UN General Assembly," *Department of State* (September 25, 1961), https://www.jfklibrary.org/learn/about-jfk/historic-speeches/address-to-the-united-nations-general-assembly.

80. For traditional histories of the Cuban missile crisis see Robert F. Kennedy, and Arthur M. Schlesinger. For revisionist histories see Michael R. Beschloss and Garry Wills. For post- revisionist accounts see Michael Dobbs and Ernest May and Philip Zelikow. For a post-post-revisionist or "new" history see Sheldon Stern. Beschloss, *The Crisis Year*. Michael Dobbs, *One Minute to Midnight: Kennedy, Khrushchev, and Castro on the Brink of Nuclear War* (New York: Alfred A. Knopf, 2008). Robert F. Kennedy, *Thirteen Days: A Memoir of the Cuban Missile Crisis* (New York: W.W. Norton & Co., 1969). Ernest R. May and Philip D. Zelikow, *The Kennedy Tapes: Inside the White House During the Cuban Missile Crisis* (Cambridge, MA: The Belknap Press/Harvard University Press, 1997). Arthur M. Schlesinger, Jr., *A Thousand Days: John F. Kennedy in the White House* (Boston, MA: Houghton Mifflin Company, 1965). Sheldon M. Stern, *The Cuban Missile Crisis in American Memory: Myth Versus Reality* (Stanford, CA: Stanford University Press, 2012). Garry Wills, *The Kennedy Imprisonment: A Mediation on Power* (Boston, MA: Little, Brown, & Co., 1982).
81. Lawrence Freedman, *Kennedy's Wars: Berlin, Cuba, Laos, and Vietnam* (New York: Oxford University Press, 2000), 168.
82. The presence of intermediate-range nuclear warheads so close to the United States gave the Soviets not only increased accuracy, but first-strike capability. As the crisis intensified, Secretary of Defense Robert McNamara estimated that if these missiles were used against the United States, the number of deaths would have been roughly proportionate to that of the Civil War, when out of a total population of 31 million, 600,000 had died. See Henry Chamberlain, "A Leader's Role," *The Wall Street Journal* (October 26, 1962).
83. Stern, *The Cuban Missile Crisis in American Memory*, 16.
84. Birch Bayh, Interview with author, November 11, 2014.
85. Ralph E. Lapp, "The Strategy of Overkill," *Bulletin of the Atomic Scientists* (April 1963): 4–11. As quoted in Mann, *Daisy Petals and Mushroom Clouds*, 10.
86. Stern, *The Cuban Missile Crisis in American Memory*, 90.
87. See Ted Sorensen's *Kennedy* for a discussion of Kennedy's attitude toward war and how he was "acutely" aware of the fact that

governing in the nuclear era had changed the stakes. Theodore C. Sorensen, *Kennedy* (New York: Harper & Row, 1965), 512.
88. "The President's News Conference," March 21, 1963, *The American Presidency Project*, www.presidency.ucsb.edu/ws/index.php?pid=9124.
89. "Commencement Address at American University, June 10, 1963," John F. Kennedy Presidential Library and Museum. https://www.jfklibrary.org/Asset-Viewer/BWC7I4C9QUmLG9J6I8oy8w.aspx.
90. Kennedy signed the treaty into US law on October 7, 1963.
91. In a nationally televised speech after the Berlin crisis requesting the congressional funding, the president also requested the participation of all Americans at the federal, state, city, and individual levels. The speech was televised on July 25, 1961. Drew Pearson, "Kennedy Will Call for Shelters," *The Washington Post* (July 20, 1961).
92. For example, *The Washington Post* reported that a NJ. resident, Arthur V. Wynne, had written to the Office of Civil Defense Mobilization for advice on how to construct one in his basement, stating that Wynne's "attitude is typical" because of the grim possibility of war over Berlin. These pamphlets were distributed by civil defense officials in bulk shipments to state and local government offices. By request, one could receive a pamphlet on proper shelter-building in brick rather than concrete. The paper added that government assistance to build shelters was available in the form of home improvement loans insured by the Federal Housing Administration. Edward Cowan, "Interest in Fallout Shelter Increases Since Berlin," *The Washington Post* (August 12, 1961).
93. "County of Union Civil Defense and Disaster Control, Received January 9, 1965 Central Files," LBJL, National Security-Defense (EX ND 2 9/24/62), Box 4, Folder "ND 2 Civil Defense 11/22/63- 4/19/66." As for other state planning measures: In a memorandum for the president on the briefing of governors dated May 15, 1964, Office of Emergency Planning (OEP) Director McDermott reported that forty-nine states "[had] already adopted some or all of the legislative measures which we proposed to preserve state and local governments in an emergency, but much remains to be done." "Memorandum for the

President from Edward A. McDermott," LBJL, EX FE 10-3 National Motto, Box 14, Folder "FE 11 National Emergency."
94. "Memorandum to W. Marvin Watson August 3, 1965 from Buford Ellington Director Office of Emergency Planning," LBJL, National Security-Defense (EX ND 2 9/24/62), Box 4, Folder "ND 2-1 Civil Defense Plans."
95. "Memorandum to W. Marvin Watson August 3, 1965 from Buford Ellington Director Office of Emergency Planning."
96. Dobbs, *One Minute to Midnight*, 310.
97. It is assumed the Supreme Court would have been relocated to Mount Weather as stated above; however, one work suggests a contingency plan was arranged with a hotel, the Grove Park Inn, in Asheville, North Carolina. David Krugler, *This is Only a Test: How Washington D.C. Prepared for Nuclear War* (New York: Palgrave Macmillan, 2006).
98. "Memorandum for Honorable Bill B. Moyers, from Buford Ellington, Director, May 14, 1965," LBJL, Office Files of Bill Moyers, Box 3 (1340), Folder "Office Files of Bill Moyers: Special Message on Office of the President."
99. "Memorandum for Honorable Bill B. Moyers, from Buford Ellington, Director, May 14, 1965."
100. "Letter to the President from Robert F. Kennedy, Attorney General," NA, CJ, SCA, Box 4, Folder "88th- Kefauver, PI Correspondence Aug 1961- June 1963."
101. "Letter to the President from Robert F. Kennedy, Attorney General."
102. "Letter to the President from Robert F. Kennedy, Attorney General."
103. "Immediate Release August 10, 1961, Office of the White House Press Secretary," NA, CJ, SCA, Box. 4, Folder "88th-Kefauver PI Aug 1961–1963."
104. In, *Six Crises*, Nixon explained that the intent behind the letters, in Eisenhower's mind, was "on solving the practical problem of giving his vice president the authority to act immediately in a [nuclear] crisis, if necessary." Richard M. Nixon, *Six Crises* (Garden City, NY: Doubleday & Company, Inc.) 178.
105. "Civil Defense: A Place to Hide," *Time* (December 18, 1950). http://content.time.com/time/magazine/article/0,9171,858974,00.html.

106. Father Oscar L. Huber performed last rites at 12:50 p.m. That Kennedy was officially declared dead at 1 p.m. is the last line of Richard Reeves' work, *President Kennedy: Profile of Power*. Richard Reeves, *President Kennedy: Profile of Power,*" (New York, Simon & Schuster, 1994), 662.
107. Cabinet en route to Japan: Gillon, *The Kennedy Assassination*, 83. Johnson reported to suffer severe heart attack: Gillon, *The Kennedy Assassination*, 101.
108. Kennedy was dead by the time his car reached the hospital, but doctors attempted to resuscitate him before officially declaring him dead.
109. "White House Statement and Text of Agreement Between the President and Vice President on Procedures in the Event of Presidential Inability," Public Papers 561, August 10, 1961.
110. This relationship of mistrust began, as Robert Caro in *The Passage of Power* contends, during their first encounter when RFK refused to greet Johnson with the customary salutation "Leader," and stand and shake his hand in the Senate Office Building in January 1953. It continued when RFK visited the LBJ ranch to go shooting, was knocked down by the kick of the gun, and LBJ derided him for it. Robert Caro, *The Years of Lyndon Johnson: The Passage of Power* (New York: Alfred A. Knopf, 2012), 61–63. See also Jeff Shesol, *Mutual Contempt: Lyndon Johnson, Robert Kennedy, and the Feud That Defined a Decade* (New York: W.W. Norton & Company, 1997).
111. Numerous conflicting accounts of when Johnson learned of Kennedy's death exist. Johnson told the Warren Commission that Kenny O'Donnell and Roy Kellerman told him at 1:20 p.m. Emory Roberts said he was the person that informed Johnson he was now president at 1:13 p.m. Steven Gillon suggests that the latter account is correct, and Johnson pushed back the clock by seven minutes so that he did not look over-eager to assume the presidency. Gillon, *The Kennedy Assassination*, 107–110.
112. Jeffrey T. Richelson, "CIA Reactions to JFK Assassination Included Fear of Possible Soviet Strike against US." *Studies in Intelligence: New Articles from the CIA's In-house Journal*, National Security Archive No. 493, (Updated November 20, 2014), 2. http://www2.gwu.edu/~nsarchiv/NSAEBB/NSAEBB493/.

113. Richelson, "CIA Reactions to JFK Assassination Included Fear of Possible Soviet Strike against US," 4.
114. Richelson, "CIA Reactions to JFK Assassination Included Fear of Possible Soviet Strike against US." *Studies in Intelligence: New Articles from the CIA's In-house Journal*, 3.
115. Later declassified documents suggest that CIA director John A. McCone was not concerned about a Communist conspiracy because signals intelligence had revealed that Kennedy's murder had shocked Soviet and Cuban leaders. David Robarge, "DCI John McCone and the Assassination of President Kennedy," *Studies in Intelligence*, Vol. 57, No. 3 (September 2013), Approved for release 2014/09/29. http://nsarchive.gwu.edu/NSAEBB/NSAEBB493/docs/intell_ebb_026.PDF.
116. Richelson, "CIA Reactions to JFK Assassination Included Fear of Possible Soviet Strike against US," 3.
117. David Robarge, "DCI John McCone and the Assassination of President Kennedy," *Studies in Intelligence*, Vol. 57, No. 3 (September 2013), Approved for release 2014/09/29. http://nsarchive.gwu.edu/NSAEBB/NSAEBB493/docs/intell_ebb_026.PDF. Both to quell fear and uncover further answers, Johnson formed the President's Commission on the Assassination of President Kennedy, which became known as the Warren Commission: he cajoled Supreme Court Chief Justice Earl Warren into leading it, to add a strong sense of legitimacy to the Commission's findings. Even after the Commission ruled that a conspiracy had not transpired, a Harris survey showed that 66% of Americans still believed one had occurred. Louis Harris, "The Harris Survey: 66% See Conspiracy in Kennedy slaying" *The Washington Post* (Monday morning, May 29, 1967), LBJL, Box 179 "Office Files of Frederick Panzer," Folder "Office Files of Fred Panzer ASSSASSINATION/OSWALD."
118. Johnson first displayed his anxiety over conspiracy rumors while watching NBC's news broadcast; he started talking back to anchormen Chet Huntley and David Brinkley: "Keep talking like that and you'll bring on a revolution just as sure as I'm sitting here." See David Robarge, "DCI John McCone and the Assassination of President John F. Kennedy," *Central Intelligence Agency* (9/29/2014). https://archive.org/details/DCIJohnMcConeAndTheAssassinationOfPresidentJohnF.Kennedy.

119. "[Johnson] repeated that point in a 1970 interview with Walter Cronkite. 'I think the first thought that I had was that this is a terrifying thing that may have international consequences, and the problems that we'd had with Castro and what I had seen in intelligence reports and other things that concerned me, that this might be an international conspiracy of some kind.'" As quoted in Gillon, *The Kennedy Assassination*, 60–61.
120. James Reston, "The Problem of Succession to the Presidency," *The New York Times* (December 6, 1963).
121. "Memorandum for Bromley Smith 4 December 1963," LBJL, NSF Subject File Box 20, Folder.
 "Kennedy Death DEFCON PROCEDURES."
122. Remarkably, after hearing of the assassination at 2:15 p.m. from the Joint Chiefs of Staff, it took the Department of Defense's US Southern Command a full thirty-five minutes to order the change and another ninety-eight minutes for it to be accomplished at 4:28 p.m. "Memorandum for Bromley Smith 4 December.
 1963," LBJL, NSF Subject File Box 20, Folder "Kennedy Death DEFCON PROCEDURES."
123. Night Duty Report Major Leo J. Parent 25 November 1963," LBJL, NSF Subject File Box 20, Folder "Kennedy Death DEFCON PROCEDURES." See also "Letter to Mr. Bundy December 4, 1963," LBJL, NSF Subject File Box 20, Folder "Kennedy Death DEFCON PROCEDURES." This explains why Reston began the statement on instantaneous attack with the incorrect claim that "no additional atomic bombers were flushed, as during the Cuban crisis." James Reston, "The Problem of Succession to the Presidency," *The New York Times* (December 6, 1963).
124. Gillon, *The Kennedy Assassination*, 107.
125. See Ted Sorensen's *Counselor* for an account of a Kennedy aide who stayed on with Johnson through the transition (and for a cogent account of the Kennedy administration crises). Sorensen submitted his resignation letter on the day after the assassination, but Johnson did not accept it. He was the first to resign on February 29, 1964. Sorensen, *Counselor*.
126. Studying Johnson's doodles, historian David Greenberg later observed these dual sides of the president's character: while many of the doodles reflected the president's "explosive personality,"

Johnson's drawings depicting regimented boxes and lines demonstrated a "different side of his character" which was "coolly measured and systematic." David Greenberg, *Presidential Doodles* (New York: Basic Books, Perseus Books Group, 2006), 161. On Johnson's success in checking his temper and appearing calm and in control, see historian Robert Caro's conclusion, suggesting Johnson pulled off this feat "long enough." Caro, *The Years of Lyndon Johnson*, 598–605.

127. The author has contacted the Capitol Police, Metropolitan Police, Senate Historian Don Ritchie, NARA archivist Tom Eisinger, LBJ Library archivist Allen Fisher, a Secret Service Historian, and others, but has found records elusive. Additionally, she corresponded with Steven M. Gillon; he is of the opinion that security around the speaker and Senate president pro tem was increased but cannot find official supporting documentation either.

128. John D. Morris, "McCormack, Next in Line to the Presidency," *The New York Times* (November 23, 1963), 11.

129. William Manchester, *The Death of a President: November 20–November 25, 1963* (New York: Arbor House, 1967), 247.

130. *Congressional Quarterly Almanac 88th Congress 1st Session 1963*, Volume XIX (Washington, DC: Congressional Quarterly Inc., 1963), 65.

131. Salinger also confirmed that Hayden would be attending weekly congressional meetings of White House officials now that he had succeeded Johnson as the presiding officer in the Senate. Nan Robertson, "McCormack Asked to Join on Key Meetings of Policy," *The New York Times* (December 4, 1963).

132. Johnson ordered a Secret Service detail to protect former President Eisenhower at about seven thirty in the evening of November 22. 1965. This was the first time the federal government provided Secret Service to former presidents, even to ones that had death threats against them.

133. "For Mr. McGeorge Bundy, White House, From Benjamin H. Read, Executive Director, Department of State," LBJL, NSF Speech File, Box 1, Folder "Speech, President's Joint Session of Congress (11/27/63)," 7.

134. "Office of the White House Press Secretary, Remarks of the President to a Joint Session of Congress (As Actually Delivered),"

LBJL, NSF Speech File, Box 1, Folder "Speech, President's Joint Session of Congress (11/27/63)."
135. "Daily Report Supplement, World Reaction Series: Foreign Radio and Press reaction to President Johnson's Speech of 27 November 1963," No. 9—1963. LBJL, NSF Speech File, Box 1, Folder "Speech, President's Joint Session of Congress (11/27/63)," 2.
136. "Worldwide Reaction to President Johnson's Speech to Congress—November 27, 1963," (United States Information Agency Research and Reference Service, November 29, 1963), LBJL, NSF Speech File, Box 1, Folder "Speech, President's Joint Session of Congress (11/27/63)," 5.
137. Robert Caro argues that the Johnson transition period lasted seven weeks, ending with his State of the Union Address on January 8, 1964. See Caro, *The Years of Lyndon Johnson*.
138. "To Senator and Larry Conrad from Jerry Udall and George Condon," NA, CJ, SCA, Box 9, Folder "88th Congress, PI - Memo (Staff) 1964."
139. "To Senator and Larry Conrad from Jerry Udall and George Condon."
140. "LBJ Ascends to the Presidency," White House Historical Association, https://www.whitehousehistory.org/teacher-resources/lbj-ascends-to-the-presidency.
141. "Acceptance Speech at the Democratic National Convention (August 27, 1964), Lyndon B. Johnson," *Miller Center* (University of Virginia), http://millercenter.org/president/speeches/speech-5660.
142. In bold letters under "Building The Peace," the pamphlet argued that these nuclear weapons must remain with the president. The statement was a direct counter to many made by the Republican nominee, Arizona Senator Barry Goldwater, who argued in a 1960 book written on his behalf, *The Conscience of a Conservative*, that because of the split-second timing needed to make decisions regarding the use of nuclear bombs, smaller ones should be under the control of NATO commanders in the field. "One Nation, One People: Democratic Platform, 1964," LBJL Office Files of Frederick Panzer Box 145, Folder "1964 Democratic Platform," 8–9.
143. Mann, *Daisy Petals and Mushroom Clouds*, 21. Goldwater's language regarding relations with the Soviet Union recalled

Eisenhower's brinkmanship—a Goldwater presidency would not feel like a natural progression from Kennedy's flexible response. Quite the opposite, Goldwater had made a name for himself in the Senate as one of the main opponents of Kennedy's Limited Nuclear Test Ban Treaty.

144. According to the Senator, the US "should make every effort to achieve decisive superiority in small, clean nuclear weapons." Barry M. Goldwater, *The Conscience of a Conservative* (Mansfield, CT: Martino Publishing, 1960), 119.
145. Goldwater, *The Conscience of a Conservative*, 118.
146. Fendall W. Yerxa, "President Finds G.O.P. 'Smearlash,'" *The New York Times* (October 22, 1964).
147. Mann, *Daisy Petals and Mushroom Clouds*, 27.
148. Mann, *Daisy Petals and Mushroom Clouds*, 27.
149. "*K Trigger-Wary About Goldwater*," *New York Herald Tribune*, July 22, 1964. LBJL Goldwater Files Series 1 Goldwater: Press Relations, Politics Polls, & Foreign Policy Box 318, Folder "Goldwater, Sen. Barry: Foreign Policy Khrushchev And Russian Criticism Of 1964."
150. "*K Trigger-Wary About Goldwater*."
151. John G. Geer, *In Defense of Negativity: Attack Ads in Presidential Campaigns* (Chicago: University of Chicago Press, 2006), 3. As quoted in Mann, *Daisy Petals and Mushroom Clouds*, 115.
152. Additional Johnson ads reflected this fear. For example, the "Telephone Hotline Spot," pictured an unanswered phone ringing (meant to mimic the hotline installed between Washington and Moscow after the Cuban missile crisis) with the announcer concluding that it only rang in a crisis and should be answered by a president well-equipped to handle it. "The decisions they make here [in the office of the president] can change the course of history or end history altogether," the voiceover in the "Our President" spot stated. "Type of Commercial Commander-in-Chief: 'Our President,'" *Museum of the Moving Image: The Living Room Candidate* (2012), February 3, 2016. http://www.livingroomcandidate.org/commercials/type/commander-in-chief.

153. See Laurence Stern, "Johnson to Remain in Hospital for Rest," *The Washington Post* (January 24, 1965).
154. Senate Swearing-In 1963 (448–1074), January 9, 1963, Photograph Collection, Birch Bayh Senatorial Papers, Modern Political Papers Collection, Indiana University Libraries, Bloomington, Indiana.

CHAPTER 4

Ingraining Anxiety: Ratifying the Twenty-Fifth Amendment in the Nuclear Age

Even prior to the assassination of President John F. Kennedy, momentum had begun to build for a new constitutional amendment to solve the presidential succession and inability issues that had existed since the nation's founding. From December 1963 through February 1967, references to the shock of Kennedy's assassination lessened, but direct and indirect allusions to the nuclear anxiety that permeated American culture and politics continued unabated. Focused on the shock of the Kennedy assassination, traditional histories of the Twenty-Fifth Amendment, however, have missed the fact that before the president's sudden death, congressmembers and expert witnesses already were framing the urgent need for a solution to the succession and inability problem in language that displayed society's deep undercurrent of nuclear anxiety.

Dwight Eisenhower and Richard Nixon—leaders formerly in the presidential line of succession—provided statements in hearings that the Nixon/Eisenhower and Kennedy/Johnson letter agreements were an insufficient solution. The major architect of the amendment, Birch Bayh, believed that S.J. Res. 35—introduced before Kennedy's assassination by Senators Estes Kefauver of Tennessee and Kenneth Keating of New York—did not solve the problem either. But what appeared to be a typical legislative dead end changed when Bayh harnessed nuclear anxiety to the passage of the bill. Bayh reflected in a 2014 interview that nuclear anxiety was an important, continuous factor that provided a sense of urgency and also helped to speed the process of ratification.[1] It was this nuclear anxiety that contributed to each stage of the process from Bayh's original drafting, passage through committees and the Senate in 1964, debate over time limits, the passage through both Houses of Congress in 1965, and finally ratification in the states in February 1967.

Oral interviews of key actors and examination of the Subcommittee on Constitutional Amendments files and other previously unexamined archives reveal that senators shared concerns about presidential succession and inability in a nuclear age, but the archives also uncover contradictions that complicated the amendment's progress: different ways of thinking about nuclear anxiety manifested in strong, and sometimes opposing, suggestions for the language and structure of the succession and inability plan. Congressmembers disagreed about the amount of detail the amendment should contain. In some cases, greater detail appealed to congressmembers as a solution to the problem of ensuring presidential continuity, while to others, the detail seemed like a liability. Different institutional values held by each House also contributed to a stalemate in Conference Committee. The urgency of concern about presidential stability amid the real possibility of instant nuclear destruction directly contributed to ratification and complicated the process of ratification. In Colorado, for example, those who were worried about a nuclear attack tended to be pro-amendment. However, a significant subset of those who were *really* worried about a nuclear attack took positions against the amendment on the grounds that it did not go far enough in protecting the continuity of the presidency. Despite these different reactions to the prospect of nuclear destruction, after more than two decades at the forefront of America's psyche, nuclear anxiety became ingrained in the constitutional framework of American government.

* * *

A year after the Sputnik launch, and after Eisenhower and Nixon signed their letter agreement on March 3, 1958, Senator Kefauver, chairman of the Judiciary Committee's Subcommittee on Constitutional Amendments, had made it clear that he believed the time had come to pass inability and succession legislation. In April 1958, Kefauver had introduced S.J. Res. 28, which embodied the spirit of the letter agreements with few modifications.[2] He reintroduced the bill in the 86th Congress (1959–1960).[3] Both times, the chairman was able to move the bill out of his subcommittee to the wider Judiciary Committee but no further. Congress adjourned in 1960 with the legislation still on the Committee's agenda.

Then, in early 1963, Kefauver announced that he would join Republican Senator Kenneth Keating to cosponsor a bill, S.J. Res. 35, endorsed by the American Bar Association, that "simply authorizes Congress to pass laws on how to decide when a president is disabled," or, in other words, enabled Congress to establish procedure.[4] The thrust of the release was that "this is the time to do it—when we have a young, healthy president, when extensive hearings on this subject would not be embarrassing to anyone."[5] In a private correspondence, Kefauver stated that he had "managed to obtain a tentative commitment from the administration that it will go along with [S.J. Res. 35]" and repeated that the president was "obviously healthy" and therefore "no inferences can be drawn from our interest in this matter that the president might be in poor health."[6] A healthy president would not take succession planning as a slight. Legislating a solution now was imperative.[7]

On June 10 and 18, 1963, the Senate Subcommittee on Constitutional Amendments held hearings on presidential succession and inability bill S.J. Res. 35, sponsored by Kefauver and Keating. The bill was less detailed than many pieces of legislation pending in the Subcommittee, drawn up that way in the hope that Congress would be more inclined to pass a less-complicated piece of legislation. It did not deal with vice presidential vacancy, nor did it guard against the contingency that Congress may not act in the case of a succession crisis. But it had the tacit support of former Vice President Richard Nixon, who experienced firsthand the issues involving an incapacitated president when Eisenhower was ill. Nixon wrote to Kefauver before the hearings began, saying: "With the advent of the terrible and instant destructive power of atomic weapons, the nation cannot afford to have any period of time when there is doubt or legal quibbling as to where the ultimate power to use those weapons resides."[8]

Pointing to the "constitutional defect" in his opening statement, Keating agreed with the former vice president; failing to take action in this era could result in paralysis at the very time that quick and cogent decision-making was imperative.[9] With these fears in mind, the subcommittee as a whole came to that conclusion as well; the bill was voted out of the subcommittee to the full Judiciary Committee.

On August 10, 1963, two weeks after his sixtieth birthday, Kefauver died of a heart attack; the hope of a more solid succession and inability plan almost died with him. Senator James O. Eastland of Mississippi, chairman of the Senate Judiciary Committee, decided to dissolve the panel. Staff and resources would be distributed elsewhere.[10] Yet a memorandum written in round cursive handwriting on US Senate letterhead in the last of Kefauver's files noted, confidentially, that presidential disability had "prospects at this time."[11]

At the same time, Birch Bayh, the freshman senator from Indiana, and his staff were searching for their own opportunities to resolve the succession and inability issue, hoping to fill the void Kefauver's death created. In an interview in 2014, Bob Keefe, Bayh's office manager, confessed that "being so junior, [Bayh's staff members] weren't yet aware of the opportunities that lay before them; they weren't yet attuned to moving when the corpse was still warm."[12] Upon learning of Eastland's decision, Keefe urged Bayh to go see the chairman immediately, that very afternoon. When Bayh returned about two hours later,[13] he was the newly named Chairman of the Subcommittee on Constitutional Amendments.[14] On September 30, 1963, the Judiciary Committee ratified his appointment.

Kennedy's sudden death elicited calls for legislation to remedy the confusion surrounding presidential succession and inability; these were coupled with direct and indirect references to the tense cultural and political mood of the era surrounding the potential for nuclear war. "Has the Congress prepared the presidency adequately for the possibilities of a violent age?" James Reston asked in a column on December 5, 1963. "Is the rule of presidential succession satisfactory for these days of human madness and scientific destruction?"[15] Similarly, a *Washington Post* editorial insisted that "the whole problem of succession to the White House needs a fresh analysis … in these days of hair trigger defense few things would be more perilous than uncertainty as to where the powers of the presidency would lie in case of disaster or a succession of disasters."[16] These articles served as a motivating factor for Bayh.[17]

At first, Bayh questioned his ability as a junior senator to achieve any steps toward a succession and inability solution. He was well aware that even if an amendment passed through Congress, it needed to be ratified by three-fourths of the states. The amendment would take a minimum of two to three years because some legislatures met only biannually.[18] Another constraint: the amendment would have to be ratified by the necessary thirty-eight states within seven years.[19] Yet, in addition to the articles, Bayh was also spurred on by President Johnson's November 27 address after Kennedy's assassination. Although the speech was intended to soothe the nation, the television cameras panned from Johnson to House Speaker John McCormack and Senate President pro tempore Carl Hayden, ages seventy-one and eighty-six, respectively, behind him as he delivered the speech. Bayh saw the absolute necessity of finding a solution to the succession and inability issue, which would be the focus of his work for the better part of two years and beyond.

Bayh had been thrust into a centuries-old constitutional conundrum.[20] On December 4, after listening to debate in a Judiciary Committee meeting that focused mainly on other matters but included references to the succession bill that Kefauver and Keating had introduced earlier in the year, Bayh decided to draft his own measure. He believed that the succession bill, with Keating as its key sponsor now, simply gave Congress a power it already had—to establish procedures to determine inability—and did not solve the inability problem, nor the one of succession. On a yellow-lined eight-by-five tablet he scrawled the first points of what would become the Twenty-Fifth Amendment: Presidential succession should be kept within the executive branch. Vice presidential vacancies must be filled. Disability dealt with.[21]

The second week in December, the senator gathered his team together and began the herculean undertaking.[22] Bob Keefe explained that it was clear to Bayh that the subcommittee he now led, composed of Democrats James O. Eastland of Mississippi and Thomas J. Dodd of Connecticut, and Republicans Everett McKinley Dirksen of Illinois, Hiram L. Fong of Hawaii and New York's Keating, would be given neither a budget for staff nor space until they found "something to do."[23] John D. Feerick[24] became the chair of the American Bar Association's (ABA's) Junior Bar Conference Committee on Presidential Inability and Vice Presidential Vacancy in the spring of 1964.[25] He made it the Junior Bar Association's mission to garner further support for a presidential succession and inability amendment.[26] Donald E. Channell, Lowell Beck, Jim Kirby, Lewis Powell, Dale Tooley, Martin Taylor, and other members of the ABA would become instrumental in conducting the campaign—in Congress, among the state legislatures, and with the public—to get presidential succession and inability measures written into the Constitution.

In his book *One Heartbeat Away*, Bayh wrote that his reason for proposing succession and inability legislation was inspired by Kennedy's murder. In his press release of December 12, 1963, although it was a factor, no mention was made of the assassination. Significantly, the statement referred to the increased pace of communications and technology (and therefore warfare) in the modern era of globalization and concluded that the tense international atmosphere called for immediate action: "The accelerated pace of international affairs, plus the overwhelming problems of modern military security, make it almost imperative that we change our system to provide for not only a president but a vice president at all times."[27] Bayh's statement highlighted the increased importance and responsibilities of the vice president during the Cold War, pointing out that the vice president was a statutory member of the National Security Council and National Aeronautics and Space Administration, requiring him to decide key issues of the day.[28] In testimony later, members of the public and Congress alike would amplify Bayh's point: even if it had not been the case in the past, now, during the atomic age, having a successor in place was vital to the nation's security.[29]

Nuclear anxiety was a key motivating factor driving the amendment forward from the outset. As Bayh got to work with his team to perfect his first draft, he, too, reflected that, for the sixteenth time in US history, the nation was without a vice president, but that, as Bayh wrote, "this was a different and dangerous age. The possible consequences of inaction were… terrifying."[30] They began by using the letter agreements as a template for the amendment. The first point would permit a vice presidential vacancy to be filled when it occurred, rather than the position standing empty until the next presidential inauguration, as had happened in 1963. The second goal was to try to address the issue of presidential disability. The third was to revise the 1947 succession law to eliminate the possibility for congressional succession and a potential violation of the separation of powers found in the Constitution. In this draft, the secretary of state, followed by Cabinet secretaries in order of creation of the department, would replace the speaker of the House and the Senate president pro tempore.

The question of whether these succession and inability concerns could be remedied by a simple statute did not arise within Bayh's tight-knit group. In June of that year, in addition to emphasizing potential paralysis of the executive branch during a crisis if action was not taken immediately, Keating had made an eloquent argument favoring an amendment. He believed the American people would question any assumption of power under a statute and the "uncertainties of the present situation would persist." A statute would only suffice as an interim measure until an amendment could be ratified. Worse still, he argued, was the "hazard" of having only the letter agreements in place. It was a "minimum safeguard" that would be useless in the event of a disagreement between the president and vice president as to whether the president's inability had ended.[31] Bayh's first attempt at constructing an amendment amounted to six pages consisting of seven detailed sections—longer than all previous amendments taken together.[32]

Bayh introduced Senate Joint Resolution 139 on December 12, 1963.[33] Concerns at this time revolved around a perceived weakness in the 1947 succession law: the potential for the presidency to switch parties suddenly during the nuclear age. On the day it was introduced, Walter Lippmann poked holes in the current succession legislation. "Under the badly considered 1947 law," he wrote, "the whole administration of the government can be transferred from one party to another by the act of one sniper."[34] The Committee for Economic Development, a public policy think tank, suggested avoiding a potential sudden switch in parties by altering the line of succession so that Congress was cut out. In the think tank's proposal, the secretary of defense would be third in line behind the vice president and secretary of state, removing the speaker of the House and Senate president pro tempore put in place by the 1947 law.[35] Notably, the proposal pointed out: "[As commander-in-chief] of the armed forces, the president must keep his finger on the nation's nuclear trigger. If that grip should loosen even for a brief period, the resulting slowness of our response to nuclear aggression might well prove disastrous."[36] The proposal underscored the urgency of finding a solution to presidential succession and inability because of the power the president had at his fingertips.

Despite these concerns, Bayh complained that his early press conferences on S.J. Res. 139 were not well attended. One way to publicize the effort and build support, Bayh thought, was to alert the public to star witnesses invited to testify at the subcommittee hearings. Hearings on the measure began on January 22, 1964, and stretched over six sessions, lasting until March 5; Bayh hoped that one of the stars of the hearings would be former President Dwight Eisenhower, who, he believed, was "the only person alive that could adequately describe the need for an inability amendment."[37] Although Eisenhower declined the invitation to appear in person,[38] explaining that he was spending the winter in Southern California, he agreed to submit a letter for the record. In that letter, Eisenhower pointedly did not suggest that the letter agreements signed by himself and Nixon in 1958 would suffice to solve the succession and inability problem. Instead, he stated that the "bothersome" possibility of a disaster removing the president and vice president simultaneously meant that changes should be made by constitutional amendment.[39] He admitted the issue was complex: "There is no completely foolproof method covering every contingency and every possibility that could arise in the circumstances now under discussion."[40] But the former president believed that, in a time of disaster, the "individuals concerned" would be men whose chief concern would be the public good.[41]

Among those who testified at the subcommittee hearings was Laurens Hamilton, a former legislator from New York and the great-great-grandson of Alexander Hamilton; he emphasized the nuclear question in arguing for immediate action on succession as the president was the key to the nation's survival in the case of an attack. Pointing out to the subcommittee that: "we live in a day when lightning sneak attack might be made on us by an aggressor," he said the president served as the nation's greatest defense because: "he and he alone has the authority to push the vital button or to deliver the agreed code word over hot line telephones."[42] Hamilton was so anxious for action, he followed up with similar language in a letter dated five days later, April 13, 1964.[43]

Testimony from members of Congress on both sides of the aisle was rife with similar remarks that nuclear war was a grim possibility, and, as such, the United States required an immediate solution to the succession and inability problem. Republican Louis C. Wyman of New Hampshire went on at length, stating that a "crippling inability is a daily possibility with any president" and concluded that Congress must act because "in this atomic era seconds can be crucial."[44] Republican Senator Jacob K. Javits of New York stated "the split-second exigencies of this nuclear age do not permit the luxury of further incomplete solutions."[45] And Senator James B. Pearson, Republican of Kansas, argued that "in an era when defense of the entire free world through the use of our nuclear deterrents, rests on the spoken word of one man, the President of the United States, we cannot leave any doubt about the fact of succession or the capabilities of the president's successor."[46] The Kennedy/Johnson letter agreement of August 10, 1961, was included in the testimony.[47] The agreement had concluded by underscoring that, "obviously," not having a plan in place "is a risk which cannot be taken in these times."[48] The voices calling for action were building.[49]

One expert witness, Professor Ruth Miner of Wisconsin State College, was adamant that a solution to the issue was needed because of the tense public mood of the era and suggested—due to her worry that an atomic attack would occur when all officials in the line of succession were in DC—that the line of succession after the vice president include state governors.[50] Miner, however, expressed a concern that those who argued in favor of an executive branch line of succession did not mention: Cabinet members, she noted, are specialists in their field, but not in all fields. The secretary of state, for example, was qualified only as an expert in international affairs.[51] Further, she argued that because of the danger that a nuclear attack could occur when all those in the line of succession were in range of the attack, after the vice president, the line of succession should include the governors in the order of their states' population.[52]

The governors who testified did not discuss Miner's succession idea, but they also argued that the 1947 Presidential Succession Act was inadequate in light of nuclear anxiety. Governor Edmund Brown of California testified that it "would be tragic, in this day of nuclear weapons when foreign policy decision literally can mean life or death, not to provide the machinery in all contingencies for a sure and smooth transition of executive power."[53] And Governor Nelson A. Rockefeller of New York echoed Brown's sentiments: "In my view, the present succession statute, enacted in 1947, does not adequately cope with the nation's needs at a time of international crisis and tension when the 'hot line' to Moscow might have to be used on short notice by the nation's chief executive."[54] Rockefeller's support was important because of speculation that he would be the Republican nominee for president that year.

The only witness to eclipse Rockefeller's star power was scheduled for the last day of the hearings, March 5. Bayh had enlisted former vice president Richard Nixon to talk about the dire need for the succession and inability amendment. "He was going to be our clean-up hitter," Bayh said, "Here was living proof of a president and a vice president who had been in that situation."[55] Nixon's views on succession had not changed since his letter to Senator Kefauver over the summer, before JFK's assassination.[56] In fact, he was even more adamant that the existence of atomic weapons made it imperative to ratify an amendment. After stating that the president was the defender of the free world, he continued: "The United States and the free world can't afford 17 months or 17 weeks or 17 minutes in which there is any doubt about whether there is a finger on the [nuclear] trigger."[57] Nixon also made the case in an essay for the *Saturday Evening Post* "Fifty years ago the country could afford to 'muddle along' until the disabled president either got well or died," he wrote. "But today when only the president can make the decision to use atomic weapons in the defense of the nation, there could be a critical period when no finger is on the trigger because of the illness of the chief executive,"[58] he added. Those that had the experience of being in the presidential line of succession shared the belief that lack of planning for such a crisis was unacceptable.

Keating's resistance was the final barrier to successfully getting S.J. Res. 139 out of the subcommittee and in front of the full Judiciary Committee for consideration; therefore, to get Keating to abandon S.J. Res. 35 that simply enabled Congress to establish procedure, and support S.J. Res. 139, Bayh made a strategic concession. Keating had written to Bayh that he was inclined to support Bayh's S.J. Res. 139 on one condition: Bayh's preliminary version called for succession to pass to the secretary of state and other Cabinet members if the presidency and vice presidency were both vacant, a change from Truman's 1947 Presidential Succession Act that allowed the vacancy to be passed to Congress. Bayh must relent on his conviction that the line of succession remains in the executive branch. Bayh was ready to compromise. To reach an agreement with Keating, Bayh abandoned this point, one he had thought necessary as he scrawled notes on the plane in December 1963. Bayh conceded this point even though some witnesses had called for an executive line of succession during the subcommittee hearings.[59]

Bayh's concession was not just political, it was also a reaction to the apprehension in the media surrounding McCormack's abilities. The Massachusetts media was lambasting the speaker as a leader who was past his prime and usefulness.[60] McCormack was reportedly "shaken" when asked by reporters if rumors were true that he would quit his post in order for someone younger to take his place.[61] A national newspaper added to the fray by suggesting that McCormack must "feel a sense of dread that the presidency in a time of fearful responsibility and extraordinary peril might by some tragic mischance devolve on [him]."[62] McCormack, mistakenly thinking for a moment after the Kennedy assassination that he had succeeded to the presidency, did, indeed, experience dread.[63] By mid-March, however, newspapers such as *The New York Times* were predicting that Bayh's amendment would not advance further in the House because the chances that the speaker (and those that did not want to offend him) would block the bill were higher than the possibility of dual presidential and vice presidential vacancies.[64]

Johnson, who was seeking a term in his own right in 1964, reminded Bayh to be mindful of McCormack's position when strategizing about passage. Nobody knew the flaws in the succession process better than Johnson. But Johnson had not provided any support during the subcommittee hearings forcing Bayh to incorporate an earlier letter of Deputy Attorney General Nicholas deB. Katzenbach's dated June 18, 1963, into the record in the hopes that critics of his succession and inability bill would not make note of the administration's silence. Katzenbach had expressed support for the Kefauver-Keating succession legislation prior to Bayh's introduction of S.J. Res. 139. Katzenbach's main reason for supporting the earlier bill, Bayh knew, could also be applied to S.J. Res. 139. "The primary purpose," the Attorney General had said, "is to confer broad discretion on the Congress" when "the president and vice president have reached an impasse, or an atomic attack or like holocaust prevents communication and agreement between the president and vice president."[65] Yet the president recognized that some members of the House would not vote favorably for S.J. Res. 139 out of respect for McCormack, despite fears of a chaotic transfer of presidential power in the nuclear age. Johnson relayed this advice to Bayh in late March 1964, after the hearings were finished, when they met in Atlantic City at a convention of the United Auto Workers. In an interview many years later, Bayh recalled their conversation on Marine One during the return trip to DC:

> I thought I would lobby him to come out in support of the Twenty-Fifth Amendment. [The president] said, "You know, Birch, you're not going to get that passed, not now." He said you're not going to get that passed as long as there's no vice president because the House of Representatives is not going to vote for a measure that will take the speaker out of the chain of command because he's their leader. So basically, we didn't push it that way because that would've happened…. He said to wait until Hubert [Humphrey] and I are elected and Hubert is vice president and you can get it passed, the House will go along with it. And so that's exactly what we did.[66]

Two months later, on May 27, 1964, S.J. Res. 139 was reported out of the subcommittee to the full Senate Judiciary Committee. The *Congressional Quarterly* noted that a Senate subcommittee had approved a measure that "would provide a means of filling vice presidential vacancies, unsolved problems of paramount importance in a push-button-war age, in the opinion of some."[67] With Johnson's advice in mind, however, Bayh was content to see S.J. Res. 139 unanimously pass the Judiciary Committee on August 4, 1964, and then pass the Senate with a roll call vote of 65–0 on September 30, 1964, about five weeks before the presidential election and only days before Congress adjourned for the campaign season on October 3. Bayh now intended to "introduce the amendment at the beginning of the following session, pass it rapidly through the upper chamber, and bring [the] entire effort to bear upon the House of Representatives."[68] Heightened nuclear anxiety would allow him to do just that.

* * *

Bayh felt the administration's support was crucial to passage in the House. He managed to secure another brief meeting with the president to discuss succession and inability legislation on December 10, 1964. Johnson, seated in his rocking chair, was preoccupied with his hand, which was healing from the removal of a small growth. He made no promises to Bayh, instead directing the senator to talk to his aides, Press Secretary Bill Moyers, and Deputy Attorney General Ramsey Clark. Bayh eventually got Clark on the phone and confessed that during the last session, congressmembers were "jittery of the speaker's feelings," and although he didn't think that would be the case this time, "we couldn't afford to take any chances." Bayh emphasized that if the administration acted, "we'll be home free."[69] Bayh's pleas were successful. The president—who does not have a constitutional role in the amending process—mentioned the succession and inability legislation in his State of the Union address on January 4, 1965, saying: "I will propose laws to insure the necessary continuity of leadership should the president be disabled or die."[70] With those eighteen words, Johnson sounded as though he were promising a statute, not an amendment, but Bayh thought that was unlikely.

When the president's State of the Union Address concluded, the House stayed in session and House Judiciary Committee Chairman Emanuel Celler introduced House Joint Resolution 1. Bayh introduced the companion bill, S.J. Res. 1, two days later, on January 6. They were identical to one another and to S.J. Res. 1 as passed by the Senate in September 1964. The bill read as follows:

Section 1. In case of the removal of the president from office or of his death or resignation, the vice president shall become president.
Section 2. Whenever there is a vacancy in the office of the vice president, the president shall nominate a vice president who shall take office upon confirmation by a majority of both houses of Congress.
Section 3. If the president declares in writing that he is unable to discharge the powers and duties of his office, such powers and duties shall be discharged by the vice president as acting president.
Section 4. If the president does not so declare, and the vice president with the written concurrence of a majority of the heads of the executive departments or such other body as Congress may by law provide, transmits to the Congress his written declaration that the president is unable to discharge the powers and duties of his office, the vice president shall immediately assume the powers and duties of the office as acting president.
Section 5. Whenever the president transmits to the Congress his written declaration that no inability exists, he shall resume the powers and duties of his office unless the vice president, with the written concurrence of a majority of the heads of the executive departments or such other body as Congress may by law provide, transmits within two days to the Congress his written declaration that the president is unable to discharge the powers and duties of the office, the vice president shall continue to discharge the same as acting president; otherwise the president shall resume the powers and duties of his office.[71]

Bayh had been gathering outside support. In a letter dated December 21, 1964, he informed colleagues that a range of groups were already on board such as the American Bar Association, cities, and counties.[72] Responses from colleagues adding their support trickled in.

Along with Bayh's letter, the president's resounding win (which brought Democratic supermajorities in both houses[73]) and his subsequent support for Bayh's bill helped Bayh collect cosponsors for S.J. Res. 1. S.J. Res. 1 became a "hot item," according to Keefe.[74] Bayh received just a handful of rejection letters.[75] A short, perfunctory "no thank you" letter typed by a secretary was customary in the early 1960s, leaving Bayh and his staff to guess as to the reasoning behind the rejections. Overall, however, it was such a popular piece of legislation, according to one preparatory document, that fifty-three of sixty-eight Democrats in the Senate allowed their names to be added to the bill by mid-January 1965.[76]

Three weeks after delivering the State of Union Address, and after additional lobbying by Bayh and his staff, Johnson officially endorsed Bayh's amendment, sending a support message to Congress on January 28, 1965, that emphasized that a nuclear holocaust or other such catastrophe required planning in the form of an amendment. Thanks to Providence alone, America had avoided a chaotic transfer of presidential power. But, Johnson said, "It is not necessary to endure the nightmare of nuclear holocaust or other national catastrophe to identify these omissions as chasms of chaos into which normal human frailties might plunge us at any time."[77] He continued, "The potential of paralysis implicit in these conditions constitutes indefensible folly for our responsible society in these times. Common sense impels, duty requires us to act—and to act now, without further delay."[78] Highlighting the tense cultural and political mood, he urged: "Action on these measures now will allay future anxiety among our own people, and among peoples of the world."[79] Until that formal announcement, Bayh was unsure of the president's exact position on the amendment, but the president was clearly urging Congress to act before nuclear disaster struck.

By the end of January, Bayh's appeals combined with the president's endorsement had been somewhat effective[80]; yet, influential dissenters existed on both sides of the aisle.[81] Dirksen emerged as a key opponent, despite believing an amendment was urgent.[82] In a statement of his position on February 1, 1965, he wrote "we must have an amendment to deal with the problem of presidential succession and inability," but he took issue with the language in S.J. Res. 1.[83] He had been preoccupied with the Civil Rights Amendment in 1964, allowing S.J. Res. 139 to progress out of the Judiciary Committee and to a successful floor vote, but now took up the argument Keating had dropped.[84] Dirksen was in favor of the broadest language possible that would enable Congress to decide on presidential inability. He felt vagaries would remain but had an opinion on how to remedy them. "The proper way to cure these ambiguities is to omit the details that give rise to them," he counseled.[85] Bayh scribbled "advocates blank check" on the bottom of his copy of Dirksen's statement, concluding that Dirksen supported a simple enabling amendment, very similar to Senator Keating's S.J. Res. 35.[86] Dirksen then introduced his own amendment along those lines, which was debated in the Subcommittee on January 29, 1965, the day after the president sent his message to Congress.[87] Three days later, although not every senator was in agreement about the language of S.J. Res. 1, the bill was voted unanimously out of the subcommittee.[88]

During the first four days of February when the full Judiciary Committee considered S.J. Res. 1, Robert Kennedy raised similar concerns to that of Dirksen regarding the language in section five; but his solution was to add detail, not remove it as Dirksen preferred. Kennedy's first issue was that "inability" was left undefined in the amendment. He wanted the "gravity" and "duration" explained. Short of that, he wished for examples of what did not count as an inability.[89] Further, he added, "Just yesterday, Secretary [of State Robert] McNamara pointed out that a nuclear attack on this country would take 149 million lives. This terrible realization that those are the stakes we're playing for," meant that the president should not be "second-guessed" when decisive action was needed.[90] The Senators agreed that an amendment was needed because of the existence of nuclear bombs but disagreed about the language.

The same week the Senate Judiciary Committee approved the resolution containing the amended language, the House Judiciary Committee held its own hearings (on February 9, 10, 16, and 17, 1965); the testimony was replete with references to nuclear anxiety as the reason for moving forward with H.J. Res. 1. Convening the hearings, in his opening statement, Chairman Celler did not mention the tragic death of the late president. Rather, he listed the duties of the president and argued that the nation could not leave the office unfilled, even briefly, because of these responsibilities in the nuclear age. He stated: "In this nuclear age [the president's] finger rests upon the trigger…. One would have to be blind not to see and acknowledge the dangers" the nation was gambling with by not having a solution to the important problem.[91] Celler then pointed out that thirty-eight proposals were before the House on the topic of succession and inability. He concluded that a lack of a perfect solution should not, in this pressing case, be a deterrent to immediate action. Bayh agreed. "What we wanted," Bayh said, was "to have a system that would—right and wrong, without politics, without a crisis of the moment—say, 'Here it is.'"[92] Conveying this sentiment, Bayh was speaking for many of his colleagues who felt finding a solution was of the utmost urgency.

Bayh was also one of the experts who testified before the House Judiciary Committee and mentioned a nuclear nightmare. He began by discussing time limits, focusing on the number of days that might elapse between the nomination of a vice president and the vice president's confirmation. Bayh shared what the Senate Judiciary Committee was thinking, posing a nuclear holocaust scenario as follows: "What if we were engaged in nuclear war and the seat of government is destroyed? There would be a time element involved finding a place where the Congress could meet and convene despite rapid travel we take for granted."[93] Nuclear war could cause numerous problems for presidential continuity—not the least of which was convening Congress to determine a president's inability if the president and vice president disagreed—but predicting the hardships that would come in the aftermath of a nuclear attack was difficult.

The issue of time limits would become the greatest point of contention when ironing out the differences between the Senate and House versions of the bill in the Conference Committee. Colorado Congressman Byron G. Rogers, a member of the Judiciary Committee, raised the issue of the need to include provisions for dual presidential and vice presidential inabilities in a nuclear age. "Since your committee finds a need to change the present posture we are in because of the nuclear age, and since it is conceivable, though remote, that some situation like [dual incapacity] might occur,"[94] Rogers noted. Focused on the specter of nuclear war, Democratic Congressman Abraham J. Multer of New York reminded the Committee of policymakers' unease around Eisenhower's illnesses saying, "I need not document the circumstances of these occasions, for we can all recall the danger than can be sensed when a president is incapacitated, particularly in the nuclear age."[95] Howard W. Robison, another Representative from New York, suggested not only ratifying an amendment, but including a statute to specify additional procedures in the event of disability. One of the provisions Robison stipulated was a commission with the responsibility to declare the president incapacitated. He said, "I feel the latter contingency is important in view of the perilous nuclear-threatened world in which we live."[96] In another statement, California Congressman Edward R. Roybal, expressing his support for H.J. Res. 1, also tied the need for the amendment to the nuclear age. "I am sure the members of this Committee fully realize that we can no longer afford, in this nuclear-space age, to leave the fate of or [sic] government to the whims of chance."[97] Talk of time limits continue to pivot on the fact that Congress would be making the decision on inability in the nuclear age when minutes mattered.[98]

On February 19, 1965, Bayh introduced his reworked legislation, S.J. Res. 1, on the floor of the Senate. In his speech on the Senate floor,

Bayh listed the crises America was dealing with when Eisenhower had his heart attack in 1955 and then read a pertinent section of Nixon's *Six Crises* aloud, underscoring the fact that it was the president's job to react to these situations and it was he who had his finger on the nuclear button. In the section Bayh read, Nixon had written: "The ever-present possibility of an [atomic] attack was hanging over us. Would the president be well enough to make the decision? If not, who had the authority to push the button?"[99] The author of the amendment had not only pointed numerous times to nuclear attack as the reason for urgent passage but was now highlighting the nuclear anxiety of the former vice president, who was once first in the line of succession.

Bayh was deeply concerned that Dirksen or other senators might hold up his amendment—that would ascertain, without doubt, who succeeded to the presidency in a crisis and had the authority to detonate nuclear bombs.[100] This led him to ask his ally, Senator Sam Ervin who was at home in Morgantown, North Carolina, to return from vacation early, to support S.J. Res. 1.[101] Ervin agreed to return to Washington and paid tribute to Bayh's work in a speech on the Senate floor.[102] John Little McClellan of Arkansas and others also raised their voices in support of S.J. Res. 1. When McClellan rose to speak, he focused on the import of a smooth transition of executive power in a democracy and the requirement that the government be prepared for the worst possible crisis: nuclear war. The Democrat from Arkansas warned that Congress must prepare for the worst: "This was never more true [sic] than in today's nuclear age, when this morning's crisis is often relegated to the back pages of the afternoon newspapers, headlining still another crisis."[103] The senator was emphasizing the swift pace of nerve-wracking events; a succession and inability plan was an essential element in preparing for unknown crises.

Just before the vote in the Senate, however, senators proposed amendments that could have acted as temporary impediments to passage by sending S.J. Res. 1 back to committee.[104] The most seriously considered, Senator Strom Thurmond's amendment, called for the Electoral College to be convened to fill a vice presidential vacancy.[105] Thurmond may have been seeking to delay the amendment's progress out of personal animosity toward Bayh. Bayh generally recalled positive relations with his colleagues, but[106] Thurmond was an exception.[107] Ervin proved instrumental in saving the day, however. Ervin reminded senators about a moment in 1868, when a group led by president pro tempore of the Senate Ben Wade—who was in line for the presidency after Andrew Johnson had assumed the office when Lincoln was assassinated—led the impeachment process against Johnson. The clause requiring a two-thirds majority, which Wade had failed to acquire by just one vote, was all that stood between Johnson and the rival party gaining power.[108] Ervin's point eased remaining concerns: at least some detail was necessary as opposed to a simple enabling amendment, the matter was urgent, and every vote counted. The following day, with Ervin's assistance, the measure passed, 72–0. Another hurdle had been cleared.

* * *

S.J. Res. 1 was delivered to the House on February 22, 1965. The House passed a modified version of S.J. Res. 1 by a vote of 368 to 29 on April 13 and returned the bill to the Senate on April 22. In the House, Celler's statement echoed that of Johnson's January 28 endorsement. He said that while fate had been kind to America, Congress could not expect America's luck to hold out. He noted that the resolution had the support of the American Bar Association and reread earlier testimony into the record. The chairman again iterated the sentiment that, because the president's finger was on the nuclear trigger, Congress could not ignore the danger inherent in failing to enact Bayh's resolution. He said, "One would have to be blind not to see and acknowledge the danger and the risk we are faced with at this very moment."[109] He then urged the approval of the constitutional provision to ensure a smooth presidential transition.

When the House returned the bill to the Senate on April 22, moderate changes were made limiting the time in which Congress had to decide the president's disability; Bayh used the nuclear issue to sway the decision-making. The House had added the provision that if Congress did not declare within ten days that the president was incapacitated, he would resume office.[110] Bayh commented that, although he was not a doctor, time for diagnoses and discussion would be needed. He would "bet that there are some illnesses which can't even be diagnosed in ten days, let alone enough time for congressional discussion."[111] After a ten-day period, Congress could still be weighing the evidence and "we might have a president who could be completely off his rocker reassuming his powers and duties, even if it meant he could blow us all to kingdom come in an hour's time," he said.[112] Bayh had again invoked the nuclear specter as a main argument, this time for the Senate not to cave to the House.

One other time-related difference remained between the Senate and House versions.[113] In the House version, Congress was required to convene within forty-eight hours to discuss the president's inability, and Bayh, yet again, brought up the possibility of nuclear attack. Congress convening in that last instance would only occur if the president and vice president had disagreed about the president being disabled. On this point, Bayh stated, "If we're hit by an atomic attack and the Capitol building is destroyed, it might take more that forty-eight hours for Congress to convene."[114] Bayh's colleagues in the Senate felt that limitations on the time in which Congress had to decide the president's disability were unacceptable. Interested in protecting the Senate's tradition of free debate, Bayh requested a conference.[115] Though the resolution moved forward in both Houses for the same reason—a strong belief that something needed to be done to provide for smooth transitions during the nuclear age—different versions of the bill now existed and needed to be hammered out in Conference Committee.

The Joint House/Senate Committee met between May 11 and June 10, 1965, and debate ranged over issues of both physical and mental incapacity.[116] House members seemed determined that their version of the amendment should be approved by the Senate without compromise. Senators who had previously been opposed, like Dirksen, now sided with their fellow senators.[117] When Bayh had made his initial presentation to the Senate in February, he said that incidents less cataclysmic than an outbreak of nuclear war could lead to uncertainties about chain of command. He cited two recent examples: the removal of the growth on Johnson's hand on December 1, 1964, and his hospitalization due to a cold on January 23, 1965 (and then launched into discussion of Eisenhower's 1955 heart attack and the nuclear attack scenario). These and other examples of uncertainty at the top urgently required the bill's passage without further complications.[118]

Congressional debate sometimes involved somewhat farfetched scenarios; some of which stemmed from the plots of popular TV shows, movies, and books of the time. During a Conference committee meeting, the ranking Republican on the House Judiciary Committee, William M. McCulloch, referred to "not that which is probable, but that which may be possible."[119] In particular, multiple scenarios of possible usurpation of presidential power were offered—such as if someone suggested he had received a letter from the president himself declaring insanity, only to have the president announce on national television shortly thereafter that the letter was a forgery, or if the president was tricked into signing a declaration of insanity—with nuclear bombs as the backdrop.[120]

During an impasse in the debate in a Senate and House committee conference, in an attempt to keep the process moving forward, Bayh lost control of his temper, or appeared to. This scene revolved around this most controversial piece of the bill—the time limits on inability-related decisions.[121] The root of the problem was that Bayh had been assured by Celler that McCulloch, who had argued for a ten-day period of mediation by Congress, would go along with his decision on time limits. At this meeting, however, Bayh found Celler was mistaken: McCulloch was unbendable, and Celler could not overrule the ranking Republican member of the House Judiciary Committee because bipartisan support was needed for passage.[122] Bayh stormed out—"for effect," he later claimed.[123] Part of his anger was real as he, his staff, and the ABA had been working very diligently for two years and he did not want all their efforts to be for naught this late in the process. Of course, he believed it was imperative to come to a rapid conclusion to the succession and inability issue—in the form of his amendment.

Shortly thereafter, ABA president Lewis Powell was summoned away from a conference in Puerto Rico to make amends between Celler and Bayh, and a chance meeting among the three in the Washington, DC, airport brought about reconciliation and an agreement on limitations so that the amendment could move forward.[124] Bayh conceded to a thirty-day limitation, then Ervin suggested twenty-one days in response to McCulloch's push for ten days. After a two-month deadlock, twenty-one days was agreed upon.[125] In the end, "they gave a few days and we gave a few days," Bayh recollected.[126] Then the conference report was passed by voice vote in the House on June 30, 1965. Much of the earlier testimony was repeated for the record, such as Congressman Roybal's comment that "we can no longer afford" delay "in the nuclear space age."[127] What remained was for the bill to go back through the Senate with the changes. The debate in the Senate began on the same day.

Despite the need for action during the nuclear age, the amendment's passage was not guaranteed. Gore and Senator Frank J. Lausche of Ohio[128] both wanted tighter language and more specifics written into the amendment when the trend had always been to write less into the Constitution to allow future generations more flexibility.[129] In addition to Senators Gore[130] and Lausche, Senators Walter Mondale and Eugene

McCarthy of Minnesota[131] voted against S.J. Res. 1, even though they were listed as cosponsors. Mondale supported an enabling amendment of the type that Dirksen favored, as did Senator John Tower, the fifth "Nay" vote.[132] Mondale and Tower, therefore, swung in the opposite direction of Gore and Lausche, suggesting as the longest amendment to date, S.J. Res. 1 went against the basic principles of constitutional law, a desire not to write specifics into the Constitution. McCarthy went to an extreme, suggesting that a statute rather than an amendment offered the most flexibility.[133] Although McCarthy's argument may have contained a kernel of truth, a statute would not offer a solution to the succession and inability issue that would provide a sense of security. The author of the amendment believed that "One reason the Constitution adapted itself so well to changes of the time has been the breadth of language and its open-endedness."[134] The Constitution was not easily amended, but a statute could easily be changed by a second statute overriding the first.

Going into the vote, Bayh was nervous that the amendment would not pass, however.[135] This was in large part because Gore spoke at length about his opposition to the amendment.[136] Ervin, one of Bayh's most steadfast allies, alleviated some of Bayh's fear by speaking next on the floor, urging the Senate to pass the amendment.[137] Returning to the nuclear context, he reminded his colleagues, "This is a dangerous period in which we live" when a president "can start an atomic holocaust."[138] Another one of the senators causing Bayh's jittery nerves was the slain president's brother, Robert Kennedy.[139] But, as his comments earlier in the year revealed, he was concerned about the possibility of nuclear attack and this may have helped sway his vote. Robert and Edward Kennedy were both "Aye" votes in the end.[140]

In his final floor speech, Bayh concluded that during other times in history, it may not have mattered if a competent president was at the helm in times of crisis, but because of the possibility of nuclear war, the succession and inability amendment must be passed now. Juxtaposing the period before the bomb with the current era, Bayh stated, "Today, with the awesome power at our disposal... when it is possible actually to destroy civilization in a matter of minutes [with nuclear weapons], it is high time that we listened to history." The amendment would ensure "a President of the United States at all times, a president who has complete control and will be able to perform all the powers and duties of his office.[141] After his speech that once again emphasized the dangers of the nuclear era, the amendment passed by a roll call vote of 68–5 in the Senate on July 6.

Although the Twenty-Fifth Amendment was (and still is) one of the longest amendments to date, the final form of the amendment, whittled down from five sections to four, did not contain specific details on several important issues. The definition of inability and how Congress would arrive at the decision on inability were left open-ended. Further, the amendment did not revert to the executive line of succession put in place in 1886 but instead kept in place the controversial congressional line of succession as dictated by the 1947 Presidential Succession Act. The amendment states:

> Section 1. In case of the removal of the president from office or of his death or resignation, the vice president shall become president.

> Section 2. Whenever there is a vacancy in the office of the vice president, the president shall nominate a vice president who shall take office upon confirmation by a majority vote of both houses of Congress.

> Section 3. Whenever the president transmits to the president pro tempore of the Senate and the speaker of the House of Representatives his written declaration that he is unable to discharge the powers and duties of his office, and until he transmits to them a written declaration to the contrary, such powers and duties shall be discharged by the vice president as acting president.

> Section 4. Whenever the vice president and a majority of either the principal officers of the executive departments or of such other body as Congress may by law provide, transmit to the president pro tempore of the Senate and the speaker of the House of Representatives their written declaration that the president is unable to discharge the powers and duties of his office, the vice president shall

immediately assume the powers and duties of the office as acting president.

Thereafter, when the president transmits to the president pro tempore of the Senate and the speaker of the House of Representatives his written declaration that no inability exists, he shall resume the powers and duties of his office unless the vice president and a majority of either the principal officers of the executive department or of such other body as Congress may by law provide, transmit within four days to the president pro tempore of the Senate and the speaker of the House of Representatives their written declaration that the president is unable to discharge the powers and duties of his office. Thereupon Congress shall decide the issue, assembling within forty-eight hours for that purpose if not in session. If the Congress, within twenty-one days after receipt of the latter written declaration, or, if Congress is not in session, within twenty-one days after Congress is required to assemble, determines by two-thirds vote of both Houses that the president is unable to discharge the powers and duties of his office, the vice president shall continue to discharge the same as acting president; otherwise, the president shall resume the powers and duties of his office.[142]

More broadly, nuclear attack provisions were not written into the amendment but concerns about such an attack clearly affected the language and structure of the amendment that passed. The words of the framer of the amendment, congressmembers, and expert witnesses illustrate that this nuclear anxiety was an underlying cause precipitating passage. Congressmembers had recognized the need for an immediate solution in the nuclear age, and, by the summer, the Twenty-Fifth Amendment had gone to the states for ratification.

* * *

Ratification by three-fourths of the states was now all that remained for the Twenty-Fifth Amendment to become part of the Constitution, but the amendment's success was not given. Following passage in the Senate, Bayh and his American Bar Association supporters immediately launched a campaign to get the necessary thirty-eight states on board. Eventually, thirteen states would ratify the amendment in 1965, eighteen in 1966, and the final seven states in January and February of 1967. Over the course of these nineteen months, ratification of the amendment got caught up in confusion about the meaning of certain sections. Though the amendment could fail in twelve states and still become part of the Constitution, Bayh and the ABA worried that a rejection in any state would cause a domino effect, affecting the amendment's overall progress.[143] While some states ratified quickly and without issue, political and cultural tensions determined the amendment's success in others: in particular, the nuclear issue.

Nuclear anxiety was most evident in the state-level ratification process when state legislators in Colorado, Arkansas, and Pennsylvania considered ratification. In Colorado and Arkansas, legislators would have been more comfortable ratifying the amendment if succession and inability procedures in the event of nuclear attack were written into the amendment. Colorado has been singled out by other scholars because the amendment did not pass the first time it was brought to a vote, leading to procedural questions. However, previously unexamined correspondence between Colorado State Senator John R. Bermingham and members of the ABA reveal that Bermingham's letters contain pleas that specific provisions be written into the amendment to deal with a nuclear crisis.[144] In Arkansas, the amendment's lack of detail pertaining to a nuclear attack also was criticized, holding up the amendment's progress briefly. Conversely, on the floor of the Pennsylvania House, the possibility of nuclear conflict was cited as the reason why the amendment needed immediate ratification and partisan politics had to be overcome.

Bayh and the ABA went to work immediately after the legislation passed Congress, drafting letters to every member of each of the fifty state legislatures asking for their endorsement of the amendment.[145] The ABA's intense campaign was highly organized and its work during the ratification process built on earlier methods.[146] For example, during the ratification phase in Colorado, lobbying efforts—like sending letters to each legislator that had voted against the amendment the first time it was considered in the state legislature—were combined with media efforts such as securing television spots.[147] The potential need for practical application of what had originally been an academic interest of Feerick's became obvious when Kennedy's sudden death drew nationwide media attention, but that reason was not emphasized as the amendment made its way through the states.[148]

In Pennsylvania, the amendment passed through both houses of the legislature and through two additional readings before it met with delays related to concerns about the nuclear era. The cause of the amendment's pause was a lone representative, Philadelphia Democrat Eugene Gelfand, whose party controlled the statehouse.[149] Gelfand, perhaps unaware of the scrutiny and debate the amendment had undergone at the federal level, argued against ratifying Bayh's amendment too quickly without careful consideration.[150] But Gelfand's colleague, Republican Representative G. Sieber Pancoast of Montgomery County, urged the Pennsylvania state legislature to back the amendment. In the floor debate, Pancoast argued that Section 4 of the amendment might lead to a power struggle between political parties, a struggle that was unacceptable for any "length of time in our atomic age."[151] Gelfand, who spoke next argued that though anxious times called for action, the House still should not vote in haste: "I know the tenor of the times is to do something," he said, "but let us not rush pell-mell down the road to madness just for the sake of doing something, because it could mean disaster."[152] The amendment was not brought to a vote.

The ABA pushed back. It mobilized federal, state, and local bar associations, as well as other members of the Pennsylvania legislature, to put pressure on Gelfand to allow the process to move forward.[153] The ABA was able to convince Pennsylvania legislators that not ratifying would lead to more serious disaster in the dangerous age. Gelfand did not mention the Bar Association's pressure, but in a matter of weeks, Pennsylvania became the fifth state to ratify on August 18, 1965.

Kentucky was also ready to take up the issue at this time. Lieutenant Governor Harvey Lee Waterfield wrote to Bayh explaining that Governor Edward Breathitt had called a special session in part to consider the amendment, and he asked for assistance in winning over the state's legislators. "In light of what happened in Colorado," he wrote, "I would request that you send to me any material that can be presented to our legislators in support of the proposed amendment."[154] This background information may have proved persuasive. Kentucky ratified on September 16.[155]

But in Arkansas, Bayh and the ABA encountered a holdup. Bayh's personal appearance at the National Governors' Conference in July helped bring Governor Orval Faubus on board.[156] After the conference, Bayh and Faubus exchanged letters. In a letter dated August 5, Faubus stated that he had hoped that Congress would pass the amendment while Arkansas had been in special session, but now it did not look likely that Arkansas would ratify before the Arkansas legislature convened next.[157]

Speaker J.H. Cottrell disseminated a copy of an article by Professor George D. Haimbaugh that had appeared in the *South Carolina Law Review*, "Vice Presidential Succession: A Criticism of the Bayh-Cellar [sic] Plan," criticizing the amendment's lack of specific provisions to deal with a nuclear attack. In the article, Haimbaugh brought up the possibility of a nuclear crisis and the effect it would have on succession, criticizing the amendment for not addressing it. Significantly, he wrote, "Arguments for the Bayh-Celler plan for vice presidential succession must also include a ritual reference to the thermonuclear age." He continued, "The possibility of the simultaneous death of all in the line of succession is a nuclear age reality, but the Bayh-Celler plan does not meet this danger."[158] Haimbaugh suggested that the amendment was not useful because it was granting Congress powers it already had to designate successors to the presidency that would not be affected by a nuclear attack on Washington, DC. He argued that under Article II, Congress has "the power to extend the line of officials to include high-ranking officials who work outside the Washington area." Haimbaugh presumably was referring to the "necessary and proper" clause. In a rebuttal entitled "Vice Presidential Succession: In Support of the Bayh—Celler Plan," also published in the *S.C. Law Review*, Feerick agreed that Congress had the power to extend the line of succession, but the concern that a line of succession consisting of officials not in Washington did not need to be dealt with in the amendment.[159] Instead, the amendment was urgent and, Feerick charged, Haimbaugh's arguments were "invalid, inapplicable, and unrealistic." Arkansas ratified the amendment on November 4, 1965.

The amendment began to pick up steam in the states[160]; however, the ratification process in Colorado threatened the amendment's overall success. Initially, the ABA assumed that Colorado would be one of the first states to ratify because the Colorado legislature passed a memorial resolution, S.J.M. 5, asking Congress to move forward on the amendment on presidential succession and inability in February.[161] Colorado Governor John Arthur Love called another special session of the legislature in the summer of 1965 to deal with issues that had resulted from flooding but added the amendment to the agenda. At that time, with less than the usual number of members present, the legislation supporting ratification of the amendment was given surface consideration and voted down narrowly after the third reading in the Senate.[162] However, Tooley expressed great optimism that the legislature would most likely consider the amendment more favorably when it reconvened in January 1966 for its regular session and pointed to the earlier memorial.[163]

Instead, the heightened anxiety surrounding a nuclear attack caused concern. In a letter to Feerick on July 21, 1965, Tooley added an article he wrote in *The Denver Post*, a response to its article the day before, entitled "Twenty-Fifth Amendment has Serious Defects." He complained that the *Post* had reversed its earlier position in support of the amendment.[164] One notable point of the *Post's* was that the amendment did not deal directly with vice presidential inability. What if both the president and vice president simultaneously were unable to serve? It was a dangerous omission because a coherent commander-in-chief was needed when seconds mattered in the nuclear era, the *Post* argued: "In a nuclear age, the presidency must be occupied at all times by a man in full possession of his faculties."[165] In Colorado, it looked like a lack of specifics around vice presidential inability during the nuclear age might prevent ratification.

Colorado State Senator John R. Bermingham also worried about the proposal's failure to contend with a nuclear catastrophe. In a July 22 letter to Feerick, Tooley enclosed a *Rocky Mountain News* article entitled "GOP Senator Explains Vote on Amendment" published that day featuring Bermingham, one of the original sponsors of the memorial. He was now one of twelve representatives opposed to the amendment. In the article, his opposition was framed in terms of process as much as substance. Bermingham called for an open hearing, voicing his opinion that the public should have a say in any vote to amend the Constitution. Stating his opposition was misunderstood, he mentioned that he and several other senators had "serious objections" to the amendment.[166] Then, in his first letter to the ABA dated August 10, 1965, Bermingham made clear that he wanted provisions explicitly written into the Twenty-Fifth Amendment in case of a nuclear crisis. He questioned "why no provision was included in the proposed amendment to cover the situation that would occur if an atomic bomb wiped out the entire city of Washington while all our high officials were present. How would the government get started again?"[167] The senator would continue this laser-like focus on the lack of detail in the event of a nuclear attack for months.

ABA staffer Michael Spence responded to Bermingham ten days later noting that Bermingham was not the only one to have raised questions about whether the succession and inability amendment addressed nuclear attack. Spence stated that although the drafting committee did consider that possibility, the amendment "could not cover every possible situation which might be imagined." The amendment was designed to deal only with problems "which history has indicated might be likely to occur," he said.[168] He went further, stating that the amendment "does not deal with the subject of atomic holocaust specifically" but admitted that "The occurrence of atomic destruction under any circumstance would be chaotic."[169] He concluded by saying that the amendment would not cause problems during such events.

This was not the assurance that Bermingham wanted. He wrote again to Spence stating that the huge sums spent annually on defense against atomic attack were proof that the nuclear issue was an important one.[170] He then concluded his letter by asking more pointedly why the amendment could not cover an atomic attack: "Do I interpret your remarks correctly in concluding that our laws make no provision whatsoever for continuity or succession in our government [in the event of an attack]... Is there any reason why the succession law could not be amended to cover an atomic holocaust?".[171]

Spence focused on the questions related to process, rather than those related to nuclear attack. He pointed out that the Twenty-Fifth Amendment did not change the line of succession dictated in the 1947 Presidential Succession Act. Further, Section I of Article II of the Constitution allows Congress to legislate on succession and that to provide for "contingencies such as the atomic holocaust you suggest"; succession law could be amended in the future. Attempting to drive a wedge between the two issues that legislators at both the federal and state levels saw as intricately linked, Spence added that the problem of an atomic holocaust was separate from the problems the amendment addressed.

Bermingham, though not completely satisfied, did not continue the battle to add language to the amendment to cover a nuclear attack. He told Spence he agreed they were separate issues; however, he emphasized the salience of the nuclear issue to the public, and that it was Congress' duty to legislate on both. Bermingham wrote, "Nevertheless, they are not unrelated in the thoughts of the public and it seems to me that Congress has as much duty to take action with respect to the one problem as the other."[172] In Colorado's case, it seems that the dispute was between those who were worried about a nuclear attack and those who were *really* worried about a nuclear attack. The former supported an amendment, and the latter were against an amendment that did not include specific instructions to deal with a nuclear holocaust.

Spence did not fully answer Bermingham's question on a nuclear provision. As assistant to the director, Spence was following his marching orders to get the amendment ratified by any means possible. Moreover, if the amendment were redrafted to include any provisions for a nuclear attack, it would have to start again at the beginning, in a congressional subcommittee. Bermingham could have held up the amendment in Colorado, like what happened in Pennsylvania and Arkansas. On January 27, 1966, the ABA sent cards to every member of the Colorado legislature asking not only that they support ratification but also that they go beyond this by contacting a list of representatives who previously had opposed the amendment.[173] Senator Bayh's office also dictated a defense of the amendment that was distributed by the ABA to each member the following week.[174] The ABA had feared that if the amendment was not ratified in Colorado because the language was deemed deficient in some way, other states would block ratification as well. Yet, after intense focus on the nuclear issue, Colorado ratified the amendment on February 3, 1966.[175] Additional states began to fall into line rapidly.[176]

The final effort toward ratification came in February 1967. Three states—Nevada, North Dakota, and Minnesota—vied for the honor of being the thirty-eighth state to ratify. Nevada and North Dakota on February 8, and February 9, 1967, respectively, upon learning that they were only the thirty-seventh state to ratify, withdrew their ratifications. At first, the validity of North Dakota's nullification was unclear. Minnesota ratified next, followed by a second attempt an hour and thirteen minutes later (due to a difference in time zones) by Nevada. When North Dakota's nullification was finalized, Nevada became the thirty-eighth state to ratify.[177] Ultimately, the amendment was ratified by forty-seven states; only Georgia, North Dakota, and South Carolina[178] did not ratify officially.

Once three-fourths of the states have ratified, the amendment automatically becomes part of the Constitution; presidents do not need to affix their signature to an amendment. However, Johnson chose to sign the amendment anyway, in a ceremony on February 23, 1967, recognizing and signifying the achievement.[179] Technically, he served simply as witness to the signature of General Services Administrator Lawson Knott—a contrivance devised to afford Johnson the opportunity to show the public he supported this popular idea. At the signing ceremony, Vice

President Hubert Humphrey was at the president's side. Those next in the line of succession, Senate President Pro Tempore Carl Hayden and Speaker of the House John McCormack, were also present. Johnson's presence at the ceremony closed the circle he had begun when in his 1965 State of the Union Address, he made a brief inclusion of the topic. Newspapers such as *The New York Times* heralded it as a successful piece of the president's Great Society Program. Tom Wicker of *The Times*, when assessing Johnson's Great Society ideas, both new and old, wrote, "There is still a category of Great Society proposals—old ideas that at last seem to have a great chance of fulfillment.... Mr. Johnson has even tackled the oldest established permanent loophole in the Constitution by lending his support to an amendment on presidential succession and inability."[180] It is conceivable, however, that Johnson might not have been able to add the succession and inability solution to his list of Great Society accomplishments if it were not for the tense political and cultural mood.

The Twenty-Fifth Amendment became part of the US Constitution on February 10, 1967, three years, two months, and nineteen days after Bayh drafted the legislation on his flight to Chicago. The framers of the amendment had ensured that "[w]hile the light in the White House may flicker, it [would never] go out."[181] Nuclear anxiety was ingrained in the Constitution itself, even as the Constitution continued to take shape based on the needs of the era. As references to the sudden transition from Kennedy to Johnson faded into the background, nuclear anxiety remained at the forefront of political discourse at the federal and state levels. The lens of nuclear anxiety reveals new facets of the amendment's path to ratification unavailable through more traditional accounts focused on a staid legal process or that omit the cultural and political mood or attribute the anxiety that helped propel the amendment forward solely to the presidential assassination. Although the amendment in its final form did not contain specific procedures to follow in the event of nuclear attack, congressmembers attempted to strike a balance between including enough detail to provide a solid and reassuring answer to the succession and inability problem and, at the same time, allowing flexibility should unforeseen events happen, especially as a result of a nuclear attack. This desire to allow future Congresses maneuverability led to gaps and vagaries in the amendment that successive Congresses would debate within a climate of heightened nuclear anxiety.

US Senator Birch Bayh with President Lyndon B. Johnson, 1967[182]

Notes

1. Birch Bayh, Interview with author, November 11, 2014.
2. See Bayh, *One Heartbeat Away*.
3. S.J. Res. 40, 86th Congress, 1959.
4. "Memo from Washington by Senator Estes Kefauver," NA, CJ, SCA, Box 4, Folder "88th-Kefauver PI Aug 1961–1963." Senator Thomas Dodd of Connecticut also added his name to S.J. Res. 35 at this time.
5. "Memo from Washington by Senator Estes Kefauver."
6. Though the Kennedys had carefully constructed an image of tanned, vigorous president, the truth was much grimmer. Historian Robert Dallek, with the assistance of physician Jeffrey Kelman, analyzed JFK's medical records and showed, in *An Unfinished Life*, that JFK was far from healthy, relying on a

cocktail of drugs and cortisol shots for health issues, including Addison's disease, to get him through his daily responsibilities. "A *New York Times* article made the claim that a New York physician warned he would make his knowledge of Kennedy's treatments public, because "no president with his finger on the red button has any business taking stuff like that." As quoted in Robert Dallek, *An Unfinished Life*. No president: As quoted in Edward B. MacMahon and Leonard Curry, *Medical Cover-ups in the White House* (Washington, DC: Farragut 1987), 119–37. See also Brown University professor Rose McDermott's chapter in her work *Presidential Leadership, Illness, and Decision-Making*, which argues that President Kennedy's illnesses and treatments altered his behavior at the 1961 Vienna conference with Soviet premier Nikita Khrushchev. McDermott, Rose, McDermott. *Presidential Leadership, Illness, and Decision-Making*. (New York: Cambridge University Press, 2007).

7. In a moment of eerie prescience, a publisher wrote to Kefauver, agreeing that legislation was of the utmost importance: "With so many trigger-happy fanatics here and abroad together with the increasing strain of the presidency, your efforts to provide a sound basis for inability is very timely." "Letter from A.I. Boreman, Publisher, to Kefauver February 18, 1963," NA, CJ, SCA, Box 4, Folder "88th Kefauver, PI Correspondence Aug 1961- June 1963."

8. Nixon did not appear to testify in June 1963, though he was a key witness in later hearings (as described later in this chapter). "Letter from Richard Nixon to Estes Kefauver June 10, 1963," NA, CJ, SCA, Box 5, Folder "88th-Kefauver PI—Corr—June Hearings Witnesses 1963."

9. Hearing Before the Subcommittee on Constitutional Amendments of the Committee on the Judiciary, US S, 88th Cong., 1st Sess., 11. https://www.govinfo.gov/content/pkg/CHRG-88shrg203280/pdf/CHRG-88shrg203280.pdf.

10. Kyvig, *Explicit and Authentic Acts*, 358. Kefauver had been a favorite of Eastland's according to Bob Keefe. Interview with Robert "Bob" Keefe, former Administrative Assistant to US Senator Birch Bayh, November 5, 2014.

11. "United States Senate Memorandum," NA, CJ, SCA, Box 4, Folder "88th Kefauver, Memos—Briefs on Amendments."

12. Bob Keefe, Bayh's office manager, learned of the potential dissolution of the Subcommittee on Constitutional Amendments while talking with Fred Graham, who had served as Kefauver's subcommittee counsel. Bob Keefe, Interview with Author, November 5, 2014.
13. It was clear he had been drinking, which was highly unusual. In fact, Keefe said, the senator was "half-drunk." Bob Keefe, Interview with Author, November 5, 2014.
14. Asked about that turn of events in an interview in 2012, Bayh smiled and said that he and Eastland bonded over drinks, but in his recollection, he returned to the office, the phone rang, and Eastland informed him of his new title. In *One Heartbeat Away*, Bayh states it took Chairman Eastland two days to make that phone call. Bayh was not known to imbibe alcohol in great quantities; during his videotaped interviews, he enjoys his preferred drink, Diet Dr. Pepper, of which his wife Kitty tries to curtail his consumption. Regardless of the precise chronology, Bayh's elevation was the result of what he called a "series of unusual circumstances." Call: Bayh, *One Heartbeat Away*, 28. Bayh's drinking habits: Birch Bayh, Interviews with Bob Blaemire, 2012.
15. James Reston, "The Problem of the Succession to the Presidency," *The New York Times*, December 5, 1963.
16. "Presidential Succession," *The Washington Post*, December 2, 1963, A20.
17. Bayh, *One Heartbeat Away*, 32.
18. Texas is one example; see the end of the chapter for further discussion on this topic.
19. Bayh's later Equal Rights Amendment would fall short or the necessary number, three-fourths or thirty-eight states, by just three states.
20. On the day of the assassination, Bayh was working closely with Attorney General Robert Kennedy and others in the administration on the Studebaker car plant, trying to keep the jobs in South Bend, Indiana, though the factory was closing. He spoke with the attorney general by phone, boarded a Chicago-bound plane to meet with the company's CEO, and heard the morbid news from the pilot upon landing. Bayh believes he was one of the last people Robert Kennedy spoke with before receiving the news at Hickory Hill that his brother had been shot. Their efforts

were successful in retaining the jobs: the Studebaker plant became an Asanti dealership. Birch Bayh, Interviews with Bob Blaemire, 2012.
21. Bayh, *One Heartbeat Away*, 301.
22. Bernard "Bud" Fensterwald, a former Kefauver staffer, former counsel to the Subcommittee on Constitutional Amendments, and a chief counsel of the Judiciary Subcommittee on Administrative Practice and Procedure, urged the senator to push forward on the succession and inability legislation before any of his colleagues did, and volunteered to work with him. Larry Conrad, a member of Bayh's legislative staff, operating from a closet in the corner of Bayh's office, was delegated with the task of forming an agenda for the Subcommittee and became the Subcommittee's chief counsel. Steven Lescher, a temporary member of Bayh's staff because he was a recipient of a fellowship from the American Political Science Association, weighed in on Bayh's draft.
23. Bob Keefe, Interview with Author, November 5, 2014.
24. Feerick wrote a paper entitled "The Problem of Presidential Inability: Will Congress Ever Solve It?" published in the *Fordham Law Review* in 1963.
25. John D. Feerick, "The Problem of Presidential Inability: Will Congress Ever Solve It?" Vol 32, Issue 1, Fordham Law Review 1963, http://ir.lawnet.fordham.edu/flr/vol32/iss1/3/. J. William Cuncannan, "Our Younger Lawyers," *American Bar Association Journal*, Volume 50, June 1964, 573.
26. Feerick wrote to all fifty governors to inquire about their own succession laws. Their responses lead to his paper that became the lead in the program for an ABA convention in early 1964. The meeting took place January 20–21, 1964, at the Mayflower Hotel in Washington, DC. Feerick's paper was widely circulated, including to Attorney General Kennedy. In a letter to *The New York Times* that was published just five days before Kennedy's assassination, Feerick wrote: "Congress has consistently failed the American people by not acting to eliminate the possibility of a gap in the executive." Letters to Feerick: John D. Feerick. Congress has failed: John D. Feerick, "Letters to the Times: Fixing Presidential Succession," *The New York Times*, November 17, 1963.

27. For an explanation of the accelerated pace of the modern era of globalization, see Yale H. Ferguson and Richard W. Mansbach, *Globalization: the Return of Borders to a Borderless World?* (New York: Routledge, 2012). "Speech by Senator Birch Bayh proposing an Amendment to the Constitution of the United States regarding the Offices of President and Vice President," NA, CJ, SCA, Box 9, Folder "88th Congress PI—Press Releases (Bayh) 1963," and (identical to) "Speech by Senator Birch Bayh proposing an Amendment to the Constitution of the United States regarding the Offices of President and Vice President," NA, CJ, SCA, Box 6, Folder "88th Congress, PI, Bills-S.J. Res 139-Introductory Speech (Bayh) 1963 Dec 12."
28. "Statement by Senator Birch Bayh," NA, CJ, SCA, Box 8, Folder "88th Congress, PI—Hearings—Statements—Bayh, Birch, 1964 Jan 22."
29. Cornell University historian and political scientist Clinton Rossiter affirmed that the amendment was "imperative especially under conditions of modern existence.... Perhaps the single most pressing requirement of good government in the United States today is an uninterrupted exercise of the full authority of the presidency." Democratic Senator Frank Moss of Utah said that to continue with the status quo would be "foolhardy in these days of instant crisis ... I do not believe that world order in the age of the atom, supersonic flight, and instant communications can tolerate that sort of leadership strain in the most powerful country in the world." Rossiter statement: "The Problem of Succession to the Presidency," NA, CJ, SCA, Box 7, Folder "88th Congress, PI, Correspondence Rossiter, Clinton R. 1964." Moss statement: "Statement of Senator Frank E. Moss," NA, CJ, SCA, Box 9, Folder "88th Congress, PI, Hearings—Statements: Moss, Frank C 1964 Jan 23," 4.
30. Bayh, *One Heartbeat Away*, 34.
31. Hearing Before the Subcommittee on Constitutional Amendments of the Committee on the Judiciary, US S, 88th Cong., 1st Sess., 11.
32. Birch Bayh, *One Heartbeat Away*, 37.
33. Senator Edward V. Long of Missouri, who also sat on the Judiciary Committee, though not on the Subcommittee, was the original cosponsor of S.J. Res. 139 when it was introduced on

December 12, 1963. Bayh introduced S.J. Res. 139 after conferring with more seasoned colleagues, such as Speaker McCormack, Senate President Pro Tempore Hayden, and Senate Judiciary Chairman Eastland. Bayh also received advice from his father. A director of physical education in the Washington, DC, public school system, Birch Evan Bayh, Sr. told his son in a handwritten letter, "I know you consult closely with your chairman, Sen[ator] Eastland, and will have his approval for all moves. Older men like younger men to seek their advice." "Dear Son," NA, CJ, SCA, Box 6, Folder "88th Congress, PI, Bills—Correspondence 1965–64".

34. Walter Lippman, "Today and Tomorrow… The Presidential Succession," *The Washington Post*, December 12, 1963, A21.
35. "Confidential—Not For Release, First Draft Policy Statement," NA, CJ, SCA, Box 6, Folder "88th Congress, PI—Committee for Economic Development, 1964," 45. At least one piece of CED correspondence was written on Eastman Kodak Company letterhead, an indication that business executives were also concerned about the sudden transition of executive power during a crisis. See "To The Honorable Birch Bayh from Marion B. Folsom, Chairman," NA, CJ, SCA, Box 17, Folder "89th Congress, PI—Hearings—Correspondence—Witnesses 1965."
36. "Top US Priority in a Nuclear Age—Presidential Succession and Inability," NA, CJ, SCA, Box 6, Folder. "88th Congress, PI—Committee for Economic Development, 1964."
37. Birch Bayh, Interview with author, November 11, 2014.
38. John Tower, a member of the Committee on Labor and Public Welfare, was a former constitutional law professor, making him a natural for Bayh's list of potential witnesses. But in a letter to Bayh dated January 24, 1964, he, like Eisenhower, declined to participate in the hearings. Though he did express his desire that a workable solution be found, he supported a more general or "enabling" piece of legislation. A year later, when asked by Conrad to cosponsor Bayh's legislation, his staff would decline on his behalf and say "we think he supports the 1886 law." He was, a year-and-a-half later, one of the five "nay" votes on the amendment's final language. Bayh, *One Heartbeat Away*, 170.
39. "Letter from Former President Dwight D. Eisenhower… Included in the Record of March 5 Hearings," NA, CJ, SCA,

Box 9, Folder "88th Cong., PI—Hearings—Statements For the Record: Eisenhower, Dwight D."
40. "Letter from Former President Dwight D. Eisenhower."
41. "Letter from Former President Dwight D. Eisenhower."
42. "Mr. Hamilton's testimony," NA, CJ, SCA, Box 8, Folder "88th Cong., PI—Hearings—Report—Mock-Up, 398–498, 1964."
43. "Letter to Hon. Birch Bayh from Laurens M. Hamilton," NA, CJ, SCA, Box 7, Folder "PI Correspondence Hamilton, Laurens M. 1964."
44. "Statement of Congressman Louis C. Wyman 31–160 472," NA, CJ, SCA, Box 8, Folder "88th Congress, PI—Hearings—Report—Mock-Up, 398–498, 1964." It is no surprise that Congressman Wyman supported the Twenty-Fifth so strongly: in February 1962, he drafted H.R. 1164, a similar solution, though statutory, which the ABA's House of Delegates supported. Wyman requested to testify in a letter to Bayh. "To the Honorable Birch Bayh from Louis C. Wyman," NA, CJ, SCA, Box 7, Folder "88th Congress, PI—Correspondence Congressional, 1963–1964."
45. "From the Office of Jacob K. Javits," NA, CJ, SCA, Box 8, Folder "88th PI Hearings Statements: Javits, Jacob K."
46. "Statement of Senator James B. Pearson, 31–160 018," NA, CJ, SCA, Box 8, Folder "88th Congress, PI—Hearings—Report—Mock-Up, 1–22, 1964."
47. "White House Statement and Text of Agreement Between the President and Vice President on Procedures in the Event of Presidential Inability," Public Papers 561, August 10, 1961.
48. Hearing Before the Subcommittee on Constitutional Amendments of the Committee on the Judiciary, US S, 88th Cong., 1st Sess., 86, https://www.govinfo.gov/content/pkg/CHRG-88shrg20328O/pdf/CHRG-88shrg20328O.pdf.
49. Discussions of presidential succession in the context of nuclear warfare were not confined to the floor of the Senate. In May 1964, the American Bar Association hosted a conference on presidential succession at which numerous members of Congress and President Eisenhower spoke. Bayh, *One Heartbeat Away*, 111–12. LeRoy Collins, a former governor of Florida who served as permanent chairman of the Democratic National Convention in 1960 and who moderated a panel discussion at the conference,

reminded those present, "that the responsibilities of the presidency are far more awsome [sic] in this atomic age." Of the age itself, he said, "we live on a thin line between the possibility [sic] of cataclysm on the one hand, and the greatest era of human progress of all time on the other. Any missing gap in our leadership thus contributes to the peril...." "But no president in history," NA, CJ, SCA, Box 6, Folder "88th PI Bills SJ Res 139—Working File," 2.

50. "Statement of Ruth Miner, Associate Professor of political science and business law, Wisconsin State College, Whitewater, Wisconsin," NA, CJ, SCA, Box 8, Folder "88th Congress, PI Hearings—Report—Mock-Ups,. 499–567, 1964," 31 160 585.
51. "Statement of Ruth Miner."
52. The United States does, after Johnson (and with the exception of Ford) begin to see the era of former congressional leaders as president end, and former state governors begin to be elected as president. (Also note: Miner's proposal, although not widely advocated, would most likely have garnered the support of Colorado State Senator John R. Bermingham, who expressed similar concerns but was silenced by the ABA's effective campaign, as discussed later in this chapter.) "Statement of Ruth Miner, associate professor of political science and business law, Wisconsin State College, Whitewater, Wisconsin," NA, CJ, SCA, Box 8, Folder "88th Congress, PI, Hearings—Report—Mock-Ups, 499–567, 1964," 31 160 587.
53. See civil defense and Governor Brown in the previous chapter, Chapter 3. "State of California, Governor's Office, Sacramento," NA, CJ, SCA, Box 8, Folder "88th Congress, PI—Hearings—Report—Mock-Up, 494–597, 1964," 31–160 576.
54. "Dear Senator Bayh from Nelson A. Rockefeller, Governor, Feb 25, 1964, 31–160 414," NA, CJ, SCA, Box 8, Folder "88th Congress, PI—Hearings—Report Mock-Up 398–498, 1964."
55. Baseball analogies, such as referring to Nixon as "the clean-up hitter," were a norm for Bayh. Bayh, though raised in Terra Haute, Indiana, was a Washington Senators fan until they left DC in 1971; after that he followed the Baltimore Orioles. Bayh played for the Senate Democrats. Democrat-Republican baseball games at RFK stadium or "friendlies," and other examples of bipartisan picnics and dinners, point to the cordial respect senators had for

one another at the time. Bayh has said they would often "go along [with legislation] to get along." Birch Bayh, Interview with author, November 11, 2014.
56. The former vice president, who just about a year earlier had lost a bid to become governor of California and vowed to retire from politics, talked for forty minutes without notes.
57. Nixon testified on the final day of the hearings, Thursday, March 5, 1964. He stressed the import of filling vacant presidential seats and dealing with disability immediately during the early press conference, though he preferred the Electoral College rather than Congress, take up the task. "31–160 541," NA, CJ, SCA, Box 8, Folder "88th Congress, PI—Hearings—Report—Mock-Up, 494–597, 1964," 31–160 541.
58. "Speaking Out: We Need A Vice President, by Richard M. Nixon, From Saturday Evening Post, Jan. 1, 1964," NA, CJ, SCA, Box 8, Folder "88th Congress, PI—Hearings—Report—Mock-Up, 494–597, 1964," 31–160 531.
59. For example, in a letter submitted for testimony, Senator Leverett Saltonstall of Massachusetts forwarded the argument that the secretary of state be placed next in the line of succession to ensure an orderly transfer of power because a potential sudden switch to a different political party "would hardly be conducive to the smooth and uninterrupted conduct of the nation's affairs." "Honorable Birch Bayh, Chairman from Leverett Saltonstall, Senator" NA, CJ, SCA, Box 8, Folder "88th Congress, PI—Hearings—Report—Mock-Up 398–498, 1964."
60. "McCormack Prefers Current Succession," *The Washington Post*, December 8, 1963, A13.
61. "McCormack, Hayden Won't Quit: Deny Plans to Give Up Congress," *The Washington Post* December 12, 1963, A1.
62. Marquis Childs, "The Shaky Line of Succession," *The Washington Post* November 29, 1963, A20. In March 1964, Conrad and Lesher met with Marquis Childs as well as with *New York Times* editor Arthur Krock (separately) in an effort to "maintain the public interest." Bayh, *One Heartbeat Away*, 98.
63. William Manchester, *The Death of a President: November 20—November 25, 1963* (New York: Arbor House, 1967), 247.
64. Change Doubted in Succession Law," *The New York Times*, March 15, 1964, 40.

65. "Mr. Katzenbach's testimony," NA, CJ, SCA, Box 8, Folder "88th Congress, PI—Hearings—Report—Mock-Up 398–498, 1964," 31–160 442.
66. Bayh, Interview with author, November 11, 2014.
67. Bayh joined with three other Subcommittee members—Senators Dodd, Fong, and Keating—on a press release sharing with the public the news that the bill had progressed out of the Subcommittee. "Presidential Inability and Veep Vacancies," NA, CJ, SCA, Box 6, Folder "88th Congress, PI—Correspondence 1965–64 CQ Congressional."
68. Bayh, *One Heartbeat Away*, 98.
69. Bayh, *One Heartbeat Away*, 163–67.
70. Lyndon B. Johnson, "Annual Message to Congress on the State of the Union," January 4, 1965. http://www.presidency.ucsb.edu/ws/?pid=26907.
71. In its final form, the amendment would consist of just four sections. John Feerick, *The Twenty-Fifth Amendment* (1976), 246.
72. The list includes: the American Association of Law Schools; the State Bar Associations of Arizona, Arkansas, California, Colorado, Connecticut, Hawaii, Indiana, Iowa, Kansas, Louisiana, Michigan, Ohio, Rhode Island, Texas, Virginia, and Vermont; the Bar Associations of Denver, Colorado; the District of Columbia; Dade County, Florida; the City of New York; Passaic County, New Jersey; Greensboro, North Carolina; York County, Pennsylvania; and Milwaukee, Wisconsin. "To Senator-elect George Murphy from Birch Bayh, Chairman," NA, CJ, SCA, Box 7, Folder "88th Congress, PI—Correspondence Congressional 1963–1964."
73. Democrats began the 89th Congress, 1st sess., with supermajorities in both Houses of Congress: a filibuster-proof 68–32 in the Senate, and a lead of 295–140 in the House.
74. Bob Keefe, Interview with author, November 5, 2014.
75. Archival files contain these letters from Senators Richard Russell, Jr. (D-Georgia), Spessard Holland (D-Florida), Stuart Symington (D-Missouri), Joseph S. Clark (D-Pennsylvania), Wallace R. Bennett (D-Utah), Thomas J. McIntyre (D-New Hampshire), Edmund Muskie (D-Maine), Edmond Edmonton (D-Oklahoma), Albert Gore, Sr. (D-Tennessee), and John Tower

(R-Texas) declining to cosponsor the amendment. NA, CJ, SCA, Box 7, Folder "88th Congress, PI—Correspondence Congressional 1963–1964."
76. This figure, combined with 22 of 32, or 69 percent of Republicans, meant that, although it saw lively debate, 75 percent of the Senate cosponsored the amendment six months before it passed. "Background on S.J. 1," NA, CJ, SCA, Box 16, Folder "89th Congress, PI-Bills—S.J. Res. 1-Cosponsors, 1965 Jan 14."
77. "For Release on Delivery to the Senate," Box 3. Office Files of Bill Moyers: Special Message on Office of the President. LBJL.
78. "For Release on Delivery to the Senate."
79. Cong. Rec., 89th Cong., 1st sess., vol. 111, pt. 2., 1460.
80. Eventually, Bayh would get more than seventy of his Senate colleagues to cosponsor. "The Great Society Congress: 25th Amendment Legislation," The Association of Centers for the Study of Congress, http://acsc.lib.udel.edu/exhibits/show/legislation/25th.
81. Subcommittee files indicate that four of the senators he wrote—Symington, Clark, McIntyre, and Muskie—agreed to cosponsor. "Background on S.J. 1," NA, CJ, SCA, Box 16, Folder "89th Congress, PI-Bills—S.J. Res. 1-Cosponsors, 1965 Jan 14."
82. Ironically, the two men were very friendly, but they were an unlikely pairing. Dirksen was a Republican and a veteran of Capitol Hill. Bayh was a Democrat and a newcomer to a chamber that emphasized seniority. However, the two men bonded almost immediately, during the Kennedy administration. Bayh recalled a memorable experience with the minority leader aboard the presidential yacht in 1963: I remember we were going down the [Potomac] River on the Sequoia. Bobby Kennedy, the Attorney General at the time, had gotten all members of the Judiciary Committee and taken them on the river for a sunset cruise so he could get to know them. I remember being on the fantail of this boat and [Dirksen] said "Birch, do you know what we need to do?" And I said "What's that, Minority Leader?" And he said "We need to start right now getting you reelected." I think I said "What's that again! And he began to rattle off a list.... It was a sincere observation on his part." Birch Bayh, Interview with author, November 11, 2014.

83. "S.J. Res. 1 Summary of My Position—Senator Everett McKinley Dirksen," NA, CJ, SCA, Box 17, Folder "89th Congress, PI—SJRes 1 Dirksen Opinion 1965 Feb 1."
84. Keating was no longer in the Senate, having been defeated in 1964 by Democrat Robert F. Kennedy.
85. "S.J. Res. 1 Summary of My Position—Senator Everett McKinley Dirksen," NA, CJ, SCA, Box 17, Folder "89th Congress, PI—SJRes 1 Dirksen Opinion 1965 Feb 1."
86. "S.J. Res. 1 Summary of My Position—Senator Everett McKinley Dirksen."
87. The Subcommittee had held hearings for four-and-a-half hours. As Bayh noted, "nothing had come out in the second set of hearings that had not been disclosed in the first." Birch Bayh, *One Heartbeat Away*, 203.
88. Full committee debate seemed to be dragging on thanks to Dirksen's insistence on an amendment like S.J. Res. 35, so Bayh requested that the Committee vote on the amendment section by section. No changes were made to the first two sections. The third and fourth sections were changed to specify that the letter declaring disability would be transmitted to the president of the Senate and the speaker of the House of Representatives rather than the more general term, "Congress." Bayh, *One Heartbeat Away*, 209.
89. "To the Honorable Emanuel Celler from Robert F. Kennedy," NA, CJ, SCA, Box 17, Folder "89th. Congress, PI—Congressional Correspondence 1965."
90. "Friday, February 19, 1965, Robert F. Kennedy," Folder "2/65–3/65," Presidential Inability and Succession, Box 94, Robert F. Kennedy Papers, John F. Kennedy Library and Museum.
91. Hearing Before the Committee on the Judiciary on Miscellaneous Proposals Relating to Presidential Inability, 89th Cong., 1st sess., February 9, 10, 16, and 17, 1965, 2. https://babel.hathitrust.org/cgi/pt?id=ucl.$b654933;view=1up;seq=5.
92. "A Modern Father of Our Constitution: An Interview with Former Senator Birch Bayh," 79 *Fordham Law Review* 781, 2011, 790.
93. Here Bayh acknowledged not just the development of the bomb, but that the speed of travel, due to technological "advancements," had also changed since the last major presidential inability.

Hearing Before the Committee on the Judiciary on Miscellaneous Proposals Relating to Presidential Inability, 89th Cong., 1st sess., February 9, 10, 16, and 17, 1965, 67. https://babel.hathitrust.org/cgi/pt?id=ucl.$b654933;view=1up;seq=5.
94. Hearing Before the Committee on the Judiciary on Miscellaneous Proposals Relating to Presidential Inability, 89th Cong., 1st sess., February 9, 10, 16, and 17, 1965, 158. https://babel.hathitrust.org/cgi/pt?id=ucl.$b654933;view=1up;seq=5.
95. Hearing Before the Committee on the Judiciary on Miscellaneous Proposals Relating to Presidential Inability, 89th Cong., 1st sess., February 9, 10, 16, and 17, 1965, 182. https://babel.hathitrust.org/cgi/pt?id=ucl.$b654933;view=1up;seq=5.
96. Hearing Before the Committee on the Judiciary on Miscellaneous Proposals Relating to Presidential Inability, 89th Cong., 1st sess., February 9, 10, 16, and 17, 1965, 260. https://babel.hathitrust.org/cgi/pt?id=ucl.$b654933;view=1up;seq=5.
97. Hearing Before the Committee on the Judiciary on Miscellaneous Proposals Relating to Presidential Inability, 89th Cong., 1st sess., February 9, 10, 16, and 17, 1965, 289. https://babel.hathitrust.org/cgi/pt?id=ucl.$b654933;view=1up;seq=5.
98. On the night the House Judiciary Committee Hearings concluded, Bayh and his staff nervously worked late; S.J. Res.1 was about to be introduced on the Senate floor. Causing Bayh consternation was the fact that *The New York Times* had reported that Dirksen believed Katzenbach, based on his testimony a year earlier, was opposed to Bayh's amendment, and, like Dirksen, supported an enabling amendment—even though President Johnson had given Bayh's amendment his blessing. In response, Bayh asked both Deputy Attorney General Ramsey Clark and White House aide Jack Valenti for a letter confirming Katzenbach's support. Valenti promptly sent a memorandum to the president notifying him of Bayh's call. The memo read: "Hearings are beginning tomorrow on presidential disability, etc. Senator Everett Dirksen is trying to torpedo the whole thing and use as ammunition remarks made by Attorney General Katzenbach a year ago. Katzenbach's testimony this time is perfect and aids the bill a great deal. What Bayh needs: a strong letter to Bayh from Katzenbach saying "This I believe" and setting forth

his views. Do you agree to such a letter going from Katzenbach?" Below the question appear only two words: the word "Yes," with a blank next to it, and the word "No," also followed by a blank. The blanks remain unchecked in the archived memorandum; it is unclear exactly how Johnson reacted. Katzenbach, following two of his predecessors in the Justice Department, Herbert Brownell, and William P. Rogers, ultimately agreed with Bayh that his amendment was necessary. Bayh planned to pull the letter out of his pocket on the floor of the Senate should he be challenged. Dirksen: "Dirksen Opposes Disability Plan," *The New York Times* (February 12, 1965), 8. Memo: "To Mr. President from Jack Valenti, February 17, 1965," LBJL. Legislative Background, Presidential Disability Box 1, Folder "Presidential Disability—4. Legislative Struggle." Bayh would use letter: Bayh, *One Heartbeat Away*, 246–47.
99. *Cong. Rec., 89th Cong., 1st sess.*, 1865, vol. 111, 3251.
100. Bayh, *One Heartbeat Away*, 245.
101. Bayh, *One Heartbeat Away*, 245.
102. Bayh, *One Heartbeat Away*, 252.
103. *Cong. Rec., 89th Cong., 1st sess.*, 1965, vol. 111, 3274.
104. Democratic Senator Ross Bass of Tennessee, who was concerned that congressional control by one party would hold up the selection of a vice president, offered one such amendment. Congressman Clarence Brown of Ohio expressed a related concern to that of Bass, one of the biggest issues when it came to House passage of the joint resolution: it would take away from Congress the constitutional right it had to select a president. John O. Pastore of Rhode Island wanted the words "and no other business shall be transacted until such issue is decided upon" inserted into Bayh's amendment. Fellow Democrat Joe Tydings passed Bayh a note which told him to "stick to [his] guns, Pastore [is] wrong." "Note from Senator," NA, CJ, SCA, Box 16, Folder "89th Congress, PI—Note from Senator During Floor Debate 1965 Feb 14."
105. Many before, during, and after the Twenty-Fifth's journey through the ratification process called for, if not an Electoral College vote, then a vote of the general electorate to decide who would succeed to the presidency. Often this suggestion was contingent upon the number of months between the death,

removal, resignation, or inability of the president and the next quadrennial election.
106. This is true not just of my interactions with Bayh, but of other interviews I have been privy to. See Bayh, Interview with author, November 11, 2014, and Bayh, Interviews with Bob Blaemire, 2012.
107. When asked generally about his relationship over the years with Senator Strom Thurmond, Bayh confessed to the author: "Strom and I were not close." Bayh, Interview with author, November 11, 2014.
108. Bayh, *One Heartbeat Away*, 258.
109. *Cong. Rec., 89th Cong., 1st sess.*, 1965, vol. 111, pt. 6, 7937.
110. One House delegate later reasoned the lengthy debate around the Civil Rights Act, which had taken place the year before, indicated the need for some time limit on whether the president was incapacitated. See Bayh, *One Heartbeat Away*, 289.
111. Bayh, *One Heartbeat Away*, 285.
112. Bayh, *One Heartbeat Away*, 285. Twenty-one days was eventually agreed upon.
113. Additionally, the House wanted the vice president and Cabinet's transmission to the president pro tem of the Senate and the speaker of the House regarding the president's continued disability to occur within two days. Two days originally appeared in the Senate's version of the bill, before Senator Hruska had suggested ten and the Senate compromised on seven. At this point, Bayh privately told his staff that the Senate ought to compromise with the House on four days. Four appears in the amendment's final form. Bayh, *One Heartbeat Away*, 283.
114. Bayh, *One Heartbeat Away*, 283.
115. Bayh, *One Heartbeat Away*, 279.
116. The Conference Committee consisted of Senators Bayh, Eastland, Ervin, Dirksen, and Hruska and Congressmen Celler, Rogers, and McCulloch, as well as John Corman of California and Richard Poff of Virginia.
117. This was particularly true of Dirksen, who had favored a simple enabling amendment, without any specifics, from the outset. Yet further investigation has unveiled another version of the story. Bayh, when interviewed in 2012, explained that he went to Dirksen's office to lobby him directly and discovered Dirksen's

cooperation on the matter was linked to an amendment that would allow prayer and Bible reading in public schools, overriding recent Supreme Court rulings deeming such activities unconstitutional. Birch Bayh, Interviews with Bob Blaemire, 2012. Substitute amendment: Sam Ervin, *Preserving the Constitution: The Autobiography of Senator Sam Ervin* (Charlottesville, VA: The Michie Company, 1984), 241.
118. Bayh, *One Heartbeat Away*, 248.
119. McCulloch had turned down an offer to testify in January 1964, but this quote appears with a few others in a handwritten note on United States Senate letterhead. It seems one of Bayh's staff members, most likely Larry Conrad, Counsel to the Subcommittee, was charged with the task of collecting key statements during the debate in 1965. "Note that the House," NA, CJ, SCA, Box 16, Folder "89th Congress, PI—S.J. Res. 1-Conference—Meetings 1965, May–June."
120. Bayh, *One Heartbeat Away*, 233.
121. During the Conference Committee, Bayh pounded the pavement, at times literally walking from office to office, to persuade Eastland, Dirksen, Ervin, and Hruska to agree to a four-day limitation on the vice president and Cabinet so that the Senate conferees could present a united front. At the time of this conference committee meeting, the House wanted a two-day meditation period; Senator Bayh considered agreeing to Senator Hruska's suggestion of seven but met with him privately late on the night of June 9, 1965, explaining he felt the full Senate body would not accept a period longer than four days as the Senate was hesitant to accept any limitations. Hruska reluctantly agreed to the four days which appears in the final Amendment. Bayh, *One Heartbeat Away*, 288–297.
122. Bayh, *One Heartbeat Away*, 288–297.
123. Bayh, *One Heartbeat Away*, 298.
124. Bayh, *One Heartbeat Away*, 303.
125. John Feerick, *The Twenty-Fifth Amendment* (1976), 104. This appears in the amendment's final form.
126. Bayh, Interviews with Bob Blaemire, 2012.
127. Congressman Poff listed the changes that had been made, including that at this point Sections 4 and 5 were combined into

a single section, Section 4. Fordham Law School Dean Emeritus John Feerick has what appears to be the only copies of his correspondence with Poff on this issue at his private office in Larchmont, New York. *Congressional Record*, Vol. 111, Part II. 89th Congress, 1st Session (June 30, 1965), 15,213. See also: John Feerick, Interviews with author, February 24, and May 27, 2015.

128. Lausche suggested "having both a majority of the members of the Cabinet *and* a majority of the members of the body created by Congress" determine whether the inability had ended. Of Lausche, Bayh said, "It was pretty hard to nail him down. He was a Democrat, but pretty conservative. It was his way or the highway often." Birch Bayh, Interview with author, November 11, 2014.

129. Gore was able to obtain postponement of further debate on the floor to have time to study the legal connotation of the language in the disability clause until July 6, 1965. On that day, he noted that it was impossible to provide for every contingency, but that changes could not be made after ratification. This fact, he claimed, would have added uncertainty, rather than certainty, to a sudden presidential transition. Urging others to join with him in opposing S.J. Res. 1, he concluded "should the Conference Report, with its present language, be approved, doubt and uncertainty will, upon ratification, become embedded in the Constitution." "Remarks of Senator Albert Gore Prepared for Delivery on the Floor of the United States Senate," NA, CJ, SCA, Box 16, Folder "89th Congress, PI, S.J. Res. 1 Floor Statement: Gore, Albert 6 July 1965".

130. In retrospect, his opposition was inexplicable to Bayh. "You know I don't know why that was the case either because … he was a very liberal senator for a senator from Tennessee. He was for civil rights at a time when it wasn't popular down there and he was a fighter…. I'm sure I knew at the time; I don't remember why he took that position." Birch Bayh, Interview with author, November 11, 2014.

131. Additionally, Mondale likely would have had difficulty voting against his senior Senator, McCarthy. Bayh, Interview with author, November 11, 2014.

132. Others, such as Democratic Senator Allen J. Ellender of Louisiana, were of the same mindset as McCarthy, but did not ultimately vote against the resolution. Reacting to his opponents, Bayh did not want to leave open the possibility of easily removing the president for partisan reasons: this is one of the two main reasons a constitutional amendment, rather than an act, was the chosen remedy. In *Explicit and Authentic Acts*, David Kyvig comes to another conclusion about whether Bayh and the ABA knew that it was more difficult to challenge an amendment once it was ratified. They were "convinced that a constitutional amendment offered the best prospect for a clear and unchallengeable remedy to most potential crises." Both additional protection for the president and the fact that it provided a more secure plan, taken together, are the reasons that an amendment was the chosen plan. See Kyvig, *Explicit and Authentic Acts*, 362. Mondale: "SJRes 6 Hruska (Allott, Curtis, Dirksen, Mondale)," NA, CJ, SCA, Box 16, Folder "89th Congress, PI-Bills—S.J. Res. 1-Cosponsors, 1965 Jan 14."
133. In March 1964, when Bayh had asked McCarthy if he wanted to testify before the Subcommittee, McCarthy declined, reminding Bayh that he believed that an act of Congress, rather than an amendment to the Constitution, was the correct course of action. "Letter to Birch Bayh from Eugene McCarthy, March 18, 1964," NA, CJ, SCA, Box 7, Folder "88th Congress, PI—Correspondence—Congressional 1963–64."
134. Bayh, *One Heartbeat Away*, 66.
135. Bayh, *One Heartbeat Away*, 319.
136. While Bayh's staff kept track of the votes, they did not know the mindset of every senator.
137. Reminiscent of his February 19 testimony, Ervin told his fellow senators to pass the amendment without making further changes, stating, "We were convinced of the old adage that too many cooks spoil the broth. We had more cooks with more zeal concerned with preparing this 'broth' than any piece of proposed legislation I have ever seen in the time I have been in the Senate." *Cong. Rec., 89th Cong., 1st sess.*, 1965, vol. 111, pt. 2,. 15,590.
138. *Cong. Rec., 89th Cong., 1st sess.*, 1965, vol. 111, pt. 2, 15,590.
139. Bayh told the author, "Well, I don't know if we ever got his vote. I was down in the leader's seat, the seat that leaders were

issued, the front corner aisle seat, and somebody came down and said, "you better see what those folks are doing back there." And Bobby and Phil Hart [D-Michigan] and some others were saying this would make it possible for a coup to take place and that these were people [the Cabinet] that the president never really knew. That's not true: the president knew all of them. Some of them he knew very well. Bobby was just way off base on that. Birch Bayh, Interview with author, November 11, 2014.
140. ""Mr. Kennedy of Massachusetts."— "Aye." Mr. Kennedy of New York."— "Aye."" Birch Bayh, *One Heartbeat Away*, 332. The Congressional Record confirms his assertion. *Cong. Rec.,89th Cong., 1st sess.*, 1965, vol. 111, pt. 2,15,590.
141. Bayh, *One Heartbeat Away*, 331.
142. The Constitution of the United States, Amendment XXV.
143. "As you know, the rejection of the amendment in any state… might have a snowball effect." "Letter to R. Dale Tooley from John D. Feerick," July 20, 1965. Personal Files of John D. Feerick, Folder "JBC-ABA II through Sept. 1965."
144. The author interviewed Colorado State Senator John R. Bermingham on February 2, 2015. At the time, he was 91 years old and did not remember the specifics of Colorado's vote on the Twenty-Fifth Amendment. However, he was eager to speak about how nuclear anxiety affected a great portion of his career, including his naval service in the Pacific at the end of WWII.
145. This was a tremendous undertaking. And it was not the first time Bayh and the ABA had been in touch with state legislators: in 1964, long before passage, they had taken the clever step of polling every speaker and senator pro tem in each of the fifty state legislatures, to ask whether Bayh's S.J. Res. 139 or Keating's S.J. Res. 35 would more easily pass at the state level and this study had proved helpful in obtaining Johnson's support prior to his 1965 State of the Union Address. As Bayh and his allies assumed, S. J. Res. 139 was overwhelmingly preferred, in large part because the official endorsement of the Bar Association came down to the support of eminent attorneys in each state and, collectively, their opinions carried weight. "To Members of the Committee on Presidential Disability and Advisory Committee, Report # 1— 1964–65, from Donald E. Channell, September 3, 1964" NA,

CJ, SCA, Box 7, Folder "88th Congress, PI Correspondence Channell, Donald E. ABA 1964." See also Feerick.

146. The ABA's effort was based out of the association's Washington, DC, office and run by ABA lawyers Donald Channell and Lowell Beck, together with their assistant Michael Spence a clearinghouse," as Feerick.

147. During the passage of Bayh's bill through Congress, ABA members lobbied and fielded calls from both the executive and legislative branches of the federal government; asked state and local bar associations and fellow constituents to write letters to members of Congress; spoke in front of civic organizations; and published articles and editorials in newspapers across the country. In Nebraska alone, ABA member Richard Hansen appeared more than fifty times to deliver speeches across the state in support of ratification. Hansen was a longstanding advocate of succession reform, having published in 1962 a book called *The Year We Had No President* that documented periods in which the president was not able to carry out his responsibilities. He had testified as an expert before Congress in 1963 and advocated for the amendment throughout the process. Nebraska became the first state to ratify at 12:15 p.m. on July 13, 1965. Wisconsin ratified just four minutes later, at 12:19 p.m. Oklahoma followed three days later. Massachusetts ratified next, on August 9, 1965. All four ratified without major incident, though the specifics of the nature of debate have been lost to history. Instead, newspapers such as *The New York Times* in the case of Nebraska and Washington, focused only on the race to ratify. See, for example: "Wisconsin First State on Twenty—Fifth", July 14, 1965, *The New York Times* (1923-Current File). "Nebraska Says it was First to Ratify 25th Amendment" July 15, 1965, *New York Times* (1923-Current File). "5th State Ratifies Amendment", August 19, 1965, *New York Times* (1923-Current File). See also: Feerick.

148. No provisions existed in the current law for the possibility of Kennedy remaining alive in a comatose state, for example. Arthur Krock, in his *New York Times* article of November 24, 1963, was one of the media icons that drew attention to Feerick's work. Arthur Krock, "The Continuum: Kennedy's Death Points Up Orderly Progression in US Government", November 24, 1963, *The New York Times* (1923-Current File).

149. "Notes of Meeting held in Miami Florida, August 9, 1965," Personal Files of John D. Feerick, Folder. "JBC—ABA II Through Sept. 1965."
150. Commonwealth of Pennsylvania Legislative Journal, Session of 149th of the General Assembly, vol. 1, no. 64 (re Senate bill 1001, printer's No. 1203), August 18, 1965, 1560.
151. Commonwealth of Pennsylvania Legislative Journal, Session of 149th of the General Assembly, 1560.
152. Commonwealth of Pennsylvania Legislative Journal, Session of 149th of the General Assembly, 1563.
153. "Notes of Meeting held in Miami, Florida, August 9, 1965," Personal Files of John D. Feerick, Folder "JBC—ABA II Through Sept. 1965."
154. In Colorado, early ratification of Bayh's amendment seemed likely, but a protracted battle ensued at the same time Kentucky was considering ratification. "Letter to Senator Birch Bayh from Harvey Lee Waterfield, July 23, 1965," NA, CJ, SCA, Box 18, Folder "PI Rat Corres Govs and State Officials Jul 1965."
155. Arizona and Michigan followed Kentucky in quick secession. They were the seventh and eighth states to ratify, on September 22 and October 5, respectively. Bayh's home state of Indiana was the ninth to ratify on October 20, 1965. Governor Roger Branigin called a special session for the purpose of ratifying the amendment, which Bayh addressed, and they voted in favor the same day. Then the California legislature followed suit the next day, becoming the tenth state to ratify. State governmental officials whose states contained the more major metropolises may have felt added pressure to support the amendment because evacuation was more difficult. (See California Governor Edmund G. Brown, Jr.'s comments.) Indiana: Bayh, *One Heartbeat Away*, 338.
156. The National Governor's Conference took place in Minneapolis that year; Senator Bayh's attendance enabled him to directly lobby a great number of governors at the same time. "Letter to Senator Birch Bayh from Orval E. Faubus, August 5, 1965," NA, CJ, SCI, Box 18, Folder "P In Rat Corres Govs and State Officials 1965."

157. "Letter to Senator Birch Bayh from Orval E. Faubus, August 5, 1965," NA, CJ, SCI, Box 18, Folder "P In Rat Corres Govs and State Officials 1965."
158. George D. Haimbaugh, "Vice Presidential Succession: A Criticism of the Bayh-Cellar [sic] Plan," Vol. 17, Rev. 315, *South Carolina Law Review Journal*, 1965.
159. John D. Feerick, Vice Presidential Succession: In Support of the Bayh—Celler Plan," (New York: Fordham University Press, 1966), The Fordham Law Archive of Scholarship and History, http://ir.lawnet.fordham.edu/cgi/viewcontent.cgi?article=1381&context=faculty_scholarship.
160. New Jersey, Delaware, Utah, West Virginia, Maine, and Rhode Island all ratified in the span of two months between November 1965 and January 1966. Delaware ratified on December 7, the 178th anniversary of its ratification of the Constitution. Bayh smoothed over questions about the disability provisions (Sections. 3 and 4) in the West Virginia Senate, by phone. Bayh, *One Heartbeat Away*, 339.
161. According to Colorado Office of Legal Legislative Services aide Robert Garcia, a memorial is introduced by the Colorado House of Representatives solely for one of the following three purposes: to propose amendments to the constitution of the state of Colorado; to recommend the holdings of state constitutional conventions; or to ratify proposed amendments to the Constitution. This memorial was designed for the latter purpose, R. Dale Tooley, head of the Colorado Bar Association, wrote in a letter to Feerick on February 3, 1965.157 Purposes of memorial: Email to Author from Robert Garcia (December 23, 2016). Purpose for this memorial: See "Page 72 Senate Journal— 14th Day— January 19, 1965," and "Letter to Mr. John Feerick from R. Dale Tooley, February 16, 1965," Personal Files of John D. Feerick, Folder "JBC—ABA II Through Sept. 1965."
162. The third reading is the third and final reading of the bill when the final vote is taken. Not all members need be present, only a quorum is required. Opponents argued that the timing was inappropriate as the special session had been called explicitly to deal with flood-related matters. Colorado Representative Allen Dines' letter to Birch Bayh provided additional detail: only twelve senators had voted against the resolution, they were all Republicans,

and consequently, the House did not get to consider it during the special session. Third reading defined: Email to Author from Robert Garcia (December 23, 2016). Opponents' reason: "Letter to Senator Birch Bayh from Allen Dines, July 29, 1965," NA, CJ, SCA, Box 18, Folder "Ratification—Correspondence State Legislatures 1965."

163. "Letter to John Feerick from R. Dale Tooley, July 22, 1965," Personal Files of John D. Feerick, Folder "JBC—ABA II Through Sept. 1965."
164. In his letter of July 21, 1965, Tooley quoted *The Denver Post's* editorial position as of April 15, 1965. The *Post* stated that "ratification will be forthcoming" and "it will come none too soon." "Letter to John Feerick from R. Dale Tooley, July 21, 1965," Personal Files of John D. Feerick, Folder "JBC—ABA II Through Sept. 1965."
165. *The Rocky Mountain News* stated that the current speed of communications should allay the concern that Congress might decide inability on the basis of partisan politics. Congress, in this case, would not get away with such a course of action because the nation would know the details instantaneously. It read: "With today's instant communication, when the whole country would know every detail of congressional behavior (and a president's illness), the risk is enormously reduced." Full Possession of his Faculties: "Twenty-Fifth Amendment has Serious Defects," *The Denver Post*, July 22, 1965. Personal Files of John D. Feerick, Folder "JBC—ABA II Through Sept. 1965." Speed of communications: "The Bayh Amendment Passes," *The Rocky Mountain News*, February 23, 1965. Personal Files of John D. Feerick, Folder "JBC—ABA II Through Sept. 1965."
166. "GOP Senator Explains Vote on Amendment," *Rocky Mountain News* (Denver, Colorado: July 22, 1965), Personal Files of John D. Feerick, Folder "JBC—ABA II Through Sept. 1965."
167. "Letter to American Bar Association from John R. Bermingham, August 10, 1965," NA, CJ, SCA, Box 6, Folder, "PI ABA Junior Bar Conference 3 of 4, Dale Tooley File 1965 Jun-Dec."
168. "Letter to American Bar Association from John R. Bermingham, August 10, 1965."

169. "Letter to the Honorable John R. Bermingham from H. Michael Spence, August 20, 1965" NA, CJ, SCA, Box 6, Folder, "PI ABA Junior Bar Conference 3 of 4, Dale Tooley File 1965 Jun-Dec."
170. "Letter to Mr. H. Michael Spence from John R. Bermingham, August 26, 1965," NA, CJ, SCA, Box 6, Folder, "PI ABA Junior Bar Conference 3 of 4, Dale Tooley File 1965 Jun-Dec."
171. "Letter to Mr. H. Michael Spence from John R. Bermingham, August 26, 1965."
172. "Letter to Mr. H. Michael Spence from John R. Bermingham, September 9, 1965," NA, CJ, SCA, Box 6, Folder, "PI ABA Junior Bar Conference 3 of 4, Dale Tooley File 1965 Jun-Dec."
173. Letter to Mr. Charles Gallagher from R. Dale Tooley, January 27, 1966" Personal Files of John D. Feerick, Folder "John D. Feerick JBC-ABA III, From October 1, 1965 to January 26, 1967."
174. Bayh, *One Heartbeat Away*, 340.
175. The ABA was so consumed by the problems in Colorado, that in a memorandum containing notes from their annual meeting, the update on Utah was simply that it did not have a "Colorado-type problem." Bayh and the ABA were able to breathe easier when the halfway mark was reached with New Mexico's ratification on February 3, the same day as Colorado. Kansas, Vermont, and Alaska all ratified in February as well. Idaho, Hawaii, Virginia, Mississippi, New York, Maryland, and Missouri all ratified the next month, March 1966. But in Alabama, Bayh and Feerick feared Governor George Wallace might opportunistically seize on the amendment as a way to gain national attention and shore up states' power. In this case, Wallace, who had sought the presidency in 1964, was planning to run again. In southern states, civil rights had become a battle between federal and state power. In 1963, on the topic of civil rights, Bayh had written in a press release stating: "Too often in the past, states' rights has been falsely invoked to block and delay progress." Here they were afraid Wallace might make a call for states to avoid ratification or purposefully withhold ratification. Alternatively, Wallace might demand that the amendment be rewritten to empower states—perhaps by the inclusion of a special election that would involve state delegates; or by the substitution of state governors in the line of succession; or by the invention of a committee of governors that would help determine presidential inability. But Alabama did

not consider ratification in its 1965 session, or in its special session that had been called specifically to deal with legislative reapportionment. Attorney Bert Nettles, the ABA's contact in Mobile, told Feerick in a letter of September of that year that it would be considered in the next regular session in 1967. "Colorado—type problem": "Notes of Meeting held in Miami Florida, August 9, 1965," Personal Files of John D. Feerick, Folder "JBC—ABA II Through Sept. 1965." Kansas, Vermont, and Alaska: Birch Bayh, *One Heartbeat Away*, 340. Bayh press release: "From the Office of Senator Birch Bayh for Release upon Delivery, October 12, 1963," US Senate Historian's Office. Folder, "Bayh Newspaper Clippings." They were afraid: John D. Feerick, Interview with author, February 28, 2016. "Letter to John Feerick from Bert S. Nettles," September 20, 1967. Personal Files of John D. Feerick.

176. The remaining states ratified the amendment without issue, with the exception of a hiatus from July 6, 1966, the first anniversary of the Senate vote, until January 1967 because many state legislatures only convened biannually. New Hampshire became the 30th state to ratify on June 13, 1966. Louisiana, the 31st state to ratify, ratified at the end of their session on July 5, 1966. After success in Louisiana, Bayh and the ABA began to prepare for regular legislative sessions to reconvene in 1967. "Preparation continued on the necessary groundwork to do battle then," This preparation included more successful letter-writing to the governors and legislators in the states that had yet to ratify. Bayh, *One Heartbeat Away*, 341.

177. Feerick stated that formal efforts by the ABA to ratchet up additional states ended at this point, but he speculated that some ABA members kept up efforts in their own states. In some states this may have happened for symbolic reasons, but, more than likely, in other states, the Bar Associations would have wanted to see the process through to ratification simply because they had been in favor of Bayh's amendment since early 1964. For example, Alabama ratified the amendment on March 14, 1967, after the amendment had already become part of the Constitution. Texas did not hold a regular legislative session from May 31, 1965 (before the Twenty-Fifth Amendment passed Congress) through January 10, 1967, but Governor John Connally listed ratification of the amendment as "one of the key items" of his 1967 agenda.

Texas ratified the amendment on April 25, 1967. John D. Feerick, Interview with author, February 28, 2016.

178. A procedural error caused Georgia not to be added to the ratification list, though it appears that both houses of the legislature approved the measure just prior to their session's adjournment. In South Carolina, ABA member William "Bill" Able followed the campaign procedures used by the ABA in other states as evidenced from a letter in Feerick's personal files. Georgia: See Birch Bayh, *One Heartbeat Away*, 40 fn. South Carolina: See "Letter to Hon Robert T. Ashmore from William F. Able, March 8, 1965."

179. Until 1950, the secretary of state handled the duty of administering the ratification process. From 1950–1985, the General Services administrator took on this responsibility, which is currently in the hands of the Archivist of the United States, the head of the National Archives and Records Administration. National Archives, "The Constitutional Amendment Process," *The Federal Register*. http://www.archives.gov/federal-register/constitution/.

180. Tom Wickers, "Johnson's Great Society: Lines are Drawn," *The New York Times*, March 14, 1965, E3.

181. Jack Valenti, "The Unforgettable Afternoon," *The New York Times*, November 22, 1998, w17. As quoted in Steven M. Gillon, *The Kennedy Assassination: 24 Hours After Lyndon B. Johnson's Pivotal First Day as President* (New York: Basic Books, 2009), 142.

182. Bayh with President Lyndon Johnson (127–1074), September 18, 1967, Photograph Collection, Birch Bayh Senatorial Papers, Modern Political Papers Collection, Indiana University Libraries, Bloomington, Indiana.

CHAPTER 5

"A *Dr. Strangelove* Situation": The Twenty-Fifth Amendment in Practice

"This is a true *Dr. Strangelove* kind of situation,"[1] Birch Bayh said to his fellow congressmembers when the debate over passage of the amendment had turned to inability issues. The 1964 film *Dr. Strangelove or How I Stopped Worrying and Learned to Love the Bomb* dramatized an inconceivable event, nuclear catastrophe, with gallows humor.[2] Dr. Strangelove represented a scientist—an individual in a field Americans love to trust—that had become "strange," or gone insane. In invoking the popular film, Bayh pointed to Cold War anxieties about the collision of military and scientific power, as it focused on the ability of the president who wielded that power. The Twenty-Fifth Amendment was designed to secure the line of presidential succession in case of a sudden strike and prevent a president who had become crazy or incapacitated from having control of the bomb. Yet the amendment in practice did not completely succeed in stopping lawmakers from "worrying" nor was it always used when a president was incapacitated.

The first applications of the amendment in the 1970s revealed gaps and vagaries in Sections 1 and 2 of the amendment but resulted in smooth executive transitions. Section 3 of the amendment was invoked in 1985, 2002, and 2007, respectively, and these applications, too, raised questions. The amendment was invoked seven times between 1967 and 2025, three times to replace an elected official, and four times to deal with temporary presidential inability. The need for a stable chief executive at the nuclear trigger conflicted with political concerns, namely the president's desire to project an image of health and competency.[3] Presidents and their advisors—whose power relied on that of the president—consistently failed to demonstrate willingness to put presidential continuity, and thus the safety of the nation, over their desire to hold on to power.

To understand the Twenty-Fifth Amendment as a product of an era of nuclear anxiety requires careful consideration not only of the times that the amendment was invoked but also of the times it might have been invoked but was not. Evidence suggests that the higher the nuclear anxiety, the less likely it was that the amendment would be invoked. Further, during periods of heightened nuclear anxiety, government officials intensified their search for solutions to perpetually challenging presidential succession and inability issues, sometimes stretching the flexible boundaries of the Constitution itself.

* * *

The year after the Twenty-Fifth Amendment became part of the Constitution, former Vice President Richard Nixon was elected president. But his victory raised issues about a president's mental stability in a nuclear age. Nixon's volatile state of mind, and therefore his ability to provide stable leadership, was not a new concern, but rather a continued source of anxiety. Although Nixon had reinvented himself as a mature statesman, many Americans remembered his hot-tempered style from earlier in his career. Moreover, in an article published in July 1969, Arnold A. Hutschnecker, who functioned as Nixon's psychotherapist, suggested that "the survival of the human race" depended on the "emotional stability" of the US president. He warned of "hostile-aggressive" leaders in whom ambition "can reach a degree of madness."[4] It was not hard to read the remark as a thinly veiled reference to his famous patient.

That summer, the Paris Peace Talks intended to end the war in Vietnam collapsed and, in the autumn, Nixon purposefully feigned madness. To force the Soviets to bring the North Vietnamese back to the negotiating table, the "madman theory," based on game theory, aimed to convince them that nothing, not even a nuclear attack, was off-limits to the president. Nixon ordered the Pentagon to perform a series of measures that would put the US nuclear forces on a higher state of readiness, meant to attract the Soviet's notice, but not the attention of allies nor the public. For three weeks, the Joint Chiefs of Staff (JCS) Readiness

Test meant that US nuclear bombers were on higher alert and tactical aircraft and nuclear missile submarines in the Pacific raised their combat preparedness while US destroyers and other naval crafts in the Atlantic, Mediterranean, Adriatic, and Sea of Japan engaged in similar activities. National Security Advisor Henry Kissinger issued a series of strategic measures that escalated toward the end of October when sorties of six-armed B-52 bombers orbited Alaska, the first time in nearly two years that nuclear bombers had remained in the air. Then, just as suddenly as they began, the exercises ended.[5] The global nuclear alert did not mark a conclusion to the war in Vietnam, and, had the Soviets been convinced of Nixon's madness, it could have caused them to issue a preemptive strike.

An incident that raised a red flag at home about the president's mental health occurred in the pre-dawn hours of May 9, 1970, when students gathered in Washington to protest the war in Vietnam and the murders of four students at Kent State University by National Guard troops.[6] Much to his Secret Service detail's consternation, Nixon decided to take a walk to "rap" with student demonstrators near the Lincoln Memorial.[7] While Nixon's version of his sojourn to the Memorial was printed in the major papers on May 10, his closest aides and the students he mixed with questioned his incoherence, choice of topics, and overall sanity.[8] The incident fueled public debate about the president's ability to make clear decisions about war.

During the nuclear age, mental inability—including issues like lack of comprehension, a need for anger management or the inability to cope with a particularly stressful day (as Nixon's behavior suggested)—was proving to be more dangerous in a president than physical limitations.[9] In Nixon's case, however, illegal activity and not insanity or physical ailment put an early end to his term after five men were arrested and charged with second-degree burglary at the Democratic National headquarters in the Watergate hotel and office complex and the order for the break-in was traced to the top echelon of the executive branch. Between May and August 1973, the Select Committee on Presidential Campaign Activities chaired by Senator Sam Ervin investigated potential links between the president himself and the break-in at the Watergate hotel.[10] During 1973 and 1974, all of Washington became engulfed in the drama as Americans tried to understand the complex events, the clash between Congress and the White House, and what the implications might be for the presidency. The removal of the president from office, which would trigger Section 1 of the Twenty-Fifth Amendment, appeared increasingly likely.[11]

Then, suddenly, on October 10, 1973, Vice President Spiro T. Agnew resigned amid charges of wrongdoing unrelated to the Watergate scandal,[12] initiating Section 2 of the Twenty-Fifth Amendment instead. Richard Nixon became the first president to fill a vacancy in the office of the vice president, subject to confirmation by Congress. Agnew's resignation also seemed to increase the likelihood of Nixon's impeachment or resignation, since the general lack of regard for Agnew had acted as a kind of insurance policy for Nixon. Agnew resigned on what was the fifth day of the Yom Kippur War between Israel and its Arab enemies, which could have become a nuclear conflict.[13] The day after accepting Agnew's resignation, Nixon left for Camp David, the presidential retreat in Maryland. Feeling increasingly burdened by incessant bad news, the president began drinking heavily, a practice which apparently had become a habit. At 7:55 p.m., British Prime Minister Edward Heath requested a return call within thirty minutes to discuss the Middle East. Secretary of State Kissinger asked privately if the prime minister's call could be declined because the president "was loaded," and, therefore, mentally incapacitated to the point where he could not perform his duties.[14] Nixon also was taking sedatives regularly in this period, compounding his inability to function at full capacity.[15] Instead, Chief of Staff Alexander Haig seemed to be unofficially in charge, having for months regarded himself as a "surrogate [p]resident." Much like President Woodrow Wilson's wife and physician half a century before, he decided which issues he would handle and which ones he would bring to the president's attention.[16] Lawrence Eagleburger, who served as secretary of state under President George H. W. Bush, later reflected that US ability to deal with any potential nuclear crisis had been completely compromised.[17]

The image of a president not fully in command affected not just politics within the administration but also diplomatic relations. Key stakeholders outside the administration also knew that Nixon was not at the helm making the foreign policy decisions. Prime Minister Golda Meir of Israel sent her requests for weapons and supplies to Kissinger, not Nixon.[18] On October 24, in the middle of one meeting, which took place at 2:00 a.m. while the president was sleeping, the president's men, without the president's input, instructed the US military to raise the Defense Condition from DEFCON IV to DEFCON III. DEFCON III was "the highest stage of readiness for essentially peacetime conditions," according to Kissinger.[19] Raising the alert sent a message in and of itself. But by the meeting's conclusion, they disseminated the following explicit message to the Soviets: Sending troops would be considered a "matter of the gravest concern involving incalculable consequences."[20] American intelligence had detected Soviet ships carrying nuclear arms in the Dardanelles and the Arab–Israeli War had ended, according to policy hand William Quandt, in "near-confrontation of the two nuclear superpowers."[21]

Legally, Nixon's advisors could not take this step. Kissinger, Haig, and other (unelected) officials were making foreign policy decisions as the United States and Soviets continued to arm their respective proxies.[22] Kissinger had decided the president was "too distraught to participate in the discussion."[23] During this critical time, final decisions were being made only by advisors. Unlike Wilson's inability after World War I when foreign policy emanating from the White House stagnated, the Yom Kippur War occurred during the nuclear era when any improper decision or a president's degraded mental capacity could have immediate and disastrous national security implications. Nixon was, without a doubt, not functioning at full capacity, and his incapacity could not have come at a more dangerous time. At this point, the president's condition and the increased potential for a nuclear catastrophe should have initiated discussions about invoking Section 3 or 4 of the Twenty-Fifth Amendment.

However, Nixon did not declare himself incapacitated, nor was a vice president in place to do so. Had there been a vice president, nuclear anxiety would have made White House officials less inclined to invoke the amendment. While Nixon was "unhappy at Kissinger's assumption of presidential power," he was entirely preoccupied and completely beleaguered by the Watergate scandal, historian Robert Dallek argues in *Nixon and Kissinger: Partners in Power*.[24] Kissinger and the Cabinet did not want to call attention to the matter of Nixon's potentially compromised judgment for fear of losing their prime decision-making positions or signaling to the world that any unsteadiness in leadership existed at a critical juncture. Their power was linked to Nixon remaining in the Oval Office. No guarantees existed that the next president, even if he were hand-picked by Nixon, would allow them to exercise as much power. The vice presidential vacancy made the situation even more complex.[25] Section 3 of the amendment requires that a vice president be in place, and Section 4 revolves around the vice president's decisions.

Nixon arrived at a decision regarding his vice presidential nominee after his drunken episode at dawn on October 12, 1973.[26] He selected

Minority Leader Gerald R. Ford. Section 2 of the Twenty-Fifth Amendment does not provide direction to Congress as to how to consider the president's nominee for vice president to arrive at a majority vote of both Houses. Congress found that the structure of the process needed to be created. That day, having canceled a recess, the question was raised in the Senate, specifically regarding whether to refer Ford's nomination to the Senate Rules Committee or to establish a special committee for that purpose.[27] A three-and-a-half-hour debate ensued—the Democratic caucus decided on a compromise. The compromise designated a special committee composed of the full membership of the Rules Committee plus three senators from each party. It passed by a vote of 40–24. Republicans held their own two-hour caucus and suggested the Rules and Administration Committee, not an augmented version of it, was enough. The Republican version prevailed.[28] Because of a lack of specifics in the amendment, however, another committee could have been chosen in either House and produced different results, perhaps leading to a rejection of the nominee, a repeat of the entire process, and a much longer vacancy in the vice presidency when time was of the essence.

The Senate Rules Committee held hearings throughout the first two weeks of November in 1973. Both the senators and witnesses were aware that they were probably choosing Nixon's successor and were concerned about Ford's experience in foreign affairs, especially given the responsibilities of the president in the nuclear age.[29] For example, Vice Chairman of Americans for Democratic Action Joseph L. Rauh, Jr. stated that Ford's confirmation, because he was much less experienced than Nixon, was insurance that Nixon would not be impeached. He said, "I think as time goes on people will recognize that to put a foreign affairs neophyte in the president's seat... is unthinkable."[30] Rauh concluded Ford should not be confirmed because a mistake "could mean nuclear holocaust."[31] Representative George H. Mahon, testifying before the Senate Committee, eased senators' concerns on this issue by telling them that, having served closely with the nominee, Ford understood America's nuclear capabilities and how they affected America's role in international affairs.[32] Confirming Ford would not mean an inexperienced finger would be on the trigger if he should succeed Nixon, Mahon reassured his colleagues.

In addition to questions about process, the hearings raised questions as to the proper depth and breadth of information Congress should require from the president's nominee. Again, the Twenty-Fifth provided no guidelines. On the one hand, Ford's privacy had to be considered.

On the other, the well-being of the nation was paramount. The Senate approved Ford by a vote of 92–3 on November 27, 1973; the approval took one month and eight days.[33] The extent to which the nominee should be questioned was not described in Section 2 of the Twenty-Fifth Amendment; congressmembers were melding the amendment to meet the situation's needs.

During the House debate, numerous speakers acknowledged that Ford would succeed to the presidency should Nixon not serve the entirety of his second term and, either way, he might be forced to make split-second decisions about nuclear warfare. One witness, Democratic Congressman Michael J. Harrington of Massachusetts, pointed out that tensions were not abating; rather, nuclear alert had been declared between the time of Ford's nomination and the hearings, and Ford might very well have to deal directly with that issue.[34] After a five-hour debate on December 6, 1973, the House confirmed Ford by a vote of 387–35.[35] Ford's swearing in as the fortieth vice president of the United States took place in the House Chamber before a joint session of Congress with Nixon, the entire Supreme Court, ambassadors, and foreign dignitaries in attendance.[36] Ironically, a nuclear attack on Washington during the swearing-in ceremony would have caused government paralysis, exactly the type of scenario expert witness Ruth Miner and others envisioned when arguing in favor of incorporating greater detail into the amendment during committee hearings prior to the amendment's ratification.

Over the next eight months, evidence implicating Nixon in serious wrongdoing mounted, and after he lost a critical Supreme Court decision that forced him to give key White House recordings to the Watergate special prosecutor, Nixon realized that impeachment and removal were inevitable. During this tumultuous time, Nixon's telecommunications advisor, Clay T. Whitehead, and Ford's closest friend, Philip W. Buchen, members of a small, clandestine team that had begun to prepare for a Ford presidency, wondered if Nixon would refuse to leave, go crazy, and try to use the military to retain office. What if it became necessary to remove the president via Section 4 of the Twenty-Fifth Amendment? They considered raising this scenario with Defense Secretary James R. Schlesinger.[37] Meanwhile, Schlesinger had been warned by Senator Alan Cranston that Nixon had made an ominous comment to congressmembers: He could issue an order and "25 minutes" later "millions of people would be dead."[38] Schlesinger, worried about the president's mental stability,[39] had decided he would not leave Washington so as to be present at the Pentagon to prevent "any series of hypothetical situations from developing,"[40] and instructed the military not to react to White House orders on nuclear matters.[41] He and Chairman of the Joint Chiefs of Staff General George S. Brown were concerned about an "improbable" situation in which Nixon would order actions while "blocking the constitutional process," or that some genuine national emergency would occur, and the military would need to go on high alert.[42] Stress around a peaceful transition of power overlapped with fears that the chain of command would be circumvented and Armageddon would ensue.

Then, on the evening of August 8, 1974, Nixon told a television audience of between 110–130 million people that he would resign the presidency the next day.[43] At 11:35 a.m. on August 9, Nixon became the first United States president to resign. The letter delivered by Haig to Kissinger contained just a single sentence: "Dear Mr. Secretary: I hereby resign the office of President of the United States. Sincerely, Richard Nixon."[44] That one sentence triggered the second implementation of Section 1 of the Twenty-Fifth Amendment.

On August 20, the new president, Ford, announced on television and radio that he was nominating the former governor of New York, Nelson Rockefeller, for vice president, and, once again, nuclear concerns loomed in the background. Rockefeller's long career in government service could help Ford establish himself as a competent executive.[45] Yet despite his experience, Congress made the nominee answer questions seventeen different times.[46] On at least one occasion, the Congressional Record suggests that Rockefeller was questioned about his position on nuclear weapons. The extensive appendix to the hearing testimony includes questions such as: "In what circumstances, if any, would [he] resort to the first use of nuclear weapons? What nuclear weapons would be treated as conventional?"[47] Some of his gubernatorial papers were inserted into the record, including one dating to February 1963 that dealt almost entirely with nuclear parity with the Soviets.[48] On August 20, 1974, Rockefeller was confirmed by majority vote of both houses of Congress. For the first (and, so far, only) time in American history, both the president and vice president were appointees not elected by the entire American electorate.[49]

The Twenty-Fifth Amendment had functioned as planned in the appointments of Ford and Rockefeller. But some were unhappy that the nation lacked a popularly elected official in either top post. Early the following year, a concerned mood in Congress and among the public led to both a hearing on the first implementation of Section 2 of the Twenty-Fifth Amendment and the introduction of various bills in Congress calling for changes to the amendment. For example, on November 9, 1973, Senator William Hathaway (D-ME) introduced S. 2678, which called for a special election of the president and vice president when both offices were vacant as well as for an "interim president" of the same party as the president.[50] On February 25, 1975, during a hearing before the Judiciary Subcommittee on Constitutional Amendments, Bayh alluded to the fear of nuclear war: "The way I understand your proposal, Senator Hathaway, is that you feel we should continue to implement the provisions of the Twenty-Fifth Amendment, in the event there is... some crazy catastrophe of violence."[51] When Hathaway responded, "That is correct," Bayh endorsed the sentiment. Bayh then spoke about what he and the other framers of the Twenty-Fifth were thinking about the delicate balance the amendment tried to establish. Bayh said, "We had to draw the line as to what we felt had traditionally been constitutionally established and what we felt could be indeed enacted by statute." Further, he suggested that Hathaway's statute pointed to a weakness in the Twenty-Fifth Amendment—"that perhaps it did not go far enough."[52] The architect of the amendment may have been recalling the moments during the ratification of the amendment when legislators called for additional language that would outline procedures in the event of a nuclear attack.[53]

Along with his admission that the amendment did not cover all potentialities, Bayh supported Hathaway's suggestion that Congress enact a statute to deal with gaps in the line of succession in the event of a nuclear catastrophe. But Bayh did not support a statute that would allow for a special election. Bayh clarified his views when he testified in February on a different bill, S.J. 26, sponsored by Senator John Pastore of Rhode Island. It modified the Twenty-Fifth Amendment under the circumstances like those in which Ford became president; in such cases, the bill proposed, the vice president would serve as president only until a president elected in a special election took the oath of office.[54] Bayh argued that an election would be divisive "at a time when we really need something to pull us together."[55] The bills designed to change portions of the Twenty-Fifth Amendment did not become law, but the debate around them showed congressmen's continued anxiety surrounding both nuclear war and succession and inability issues. The consensus during the hearings on the first applications of the Twenty-Fifth Amendment was that the Twenty-Fifth Amendment had "worked" when applied—the unplanned executive transitions had gone smoothly—but constitutional questions still needed ironing out and the threat of nuclear apocalypse was constantly weighing on lawmakers' minds.[56]

* * *

After the next (planned) presidential transition—Jimmy Carter was sworn in as president in January 1977—an accident occurred at Three Mile Island nuclear power plant in Pennsylvania. This accident increased popular resistance to the idea that nuclear power could ever be harnessed for good, resistance that had already been building at the local level for years. A popular thriller, *The China Syndrome*, released the same month, depicted a reporter who uncovered safety violations at a nuclear plant and became entangled in a plot to hide from the public the truth about the extent of the damage. In the minds of the public, issues of nuclear power and nuclear war were entangled.[57] Later that year, on June 17, 1979, Carter and Soviet Premier Leonid Brezhnev signed SALT II in Vienna. SALT II limited the number of nuclear delivery forces and placed other restrictions on strategic nuclear forces.[58] After the Soviets invaded Afghanistan on December 5, however, Carter asked the Senate not to consider the treaty.[59] Nuclear tensions were building.

During the presidential campaign that year, Republican nominee Ronald Reagan had employed tough language directed at the Soviets, renewing fears of a nuclear confrontation. He appeared on televangelist Jim Bakker's *The PTL Club* and said, "We may be the generation that sees Armageddon."[60] Reagan believed in a heroic figure that could change the outcome of Armageddon; the president's mission was to protect Americans from nuclear catastrophe.[61] (It was for this reason that many congressmembers had voted in favor of the Twenty-Fifth Amendment fifteen years earlier—the need to have a competent president manning the nuclear button.) These tensions combined with the overall unpopularity of Carter's foreign policies, as well as the depressed mood of the electorate, and the declining economy, paved the way for Reagan's victory. He was the oldest man who had been chosen for the presidency to that date.[62]

Concerns about a smooth transition of presidential power were evident during the Carter-Reagan transition, which highlighted the fact that the Twenty-Fifth Amendment did not address a potential crisis on Inauguration Day.[63] In April 1980, the Director of the White House Military

Office had ordered the Federal Emergency Management Agency to "monitor locations and recommend procedures to the president for presidential successor attendance" at "publicly announced scheduled events outside the White House complex... at which the president and other officials in [the] legal line of succession [would] be assembled."[64] If all members in the line of succession planned to attend a State occasion, one or more designated official(s) would be requested not to attend the event in order to protect the succession.[65] Reagan's inauguration provided the first opportunity to test the "designated survivor" program, which would become more detailed over time.[66] This Continuity of Government plan reflected the desire to protect the line of succession as nuclear tensions between the superpowers increased.

In his autobiography *An American Life*, Reagan later recalled the heightened nuclear anxiety in the spring of 1981. The United States was modernizing its nuclear weapons capabilities and sending weapons to its NATO allies so that they could defend themselves against Soviet missiles. It was imperative that the United States best its rival in the intensifying arms race. He concluded doomsday had come: "There didn't seem any end to it, no way out of it." War "would incinerate much of the world and leave what was left of it uninhabitable forever."[67] The president was not only identifying his own nuclear anxiety, he was speaking for the nation as the tensions between the superpowers appeared to be approaching heights similar to those the United States had experienced exactly twenty years earlier.

On top of this apocalyptic threat, power struggles over who was in charge of the foreign policy agenda ensued. White House aides vied to influence the man whose finger was on the nuclear trigger. Secretary of State Alexander Haig had already had a taste of foreign policy decision-making control in the Nixon administration. He asked the president to sign "National Security Decision Directive 1," which would have given him sole control over diplomacy and national security. Reagan refused, and Haig threatened to resign, something he did repetitively throughout his eighteen months in the administration. Reagan placated Haig by issuing a statement that Haig was his "primary adviser" on foreign matters but felt Haig wanted control over foreign affairs beyond even the president's reach.[68]

Against this backdrop, the power struggle over who was advising the president on life and death matters, on March 30, 1981, the nation nearly lost its president. Outside the Washington Hilton where Reagan had just delivered a speech to Construction Trades Council representatives, a twenty-five-year-old man, John W. Hinckley, Jr., fired a handgun at the president, puncturing his left lung.[69] By the time doctors got to Reagan at George Washington University Hospital's emergency room, the lung had collapsed.[70] The assassination attempt was caught on camera. Rallying around the wounded president, the nation was ready to believe television reports asserting that the president was conscious and still capable of conducting business.

Reporters were told that no formal transfer of presidential power was being considered. But officials in the White House Situation Room also were getting most of their information from TV. Vice President George Bush was on Air Force II between Dallas-Fort Worth and Austin, Texas, when the assassination attempt occurred. With Press Secretary James Brady also wounded in the shooting, reporters cornered Acting White House Press Secretary Larry Speakes on his way back to his office from the hospital. Speakes decided to hold an impromptu press conference,[71] but when asked if the military had been put on higher alert readiness, who was running the government, and who would determine whether the vice president would take over as acting president, he failed to answer any of the questions with confidence. He said he was not aware of any increased military readiness, declined to answer the next question about who was heading up the government, and stated he did not know the details on the last. Shortly after arguing with Secretary of Defense Casper Weinberger over who was in charge of the country, Haig, shaking and sweating profusely, burst into the press conference, suddenly live on camera. He said "constitutionally, gentlemen, you have the president, the vice president, and the secretary of state in that order.... As of now, I am in control here, in the White House, pending the return of the vice president and in close touch with him." Haig's assertion stunned not only those watching on television across the country, but the president's advisors huddled in the Situation Room.

Haig had informed the American people he was in charge; but not only was his statement incorrect, his physical appearance revealed a man who was not in control. Watching on television downstairs in the Situation Room, Secretary of the Treasury Donald T. Regan asked Weinberger: "Is he mad?"[72] Military National Command Authority went from the president to the secretary of defense, known as the deputy commander-in-chief. However, because of the 1947 Presidential Succession Act, Haig as secretary of state was fourth in the line of succession after the vice president, speaker of the House, and Senate president pro tempore.[73] White House Counsel Fred Fielding had already told Weinberger that, in fact, Weinberger was correct: The Constitution did not dictate that Haig was now in charge.

Fielding rushed to his office to gather the prewritten letters to Speaker Tip O'Neill and Senate President Strom Thurmond that invocation of Section 4 of the Twenty-Fifth Amendment required, in case the Cabinet agreed that the president was incapacitated and a temporary transition of power was warranted. But when White House aide Richard Darman saw the papers, he removed them from the table and, after conferring by phone with his boss, Chief of Staff James A. Baker III, placed them in his personal safe with the intention of stopping the media from finding out the severity of the president's injury.[74] Baker, an unelected staff member, one without Senate confirmation, made a decision about presidential inability which could have had calamitous results. This unilateral action by the chief of staff circumvented the clear responsibility that the amendment places on the president's Cabinet to make these decisions.

The president, for his part, had managed a convincing act; for those watching on television, he did not appear seriously incapacitated. He walked twenty feet between the limousine and the building (only to collapse inside the front doors) and joked with the first lady and Dr. Joseph Giordanno, the chief of George Washington University Hospital's trauma unit. Significantly, when he spied Baker, Counsel to the President Edwin Meese III, and Deputy Chief of Staff Michael K. Deaver at the hospital he quipped, "Who's minding the store?"[75] The triumvirate wielded authority on the president's behalf; their presence at the hospital meant that a power vacuum existed at the White House.[76]

As Fielding's documents indicated, the Twenty-Fifth Amendment was designed to be invoked during a sudden crisis such as this. Vice President Bush should have assumed the duties of the presidency.[77] But the framers of the amendment, under Section 3, had left the decision to turn over the duties of the office in the president's own hands. Giordano told Baker and Meese that the president would not be able to function immediately because the anesthesia would affect brain function for a few days, potentially up to a week. However, hospital spokesman Dennis O'Leary denied that Reagan was ever in danger of dying and stated his "prognosis for recovery was excellent."[78] In retrospect, it appears as if O'Leary was following orders from the Reagan administration to downplay the seriousness of his condition, with the goal of allowing the president to retain his powers and duties. The president's physician, Daniel Ruge, admitted that a "little pressure" "might have been applied" to make the situation seem slightly rosier than it was in reality.[79]

Those close to and appointed by the president were unwilling to invoke Section 4 of the amendment, let alone risk a possible leak to the public that such measures should be considered. The president's advisors feared that his physical weakness would be splashed across the papers in the days after the assassination attempt, forever imprinted on the minds of the public; and while he might recover from his punctured lung, his presidency would not survive the negative imagery. Darman, for example, thought that if the Twenty-Fifth Amendment was invoked, Reagan would never again be viewed by the public as a completely able president.[80] So, they continued to mislead the public as to the president's condition. The vice president was calling the president's recovery "amazing"[81]; but, in truth, soon after the first surgery, the doctors were considering a second. Historian Gil Troy argues that Reagan's miraculous recovery stood as a "bookend" to Kennedy's assassination, helping to elevate the national mood by lifting some of the "sixties defeatist spirit."[82] But, although an assassin's bullet did not kill the president and, instead, the president's advisors and doctors reassuringly convinced Americans that the president could still do his job, the ever-present fear of nuclear attack had not dissipated. In fact, according to Troy, Americans "worried more than they had in years" about nuclear annihilation.[83] During this period of heightened nuclear anxiety, those around the president colluded to avoid invoking the amendment during a crisis of the type the amendment was clearly designed to be mitigate.

In the Situation Room, Haig and National Security Adviser Richard Allen were also concerned about a nuclear attack and wondered about the status of the nuclear football.[84] Haig told Allen that the vice president had one football, and they hunted for another for themselves, which they found in the White House Military Office.[85] The public was not aware of this panic behind the scenes. *The New York Times* reassured Americans that Lieutenant Colonel Jose Muratti, who was in charge of the briefcase, had traveled in the president's motorcade to the hospital and remained with the president.[86] The statement was true. However, once at the hospital, Muratti had lost control of the president's plastic card with the printed codes. It was taken by the FBI as "evidence."[87]

The White House tried to keep up a business-as-usual appearance, but global tensions remained elevated. During his infamous press briefing,

Haig had also informed reporters that no measures had been taken to raise the military alert after the shooting,[88] but during the briefing, Weinberger received a critical piece of intelligence: he two Soviet submarines that patrolled an area off the east coast of Poland had "multiplied and become four submarines."[89] Though it turned out that the two new submarines were simply relieving the other two, a routine procedure on the last day of the month, Weinberger requested the "fly times." This distance of an adversary's submarines was measured in the amount of time it would take for a nuclear missile to reach Washington.[90] Thus, the request alone was an indication of increased tensions. US government officials also were watching closely as troops massed on the Soviet border ostensibly to invade Poland. In fact, the last question Reagan fielded before being struck by Hinckley's bullet was from *ABC News* Chief White House Correspondent Sam Donaldson, who asked about Poland's status.[91] The Soviets did not invade Poland that spring, but the incident served as a reminder that a presidential inability could occur at any moment amid international crises.

Although Reagan's team continued to convey to the media that Reagan was working for multiple hours daily, this was not the case until at least nineteen days after he was shot.[92] The president remained hospitalized for thirteen days, and even when he returned to the White House residence, it seemed to some of his top aides that, like First Lady Edith Wilson after President Wilson's inability, First Lady Nancy Reagan was controlling and curtailing access to the president. This time, the assassination attempt made the president confront not just his own mortality but consider the continuity of mankind. During this period of inability, the president came to the conclusion that he should do "whatever [he] could in the years God had given [him] to reduce the threat of nuclear war," suggesting that it was "perhaps the reason God had spared him."[93] A week after the assassination attempt, in a response to an earlier letter of Brezhnev's, Reagan felt compelled to warn his Soviet counterpart that the nations were teetering on the edge of nuclear disaster.[94]

Nuclear war continued to be at the forefront of political planning and public debate. On January 16, 1982, in an article entitled the "US Could Survive War in Administration's View," *Los Angeles Times* staff writer Robert Scheer interviewed Deputy Undersecretary of Defense for Strategic and Nuclear Forces Thomas K. "T.K." Jones and observed, "As tension increases between the superpowers… there seems to be an inclination, at least within the administration, to look upon nuclear conflict as something less than a terminal holocaust (or the biblical prediction for Armageddon)."[95] In May 1982, Pentagon correspondent Richard Halloran of *The New York Times* broke a story about a five-year plan based on a "protracted" nuclear war, signed by Weinberger.[96] At the same time that this contentious five-year plan was brought to light, Reagan issued National Security Decision Document 13 (NSDD 13), written to proclaim that US strategic forces must be able to win a protracted nuclear war.

Despite the disclosure of the five-year plan and NSDD 13, in 1991, *CNN* first uncovered a secret presidential directive signed by Reagan that would have circumvented the 1947 Presidential Succession Act and the Twenty-Fifth Amendment in the event of nuclear war.[97] William Arkin, a nuclear weapons scholar featured on the *CNN* segment, said that the Constitution did not allow for the flexibility necessary to ensure that the line of succession would survive nuclear attack. Because of the existence of nuclear weapons, "we're going to have to fudge on the Constitution,"[98] he said. In his 2017 book, *Raven Rock: The Story of the US. Government's Secret Plan to Save Itself—While the Rest of Us Die*, historian and journalist Garrett M. Graff revealed additional information about this COG plan code-named TREETOP, that the National Program Office called the Presidential Successor Support System (PS3).[99] This highly classified program was designed to reestablish the executive branch in the event of the president and vice president's deaths. Under this secret order, Congress was elided from the line of succession in favor of an executive line of succession—almost certainly illegally.[100]

According to the plan, key advisors to the president would run the entire government in Reagan's stead, their fingers on the nuclear trigger. Each team contained a Cabinet secretary and at least one of Reagan's trusted advisors. The Cabinet secretary would be the "new president," but was really a puppet of one of Reagan's men who would be giving the strike orders. Foreign policy expertise was not a requirement of the Cabinet member that was slated to become the new president, but it was one of the distinguishing traits of the advisors on each team. Those chosen based on their judgment for team leader, such as Dick Cheney and Donald Rumsfeld, had already held top positions in the executive branch and had enough experience in national security to carry out the elaborate exercises.[101]

In the event of an attack, the leaders were responsible for moving the new president, along with complicated communications equipment, to undisclosed locations to protect the line of succession. Although the US government had built underground bomb shelters at Mount Weather in the Blue Ridge Mountains of Virginia and near Camp David, no guarantee existed that the president would make it to these shelters in time. Like the shelters for the president, the bomb shelter under the Greenbrier Hotel in the Allegheny Mountains of West Virginia was designed for Congress, but the unidentified individuals who devised Reagan's program decided that if enough members of Congress were killed so that a quorum could not be convened, decision-making would move forward without the legislative branch.[102] After all, the election of a new speaker of the House would likely create rival claims to the presidency.[103]

Without doubt, the highly classified program was both unconstitutional and illegal.[104] No matter how far the elastic clause is stretched, nowhere in the Constitution does it allow the president to establish a process for designating a new president. These Continuity of Operations Planning (COOP) exercises were happening without the knowledge of the other two branches of government as well as out of the view of the public while nuclear anxiety continued to build. In fact, while these secret exercises were underway, tension peaked on June 23, 1982, when the largest anti-war demonstration in American history took place in New York's Central Park. Carrying signs that read "arms are for hugging" and other similar slogans, a million people rallied for nuclear disarmament prior to the opening of the United Nations Special Session on Disarmament.

The public was not alone in its desire to manage nuclear anxiety. Journalists on both sides of the ideological divide, such as the *New York Review of Books*, the *New Republic,* and the *National Review*, published major pieces on nuclear issues in the early 1980s. Television series and movies such as *War Games*, *The Apocalypse Game*, *Threads,* and an episode of NBC's *Lou Grant* dramatized the effects of the nuclear threat. Reagan's Strategic Defense Initiative, announced in March 1983, conjured up images of the popular movie *Star Wars* because it was designed to use laser beams to destroy incoming missiles.[105] The president himself screened the television drama *The Day After* in November 1983, a couple of weeks before one hundred million people viewed it on ABC. Reagan wrote in his diary that the drama, which showed the devastation in the wake of nuclear war on Lawrence, Kansas, was "very effective and left me greatly depressed."[106] The following year, Reagan found Tom Clancy's *The Hunt for Red October*, a novel about the dangers of miscalculation, more enjoyable, calling it "my kind of yarn."[107] Powerful anti-war messages were encapsulated in songs too. The German "99 Red Balloons" by Nena, released in English in 1984, told the story of balloons that were mistaken for enemy aircraft with nuclear payloads that, like Lawrence, turned a city to dust. In "Russians," released in 1985, Sting sang mournfully about Khrushchev's threats and Reagan's promises of protection, and he wondered aloud how to save children from "Oppenheimer's deadly toy." Meanwhile, protests continued across the globe.[108]

Amid this tense atmosphere, just six months into Reagan's second term, on July 13, 1985, the president underwent an operation at Bethesda Hospital to remove polyps from his colon. Although he could have invoked the Twenty-Fifth Amendment, he did not. Vice President Bush was "standing by" in Kennebunkport, Maine. During the surgery, the doctors found that Reagan needed major abdominal surgery to remove two feet of intestine around a polyp that was infected with cancer.[109] General anesthesia was required. Still, White House spokesman Speakes stated that no plans had been made to invoke the Twenty-Fifth Amendment.[110] Reagan informed Congress via identical letters to O'Neill and Thurmond as is required in Section 3 of the Twenty-Fifth Amendment that he would be transferring presidential powers to the vice president. In the letter, however, Reagan specifically stated that he was enforcing a "long-standing agreement" between himself and Vice President Bush; he was not invoking the Twenty-Fifth Amendment: "I do not believe that the drafters of this amendment intended its application to situations such as the instant [sic] one," he added.[111] Bayh later criticized Reagan administration officials, stating they "were acting unconstitutionally when they did not invoke [the Twenty-Fifth] when the president went under anesthesia."[112] Although this continues to be a source of debate for constitutional law scholars, because a letter was sent to the speaker and president pro tem and duties were temporarily transferred to the vice president, the Twenty-Fifth Amendment was invoked de facto if not de jure.

Situations such as this one were exactly what Bayh had in mind when crafting Sects. 3 and 4 of the amendment; but one complication was becoming increasingly clear: presidents do not like to give up power voluntarily.[113] In an interview, Bayh pointed out that Reagan, "absolutely refused to recognize that in a situation where he was going to be *non compos mentis*, somebody else should be running the shop."[114] While

Section 4 of the amendment allows the vice president and a majority of the Cabinet to declare the president incapacitated, both Nixon and Reagan's advisors, aware of dire situations, did not rally the respective vice presidents and Cabinets to do so. Like Edith Wilson, First Lady Nancy Reagan chose to keep her husband's health as private as possible and may have curtailed access to the president. During their administrations, loyal advisors, motivated to retain the status quo in the White House, also had undue influence in the moment as to whether the Twenty-Fifth should be invoked. Therefore, those around the president are more likely to cover up the president's condition, rather than invoke the amendment or encourage the president to do so.

Thus, Vice President George Bush became "acting president" from 11:28 a.m. to 7:22 p.m., but Reagan resumed his presidential duties within eight hours; the White House communications team, as well as the nuclear football, both nearby at all times in case of need.[115] The president remained in the hospital for seven days.[116] Reagan's autobiography later contained his admission that he "signed a letter invoking the Twenty-Fifth Amendment, making George Bush acting president during the time [he] was incapacitated under anesthesia."[117] At the time of the surgery, however, Reagan avoided appearances of invoking the amendment. Bayh concluded the reason Reagan did not invoke the amendment was a "tenacious" desire to retain power and a decision "not to trust" anyone else to wield that power.[118] This is true, but it was more than that. As after the assassination attempt, Reagan and those around him did not want the public, or foreign leaders, to question the physical and mental capabilities of the oldest man chosen for commander-in-chief. This would be a public relations nightmare; once the lid on this line of questioning was opened, it would be hard to close it again for the remainder of his term.

During the first five years of Reagan's presidency, three Soviet leaders had died (all septuagenarians like Reagan),[119] and with a new Soviet premier, Mikhail Gorbachev, in power, American political commentators increasingly called on Moscow and Washington to do more to ease nuclear tensions. In an article that month entitled "Reagan's Ticking Clock," *New York Times* columnist James Reston linked rumors of the potential amelioration of nuclear tensions with Reagan's advanced age, concluding that at age seventy-five, Reagan should ensure that his legacy on disarmament included more than just a "wave and a smile."[120] After years without a summit, Reagan and Gorbachev met in Geneva, Switzerland, in November 1985, and then again on October 11–12, 1986, in

Reykjavik, Iceland, to discuss the reduction of nuclear arms.[121] The ultimate result of this summit meeting was the signing of the Intermediate Range Nuclear Forces Treaty to eliminate all land-based missiles.

The year 1987 commenced with investigations into Iran-Contra by the Tower Commission, and the congressional Iran-Contra hearings began on May 5. The commission examined decisions that had been made by the White House during the president's inability that could have led to the president's impeachment. The joint committee chairman, Senator Daniel Inouye of Hawaii, stated that he believed the president was aware of the funneling of funds to the Contras[122]; but in the end, nothing stuck—his closest aides took the fall.[123] Chief of Staff Don Regan resigned. When Howard Baker replaced Regan, members of the outgoing chief's team told Baker that he should read the Twenty-Fifth Amendment in case he needed to claim the president had been incapacitated when arms deal decisions were made after the president's cancer surgery.[124]

Baker arranged for observations of the president to judge his ability to discharge the duties of his office. These evaluations only convinced Baker that Reagan was mentally fit. Therefore, he did not recommend that the vice president and Cabinet invoke the Twenty-Fifth Amendment. Later it would become known that Reagan may have been suffering from an inability; it is possible that he was in the early stages of Alzheimer's disease, though it remains unclear whether it affected his mental acuity while he was in office, or his memory with respect to Iran-Contra.[125]

Fielding suggested that during these periods of presidential inability the Cabinet had avoided the use of the Twenty-Fifth Amendment. Fielding related his experiences with the Twenty-Fifth Amendment during Reagan's presidency to the Miller Center Commission on Presidential Disability and the Twenty-Fifth Amendment Commission established by the White Burkett Miller Center of Public Affairs at the University of Virginia in 1985. The Commission was co-chaired by former US Attorney General Brownell and Bayh and included health and legal experts. Fielding made the Commission aware of the existence of an emergency book that he drafted after Cabinet members "eyes glazed over"[126] when he mentioned the need to invoke the Twenty-Fifth Amendment during Reagan's surgery after the assassination attempt. The book contains potential scenarios in which the amendment might need to be used and has been handed down to future administrations.[127] After six sessions, the Commission issued a final report of its findings in 1988, concluding that America "must be better prepared to cope with the frailties of man in this nuclear age; the national interest demands it; the Twenty-Fifth Amendment can help."[128] Among the many recommendations the Commission put forth was that Americans, as well as presidential candidates, should familiarize themselves with the amendment.

Because Section 4 of the Twenty-Fifth Amendment is vague, to provide direction to Congress, the Miller Commission also took a close look at the players involved in determining inability, identifying two that the framers of the amendment had not: the first lady and the White House physician. The commission recommended consultations with the president's partner on ability-related matters, a hitherto-mentioned suggestion.[129] The group then argued that the White House physician fulfills two roles. The first was the "traditional role" of a confidential doctor-patient relationship, one in which the president could confide his medical concerns to a physician and receive advice that would not be made known to others. The second role, the commission suggested, was that the White House physician be a representative "in strictly nonpolitical terms" of the interests of the nation.

In 1993, historian Arthur S. Link and others convened another study group to examine the potentially conflicting roles of the White House physician.[130] The group, called the Working Group on Presidential Disability, which included former president Jimmy Carter, recommended that not only should a formal obligation be put in place so that the facts are released to Congress, but also the White House physician should be overseen on final decisions regarding disability by an official consultation group. Carter's conclusion, that the president's subordinates—including the White House physician who is below the president in the military chain of command—are inclined to "hide from the public the extent of any inabilities from which the president might suffer," appears to be correct.[131]

In between these study group meetings focused on medical decisions, doctors encountered a cut-and-dried situation and almost recommended that President George H.W. Bush turn over the powers and duties of the presidency under Section 3. On May 4, 1991, Bush was rushed to Bethesda Naval Medical Center. His rapid heartbeat after a run led to a diagnosis of atrial fibrillation related to thyroid disease. Doctors thought that they might need to put the president under general anesthesia to give his heart an electrical jolt. Bush's staff drew up the necessary paperwork for Vice President Dan Quayle to become acting president, but, in the end, medication worked, anesthetization was not necessary, and Section 3 invocation was avoided.[132]

President George H.W. Bush's predecessor, William Jefferson Clinton, also avoided invoking Section 3. On March 14, 1997, after stumbling on stairs and tearing the quadriceps tendon in his right knee, he underwent emergency two-hour knee surgery. But because he did not need general anesthesia, no temporary transfer of presidential powers occurred. In 1998, the possibility of a permanent transfer occurred when Clinton became the first president to be impeached since Andrew Johnson in 1868. On October 8, the House approved perjury and obstruction of justice articles, but the Senate did not remove him from office. Had Clinton been removed, Vice President Al Gore would have assumed the powers and duties of the presidency as per Section 1 of the Twenty-Fifth Amendment.

Although the Twenty-Fifth Amendment was not invoked during the 1990s, its use was dramatized in cultural portrayals throughout the decade, and these often intersected with fears of terrorists detonating nuclear bombs or nuclear anxiety more generally. In fact, the 1990s can be regarded as the golden age of nuclear war themes in popular culture, representing the zeitgeist of the decade. The 1990 TV movie *By the Dawn's Early Light* begins after an accidental missile launch and examines decisions leading to nuclear war; the 1994 movie *The Enemy Within*, a remake of the 1964 screenplay *Seven Days in May*, tells the tale of a president with a heart condition who pursues a nuclear disarmament treaty with the Soviet Union, the military threatens a coup, and the coup leads to a potential Soviet first strike; the 1995 thriller *Crimson Tide* portrays a US nuclear submarine crew unsure whether nuclear launch orders are legitimate; and the 1997 thriller *The Peacemaker* focus on the fragile security around nuclear weapons. The blockbuster movie *Air Force One* was released the same year as *The Peacemaker*. The terrorist hijacking of Air Force One prompts the defense secretary to urge a reluctant vice president to invoke Section 4. The president emerges heroically after Air Force One suffers severe damage by an F-15 when the pilot sacrifices himself to intercept a missile.

Some writers made invocation of more than one section of the Twenty-Fifth Amendment central to their plots. Notably, *Godfather* author Mario Puzo's *The Fourth K* combines Section 1 and 4 actions with the detonation of a nuclear bomb. The book spent a number of weeks on *The New York Times Best Seller List* when it was published in 1990, and an additional three weeks on the paperback list at the end of 1991.[133] In this tale, a fictitious nephew of President John F. Kennedy becomes president and, after terrorists murder his daughter, his grief turns to increasing authoritarianism and his disproportionate response causes a majority of the Cabinet to declare him incapacitated. The vice president hesitates to support a Section 4 action because of fears she will be considered a usurper, and the Section 4 action leads Congress to "impeach" the president—the novel mistakenly conflates the Twenty-Fifth Amendment with impeachment. Section 1 also implicitly, but not explicitly, features in the conclusion, when Kennedy is assassinated during his second inauguration and the vice president assumes the presidency. Puzo's everything-but-the-kitchen-sink approach includes the shadow of Kennedy's assassination, terrorists, an atomic bomb, and the invocation of the Twenty-Fifth Amendment, not once, but twice.[134] A *New York Times* review correctly posits that Puzo should be given "an A for touching on many timely issues" (but an "F for writing a garish comic book without pictures").[135] The books and movies of the 1990s reflect the ongoing anxieties surrounding the potential for nuclear apocalypse and the desire for clear leadership at the helm.

* * *

Concern over nuclear attacks and succession and inability planning continued during George W. Bush's administration. This subject was of such particular interest to Vice President Cheney, who had been intimately involved in Reagan's secret directive, that just sixty-seven days into Bush's presidency, on March 28, 2001, Cheney wrote a "pending" resignation letter to be used if a heart attack left him incapacitated.[136] The Twenty-Fifth Amendment does not provide for vice presidential inability, but by September, the letter looked increasingly necessary. On the morning of September 11, 2001, Cheney's cardiologist Jonathan Reiner had received the results of a blood test showing his potassium levels were dangerously high, a potentially fatal condition called hyperkalemia.[137] Then came the terrorist attacks of September 11, 2001.[138] Planes hit the World Trade Center in New York. When word that one hijacked plane was headed to the White House (it eventually struck the Pentagon), the Secret Service for the first time implemented the procedures in place to protect the presidential line of succession. Cheney was taken to a bunker under the White House. Next in line of succession,

House Speaker Dennis Hastert was taken to Andrews Air Force Base. In line after the Speaker, the president pro tempore of the Senate, Robert Byrd, went home, refusing to be moved to a secure location.[139]

The president's security was of paramount importance. Bush was taken to Air Force One and US air space was closed. He eventually recorded a public address from Barksdale Air Force Base in Louisiana before returning to the White House, though not before he was criticized by the media and the public for failing to evoke an image of steadiness and strong leadership in the midst of the crisis.[140] When the president returned, Cheney was transferred to Camp David to ensure that they were not in the same location should more attacks occur. Secretary of Defense Donald Rumsfeld raised the nation's Defense Condition level from DEFCON IV to DEFCON III. National Security Advisor Condoleezza Rice made a call to Russian President Vladimir Putin advising him of this fact; Putin agreed to halt all military exercises in light of the attacks. As Cheney wrote in his memoir *In My Time*, "We had all lived through the Cold War and knew the possibility of a mistaken nuclear launch had to be kept in mind."[141] The friction between the importance of preserving the presidential line of succession and the need to visibly convey to the world the image that a competent president was in full command of the country during an attack was evident.

Later in his presidency, Bush formally give up his powers, albeit briefly, under the Twenty-Fifth Amendment.[142] Knowing that unlike the era of President Cleveland, it would be difficult to shield the public from the knowledge that he needed general anesthesia, he invoked the amendment twice for colonoscopies on June 29, 2002, and again on July 21, 2007.[143] In both cases, he followed Section 3 of the amendment, submitting letters to the House speaker and Senate president pro tem. Cheney, acting president for about two hours each time, spent his second shift as acting president not in DC, but in Maryland. The public was not informed as to the exact time the procedure was taking place and Cheney was temporarily in power. In both circumstances, Bush took back presidential powers the same day, again underscoring the fact that presidents do not like to give up power. Bush sought to portray an image of excellent health and would not relinquish presidential powers and duties short of being rendered completely unconscious by anesthesia.[144] Prior to the events of September 11, 2001, presidents and those close to the president avoided invoking the Twenty-Fifth Amendment even during times when the president was unconscious during surgery and the world knew the exact time an absence at the helm would occur.

The September 11 terrorist attacks had brought fears of presidential discontinuity and nuclear anxiety to the fore. After the attacks, nuclear anxiety drove activity on succession planning within the executive branch. In November 2001, *The New York Times* assessed the threat. A team of reporters interviewed officials, such as John Bolton, the State Department's top arms control official, who stated he and others were "significantly more concerned" than ever about the possibility of a nuclear attack.[145] The article went on to say that Osama bin Laden's Al Qaeda group, which had carried out the attacks, had tried unsuccessfully to purchase nuclear materials in the mid-1990s. This attempt was seen as a clear indication of Al Qaeda's intentions. Separately, Vice President Dick Cheney confirmed that "even a 1 percent chance of terrorists gaining weapons of mass destruction now had to be treated as a certainty."[146] *The New York Times* authors reminded their readers that "nuclear terrorism may represent the darkest fear of all, simply because of the degree of destruction and huge number of casualties that are possible."[147]

It was not only the media that dwelled on the possibility of nuclear terrorism and the devastation it could bring; popular television series such as *The West Wing* and *24* wove this theme together with dramatic, and often inaccurate, portrayals of the Twenty-Fifth Amendment. The American political drama *The West Wing* got the amendment wrong at the beginning of season 2.[148] Democratic President Josiah "Jed" Bartlet, played by award-winning actor Martin Sheen, was rushed to the hospital following a shooting and a staffer recommends that the vice president issue military orders in Bartlet's stead. Bartlet's national security advisor states that since the president did not sign a letter turning over the powers of the presidency in advance of his inability, nothing could be done. Section 4, designed for crisis such as this, was elided completely. However, after the September 11 attacks, the show took a short, three-week hiatus before airing an episode entitled "Isaac & Ismael" focused on America's response to terrorism. And throughout the series, the show touches on Iranian and North Korean nuclear ambitions. The finale of season 4 depicts Bartlet invoking Section 3 because he is distracted by a personal concern, the kidnapping of his daughter. Because no vice president exists at the time, Republican Speaker Glen Allen Walken assumes the presidency as per the dictates of the 1947 Presidential Succession Act. The presidency switches parties, highlighting a concern with the line of succession that remains unresolved in real life. In season 5, Bartlet resumes power and Section 2 is invoked to nominate a new vice president. An episode later in that season begins with a nuclear bomb explosion, and after Russia, China, and North Korea are ruled out, it is determined that Iran detonated the bomb. *The West Wing* also explored America's relationship with nuclear energy via an accident at a fabricated San Andreo Nuclear Generating Station in California in an episode named "Duck and Cover" during season 7. The show won 26 Primetime Emmys, several Screen Actors Guild Awards, two Golden Globes, two Peabody Awards, and numerous other accolades leading *TV Guide*, *Rolling Stone*, and other publications to call it one of the best TV shows of all time.[149]

The political thriller *24*, starring Kiefer Sutherland as counterterrorist agent Jack Bauer, also won numerous Emmys, two Golden Globes, and many other awards further underscoring viewers' fascination with the possibility of a nuclear attack by an unknown agent and the decapitation of the head of state when split-second reactions would be crucial.[150] It was also the first show to call attention to Section 4.[151] In season 2, after Bauer saves the country from a terrorist attack, the president orders a retaliatory strike, only to cancel it when Bauer informs him that a recording he based his decision on was a fake. The vice president and Cabinet decide that the president is paralyzed by indecision, invoke Section 4, and the vice president, now acting president, orders the strike. At the last moment, Bauer presents evidence convincing the acting president to call the strike off, and he and the Cabinet "annul" their earlier action restoring the president to power. In reality, the Twenty-Fifth Amendment does not have an annulment mechanism. In season 4, the president is seriously injured, and the vice president and Cabinet properly invoke Section 4, the sole time this happens in *24*. In season 6, the president is again gravely wounded, this time by a bomb, but despite the vice president taking the reins of power, he is still referred to as "vice president," and no mention of the Twenty-Fifth is made at this point. The president then awakes from his coma to call off a nuclear attack that the vice president ordered, but Section 4 does not work this way. If the president had relinquished power under Section 3, he could have taken it back, but the bomb had rendered him unconscious. The vice president argues that the president is unable to defend the country because he will not order the nuclear strike. The president retorts that it is nothing more than a policy disagreement. The vote to invoke the amendment results in a tie that goes to the Supreme Court; however, Section 4 requires a majority so in real life the decision would not have been left to the judicial branch. No provision exists in the amendment providing for judicial review, and if a lawsuit were brought related to uses of the amendment, it is likely a court would dismiss it. The Supreme Court case ends up being withdrawn, but the president relapses and Section 4 is invoked by order of the vice president, rather than by a vote as portrayed correctly in season 4.[152] With the exception of the season 4 dramatization, the Twenty-Fifth Amendment's mechanisms were not accurately displayed on television; what these shows did get right was the critical nature of the decisions, the tense timing in which they would need to be made, the very real possibility that they would coincide with the need for a response to terrorist activity, and how deeply this fear would resonate with the viewing audience.

The heightened anxiety also led several foundations to join together to form a Continuity of Government Commission to study succession and disability issues. Former presidents Ford and Carter were honorary chairs.[153] The commission's report began with a potential crisis scenario—an attack on Washington during the State of the Union address—to illustrate the problems they found with the line of succession. A salient problem the commission identified was that those in line of succession are based in Washington, DC. An attack with a nuclear weapon would potentially wipe out a large geographical radius, encompassing all the Washington metro area, if not the Eastern Seaboard. Despite the influence of the commission's members and the panel's bipartisan nature, none of the recommendations in the commission's reports of 2003 and 2009 were implemented. Congressmembers have continued to leave decisions to temporarily give up presidential powers during instances of inability to the president and the vice president and Cabinet, leaving the nation vulnerable to danger.

Some congressmembers, such as Republican Senator Trent Lott of Mississippi, felt strongly that succession law needed to be altered to deal with these new problems. Several bills were introduced in the 108th Congress proposing major changes in succession law (such as H.R. 2749, S. 2073 and S. Res. 419). On September 16, 2003, the Senate Committees on the Judiciary and Rules and Administration held a joint hearing to debate the merits of the succession system. The committee hearing commenced with Lott's statement that the nation had been living under the threat of a nuclear attack since 1947, and that responsible senators must prepare for "a dirty bomb or a nuclear bomb or some other travesty that could occur."[154] Lott's co-chair, Republican Senator John Cornyn of Texas, also believed in the need for revisions to the amendment. Cornyn reiterated the Continuity of Government Commission's concern that most individuals in the line of succession resided in Washington, and, therefore, could all be killed at the same time in the event of a nuclear attack. During House hearings on October 6, 2004, many of the same questions were debated.[155] Bayh was invited back to testify. He explained that the framers of the amendment envisioned the following nuclear scenario as a reason why an amendment was needed in the 1960s: "The president's plane goes down on a deserted island, there's no communication, you can't find him, and missiles are being launched."[156] Later, Bayh was questioned in a *Fordham Law Review* interview about rumors of a classified plan that involved a secret government. He was asked: "Even if a law providing for the president to set up a shadow government was passed on to [future administrations]... what has Congress' role been in approving this plan? What is their knowledge of this plan?" Bayh responded, "The question is: what is the plan?"[157] The lack of transparency around succession planning for a nuclear attack was troubling. And yet it was also a feature of nuclear preparedness in succession planning.

Bayh's pointed answer underscoring the fact that presidents have kept the public in the dark about succession planning highlights the fact that modern presidents and their advisors have made unchecked decisions regarding inability and succession, in large part to avoid even the temporary transfer of presidential power. Public opinion concerns, and the personal ambitions of those close to the president, have stymied the use of Sects. 3 and 4 of the Twenty-Fifth Amendment. Even with the advice of experts, Congress has not been able to address the new perils created, in part, by the framers' intention of leaving the surrendering and retaking of executive power in the hands of the president himself. Pressure stemming from the fear of nuclear attack led administrations to cling to the appearance of control under any circumstances, especially during chaotic moments when presidents wanted to convey to the public the appearance that order and stability was emanating from the White House. Thus, the nation remains at risk of a contested, or otherwise unsuccessful, sudden transition of presidential power in the event of a nuclear attack. Examining cases of inability through the magnifying glass of nuclear anxiety identifies circumstances in which the amendment is less likely to be invoked. While some historical accounts have studied the effect of political machinations on the implementation of the Twenty-Fifth Amendment, these accounts have not considered the cultural climate. A greater appreciation of the fact that the Constitution, a timeless instrument, is subject to both the political and cultural mood is warranted. Stopping up gaps in the amendment that could lead to peril—such as what constitutes inability and who determines whether the president is incapacitated, the dual incapacity of the president and vice president, and the fact that the presidency might switch parties if the second in line becomes acting president and steers the country in a different direction—is necessary.

Notes

1. *Hearing Before the Subcommittee on Constitutional Amendments of the Committee on the Judiciary*, SJ Res 26, Proposing Modification of the Twenty-Fifth Amendment of the Constitution of the United States, 89th Cong., 1st sess., February 25, 26, and March 11, 1975. Printed for the use of the Committee on the Judiciary. (Washington: US Government Printing Office, 1976). See also: Chapter 3.
2. Another 1964 film, *Fail-Safe*, also dealt with the loss of control over the bomb, leading to catastrophic results. These films are just two of the myriad representations of fear around the bomb prevalent in politics and pop culture since the bomb's use in 1945. For a discussion of representations of nuclear anxiety in politics and culture, see Chapter 3.
3. For a study on the history of an image, see: David Greenberg, *Nixon's Shadow: The History of an Image* (New York: W.W. Norton & Company, 2003).
4. William Burr and Jeffrey Kimball, eds. "Nixon's Nuclear Ploy: The Vietnam Negotiations and the Joint Chiefs of Staff Readiness Test, October 1969," *National Security Archive*. Book No. 81. December 23, 2002. https://nsarchive2.gwu.edu/NSAEBB/NSAEBB81/index2.htm.
5. Garrett M. Graff, "The Madman and the Bomb," *Politico Magazine*, August 11, 2017. https://www.politico.com/magazine/story/2017/08/11/donald-trump-nuclear-weapons-richard-nixon-215478/.
6. Arnold A. Hutschnecker, "The Mental Health of Our Leaders," *Look*, July 15, 1969, 51–54. As quoted in Greenberg, *Nixon's Shadow*, 244.

7. For a discussion of this episode, see: Greenberg, *Nixon's Shadow*, 232–234. See also: Joe Eszterhas and Michael Roberts, *Thirteen Seconds: Confrontation at Kent State* (Cleveland: Gray and Company, 1970). James A. Michener, *Kent State: What Happened and Why* (New York: Fawcett Crest, 1971). Howard Means, *67 Shots: Kent State and the End of American Innocence* (Boston: Da Capo Press, 2016). Rick Perlstein, *Nixonland: The Rise of a President and the Fracturing of America* (New York: Scribner, 2008). William Safire, *Before the Fall: An Inside View of the Pre-Watergate White House* (Garden City, NY: Doubleday, 1975), 202.
8. Nixon's erratic behavior during the Lincoln Memorial visit had his closest aides wondering if he was mentally unstable. Nixon's Chief of Staff H. R. Haldeman wrote in his diary hours after the Lincoln Memorial visit, "I am concerned about his condition," and noted that Nixon's behavior that morning constituted "the weirdest day so far." Tom McNichol, "I Am Not a Kook: Richard Nixon's Bizarre Visit to the Lincoln Memorial" *The Atlantic* (November 14, 2011). https://www.theatlantic.com/politics/archive/2011/11/i-am-not-a-kook-richard-nixons-bizarre-visit-to-the-lincoln-memorial/248443/.
9. But it is important to note that medicine the president might take to mitigate the symptoms of a physical illness, such as some of Kennedy's treatments for his back, can cause mental incapacitation or severe disorientation. According to presidential historian Robert Dallek who was given unique access to JFK's prescription records: "In particular during times of stress, such as the Bay of Pigs fiasco, in April of 1961, and the Cuban Missile Crisis, in October of 1962—Kennedy was taking an extraordinary variety of medications: steroids for his Addison's disease; painkillers for his back; anti-spasmodics for his colitis; antibiotics for urinary-tract infections; antihistamines for allergies; and, on at least one occasion, an anti-psychotic (though only for two days) for a severe mood change that Jackie Kennedy believed had been brought on by the antihistamines." Robert Dallek, "The Medical Ordeals of JFK," *The Atlantic*, December 2002. http://www.theatlantic.com/magazine/archive/2002/12/the-medical-ordeals-of-jfk/305572/.

10. On October 10, staff writers Carl Bernstein and Bob Woodward of The Washington Post revealed "spying and sabotage" conducted on behalf of President Nixon's reelection, directed by officials of the White House and the Committee for the Re-Election of the President. Despite these disconcerting revelations, Nixon won reelection in November 1972. Carl Bernstein and Bob Woodward, "FBI Finds Nixon Aides Sabotaged Democrats," *The Washington Post*, Times Herald (1959–1973), Washington, DC, 1972.
11. See Journalist Elizabeth Drew's diary of this period, *Washington Journal: Events of 1973–1974*, which provides a window into the anxiety of the nation surrounding Nixon's potential inability. Elizabeth Drew, *Washington Journal: The Events of 1973–1974* (New York: Random House, 1975).
12. The vice president was accused of bribery, conspiracy, and tax evasion. Agnew pleaded "no contest" to a tax evasion count and resigned.
13. The Nuclear Proliferation International History Project of the Woodrow Wilson International Center for Scholars argues that Israel considered using an atomic bomb in the 1967 war, which makes it plausible that Israel also considered using this weapon in the later war. Aron Heller, "US Think Tank: Israel had Plans to Use Atomic Bomb in 1967," *Associated Press* (June 5, 2017). The Wilson Center argued that "according to some historical accounts, Israel came very close to deploying nuclear weapons during the Yom Kippur War. Avner Cohen, "Nuclear Weapons: Lessons from the Yom Kippur War," (Wilson Center, October 3, 2013). https://www.wilsoncenter.org/article/nuclear-weapons-lesson-the-yom-kippur-war. On the Yom Kippur War, see also: Simon Dunstan, *The Yom Kippur War: The Arab–Israeli War of 1973* (Oxford: Osprey Publishing, 2007). Mohamed Abdel Ghani El-Gamasy, *The October War: Memoirs of Field Marshal El Gamasy* (Cairo: The American University in Cairo Press, 1993). Chaim Herzog, *The Arab–Israeli Wars: War and Peace in the Middle East from the 1948 War of Independence to the Present* (London: Arms and Armour Press, Lionel Leventhal Limited, 1982). William B. Quandt, *Peace Process: American Diplomacy and the Arab–Israeli Conflict Since 1967* (Berkeley: University of California Press, 2005). Abraham Rabinovich, *The Yom Kippur War: The Epic*

Encounter That Transformed the Middle East (New York: Shocken Books, 2005). Anwar el Sadat, *In Search of Identity: An Autobiography* (New York: Harper & Row, 1978). Asaf Siniver, *The Yom Kippur War: Politics, Legacy, Diplomacy* (Oxford: Oxford University Press, 2013). Kenneth Stein; *Heroic Diplomacy: Sadat, Kissinger, Carter, Begin, and the Quest for Arab–Israeli Peace* (New York: Routledge, 1999).
14. Tim Weiner, *One Man Against the World: The Tragedy of Richard Nixon* (New York: Henry Holt and Company, 2015).
15. Robert Dallek, *Nixon and Kissinger: Partners in Power* (New York: HarperCollins Publishers, 2007), 530.
16. Bob Woodward and Carl Bernstein, *The Final Days* (New York: Simon and Schuster, 1976), 323–24.
17. Weiner, *One Man Against the World: The Tragedy of Richard Nixon*.
18. Often these requests went through the US Ambassador to Israel, former Senator Kenneth Keating, who, in 1962, had cosponsored the "enabling" amendment, S.J. Res. 35. Keating and Meir: Henry Kissinger, *Crisis: The Anatomy of Two Major Foreign Policy Crises* (New York: Simon & Schuster, 2003), 14. Enabling amendment: see Chapter 4.
19. Kissinger, *Crisis: The Anatomy of Two Major Foreign Policy Crises*, 350.
20. The Soviets stood down and the cease-fire days later included an agreement for increased United Nations involvement. Dallek, *Nixon and Kissinger: Partners in Power*, 520–533.
21. Quandt, *Peace Process: American Diplomacy and the Arab–Israeli Conflict since 1967*, 104.
22. The US' goal was to dissuade the Soviets from sending a ground force to Egypt. See "Memorandum of Conversation, Henry Kissinger, 7,320,337," *National Security Archives*, October 22, 1973. http://nsarchive.gwu.edu/NSAEBB/NSAEBB98/octwar-56.pdf.
23. Dallek, *Nixon and Kissinger: Partners in Power*, 526.
24. The White House was focused on convincing the public of the benefits of keeping Nixon at the helm. As long as Kissinger would go along with the story that the president was making the foreign policy decisions, the chief of staff had free rein. For an account of the conversation in which Nixon tells Kissinger to

make the situation appear as if the president was consulted in Kissinger's decision-making on Yom Kippur, see: Kissinger, *Crisis: The Anatomy of Two Major Foreign Policy Crises*.
25. If Nixon was determined to be incapacitated, House Speaker Carl Albert, a Democrat, would have assumed presidential responsibilities. The possibility that the presidency would switch parties was a concern of those critical of the amendment who preferred that Congress be elided from the line of succession as in the 1886 law.
26. Elizabeth Drew points out that "dawn" came with disturbing connotations: Nixon had confronted the students at the Lincoln Memorial at dawn as well. Elizabeth Drew, *Washington Journal*, 40.
27. Recess had been scheduled from October 12–29, 1973.
28. John D. Feerick, *The Twenty-Fifth Amendment: Its Complete History and Earliest Applications* (Fordham University Press, 1976), 129–153. See also: Lester A. Sobel, *Presidential Succession: Ford, Rockefeller, and the Twenty-Fifth Amendment* (New York, NY: Facts on File, Inc., 1975), 41. Jules, Witcover, *Crapshoot: Rolling the Dice on the Vice Presidency* (New York: Crown Publishers, 1992), 266–268.
29. Drew, *Washington Journal*, 134.
30. *Hearing Before the Committee on Rules and Administration*, United States Senate, The Nomination of Gerald R. Ford of Michigan to be Vice President of the United States, 93rd Cong., 1st sess., November 1, 5, 7, 14, 1973, (Washington: US Government Printing Office, 1973), 333.
31. *Hearing Before the Committee on Rules and Administration*, 330.
32. *Hearing Before the Committee on Rules and Administration*, 165.
33. Only Democratic Senators Thomas Eagleton of Missouri, William Hathaway of Maine, and Gaylord Nelson of Wisconsin voted against his nomination. Hathaway argued that because of the Watergate scandal, Nixon was not fit to choose a vice president, but most senators focused on whether the nominee was fit for the position.
34. *Hearings Before the Committee on the Judiciary*, House of Representatives, on Nomination of Gerald R. Ford to be the Vice President of the United States, 93rd Cong., 1st sess., November 15, 16, 19, 20, 21, 26, 1973, Serial No. 16 (Washington, DC, US Government Printing Office, 1973), 180.

35. Senator Bayh, who was the leadoff witness in the House hearings, later recalled that "with Republicans it was a knock-down, drag out fight over [implementing] the Twenty-Fifth Amendment." Birch Bayh, Interview with Author, November 11, 2014.
36. House Speaker Carl Albert, next in line of succession to the presidency until Ford was officially sworn in, announced Ford's resignation as the US representative of Michigan's Fifth Congressional District. Chief Justice Warren E. Burger performed the swearing in.
37. Bob Woodward and Carl Bernstein. *The Final Days* (New York: Simon & Schuster, 1976), 215.
38. Garrett M. Graff, "The Madman and the Bomb," *Politico Magazine*, August 11, 2017. https://www.politico.com/magazine/story/2017/08/11/donald-trump-nuclear-weapons-richard-nixon-215478/.
39. William V. Shannon, "Seven Days in August," *The New York Times*. September 1, 1974. https://www.nytimes.com/1974/09/01/archives/seven-days-in-august.html. Note that the title, "Seven Days in August," is a play on the book and movie "Seven Days in May." Other newspapers across the country made mentions of "speculation about the president's health" at this time. See for example "Secret Planning of Ford's Succession," *SF Chronicle*. August 26, 1974.
40. Shannon, "Seven Days in August." See also Bernard, Gwertzman. "Pentagon Kept Tight Rein in Last Days of Nixon Rule: Schlesinger and the Joint Chiefs Acted to Insure White House Gave Military Units No Unauthorized Orders," *The New York Times*, August 24, 1974.
41. *Huff Post* contributor Stanley Kutler, refutes this, arguing that Schlesinger's made these claims, but they are not backed up by statements from other public officials or a paper trail. See Stanley, Kutler, "The Imaginings of James R. Schlesinger," *Huff Post*. August 1. 2014. https://www.huffpost.com/entry/the-imaginings-of-james-r_b_5066130.
42. Gwertzman, Bernard. "Pentagon Kept Tight Rein in Last Days of Nixon Rule: Schlesinger and the Joint Chiefs Acted to Insure White House Gave Military Units No Unauthorized Orders," *The New York Times*, August 24, 1974.

43. Sobel, *Presidential Succession: Ford, Rockefeller, and the Twenty-Fifth Amendment*, 189.
44. David Gergen drafted the letter and gives his account in *Eyewitness to Power: The Essence of Leadership, Nixon to Clinton*. When Ford was sworn in as President by Chief Justice Warren Burger a half hour later, he acknowledged that he had only been elected by the people of Michigan's 5th congressional district. Ford said he was "acutely aware that you have not elected me as your president by your ballots, and so I ask you to confirm me as your president with your prayers." Letter drafting: David Gergen, *Eyewitness to Power: The Essence of Leadership, Nixon to Clinton* (New York: Simon & Schuster, 2000), 74–75. Ford speech: "Gerald R. Ford's Remarks upon Taking the Oath of Office as President," Gerald R. Ford Library and Museum. https://www.fordlibrarymuseum.gov/library/speeches/740001.asp.
45. Though the nomination did not boost Ford's overall popularity or help his presidency, he had several reasons for choosing Rockefeller. Many potential nominees within the Republican Party were associated with Nixon, but Rockefeller was not. In fact, Rockefeller was a better-known figure than Ford himself. However, Ford removed Rockefeller from the ticket in 1976.
46. Questions were split into groups such as "Nelson Rockefeller as Family Member," and "Nelson Rockefeller as Governor, Politician, and Executive."
47. Hearings Before the Committee on the Judiciary, House of Representatives, on the Nomination of Nelson A. Rockefeller to be Vice President of the United States, 93rd Cong., 2nd sess., November 21, 22, 25, 26, 27; December 2, 3, 4, 5, 1974, Serial No. 45 (US Government Printing Office, 1974), 1093.
48. This February 1963 document was entitled "Statement from the Governor Concerning the Current Disarray within the Atlantic Alliance." The confirmation hearings lasted more than two months. "*Hearings Before the Committee on the Judiciary*, House of Representatives, on the Nomination of Nelson A. Rockefeller to be Vice President of the United States, 93rd Cong., 2nd sess., November 21, 22, 25, 26, 27; December 2, 3, 4, 5, 1974, Serial No. 45 (US Government Printing Office, 1974), 1387.
49. The framers had considered vacancies in both offices during one administration highly unlikely. In 1791, Congressman Aedanus

Burke of South Carolina, stated that—having consulted with "a gentleman skilled in the doctrine of chances,"—the probability of such an event could occur once every 840 years. Democratic Senator Theodore Francis Green of Rhode Island repeated this assertion of Burke's in 1945 and added it as an "Extension of Remarks" in the Hearing in February 1975. *Congressional Record of the United States of America. Proceedings and Debates of the 79th Congress*. First Session. Appendix. Volume 91 - Part 12. June 11, 1945, to October 11, 1945. Pages A2767 to A4294. United States Government Printing Office, Washington, 1945. Page A3640. *Hearing Before the Subcommittee on Constitutional Amendments of the Committee on the Judiciary*, SJ Res. 26, Proposing Modification of the Twenty-Fifth Amendment of the Constitution of the United States. Printed for the use of the Committee on the Judiciary, 94th Cong., 1st sess., February 25, 26, and March 11, 1975. (Washington: US Government Printing Office, 1976). For an in-depth study of how chance has shaped American culture, see T.J. Jackson Lears, *Something for Nothing: Luck in America* (New York: Viking Press, 2003).
50. "In this way, whatever party mandate which attaches at the proceeding presidential election would be maintained until the people render their new judgment," Hathaway argued. S. 2678 did not advance out of the Senate Committee on Rules and Administration. *Hearing Before the Subcommittee on Constitutional Amendments of the Committee on the Judiciary*, SJ Res. 26, Proposing Modification of the Twenty-Fifth Amendment of the Constitution of the United States. Printed for the use of the Committee on the Judiciary, 94th Cong., 1st sess., February 25, 26, and March 11, 1975. Printed for the use of the Committee on the Judiciary. US Government Printing Office. (Washington: US Government Printing Office, 1976). 29–30.
51. *Hearing Before the Subcommittee on Constitutional Amendments of the Committee on the Judiciary*, SJ Res. 26, Proposing Modification of the Twenty-Fifth Amendment of the Constitution of the United States. Printed for the use of the Committee on the Judiciary, 94th Cong., 1st sess., February 25, 26, and March 11, 1975. Printed for the use of the Committee on the Judiciary.

US Government Printing Office. (Washington: US Government Printing Office, 1976), 29–30. https://www.congress.gov/bill/94th-congress/senate-joint-resolution/26?q=%7B%22search%22%3A%5B%22S.J.+26%22%5D%7D&resultIndex=21.
52. *Hearing Before the Subcommittee on Constitutional Amendments of the Committee on the Judiciary.*
53. See Chapter 4.
54. The bill stated that in such cases, "there shall be a special election for the offices of president and vice president, and the Twenty-Fifth Amendment shall not apply to the vacancy in the office of the vice president caused by such individual becoming president." *Hearing Before the Subcommittee on Constitutional Amendments of the Committee on the Judiciary*, SJ Res. 26, Proposing Modification of the Twenty-Fifth Amendment of the Constitution of the United States. Printed for the use of the Committee on the Judiciary, 94th Cong., 1st sess., February 25, 26, and March 11, 1975. Printed for the use of the Committee on the Judiciary. US Government Printing Office. (Washington: US Government Printing Office, 1976). 29–30.
55. *Hearing Before the Subcommittee on Constitutional Amendments of the Committee on the Judiciary.*
56. Congressmembers determined the amendment worked so well in practice that some bills introduced in the wake of the sudden executive transitions called for an expansion of the amendment (such as similar provisions for times when the president was abroad).
57. Paul Boyer, *By the Bomb's Early Light: American Thought and Culture at the Dawn of the Atomic Age* (Chapel Hill, NC: The University of North Carolina Press, 1985), 360.
58. Strategic Arms Limitation Talks/Treaty (SALT) I and II. The Department of State. Office of the Historian, Department of State, https://history.state.gov/milestones/1969-1976/salt.
59. Carter asked Congress not to consider the treaty on January 3, 1980. It was not ratified.
60. Lou Cannon, Interview with Robert McFarlane, December 23, 1989. As quoted in Lou Cannon, *President Reagan: Role of a Lifetime* (New York: Public Affairs, 1991), 248.
61. Cannon, Interview with Robert McFarlane, 249.

62. In 1984, when Reagan was asked during the second presidential debate—that focused on international affairs—if he was too old, at age 73, to be president, Reagan responded, "I am not going to exploit, for political purposes, my opponent's youth and inexperience." Jacob Weisberg, *Ronald Reagan: The American Presidents Series: The 40th President, 1981–1989*, (New York: Times Books, Henry Holt and Company, 2016), 113.
63. Although no mishaps occurred during Carter's inauguration, Carter worried beforehand that one would occur. Just seven days after the inauguration, Carter ordered Andrews Air Force Base to run a COG drill to practice evacuating the president and first lady from the White House. (National Security Advisor Zbigniew Brzezinski and his secretary served as stand-ins for the president and Roselynn Carter.) When Carter discovered that the Eisenhower/Kennedy era plans were rusty, the president tasked Brzezinski with updating the COG procedures during the first Carter White House staff meeting on January 21, 1977. Garrett M. Graff, *Raven Rock: The Story of the US Government's Secret Plan to Save Itself—While the Rest of Us Die* (New York: Simon & Schuster, 2017), 240.
64. "Memorandum for the Record from William D. Baird, Assistant Associate Director for Government Preparedness, July 7, 1980," Jimmy Carter Presidential Library, Staff Office Files, Hugh Carter, Subject Files, folder "Continuity of Gov't Concerns II."
65. The special assistant to the president for administration and the assistant to the president for National Security Affairs would draft a memo for the president's signature to determine the official who would sit the inauguration out. Carter's outgoing defense secretary, Harold Brown, remained in office past noon (the standard transition time), to ensure continuity in the case of nuclear attack or another catastrophic event. "Memorandum for the Record from William D. Baird, Assistant Associate Director for Government Preparedness, July 7, 1980," Jimmy Carter Presidential Library, Staff Office Files, Hugh Carter, Subject Files, folder "Continuity of Gov't Concerns II."

66. Initial problems with the "designated survivor" program included the fact that no way to confirm the identity of the designated survivor was in place. Garrett M. Graff, "Who's In Charge of America After A Catastrophe? Who Knows?" *Politico Magazine*, September 21, 2016. https://www.politico.com/magazine/story/2016/09/designated-survivor-president-succession-doomsday-plans-214271/.
67. Ronald Reagan, *An American Life* (New York; Simon & Schuster, 1990), 258.
68. "Exchange with Reporters on Foreign and Domestic Crisis Management," Ronald Reagan Presidential Library and Museum. https://www.reaganlibrary.gov/archives/speech/exchange-reporters-foreign-and-domestic-crisis-management. Control beyond the president's reach: Reagan, *An American Life*, 270.
69. The last presidential assassination attempt took place in September 1975. Ironically, Ford had also just concluded a speech in front of the AFL—CIO building tradesmen when the attempt on his life took place. See David S. Broder, "Reagan Wounded by Assailant's Bullet; Prognosis is 'Excellent,'" *The Washington Post*, March 31, 1981.
70. Two others in his entourage—Press Secretary James Brady and Secret Service agent Tim McCarthy — and a Washington policeman, Thomas Delahanty, had also been shot. "Statement by the Vice President about the Attempted Assassination of the President, March 30, 1981," Ronald Reagan Presidential Library and Museum. https://www.reaganlibrary.gov/archives/speech/statement-vice-president-about-attempted-assassination-president.
71. Speakes had also been working on President Gerald Ford's staff when two attempts were made on Ford's life. Herbert L. Abrams, *"The President Has Been Shot:" Confusion, Disability, and the 25th Amendment in the Aftermath of Attempted Assassination of Ronald Reagan* (New York: W.W. Norton & Co., 1992), 104–105 fn.
72. Donald T. Regan, *For the Record: From Wall Street to Washington* (San Diego: Hartcourt Brace Jovanovich, 1988), 167.

73. Alan Peppard, "Command and Control: Tested Under Fire," *Dallas Morning News*, May 13, 2015. http://res.dallasnews.com/interactives/reagan-bush/.
74. The bullet had come within an inch of the seventy-year-old president's heart and, in addition to the collapsed lung, he had lost half his blood. He was being kept alive by transfusions. Baker was at the president's side in the hospital and said that he and Counsel to the President Edwin Meese had rejected the idea of transferring power to Bush. It was after the call that Darman put the papers in his office safe. Del Quentin Wilber, *Rawhide Down: The Near Assassination of Ronald Reagan* (New York: Henry Holt and Company, 2011), 181.
75. Richard Reeves, *President Reagan: The Triumph of Imagination* (New York, Simon & Schuster, 2005), 38.
76. Historians often refer to Baker, Deaver, and Meese as the "troika" or "triumvirate," because of the amount of power they wielded in the White House. Historian Richard Reeves argues, however, that Reagan was "staff-dependent" but not "staff-driven." The near assassination suggests otherwise. Reeves, *President Reagan*, 13.
77. In the Situation Room prior to Haig's erroneous on-camera statement, Communications Director David Gergen argued with Haig about whether the president was on the operating table. Gergen was correct: the president was unconscious on the operating table fighting for his life. An unconscious president cannot discharge his powers and duties, but Section 4 of the Twenty-Fifth Amendment requires "the vice president and a majority of either the principal officers of the executive departments or of such other body as Congress may by law provide" to declare the president incapacitated. Gergen and Haig exchange: Reeves, *President Reagan*, 38–39.
78. O'Leary was dean of clinical affairs at George Washington medical school. "Statement by the Vice President About the Attempted Assassination of the President, March 30, 1981," Ronald Reagan Presidential Library and Museum. https://www.reaganlibrary.gov/archives/speech/statement-vice-president-about-attempted-assassination-president.
79. Abrams, "*The President Has Been Shot*," 147.

80. Historian Lou Cannon notes other cases of Reagan's advisors being hyperaware of the "public relations imperative of demonstrating that Reagan had his hand on the presidential throttle." For example, one such incident occurred when, on August 19, 1981, U.S. Navy F-14 fighters shot down two Soviet-made Libyan jets. Baker and Deaver were angered that Meese notified the vice president but failed to wake up the president. Darman: Wilber, Rawhide Down, 181. Baker and Meese: Lou Cannon, *President Reagan: The Role of a Lifetime* (New York: Public Affairs, 2000), 158.
81. By Wednesday, April 1, the president had signed a farm bill (with a signature so weak it looked like a forgery). But then the president contracted a fever and Dr. Benjamin Aaron, George Washington's chief of thoracic surgery, was considering another operation to remove the damaged lobe in his lung. This second surgery did not take place. Reeves, *President Reagan*, 46.
82. Gil Troy, *Morning in America: How Ronald Reagan Invented the 1980s* (Princeton, NJ: Princeton University Press, 2005), 76.
83. Troy, *Morning in America*, 140.
84. Abrams, "*The President Has Been Shot*," 127.
85. Reeves, *President Reagan*, 38.
86. "Nuclear Code Briefcase Remained Near Reagan," *The New York Times*, March 31, 1981, A5.
87. The FBI removed everything from the hospital as "evidence," including the president's dark blue suit containing his wallet with the codes. Although the vice president had a second card, and Secretary of Defense Weinberger a third, the president's card was not returned by the FBI for two days. Reeves, *President Reagan*, 36.
88. David S. Broder, "Reagan Wounded by Assailant's Bullet; Prognosis is 'Excellent,'" *The Washington Post*, March 31, 1981.
89. Alexander M. Haig, Jr, *Caveat: Realism, Reagan and Foreign Policy* (New York: MacMillan Publishing, 1984).
90. Alan Peppard, "Command and Control: Tested Under Fire," *Dallas Morning News*, May 13, 2015, W11. http://res.dallasnews.com/interactives/reagan-bush/.
91. In the months prior to the assassination attempt, an independent union of Polish workers, Solidarity, threatened the Polish government. Soviet General Secretary Leonid Brezhnev warned the

new Prime Minister, General Wojciech Jaruzelski, that time was running out to control the workers' strikes. In the week leading up to the assassination, the Soviets staged a landing operation on Poland's northwestern coast and contemplated an invasion to keep the Polish government in power. The United States warned of the "potential gravity" of the situation but encouraged the workers. On Sunday, April 5, Brezhnev made an unusual appearance at a Czech Communist Party meeting, where the nation's party leader Gustav Husak likened the situation in Czechoslovakia and Poland to those that led to Soviet invasions of East Germany in 1953, Hungary in 1956, and Czechoslovakia in 1968. Reagan sent a message that if Poland were to be invaded, US-Soviet arms negotiations would be "dealt a serious and lasting blow." See Abrams, "*The President Has Been Shot*," 40.
92. Reagan, *An American Life*, 267.
93. Historian James Mann, in *The Rebellion of Ronald Reagan: A History of the End of the Cold War*, argues that Reagan was "horrified by the possibility of nuclear war," even during his first term. He suggests Reagan's aversion to nuclear war can be dated even further back to his 1976 Republican National Convention speech, which Mann characterizes as "more an expression of anxiety about nuclear weapons that a specific call for their abolition." Reduce the threat: Reagan, *An American Life*, 268. Horrified about the possibility: James Mann, *The Rebellion of Ronald Reagan: A History of the End of the Cold War* (New York: Viking, 2009), 35. Anxiety about nuclear weapons: Mann, *The Rebellion of Ronald Reagan*, 40.
94. Reagan, *An American Life*, 267.
95. Robert Scheer, "US Could Survive War in Administration's View," *Los Angeles Times*, January 16, 1982.
96. Jones, having studied Soviet civil defense manuals at a previous job with Boeing, described how Americans could survive. After millions of Americans had been evacuated from the cities to the countryside, fallout shelters should be dug deep underground and once closed, piled with three feet of dirt. "It is the dirt that does it," a measured Jones assured Scheer. Richard Halloran, "Pentagon Draws Up First Strategy For Fighting a Long Nuclear War: 5-Year Overall Plan Gives Insight Into Thinking of Administration's Senior Defense Officials. Pentagon Draws Up Plans

for Long Nuclear War," *The New York Times* (May 30, 1982). T.K. Jones interview: Robert Scheer, "US Could Survive War in Administration's View," *Los Angeles Times*, January 16, 1982.
97. David Lewis, "Doomsday Government," CNN Special Assignment, *Cable News Network*, November 17, 1991. See also" "The Armageddon Plan" as described in James Mann, *Rise of the Vulcans: The History of Bush's War Cabinet*, Chapter 9. In his first footnote, he explains that he gleaned the information on Reagan's secret directive from "three separate individuals who were participants in the secret exercises." He dates the interviews to 2002. James Mann, *Rise of the Vulcans: The History of Bush's War Cabinet* (New York: Penguin Books, 2004), 389 fn.
98. As quoted in Graff, *Raven Rock*, 315.
99. Graff, *Raven Rock*, 314.
100. James Mann, *Rise of the Vulcans: The History of Bush's War Cabinet* (New York: Penguin Books, 2004).
101. Both Cheney and Rumsfeld were regular team leaders, often disappearing for a week at a time, leaving their wives mysterious phone numbers with Washington, DC, area codes to contact in case of emergency. Both had already served in the executive branch. Cheney became secretary of defense under President George H.W. Bush, and both would serve again in official positions under President George W. Bush, but when Reagan's highly classified program began, Cheney was on Capitol Hill and Rumsfeld was a CEO of a Chicago-based pharmaceutical company. Other team leaders included James Woolsey, who became a CIA director, and Kenneth Duberstein, one of Reagan's chiefs of staff. See Mann, *Rise of the Vulcans*.
102. Ted Gup, "The Ultimate Congressional Hideaway," *The Washington Post*, May 31, 1992. http://www.washingtonpost.com/wp-srv/local/daily/july/25/brier1.htm.
103. In 2011, Fordham Law Review interviewed the author of the Twenty-Fifth Amendment, asking Bayh to share his thoughts on this clandestine order for reestablishing the executive branch in the event of a nuclear war. He responded that he "still like[d] the idea of someone like [at the time of the interview in 2011, House Majority Leader] Steny Hoyer being at the Greenbrier when the State of the Union is given. Naturally, the senator believed input from Congress, the only branch of government allowed to declare

war, was crucial in the event of a nuclear attack. See "A Modern Father of Our Constitution: An Interview with Former Senator Birch Bayh," 79 *Fordham L. Rev.* 781 (2011), 797.
104. Nevertheless, Reagan poured hundreds of millions of dollars per year into the new government agency called "The National Program Office," a front for the program. James Mann, *Rise of the Vulcans: The History of Bush's War Cabinet* (New York: Penguin Books, 2004).
105. Despite claims by Reagan's top scientists that the initiative would not work, $17 billion was spent on the program by the time he left office. Robert Scheer, *With Enough Shovels: Reagan, Bush and Nuclear War* (New York: Random House, 1982), 14.
106. In one of his next entries, the president noted that a Situation Room briefing had included a "scenario for a sequence of events that could lead to the end of civilization as we knew it." (This reference was most likely to ABLE ARCHER, a November 1983 NATO exercise.) Reagan, *An American Life*, 585.
107. Schwab, Nikki. "Ronald Reagan Responsible For Tom Clancy's Rise," *US News & World Report*. October 2, 2013. https://www.usnews.com/news/blogs/washington-whispers/2013/10/02/ronald-reagan-responsible-for-tom-clancys-rise.
108. "The Bombing of the Rainbow Warrior," *Greenpeace International*, https://www.greenpeace.org/aotearoa/about/our-history/bombing-of-the-rainbow-warrior/.
109. The Constitution stipulates that presidents must be at least thirty-five years of age to assume the presidency—and senators must be thirty and representatives twenty five—perhaps the commonality of this operation for someone of his age should have raised questions about an ending temporal boundary on service in office. Yet the major papers only questioned why the cancer was not discoverable sooner.
110. Speakes had taken over from the gravely injured Brady. Gerald M. Boyd, "Reagan's Surgery Finds Second Polyp; Operation Today," *The New York Times*. July 13, 1985, https://www.nytimes.com/1985/07/13/us/reagan-s-surgery-finds-2nd-polyp-operation-today.html.
111. "Letter from President Ronald Reagan to the President Pro Tempore of the Senate and the Speaker of the House on the

Discharge of the President's Powers and Duties during His Surgery," July 13, 1985. Ronald Reagan Presidential Library.
112. "Birch Bayh, telephone interview with [Herbert L. Abrams], June 7, 1990," as quoted in Abrams, "*The President Has Been Shot,*" 293.
113. In the Working Group on Presidential Disability which first met in January 1995, Dr. Herbert L. Abrams, author of "*The President Has Been Shot,*" argued that certain circumstances such as the use of general anesthesia by the president should automatically trigger the Twenty-Fifth Amendment. See James F. Toole and Robert A. Joynt, *Presidential Disability: Papers, Discussions, and Recommendations on the Twenty-Fifth Amendment and Issues of Inability and Disability among Presidents of the United States*, (New York: University of Rochester Press, 2001).
114. This was Bayh's response after he asked Fielding, "Fred, how did you ever let the president sign a letter like that?" Fielding responded that "it was the only thing we could get him to sign." "A Modern Father of Our Constitution: An Interview with Former Senator Birch Bayh," 79 *Fordham L. Rev.* 781 (2011), 797.
115. Abrams, "*The President Has Been Shot,*" 204.
116. Reagan returned to the hospital in early August to have skin cancer removed. Again, the Twenty-FifthAmendment was not invoked.
117. Reagan, *An American Life*, 500.
118. As quoted in Abrams, "*The President Has Been Shot,*" 212.
119. Leonid Brezhnev died on November 10, 1982. Yuri Andropov died on February 9, 1984. Konstantin Chernenko died on March 10, 1985, not long before Reagan's surgery.
120. Reston, James. "Reagan's Ticking Clock," *The New York Times*, September 24, 1986, A31.
121. Although Reagan and Gorbachev privately discussed eliminating all nuclear weapons, they did not arrive at a deal. Reagan refused to put limits on the development of his Strategic Defense Initiative; Gorbachev's proposals hinged on this one condition. James Mann, *The Rebellion of Ronald Reagan: A History of the End of the Cold War* (New York: Viking, 2009), 45.
122. Bayh saw a lesson in this: "We learned from talking to doctors that anybody who has been heavily sedated should never make a

decision of any consequence within forty-eight hours. It takes that long for the brain to clear. During that period of time, he signed the Iran-contra documents." "Birch Bayh, telephone interview with [Herbert L. Abrams], June 7, 1990," as quoted in Abrams, *"The President Has Been Shot"*, 293.

123. Reagan earned the nickname "the Teflon president." Some, including the *National Journal*, charged that Regan, as well as the first lady, had been running the country like First Lady Edith Wilson and President Wilson's doctor, Dr. Grayson, earlier in the century. Regan suggested that Nancy Reagan was instrumental in his departure. She was known to tell her husband whom she did and did not trust within the administration. At times the president would listen to her, while at other times, she would use her network of friends and aides as backchannels to convince the president not to rely on those on her blacklist. Regan also suggested that the first lady was reliant on a San Francisco astrologer for White House scheduling, even when choosing the date for signing the intermediate-range nuclear forces treaty. Reagan denied his wife's influence in a televised speech on March 4: "The idea that she is involved in governmental decisions and so forth and all of this, and being a kind of dragon lady — there is nothing to that.... That is fiction, and I think its despicable fiction." Reeves, *President Reagan*, 386. See also: Donald T. Regen, *For the Record: From Wall Street to Washington* (San Diego: CA: Harcourt Brace Jovanovich, 1988).

124. Reeves, *President Reagan*, 392.

125. While younger son Ron Reagan contended that he saw evidence of the early stages of Alzheimer's three years into Reagan's first term, his older son Michael Reagan denied this. Presidential historian and editor of *The Reagan Diaries* Douglas Brinkley stated that he saw no change in the president's journal entries. However, White House reporters questioned Reagan's mental alertness during his second term—much like White House journalists' observations of President Joseph Biden in 2024, Reagan reportedly would stare off into the distance. Journalists were not sure if this was part of a hearing impairment or something else. During one photo op, when journalists asked Reagan about nuclear tensions with the Soviet Union, specifically "a perceived lack of progress on arms control talks," Reagan, lost, needed

to take a cue from Nancy Reagan who had whispered to him: "doing the best we can." Maer, Peter, "When Did Ronald Reagan Halve Alzheimer's? The Debate Goes On," (*CBS News*, February 6, 2011). https://www.cbsnews.com/news/when-did-ronald-reagan-have-alzheimers-the-debate-goes-on/. See also "Physicians Explanation of Ronald Reagan's Alzheimer's Diagnosis," *Ronald Reagan Presidential Library & Museum*. (November 5, 1994.) https://www.reaganlibrary.gov/reagans/ronald-reagan/physicians-explanation-ronald-reagans-alzheimers-diagnosis.

126. "Report of The Miller Center Commission on Presidential Disability and the Twenty-Fifth Amendment," White Burkett Miller Center of Public Affairs at the University of Virginia (VA: University Press of America, Inc., 1988), 7.

127. The Miller Commission's findings influenced George H.W. Bush's Press Secretary Marlin Fitzwater to dedicate part of a press briefing to the Twenty-Fifth Amendment on April 28, 1989. During the press conference, Fitzwater referred to an April 18 meeting at which the president "ma[d]e sure all those involved in this process are aware of the procedures, and that everyone was aware of the consultations that would have to be made [in a case of presidential inability]." Feerick, *The Twenty- Fifth Amendment*, 200. A version of this book dating to the Clinton administration can be found in the Fordham Law Archive of Scholarship and History. Office of White House Counsel, "Contingency Plans: Death or Disability of the President" (1993). Executive Branch Materials. 10. https://ir.lawnet.fordham.edu/twentyfifth_amendment_executive_materials/10.

128. "Report of The Miller Center Commission on Presidential Disability and the Twenty-Fifth Amendment," White Burkett Miller Center of Public Affairs at the University of Virginia (VA: University Press of America, Inc., 1988), 3.

129. These points are summarized in Feerick, *The Twenty-Fifth Amendment*, 223. See also "Report of The Miller Center Commission on Presidential Disability and the Twenty-Fifth Amendment," White Burkett Miller Center of Public Affairs at the University of Virginia (VA: University Press of America, Inc., 1988).

130. The panel first met in 1995, although it was formed two years earlier. "Report of The Miller Center Commission on Presidential Disability and the Twenty-Fifth Amendment," White Burkett Miller Center of Public Affairs at the University of Virginia (VA: University Press of America, Inc., 1988), 3.
131. Other panelists, such as James F. Toole, built on these ideas by suggesting presidential candidates should submit to certain physical and mental health exams that be made available to the public. Ten months after the Carter Center conference, the Working Group reconvened at Wake Forest University. This time former president Gerald Ford addressed the committee. He stated he was of the opinion that the Twenty-Fifth Amendment worked in the orderly transition of presidential power, whether temporary or permanent, though he was not opposed to discussions particularly on the idea of a plan being put into place before the inauguration of a new administration and on the White House physician being "upgraded in the White House staff structure." James F. Toole and Robert A. Joynt, *Presidential Disability*.
132. "President Dan Quayle? Yes, it almost happened, for a few hours back in 1991," *Reuters*. December 6, 2011. https://www.reuters.com/article/world/president-dan-quayle-yes-it-almost-happened-for-a-few-hours-back-in-1991-idUS1931015836/.
133. "Best Sellers: Fiction," *The New York Times*, March 10, 1991. "Best Sellers: Paperback," *The New York Times*, December 29, 1991.
134. For a discussion of the amendment in modern novels including Mario Puzo's *The Fourth K*, see Laurie Katherine Manson, "Illuminating the 25th? The Twenty-fifth Amendment to the US Constitution in Eight Novels" (Ph.D. thesis, University of Glasgow), https://theses.gla.ac.uk/83576/.
135. Lehmann-Haupt, Christopher. "Books of the Times; Oil and Terrorism in a Puzo Thriller," *The New York Times*, January 10, 1991, https://www.nytimes.com/1991/01/10/books/books-of-the-times-oil-and-terrorism-in-a-puzo-thriller.html.
136. Richard B. Cheney and David S. Addington, "Vice President Cheney's Unused Resignation Letter" (2009). Executive Branch Materials. 16. https://ir.lawnet.fordham.edu/twentyfifth_amendment_executive_materials/16.

137. "Dick Cheney Reveals Heart Defibrillator was Altered to Thwart Terrorist Hacks," *ABC News*, October 18, 2013, https://www.abc.net.au/news/2013-10-19/cheney-reveals-defibrillator-altered-to-thwart-terrorists/5033354.
138. For diverse interpretations of the September 11 attacks see, for example: Peter L. Bergen, *The Longest War: The Enduring Conflict between America and Al Qaeda* (New York: Free Press, 2011). Samuel Huntington, *The Clash of Civilizations and the Remaking of World Order* (London: Simon & Schuster, 1996). John C. Miller, Michael Stone and Chris Mitchell; *The Cell: Inside the 9/11 Plot, and Why the CIA and FBI Failed to Stop It* (New York: Hachette Books, 2002). National Commission on Terror Attacks Upon the United States, *The 9/11 Commission Report* (New York: W.W. Norton & Co., 2004). Bassam Tibi, *Islamism and Islam* (New Haven: Yale University Press, 2012). Lawrence Wright, *The Looming Tower - Al Qaeda and the Road to 9/11* (New York: Alfred A. Knopf, 2006).
139. Dick Cheney, *In My Time: A Personal and Political Memoir* (New York: Threshold Editions, Simon & Schuster, 2011), 6. The refusal of an individual in the line of succession to follow security procedures during a crisis should have raised the following question, but did not: should a statute be passed requiring those in the line of succession to follow security directions in cases of attack?
140. The president was reading to school children in Florida when the country was attacked. Coincidentally, Barksdale Air Force Base in Shreveport, Louisiana, where the president's plane was diverted, was already on the highest alert because it was in the middle of a nuclear training exercise. Jean Edward Smith, in *Bush*, says the president was "not happy" about the Secret Service's insistence that he stay away from Washington, complaining that fears about his security were being "overblown." Jean Edward Smith, *Bush* (New York: Simon & Schuster, 2016), 220.
141. Cheney had also lived through a heart attack at the age of 37 (on June 18, 1978). In a *60 Minutes* segment that aired in October 2013, Cheney discussed the fact that in 2007, when he needed his implanted cardioverter-defibrillator (ICD) replaced, Reiner ordered the manufacturer to disable the wireless feature due to concern a terrorist could assassinate the vice president by sending a signal to the device, telling it to shock his heart

into cardiac arrest. On December 2, 2012, an episode of the fictional television series *Homeland* centered on that very plot—a terrorist gained control of the vice president's pacemaker, accelerating the machine until the vice president suffered a heart attack. The entertainment news media debated the plot's plausibility. Cheney's ICD, which was designed to sound an alarm and shock the heart back into a normal rhythm should it stop beating at regular intervals, did not go off once during the eight years he was vice president. Because the vice president's health did not deteriorate suddenly, the fact that the Twenty-Fifth Amendment does not provide for vice presidential inability did not receive a lot of national attention. Cheney, *In My Time*, 7.

142. Dr. Herbert L. Abrams, author of "*The President Has Been Shot*," participated in the Carter Commission: he argued that certain circumstances such as the use of general anesthesia by the president should automatically trigger the Twenty-Fifth Amendment. Bush may have known about this recommendation. See James F. Toole and Robert A. Joynt, *Presidential Disability*.

143. In 2002, Bush transmitted letters to House speaker Hastert and president pro tem Byrd. In 2007, he did the same to House Speaker Nancy Pelosi and to Byrd again. In 2007, five polyps were found during the colonoscopy, but all were determined to be benign.

144. Bush, 55, was ill at least two additional times during his tenure, but was not put under general anesthesia and, therefore, did not invoke the amendment. The first time, he underwent surgery for the removal of skin lesions on his face. Shortly thereafter, in January 2002, he briefly lost consciousness after choking on a pretzel when alone in the living quarters of the White House. During the latter case, the public was not informed for two and a half hours. The White House quickly released the fact that Bush, just five months earlier, had a complete physical exam at which time it was determined that the president was very healthy for his age. The White House also released details of his exercise regimen, which included running at a quick pace. James Gerstenzang and Thomas H. Maugh II, "Choking on Pretzel, Bush Faints Briefly," *Los Angeles Times*, January 14, 2002. http://articles.latimes.com/2002/jan/14/news/mn-22490.

145. William J. Broad, Stephen Edelberg, and James Ganz, "Assessing Risks, Chemical, Biological, Even Nuclear: The Threats: Assessing New Risks from Nuclear Weapons to Chemicals and Germs," *The New York Times* (November 1, 2001), A1.
146. As quoted in David Greenberg. Review of John M. Schuessler, *Deceit on the Road to War: Presidents, Politics, and American Democracy*," H-Diplo, H-Net Reviews, July 2016. http://www.h-net.org/reviews/showrev.php?id=46082.
147. An expert on nuclear proliferation, David Albright, president of the Institute for Science and International Security in Washington stated in the article: "After September 11, experts began taking a fresh look at studies that largely ruled out the possibility that terrorists could obtain a nuclear device." William J. Broad, Stephen Edelberg, and James Ganz, "Assessing Risks, Chemical, Biological, Even Nuclear: The Threats: Assessing New Risks from Nuclear Weapons to Chemicals and Germs," *The New York Times*, November 1, 2001, A1.
148. For an entire chapter on the Twenty-Fifth Amendment in fiction see Chapter 7 of Brian C. Kalt's *Unable: The Law, Politics, and Limits of Section 4 of the Twenty-Fifth Amendment*. Brian C. Kalt, *Unable: The Law, Politics, and Limits of Section 4 of the Twenty-Fifth Amendment*. (New York, NY: Oxford University Press, 2019), 74–103.
149. "The West Wing: American Television Series," *Encyclopedia Britannica*. https://www.britannica.com/topic/The-West-Wing. "The West Wing. TV Series 1999–2006," *IMDb*. https://www.imdb.com/title/tt0200276/. Fretts, Bruce and Matt Roush. "TV Guide Magazine's 60 Best TV Series of All Time," *TV Guide*. December 23, 2013. https://www.tvguide.com/news/tv-guide-magazine-60-best-series-1074962/. Sheffield, Rob." 100 Greatest TV Shows of All Time," *Rolling Stone*. September 21, 2016, https://web.archive.org/web/20161024132327/http://www.rollingstone.com/tv/lists/100-greatest-tv-shows-of-all-time-w439520/the-west-wing-w439625.
150. "24 Awards," *IMDb*, https://www.imdb.com/title/tt0285331/awards/.
151. Brian C. Kalt, *Unable: The Law, Politics, and Limits of Section 4 of the Twenty-Fifth Amendment*. (New York, NY: Oxford University Press, 2019), 92.

152. Kalt, *Unable*, 94.
153. Many notable individuals familiar with the drafting, passage, ratification, or implementation of the Twenty-Fifth, as well as those involved in COOP, took part in the Commission including: President Reagan's Chief of Staff Kenneth M. Duberstein, former House Speaker Thomas Foley of Washington state, Professor Charles Fried of Harvard Law School, former House Speaker Newt Gingrich of Georgia, former Deputy Attorney General Jamie S. Gorelick, former US Attorney General Nicholas deB Katzenbach, and former House Minority Leader Robert H. Michel of Illinois.
154. *Joint Hearing Before the Committee on the Judiciary and Committee on Rules and Administration*, United States Senate, Ensuring the Continuity of the United States Government: The Presidency, 108th Cong., 1st sess., September 16, 2003, Serial No. J-108-40. (Washington: US Government Printing Office, 2008), https://www.gpo.gov/fdsys/pkg/CHRG-108shrg45948/pdf/CHRG-108shrg45948.pdf.
155. Congressional Research Service staffer Thomas F. Neale, an expert witness, explained that the hearings were necessary because of proposals made after 9/11 seeking to prevent "decapitation" of the US government "by a terrorist attack or attacks, possibly involving the use of weapons of mass destruction." Thomas H. Neale, "Presidential and Vice Presidential Succession: Overview and Current Legislation," Congressional Research Service Report for Congress. Library of Congress (Updated September 27, 2004), http://www.whitehousetransitionproject.org/wp-content/uploads/2016/04/POTUS-VP-Succession_092704-1.pdf.
156. Birch Bayh, Interview with Author, November 11, 2014.
157. "A Modern Father of Our Constitution: An Interview with Former Senator Birch Bayh," 79 *Fordham L. Rev.* 781 (2011), 812–813.

CHAPTER 6

"The [Doomsday] Clock Ticks": The Twenty-Fifth Amendment on the Precipice

This chapter traces the Amendment through the present. Although international tensions with nuclear powers and rogue terrorist groups were simmering to a boil, President Barack Obama had the good fortune of remaining healthy. Yet as soon as Donald Trump was sworn in as the forty-fifth president, questions of unfitness and calls to remove the president swirled through mainstream media, with whistleblowers daring to come forward and insiders writing exposés about the chaos in the Oval Office. Talk of invoking Section 4 of the amendment occurred at the highest levels of government. The vice president and Cabinet avoided invoking Section 4, but it was misused in cultural discourse. The media joined in the debate and scholars worked to combat under-informed arguments and mischaracterizations. The way the amendment was deployed in the political realm had parallels to its usage in the entertainment field as well. In the popular realm, the misuse was even more creative. But what was authentic about the depictions of the amendment in popular culture was that they emphasized the genuine fears around an incapacitated president's finger on the nuclear button. By December 2017, Sarah Vowell, an academic working to correct the misinformation around the amendment, recommended various books dealing with presidential incapacity as holiday gifts.[1]

The framers of the amendment had assumed that decision-makers shared a common mindset that placed the country above personal gain, and that the amendment would be invoked as a tool when needed to ensure presidential continuity. But this was not true of Trump, who prized loyalty to him above that to the Constitution. Trump's decision to avoid invoking Section 3 when undergoing a colonoscopy, despite George W. Bush's precedent, and his behavior when he contracted COVID, further underscore the pattern unveiled in Chapter 5: during these times of heightened international tensions, projecting an image of strength always took precedence. A blow to that image took place when he lost the 2020 election to Biden but refused to admit it. Concern rippled through Washington that with his loss, he had become unhinged. Domestic stressors that had been building during COVID came to a head when, on January 6, Trump inflamed his supporters causing an insurrection at the Capitol leading to Cabinet resignations, calls to invoke the amendment, and a historic second impeachment.

Tensions did not diminish as Biden assumed the presidency. In addition, concerns about Biden's mental acuity, physical health, and advancing age intensified throughout his term as well as during the 2024 presidential campaign that resulted in a second Trump administration. That year, Christoper Nolan's Hollywood blockbuster *Oppenheimer* won seven Oscars, including for best picture, at the 96th Academy Awards.[2] The story of the American theoretical physicist Robert J. Oppenheimer, a man who "risked destroying the world to save it," and his involvement in the Manhattan Project leading to the world's first nuclear detonation now seemed chillingly relevant. The resurgence of nuclear anxiety in politics and culture mirrored incandescent tensions across the globe that reached heights comparable to that of the Cold War. Having an able president's finger on the nuclear trigger was paramount.

* * *

Throughout the eight years of President Barack Obama's administration, preventing a nuclear bomb from destroying an American city had been *the* highest priority. Journalist Bob Woodward later recalled a 2010 conversation with President Obama who commented to him that

> [a] potential game-changer would be a nuclear weapon...blowing up a major American city.... And so when I go down the list of things that I have to worry about all the time, that is at the top, because that's one area where you can't afford any mistakes. And right away, coming in, we said,

how are we going to start ramping up and putting that at the center of a lot of our national security discussions? Make sure that occurrence, even if remote, never happens?[3]

In truth, Obama had little choice but to focus on the potential for nuclear attacks. He had inherited two wars from his predecessor George W. Bush—one in Afghanistan and one in Iraq. When Bush asked Congress to declare war on the latter, he claimed, erroneously, that Iraqi dictator Saddam Hussein was "reconstituting" his nuclear weapons program stating, "Facing clear evidence of peril, we cannot wait for the final proof—the smoking gun—that could come in the form of a mushroom cloud."[4] Obama began disengaging from both countries by the beginning of his second term, while simultaneously expanding the use of special forces and drones to root out terrorists.[5] He also worked to make sure that Iran would not develop nuclear weapons. In 2015, Iran signed an agreement, the Joint Comprehensive Plan of Action (JCPOA), to surrender 97% of its enriched uranium, in return for the lifting of economic sanctions.[6] The following year, Obama traveled to Cuba—the first president to do so since Calvin Coolidge in 1928—after officially recognizing the country two years earlier. As soon as he arrived, he sent a message to the White House email list underscoring the reasoning for his visit: "a Cold War confrontation over Cuba pushed the world as close as it's ever been to nuclear war"; it was time to mend the United States and Cuba's isolation from one another to "bury the last vestiges of the Cold War in the Americas."[7]

Although Obama expressed Americans' desires to put the Cold War in the past, global nuclear tensions were heating up because Iran (despite the agreement), and other rogue nations such as North Korea, continued to pursue nuclear and long-range missile capabilities. Nuclear states like Pakistan showed instability too, raising fears of their takeover by dangerous forces. Pakistan developed its nuclear triad, and, unlike its neighbors, India and China, did not have a "no-first-strike" policy.[8] However, the greater fear existed over North Korea. Secretary of Defense James Mattis called North Korea's accelerated efforts to develop a nuclear missile capable of hitting the United States a "clear and present danger."[9] Experts believed North Korean leader Kim Jong-un would have nuclear missiles capable of reaching all major US cities at his disposal by spring 2018.[10]

Coupled with the heightened nuclear anxiety was the anxiety circulating in the media and Washington not only about Kim's sanity, but about Republican presidential nominee Donald Trump's as well. The questioning of Trump's mental abilities began during the 2016 presidential election cycle, if not before. Democratic nominee and former First Lady Hillary Clinton and others argued that the Republican nominee was not temperamentally fit to make split-second decisions controlling the launch of nuclear weapons.[11] A litany of diplomats and national security experts came forward during the campaign to agree with her assessment. In October 2016, ten former nuclear launch officers or missileers who held the keys to launch on the president's order signed an unprecedented open letter questioning Trump's judgment and temperament. These officers insisted that Trump should not be entrusted with the nuclear codes.[12] But concerns about the mental ability of the next president whose finger would be on the nuclear button was not a new phenomenon.[13]

Clinton continued to press on this theme. At the end of October 2016, Clinton capitalized on Trump's own statements about nuclear weapons by using clips of them in attack ads. One Clinton ad featured Monique Corzilius Luiz, the girl who had starred in the 1964 Daisy ad, now a woman in her late fifties. Luiz said, "The fear of nuclear war that we had as children, I never thought our children would have to deal with that again."[14] Clinton believed that Luiz's concern would appeal to most voters. The desire to avoid a nuclear exchange was one of several issues that enabled Clinton to win about 2.7 million more popular votes than Trump, but Trump won the Electoral College vote, which sent him to the White House.[15]

Renewed tensions with another old enemy, Russia, increased with Trump's inauguration in January 2017. In a *Reuters* interview a month after the inauguration, continuing to employ the tough rhetoric he had used during the presidential campaign, Trump stated that he planned to increase nuclear weapons capabilities to ensure that the United States is at "the top of the pack."[16] Pointing to the president's continued tough rhetoric and call for a nuclear arms build-up, Cold War Soviet leader Mikhail Gorbachev summed up the current situation by stating: "it all looks as if the world is preparing for [nuclear] war."[17]

In May of that year, Trump divulged classified information to Russian foreign minister Sergey V. Lavrov and Russian ambassador to the US Sergey I. Kislyak about an Islamic State plot. While it is within the realm of the president's powers to declassify information, this secret was obtained by a Middle Eastern ally that guards its information so closely that the sensitive information was not even shared widely among trusted top government officials.[18] It was feared that the president's breach of "espionage etiquette" would lead to a decrease in sharing critical secrets with the United States.[19] Shortly thereafter, Deputy Attorney General Rod J. Rosenstein suggested to other Justice Department and FBI officials that he record Trump to document the chaos in the Oval Office and potentially recruit Cabinet members to invoke the Twenty-Fifth Amendment. Although Rosenstein's suggestion did not make the news for another year, talk by administration officials of invoking the Twenty-Fifth Amendment began soon after Trump assumed office and the divulging of top-secret information to America's Cold War enemy added to Americans' feelings of insecurity.[20]

Trump's rationale for sharing sensitive information with America's foe was unclear. Was it part of a disruptive, keep-the-opponent-guessing foreign affairs strategy? Was he hoping for a quid pro quo with the Russian President Vladimir Putin? Was it because he admired the Russian dictator? Was it simply to show off or demonstrate that he had the power to release top-secret information? Had he simply gone mad? It may have been a mix of these reasons. Throughout his career, Trump had admired "tough guys" and autocrats, emulating them to evoke personal strength and a sense of fear in opponents who crossed him. In her memoir, former Trump Press Secretary Stephanie Grisham confirms this assertion, tying together Trump's admiration of strongmen dictators with nuclear war. She wrote:

> Trump seem fixated on dictators.... It almost seemed as if he admired their toughness and aggression, but he was also genuinely freaked out about nuclear war. Naturally, as POTUS, he received frequent briefings about nuclear strikes and their potential impact and was (rightly) scared straight about the dangers of getting into a war with one of those guys. He said many times that nuclear war was his biggest worry. "Forget climate change," he once told me. "What we have to worry about is the bomb."[21]

Another American enemy that Trump had an unusual relationship with was North Korean supreme leader Kim Jong-un.

North Korean leader Kim's test on September 3, 2017, of a hydrogen bomb, several times more powerful than the atomic bomb dropped on

Hiroshima, precipitated a dangerous war of words between Pyongyang and Washington. Although the North Korean test received condemnation from the rest of the world including its ally China, as well as Russia, it showed that the dictatorship's nuclear plans were progressing, and this knowledge led to taunts by Trump. On the seventeenth of that month, Trump used his first United Nations General Assembly address to call Kim "Rocket Man," and stated that the United States would "have no choice but to totally destroy North Korea" if provoked.[22] The feud continued via tweets and on January 3, 2018, Trump wrote "Will someone from [Kim's] depleted and food starved regime please inform him that I too have a Nuclear Button, but it is a much bigger & more powerful one than his, and my Button works!"[23] Trump was publicly provoking Kim to brink of declaring nuclear war.

Residents of Hawaii thought Kim had pressed his nuclear button when, on January 13, 2018, mobile phone users woke up to a warning from the Hawaii Emergency Management Agency. The emergency alert text at 8:07a.m. read, "BALLISTIC MISSILE THREAT INBOUND TO HAWAII. SEEK IMMEDIATE SHELTER. THIS IS NOT A DRILL."[24] On radio and TV outlets it began, "the US Pacific Command has detected a missile threat to Hawaii…."[25] It was a false alert. The mistake caused thirty-eight minutes of panic because a new message explaining that no immediate threat existed had to be loaded into the computer program and sent out.[26] In those thirty-eight minutes, people were running for cover and fleeing through the streets, cars were abandoned on highways, parents were hiding crying children in storm drains, strangers were claiming sections in CVS' food aisles, and decisions were made as to with whom one would spend their last minutes.[27] News anchors later said that they had never covered an event of such "palpable panic."[28]

Popular movies and TV shows exploited the fears around presidential continuity by creating outlandish scenarios stemming from the invocation of the Twenty-Fifth Amendment as a result of a nuclear attack. One example is the first season of "Designated Survivor" which aired on television beginning in autumn 2016. Actor Kiefer Sutherland, star of the TV series *24* (which also aired episodes dealing with presidential succession crises), plays a Housing and Urban Development secretary chosen as the designated survivor during the president's State of the Union Address. The secretary finds himself ushered to the White House after an explosion, and the viewer sees that a mushroom cloud had engulfed the Capitol building.[29] This portrayal echoed the real anxieties that have existed since the dawn of the nuclear age around sudden presidential transitions. Throughout the decade, post-apocalyptic shows also trended upward on television.

Although North Korea had not started a nuclear war yet, fear continued to mount that the antagonizing tweets would lead to a disastrous detonation of a nuclear warhead. Some inside the beltway even pointed out that any normal military exercise might be misconstrued as an act of war. Then, at the end of January, Trump's new Secretary of the Army Mark Esper received an urgent call from the Pentagon informing him that Trump had decided to order a withdrawal of all troops from South Korea. He worried that such an abrupt, extreme measure would cause North Korea to view the evacuation as a prelude to war. In his memoir, Esper wrote that "this was a dangerous game of chicken and with nuclear roosters no less" and if Trump issued the order, America "needed to be ready for war."[30] "Who knew when the next doomsday tweet might come?"[31] he added. This type of miscalculation, feared by the framers of the amendment, could lead to a nuclear apocalypse.

While the international story was playing out publicly, it was being paralleled by discussions at home about Trump's mental stability.[32] Democratic Representative Eric Swalwell of California retweeted Trump's "my button is bigger than yours" tweet with the suggestion that members of Trump's Republican party stop his abnormal behavior before tensions with North Korea got out of hand. "If you love our country, help me put this lunacy in check," he wrote "Tell @realDonaldTrump this is not normal behavior. Any @HouseGOP want to have some say before he pushes that button?"[33] The criticism did not stem only from Democrats. Former chief White House ethics lawyer for President George W. Bush, Richard Painter, argued that Trump and Kim were "psychologically unstable men crowing about their nukes… Congress needs to deal with one of them while the U.N. Security Council needs to deal with the other."[34] Two unfit world leaders with sole control of nuclear weapons was doubly dangerous.

In June, a summit in Singapore between the two leaders bore some fruit with Kim not only agreeing in theory to ending his nuclear program, but to return the remains of Americans that had been missing in action since the Korean War.[35] Kim also embarked on a letter-writing campaign believing that the president was susceptible to flattery. By the time Christmas rolled around, Kim's letter, which referred to Trump as "Your Excellency," read that the world could expect another "historic meeting" that would be "reminiscent of a scene from a fantasy film."[36] Yet the second summit, which took place in Hanoi, Vietnam, in February 2019, was a flop. When the North Korean leader asked that all sanctions that had been placed on his country be lifted, Trump responded that he was leaving because Kim was "not ready to make a deal."[37] The line, and the cultivation of his image as a strong dealmaker, came from his book *The Art of the Deal* and his hit TV show *The Apprentice* and was reminiscent of fellow former actor President Reagan's quips. The difference was that while Reagan's zingers tended to relieve tension—such as when he was wheeled into the operating room after the March 1981 assassination attempt and turned to the surgeon to say that he hoped they were all Republicans—Trump's comments belittled those on the receiving end, turning up the heat.

In May, in advance of his next meeting with Kim, the line resurfaced when Trump decided to unilaterally pull the United States out of the 2015 Iran nuclear deal—on the grounds that it was a "disastrous deal"—while simultaneously announcing he was sending Secretary of State Michael R. Pompeo to Pyongyang.[38] National Security Advisor John R. Bolton said, "the message to North Korea" was that "the president wants to make a deal."[39] The third meeting between Trump and Kim took place on June 30, 2019, when Trump suggested a last-minute meeting in the Demilitarized Zone (DMZ). Seemingly on a whim, Trump offered to cross the demarcation line into North Korea, making history as the first sitting US president to do so. The sixty-second photo op revived stalled nuclear talks.[40]

With the heightened nuclear anxiety and concerns about Trump's mental stability,[41] the debate over the continuing challenges of the Twenty-Fifth Amendment that began immediately after the first applications of the amendment continued in Congress on the fiftieth anniversary of its ratification in 2017. In April 2017, Maryland Democratic Representative Jamie Raskin introduced H.R. 1987.[42] Similar to recommendations by the Working Group on Presidential Disability in the 1990s, the bill would create an eleven-member standing commission called the "Oversight Commission on Presidential Capacity" within the legislative branch. Designed to determine "whether the president is physically and mentally unable to discharge the duties and powers of the office," the commission would be composed of doctors, as well as two former high-ranking executive officials, such as presidents, vice presidents, attorney generals, secretaries of state, or surgeon generals. Unlike the Working Group, the bill did not get into substantive debate about the types of medical practitioners that would need to weigh in on what ailments and situations constitute an inability. The bill was referred to the Subcommittee on the Constitution and Civil Justice and received bipartisan support from congressmembers such as Senate Majority Whip John Cornyn (R-TX) and Representative Sheila Jackson Lee (D-TX) who showed interest in the succession and inability issue in the past.[43] At the end of June, Trump's tawdry tweets about talk show host Mika Brezinski—who had questioned his temperament and emotional stability—elicited additional support for the bill.[44] The bill had twenty-one cosponsors, but did not receive the support necessary to become law in the 115th Congress.

As the theatrical scenarios played out between Trump and other world leaders, and international relations seemed both uncertain and unbalanced, Trump's judgment and temperament were questioned, not just in Washington, but by journalists suggesting that he might be impaired and that the Twenty-Fifth Amendment should be invoked.[45] On January 5, 2018, journalist Michael Wolff's exposé on the first nine months of the Trump administration was published, the publication date having been moved forward a handful of days, flouting a cease-and-desist order, because it was already a number one bestseller on Amazon.[46] The title, *Fire and Fury: Inside the Trump White House*, was based on a comment Trump made when referring to North Korea—"they will be met with fire and fury like the world has never seen."[47] Despite "unsourced assertions,"[48] the book was a damaging account of both the chaos in the Trump White House and the mental stability of the man who ran it. When confronted one day after the book's publication and just days after his threatening nuclear button tweet, Trump defended his mental fitness in a tweet.[49] He tweeted:

> …Throughout my life, my two greatest assets have been my mental stability and being, like, really smart… I went from VERY successful businessman, to top T.V. Star to President of the United States (on my first try). I think that would qualify as not smart, but genius… and a very stable genius at that![50]

The tweet quickly became a meme involving a horse, using black humor to underscore a serious concern.

Scholars weighed in on Trump's fitness and ability and the applicability of the amendment. Within an hour of the "very stable genius" tweet, Pulitzer Prize-winning journalist Doris Kearns Goodwin, who, like presidential historian Robert Dallek, had written extensively on LBJ, was interviewed on *NPR*. Goodwin stated that if the people close to the president believe he is unfit because he could not control his impulses and emotions, then it is truly a serious matter. "I think it's just as important as physical illness and physical strength to understand temperament and leadership qualities," she said.[51] Goodwin was essentially concurring with Dallek's December 2017 assessment of Trump. In December, Dallek wrote that Trump, despite his own assurances to the contrary, was the least-qualified and "least-effective president since [Warren] Harding," who had held the office almost a century prior.[52] In addition to stating that the president "lacks the temperament to lead a great nation," he cited Trump's "untrustworthiness, lying, and appalling behavior," suggesting that the Twenty-Fifth Amendment's interpretation should be "expanded," and the amendment should be invoked. He argues that Trump "can and should be replaced by his vice president." In short, Trump lacks the wherewithal "to discharge the powers and duties of his office."[53]

However, while the Twenty-Fifth Amendment had been designed, like the Constitution itself, to be flexible, the amendment does not allow for the permanent removal of a president. The only circumstance in which the removal would become permanent is if the president never recovered from the inability. Even though Trump's demeanor may not have been "presidential," and his provocations of world leaders were likely ill-advised, his temperament and actions did not constitute an inability. A *Politico Magazine* op-ed, "Stop Talking About the 25th Amendment. It Won't Work on Trump. And It Might Just Set Off a Constitutional Crisis," explains that "temperamentally unfit" does not equal "incapacitated." This piece was published a few days after an anonymous *New York Times* op-ed entitled "I Am Part of the Resistance Inside the Trump Administration," claimed that senior members of the administration were "working diligently from within to frustrate parts of [Trump's] agenda and his worst inclinations."[54]

While the "resistance" op-ed created a bit of a furor, similar scenarios had occurred during Nixon's time in office when Section 4 had not been invoked; instead, those close to Nixon chose not to implement his emotional or drunken directives. These officials had, after all, sworn an oath to the Constitution, not the president himself. Trump would later challenge this notion, firing those around him not deemed sufficiently loyal to him. The *Politico* op-ed argues that the best course of action was for senior administration officials to continue to stymie the president's worst impulses and allow for the American people to make the choice not to reelect him. To rely on a never-used clause in a constitutional amendment is not the way to permanently remove an "unpresidential" chief executive.[55]

However, an instance of when Trump was going to be incapacitated and plans to invoke the Twenty-Fifth Amendment should have been made, but were not, occurred on November 16, 2019. The precedent had been set by earlier Republican presidents that they would invoke Section 3 when they were expecting to be anesthetized. President George W. Bush had done so twice for colonoscopies in 2002 and 2007, yet when Trump went to Walter Reed National Military Medical Center for a colonoscopy, he did not follow the precedent established by previous presidents. No steps were taken to invoke the amendment beyond asking Vice President Michael R. Pence to stay in Washington. Press Secretary Grisham later stated that she was not allowed to divulge the fact that the president was undergoing the procedure and that ultimately, and to maintain an image of strength, he was not put under.[56] Trump did not want to "have to be perceived as giving up power" because "in his eyes that would have shown weakness."[57] She added "he did not want to be the butt of a joke.... Pardon the pun."[58] Almost two years to the day later (November 19, 2021), President Joseph R. Biden, about to undergo a colonoscopy, would use Section 3 to transfer power to Vice President Kamala D. Harris without incident. However, throughout his entire administration, Trump continued to avoid projecting any hint of poor health or sickness and to ensure that he would not transfer the powers and duties of the presidency, even temporarily.[59]

Compounding the talk of transferring presidential powers under the Twenty-Fifth Amendment, Democratic members of Congress, without leadership's support, had introduced articles of impeachment at least three times during as many years.[60] In December 2019, the charges were different because they were both "simple and self-contained."[61] In September 2019, the public had learned of a whistleblower complaint about a July phone call, later confirmed by the acting ambassador to the Ukraine, during which the president had threatened to withhold foreign aid money until Ukrainian President Volodymyr Zelenskyy agreed to investigate Hunter Biden, the son of Trump's 2020 Democratic presidential opponent, former Vice President Joe Biden.[62] Although the

Republican-controlled Senate ultimately did not vote to remove Trump from office, on December 18, 2019, the House voted along party lines in favor of impeachment on two articles—abuse of power and obstruction of Congress[63]—giving Trump the dubious distinction of being only the third president in history (after Andrew Jackson and Bill Clinton) to be impeached and closing out the year on a shaky note.[64]

The beginning of 2020 was fraught with tensions that had carried over from 2019. On September 21, 2019, just five days before Americans learned about the whistleblower's complaint and the questionable actions of the president, Iran shot down an American drone. At the very last minute, after planes were in the air and missiles were fixed on targets, Trump called off a retaliatory strike.[65] Then on January 3, 2020, he ordered the assassination of Iran's top security and intelligence commander, Major General Qassim Soleimani, who had been spearheading attacks against American embassies, consulates, and personnel in Syria, Iraq, and Lebanon.[66] This was the second successful assassination Trump had ordered in a matter of months; in October, the United States had killed Islamic State leader Abu Bakr al-Baghdadi.[67] In the days following the strike on Soleimani, America's missile warning systems at Colorado's Buckley Air Force Base and Cheyenne Mountain were put on high alert.[68] Iran's response to Soleimani's assassination was the launching of sixteen ballistic missiles at two Iraqi bases. A collective twelve thousand pounds of rocket-mounted warheads were used in the attack, which amounted to the largest ballistic attack on Americans in history.[69] According to Secretary of Defense Mark Esper, the six-satellite space-based infrared system operated by Space Force's 2nd Space Warning Squadron provided the critical early warning for the two thousand US service members stationed in Iraq to seek cover.[70] The administration's clandestine killings had only heightened foreign tensions even more.

Another silent killer from abroad also signaled a distressing start to 2020. In January, Trump was briefed on a deadly disease that had originated in Wuhan, China, coronavirus SARS-CoV-2, or COVID-19. This new airborne disease became a pandemic by March, almost exactly a century after the influenza pandemic—which had been spread by soldiers returning home after World War I—killed more than twenty-five million people around the world. Yet the president downplayed the gravity of the disease. To veteran journalist Bob Woodward and other reporters, Trump expressed a desire to avoid inflaming already-palpable tensions abroad. He said, "Certainly I'm not going to drive this country or the world into a frenzy. We want to show confidence. We have to show strength."[71] Trump again was displaying his obsession with exuding strength, which often had the opposite effect and created stress, if not a "frenzy."

As Americans were ordered to quarantine at home, the quiet, peaceful streets belied underlying domestic tensions. In May, the killing of George Floyd by a white Minneapolis police officer brought global attention to the Black Lives Matter movement and sparked protests across the country. Throughout the following weekend, protestors' chants in Lafayette Square could be heard, reminiscent of the anti-Vietnam war demonstrations that plagued President Johnson, from the White House residence.[72] By nightfall on Sunday, May 29, the protests turned violent with people throwing rocks, bricks, and bottles, and trying to pull down police barricades. The breaching of a temporary barricade caused the Secret Service alert on the White House to be raised from "yellow" to "red"—one of the highest alerts on the White House since the September 11 terrorist attacks.[73] Trump, the first lady, and their son, Barron, were moved to the Presidential Emergency Operations Center (PEOC) under the White House where the president spent about an hour. When *The New York Times* first reported that the president had been taken to the secure shelter, Trump was furious that the news had gotten out, and claimed that he was simply inspecting the bunker, because he felt that being hidden there showed signs of weakness.[74]

Another potential threat to the president's life, and image of strength, this time in the form of illness, occurred when Trump announced via tweet that he and First Lady Melania Trump had tested positive for COVID on Friday, October 2, 2020.[75] "Trump was deeply phobic of hospitals and all things related to illness—it fell into the bucket of 'weakness' for him—and his own illness was no exception,"[76] wrote journalist and author Maggie Haberman, who had long followed Trump's rise to power. That evening, after confiding in one associate that going to Walter Reed National Military Medical Center was going to be "bad imagery," Trump was convinced by a "small army" composed of "his doctors, members of the White House operations staff, the Secret Service, and his son-in-law and senior adviser, Jared Kushner" to go to the hospital.[77] White House doctor Sean P. Conley said that he would have access to better medical treatments there. The staff even used the tactic of telling Trump that it was not about him, but rather about protecting the presidency. According to one source, they begged him to think about "the military and everyone else whose life would be upended if the state of the country's leadership was in doubt."[78] Chief of Staff Mark Meadows told Trump that it would be preferable for him to walk to Marine One for the short trip to Bethesda, Maryland, that day rather than be carried out on a gurney if his symptoms worsened in the future.[79] The fact that the imagery could go from bad to worse is probably what motivated him to go to Walter Reed.

The danger to the president's life was acute, particularly because, at the age of 74, he was at higher risk of dying from the disease, which had already taken about a quarter of a million souls and would take 150,000 by the end of the year.[80] Even before he went to the hospital, Trump's blood oxygen level became dangerously low.[81] He was given supplementary oxygen, the steroid dexamethasone, and an experimental antibody medication REGN-COV2.[82] While the administration of oxygen and even the steroid may not have been unusual—President Kennedy had been given cortisol steroid shots to help with the symptoms of Addison's disease, for example[83]—the latter course of action indicated that Trump's symptoms must have been severe to necessitate the administering of an unlicensed drug. In fact, Trump himself emphasized the seriousness of his condition while on the phone at Walter Reed; he was overheard saying "I could be one of the diers."[84] That weekend, Dr. Conley painted a rosy picture for the media,[85] but Meadows asked to speak with reporters off the record—although unbeknownst to him, a camera caught his conversation—to clarify that the president was not out of the woods yet and that the next forty-eight hours would be critical.[86]

The public was getting mixed messages about the president's health; the only thing that was apparent was the lack of transparency about whether Americans could expect an able president at the helm. At the time, Scott Jennings, who had been an aide to both President George W. Bush and Senate Majority Leader Mitch McConnell and was close to the Trump White House, even expressed that communication with the public seemed to be a confused afterthought. He remarked that

> [T]he world has to know whether the president of the United States is in good health.... You cannot have inconsistent reports about the president's health.... I am stunned that the White House put the president's doctor out there and then issued a contradictory statement.... You can't do that. This just invites questions about what's going on there.[87]

The reason for the subterfuge was the fact that Trump had placed control over his image above a seamless transition in the Oval Office. As Pulitzer Prize-winning reporters Carol Leonnig and Phil Rucker point out in their bestselling book on the final year of Trump's first term, "in deference to Trump's psychological need to always appear in complete control" no one reassured the public that a plan was in place to ensure the continuity of the presidency should the disease fully incapacitate Trump because Vice President Pence and others knew "even entertaining that notion" would "infuriate" the president.[88] At one point during the president's coronavirus crisis, Deputy Chief of Staff for Operations Anthony M. Ornato privately warned the president that if his situation "became more dire," procedures to ensure the continuity of government would have to be set into motion.[89] Yet it was clear from Trump's skirting of Section 3 when he underwent his colonoscopy the year before that, healthy or not, he had no intention of giving up the powers and duties of the presidency even for a minute.

Speculation about Trump's health, and concern about his ability to discharge the powers and duties of the presidency while positive for the virus and undergoing medical treatment was rampant in the media. One former senior congressional staffer suggested taking advantage of the moment to plug in at least one of the holes in the Twenty-Fifth Amendment: dual incapacity. As Roy E. Brownell II, former Deputy Chief of Staff and Counsel to Senate Majority Leader Mitch McConnell wrote in a timely opinion piece published on October 2, "Now is the Time to Address Presidential and Vice-Presidential Incapacity," the mechanisms of the Twenty-Fifth Amendment revolve around an able vice president and the rapidity with which COVID-19 spread and killed those that fell ill with the sickness meant that both Trump and Vice President Pence could become incapacitated simultaneously; and, if they arguably recovered, they could be in contest with the speaker of the House.[90] Earlier contingency plans suggested that the Cabinet and speaker agree on dual incapacity, but a statute would prevent any confusion.

On the Hill, members of Congress were also puzzling over related questions and reintroduced a statute to fill a different hole in the Twenty-Fifth Amendment: who would determine what constitutes "inability." On October 9, House Speaker Nancy Pelosi was joined by Democratic Congressman Jamie Raskin, a constitutional expert, at a press conference to announce the introduction of the Commission on Presidential Capacity to Discharge the Powers and Duties of Office Act. This was the bill Raskin originally introduced in 2017. The difference in bill language between the 2017 version and the reintroduced one was that, rather than a ten-member-plus-one-chair commission, the 2020 legislation called for a bipartisan commission composed of sixteen members, plus one chair chosen by those sixteen members.[91] Of the first eight members, Democrats would choose half, and Republicans, the other half. These first eight would be medical personnel, physicians, and other medical authorities.[92] The other eight members would be former high-ranking executive branch officers, from former presidents and vice presidents to attorneys general, secretaries of defense, treasury, and state, and surgeon general.[93] During the press conference, Pelosi stated that Trump was not a target of the reintroduced legislation, instead it was designed to apply to the next president, whether that was Trump or his opponent.[94] Raskin highlighted the fact that the framers of the Twenty-Fifth Amendment thought ratification was critical for the security of the country during the nuclear age, and the prevalence of the deadly coronavirus pandemic now underscored its necessity. Raskin stated:

> The authors of the 25th Amendment thought it essential in the nuclear age to have a safety valve option. And they often said, we have 535 Members of Congress, but we only have one president. In the age of COVID-19, which has killed more than 210,000 Americans and now ravaged the White House staff, the wisdom of the 25th Amendment is clear.[95]

With the added concern of a deadly coronavirus that could swiftly fell the president and vice president, filling some of the gaps in the amendment seemed urgent.

However, Trump's answer to Meadows' public admission of the president's frailty was not to address issues of continuity, but to concoct photo ops intended to highlight his strength and vitality. While at the hospital, to appear to be working diligently, he had photographs taken of him signing blank pieces of paper.[96] To announce his return to the White House, Trump came up with a plan based on singer James Brown "tossing off his cape": the president would rise and rip off a button-down shirt to reveal a t-shirt with the Superman logo.[97] He had an aide order the shirt, but his staff dissuaded him from carrying out the idea.[98] Instead, he decided to climb the stairs to the second-floor portico and dramatically rip off his mask.[99] This did little to enhance his image of being healthy and in charge; to everyone watching, he seemed to be gasping for breath.

Furthering the image of being strong and in control was particularly important as Trump was only a month out from Election Day. One reporter wrote that "statistically, the coronavirus is more likely to cost Donald Trump the White House than his life, though the threat to the latter isn't helping the former," and then quoted someone "who publicly supports Trump and considers him a friend," saying "I didn't like the way he looked on that balcony. Last week, I would've said that he was definitely going to win. Now, I don't know."[100] Ironically, as a candidate in 2016, Trump dictated a note to his former doctor that declared he would be the "healthiest individual ever elected to the presidency."[101] When he became president, his physician, Dr. Ronny Jackson, claimed the president could have lived to "200 years old" with a better diet.[102] (Trump loved burgers and Diet Coke, the latter so much so that he had a red button installed on the Resolute Desk to summon a soda. Visitors to the Oval Office worried that it was the nuclear button.[103]) Needless to say, contracting COVID did not help him to convince voters that he was hale and hearty and therefore it did not fit with his reelection plans.

As an election loss loomed closer, US intelligence showed that China believed Trump might start a war so that a foreign policy victory would cause Americans to rally around the flag thereby boosting his popularity.[104] Four days before the election, to alleviate their fear, chairman of the Joint Chiefs of Staff General Mark Milley called his Chinese counterpart, General Li Zuocheng, to "pass the message to Chinese president Xi Jinping" that America was not about to attack.[105] Two months later, the *Wall Street Journal* published an opinion piece "China is National Security Threat No. 1" written by Director of National Intelligence John Ratcliffe that argues that China should be America's "primary national security focus moving forward" because China is intent on "replacing America as the dominant superpower."[106] Relations with nuclear superpower China were on a knife-edge.

Amidst this tension in the run up to the election, reporters asked Trump directly if he would accept an election loss; he signaled he would not and questioned the bedrock of American democracy by stating, without proof, that Democrats were compromising the election's integrity.[107] Then, on November 3, 2020, Americans voted Trump out of office. Biden received 81,268,924 popular votes to Trump's 74,216,154.[108] The oldest president to that date, former Vice President Biden, who was older than Reagan in 1984, would take office in a matter of weeks. Trump, far from graciously accepting the loss and preparing the country for a peaceful transition of power, refused to concede the election. He tweeted that the election was "rigged," and complained of dead people voting and ballot-box stuffing.[109]

On the Monday after the election, just seventy-two days before Biden would take office, President Trump fired Esper, who had been elevated to defense secretary eighteen months earlier, upending the military's leadership. Trump had "terminated" him by tweet, and Meadows informed him that he lost his post because he "wasn't sufficiently loyal."[110] Meadows meant loyal to the president, not to the Constitution, and this was a benchmark that Trump would increasingly measure his advisors by going forward. National security veterans were among the most vocal critics of Esper's termination and were in general agreement that, as *The New York Times* put it, "it was a volatile move ... by a president who has made clear that he does not want to give up power... [to reassert] his waning authority over the most powerful agencies of the government."[111] Democratic Chairman of the House Armed Services Committee Adam Smith called Trump's decision to fire Esper "reckless," and Jim Stavridis, a retired four-star Navy admiral, pointed out via Twitter that, "Things are already unstable internationally, and this does not help."[112] Then, fifty-nine days out, more than one hundred national security officials from previous Republican administrations signed a letter stating that Trump's delay in accepting and authorizing the transition was a national security risk in the event of a terrorist attack or other catastrophe and urged Trump to move forward with a smooth and orderly transition of power.[113] In his effort to reassert his authority over Defense and project an image of power, he caused instability. The uncertain time between administrations would continue to get rockier.

During the transition, rather than convincing the president to admit defeat and calmly make way for his replacement, White House advisors avoided him, and he increasingly tuned out anyone that did not humor him in favor of "an infusion of new loyalists." One loyalist, former New York City Mayor Rudolph Guiliani posted a profusion of false tweets claiming that Trump had won the election and, together with Trump and the rest of his legal team, pressured state officials in several states—including Arizona, California, Georgia, Pennsylvania, and Wisconsin—to overturn the results.[114] These new advisors told him what he wanted to hear while also pandering to his paranoia.[115] They repeated what had already been suggested online even before Election Day, including that America's enemies such as China, Iran, North Korea, and Russia had coordinated a cyberwarfare attack to steal votes from Trump using two CIA programs—a foreign surveillance program called the "Hammer" and a cyberwarfare weapon called "Scorecard"—to steal US elections.[116] Venezuelan leader Hugo Chavez, who had been dead for years, was blamed for creating technology that led to voter fraud.[117] The US federal agency that oversees elections, the Cybersecurity and Infrastructure Security Agency, responded with assurances that the 2020 election was "the most secure in election history." "That an American president was even entertaining any of this, raised questions about the state of his mind and his capacity to fulfill his duties,"[118] White House reporter Jonathan Swan observed. The conspiracy theory at best was farfetched, veering into the realm of fantasy when true foreign policy threats existed.

One such foreign threat was the one on the president's life. Trump's national security and Pentagon officials were anticipating that Iran would mark January 3, the one-year anniversary of General Soleimani's death by an American drone, with violence. Iranian President Hassan Rouhani gave a speech in which he made a "thinly veiled threat on Trump's life,"[119] stating that it was "the right of the [Iranian] people to take revenge."[120] After the holidays, Trump returned to the White House from Mar-a-Lago earlier than planned due to "the dangers overseas and the nature of the Iranian leader's comments."[121]

At the same time, Milley worried that Trump's rhetoric about the "stolen" election was not just chipping away at democratic principles, it was intended to cause unrest so that he would have an excuse to invoke the Insurrection Act of 1807, which empowers the president to deploy US military and federalized national guard troops within the United States to suppress civil disorder, insurrection, or rebellion.[122] Milley received word that ten former secretaries of defense had been thinking along the same lines and had written an opinion piece that would be published in *The Washington Post* on January 3.[123] It warned that the military should never be used to resolve election disputes or interfere with the peaceful transition of power. Within days, the president would indeed stoke an insurrection that would lead to chaos at the Capitol, followed by resignations of top officials in his administration and calls to invoke the Twenty-Fifth Amendment.

* * *

Trump returned to a Washington seething with tensions as security preparations were readied for a record number of protestors whose ire had been raised by the president himself.[124] The Electoral College vote that took place on December 14, 2020, counted 306 votes for Biden and 232 for Trump,[125] and the certification of these ballots was scheduled to take place on January 6, 2021. Trump pressured Pence to overturn, or refuse to certify, the election results, and when Pence refused to do his bidding, Trump put the vice president's life at risk. Mostly a formality, Pence's constitutional role was to preside over the Senate and House as they received and certified the electoral votes sent by the states and then to announce the outcome. He did not have the power to change that outcome, and he told Trump as much over lunch on January 5, after Trump tweeted, incorrectly, that "the vice president [had] the power to reject falsely chosen electors."[126] The next day, after Trump again pressed Pence to no avail, Pence wrote a letter to members of Congress stating that he did not have the constitutional authority to count some electoral votes but not others.[127] The lack of absolute loyalty infuriated Trump who then proceeded to blacken Pence's image. "With his loyal No. 2 no longer so loyal in his eyes" as White House correspondent Maggie Haberman wrote, "Trump convinced his supporters to view the routine act of certifying the election results as an illegal affront against him and against them."[128] In an incendiary speech at the Ellipse, Trump addressed his angry supporters urging them to overturn the "stolen" election by saying things like "you will never take back our country with weakness."[129] Other Trump loyalists who spoke included Guiliani, who called for a battle royale or "trial by combat."[130] Trump sent his supporters—paramilitary organizations and white extremists such as the Proud Boys and Oath Keepers—toward the Capitol complex where violence broke out.

As Trump's supporters breached the Capitol building at about 2:00 p.m., they threatened the second and third in line of succession chanting "hang Mike Pence," and "Where's [Speaker] Nancy [Pelosi]?" Trump tweeted that Pence "did not have the courage to do what should have been done to protect our Country and our Constitution."[131] The angry mob vandalized the building, the Senate and House chambers, and Pelosi's office, and very nearly captured the vice president. Speaker Pelosi was whisked away to Fort McNair where the rest of the Senate and House leadership were taken for safety.[132] Unlike Trump, Pence's concern about image was not about personal gain, but about projecting an image of stability for foreign friends and foes or at least not contributing to the destabilizing images being aired in the media for other counties to see. The United States did not want to give terrorists an "in." Footage of Pence's escape shows that at one point the mob got within one hundred feet of both him and the nuclear football.[133] Although the insurrectionists would not have been able to order a nuclear strike, the information in the attaché case included strike options, which could be shared for ideological reasons or monetary gain or both, with America's enemies such as terrorist groups, failed states, and foreign governments.[134] Pence did not leave the Capitol building, sheltering with his family and staff first in his ceremonial office and then in an underground loading dock in part because his motorcade could have clued-in the insurrectionists to his whereabouts and in part because the image of the vice president fleeing the Capitol was not one he wanted to project to the world.[135] Although the nuclear football was not captured, nor those next in line of succession, approximately 140 Capitol and Metropolitan police officers were criminally assaulted by the rioters, and at least five people died.[136]

Once the insurrection was under way, Trump did not call in the National Guard nor the secretaries of Defense and Homeland Security nor did he try to restore order. In fact, during the speech, he had promised to join his supporters at the Capitol, and he reportedly lunged at the Secret Service agent who refused to take him.[137] While Trump was with aides mulling over whether Pence should be "hanged," it was left to the vice president to mobilize a response to the mob.[138] Speaker Pelosi, Senate Majority Leader McConnell, and soon-to-be Senate Majority Leader Chuck Schumer made repeated calls to the administration and to Acting Defense Secretary Christopher C. Miller to call the rioters off and call in the Guard.[139] Eventually the Governors of Maryland and Virginia sent their National Guards who joined the DC Metropolitan police, the Department of Homeland Security's Federal Protective Service, and other federal law enforcement officers. The rioters were expelled from the Capitol by 6:00 p.m. Pence returned to his certifying duties, and, as the National Archives states, "due to violent unrest in and around the Capitol," the Electoral College votes were not certified until 3:44 a.m. on the morning of January 7, 2021.[140] The chief executive had instigated an attack on the legislative branch and done nothing to reduce tensions, but the nation's capital was finally secured.

Some believed that since it was the president's responsibility to restore order, but Pence had done so, that meant that the vice president had taken over as acting president by assuming the powers and duties of the presidency.[141] While it is true that orders did not flow from the president to the secretary of defense to stop the attack, Pence had not assumed the presidency. The Cato Institute went so far as to suggest that Pence was wrong in not invoking the Twenty-Fifth Amendment at the very moment the president refused to take action to quell the unrest.[142] The Institute stated Pence had to act because he was "[f]aced with a president who was clearly unable to carry out his responsibilities,"[143] and rebuked him for putting "political optics" over his constitutional duty. Cato was correct in stating that political imagery seemed to be of greater import to the Trump administration than following constitutional dictates. However, in this case, Trump was "able"—he was by no means incapacitated—he just was not willing.

Almost immediately, with removal via the Twenty-Fifth Amendment not an option, but no longer wanting to serve in his administration, Trump Cabinet officials and aides considered resigning. Transportation Secretary Elaine Chao, wife of Majority Leader McConnell, resigned in protest stating that the events of the day before were "traumatic" and "avoidable."[144] A second Cabinet secretary, Department of Education head Betsy DeVos, also resigned. DeVos' letter of resignation laid the blame directly on the president stating, "there is no mistaking the impact your rhetoric had" on the "unconscionable," and "violent behavior" of the protestors and added that the government should provide an example of moral leadership to the nation's school children.[145] Some Cabinet officials stayed on because they were afraid the precarious situation would worsen.[146] Those that resigned were criticized for "running away from their responsibilities" by not staying in their posts and attempting to remove the president via the Twenty-Fifth Amendment.[147] Senator Elizabeth Warren of Massachusetts commented that DeVos had done nothing to help American students so it was not surprising that she would quit her job rather than help invoke the amendment.[148] Representative Alexandria Ocasio-Cortez of New York called the resignations little more than "attempts at self-preservation," and tweeted, "If Sec. Chao objects to yesterday's events this deeply, she should be working the Cabinet to invoke the 25th amendment—not abdicating the seat that allows her to do so."[149] Representative Ted Lieu of California wanted to know if the acting secretaries replacing Chao and DeVos would be the "kind of patriot[s]" that would invoke the amendment.[150] The problem with this chiding is that while the president was "mad" as in "enraged" for not getting his way, he was not "mad" in the sense of "insane," nor was he incapacitated. The rhetoric he employed to instigate the insurrection was calculating. Not only was the amendment not a mechanism for permanent removal, but Trump was not suffering from an inability. DeVos responded to Warren by tweeting "you know not of what you speak,"[151] and said she resigned after discussing the use of Section 4 with fellow Cabinet members and Pence and learning that the vice president would never sign off on it.[152]

Other reports concurred that discussion at the highest echelons of the White House about the possibility of the vice president joining with a majority of the Cabinet to invoke Section 4 took place during the night and into the morning of January 7.[153] In *Betrayal: The Final Act of the Trump Show*, *ABC News* Chief White House Correspondent Jonathan Karl writes that Treasury Secretary Steven Mnuchin spoke with Secretary of State Pompeo about "removing Trump from office" by invoking the Twenty-Fifth Amendment.[154] According to Karl, it was only after pointing out that the Trump administration did not deny that the conversation took place that it eventually issued a denial. He added that the officials "might not acknowledge [the fact that a discussion about invoking the amendment occurred] while Trump is still a political force."[155] This reasoning, similar to Ocasio-Cortez's above—the fear of reprisal—is a reasonable one as Trump had a history of exacting revenge: He fired Esper for a lack of loyalty and turned on Pence for not bending to his will, for example. However, Pompeo did tell a few insiders a version of Karl's story, one in which the discussion about the need to ensure a peaceful transition occurred with Trump, not Pence, and the words "Twenty-Fifth Amendment" were not uttered. In Pompeo's version, Labor Secretary Gene Scalia approached the secretary of state to say that Cabinet members should "talk to the president about taking steps to ensure an orderly transition. Pompeo responded, 'How do you think that conversation is going to go?'"[156] Mnuchin later admitted to the January 6 Committee investigating the attack that the Twenty-Fifth Amendment was discussed briefly.[157] Cassidy Hutchinson, former top aide to Meadows, told the Committee that Trump knew of the talk and recorded a video message to the nation the next day not only to preserve his legacy, but as "cover" to stave off the possibility of invocation.[158] However, discussions that the vice president join Cabinet members in invoking Section 4 would have been dead on arrival, as DeVos had learned.

Pelosi, together with Schumer, called Pence and issued a statement adding to the chorus trying to convince the vice president to use the amendment.[159] They were placed on hold for twenty minutes and he ultimately did not take their call.[160] This rejection was purposeful on Pence's part. In his memoir, Pence writes that "over the weekend the Democrats' push to use the Twenty-Fifth Amendment on the president drove the news," and added that the Democrats, having approved a resolution in the House demanding that he invoke the Twenty-Fifth Amendment, "just would not let it go."[161] Congressman Raskin introduced the resolution in the Democratic-controlled House that charged Trump with demonstrating an "inability to discharge the most basic and fundamental powers and duties of his office" including defending democracy in the wake of the insurrection.[162] The vote was along party lines with one Republican, Representative Adam Kinzinger of Illinois, voting with the Democrats. Just before the vote on January 12, Pence sent a statement to Congress "I will not now yield to efforts in the House of Representatives to play political games at a time so serious to the life of our nation.... Invoking the Twenty-Fifth Amendment is not a means of punishment or usurpation."[163] Doing so would "set a terrible precedent" at a time when "our Administration's energy is directed to ensuring an orderly transition."[164] In his letter, Pence acknowledged the tensions of the time "… in the midst of a global pandemic, economic hardship for millions of Americans, and the tragic events of January 6, now is the time for us to come together, now is the time to heal."[165] But regardless of how much the president had belittled him or put his life on the line, the vice president was not going to be persuaded.

To Speaker Pelosi, invoking the Twenty-Fifth Amendment was not a matter of "punishment or usurpation," but a critical preventative measure to ensure that a reckless president would not unilaterally start a nuclear war. On Friday, January 8, Pelosi followed up her failed outreach to Pence by speaking with General Milley, who was monitoring China, Russia, Iran, and other nations that were now on high alert.[166] "This situation of this unhinged president could not be more dangerous,"[167] Pelosi told Milley. According to the speaker, the chairman of the Joint Chiefs agreed that Trump was "erratic," and reassured her that "the military, if given an order by the president to conduct a strike overseas, including a nuclear strike, was "not going to do anything illegal or crazy."[168] He allayed her fears by explaining, "The president alone can order the use of nuclear weapons. But he doesn't make the decision alone. One person can order it, several people have to launch it."[169] Yet the concern that Trump had his finger on the nuclear trigger and could push it on a whim was a red flag that nuclear missileers had warned Americans about during the 2016 campaign. That same day as Milley received the call from Pelosi, former Secretary of Defense William J. Perry co-authored an opinion piece in *Politico Magazine* detailing the dangers of having one person, in this case an unhinged president, with his finger on the button. He posed a version of the question that members of Congress considered during hearings on the Twenty-Fifth Amendment in the mid-1960s: "Do we really think *any* president should have the godlike power to deliver global destruction in an instant?"[170] Perry suggested a few solutions: sharing authority with a select group in Congress, promising the United States would not be the first to launch a nuclear weapon, and retiring land-based ballistic missiles that are an obvious, stationary target visible to satellites.[171]

Democratic lawmakers had already introduced "no first use of nuclear weapons" legislation, but the bill suffered from a lack of bipartisan support. The sponsors of the 2017 legislation, H.R. 669/S. 200, Congressman Ted W. Lieu of California and Senator Edward J. Markey of Massachusetts, reminded members that the Constitution empowers Congress to declare war, not the president, and argued the legislation was necessary to preserve global stability during the time of Trump. Their media release zeroed in on the fact that it was Trump's finger on the trigger. Lieu stated, "It is a frightening reality that the US now has a commander-in-chief who has demonstrated ignorance of the nuclear triad and stated his desire to be 'unpredictable' with nuclear weapons."[172] Markey added that Trump had said he would use nuclear weapons first against terrorists thereby endangering Americans' survival.[173] (Prior to January 6, congressmembers were concerned that the Justice Department had issued a twenty-two page legal decision defending the president's right to order a first strike, as he had against Syria in 2017, to punish them for using chemical weapons—as long as the risk of escalation was low.[174]) On the one hand, Americans do not want a trigger-happy, crazed president at the helm making a decision that will bring about a nuclear apocalypse. On the other, the president might have to make a split-second decision and waiting for Congress to convene and vote would encumber the commander-in-chief. Congress was designed to be a slow, deliberative body, as Americans were reminded after the events of January 6.

As for removing the unstable president, Speaker Pelosi had reached an impasse with the vice president, on whom the invocation of the Twenty-Fifth Amendment depended, and lamented the fact that January 2021 was "such a different moment" than when Republican congressional leaders told Nixon that he had "lost support" over Watergate and urged him to resign.[175] In fact, Republicans had discussed privately how to remove Trump, who had become a liability to the party, and House Minority Leader Kevin McCarthy considered asking him to resign.[176] Pelosi also revealed in her memoir that as the Capitol was being ransacked, members of Congress were looking to remove the president by other means. Representatives Raskin, David Cicilline, and Ted Lieu were texting each other from their respective hiding places (under furniture) about bringing new impeachment charges against the president.[177] On January 11, joined by 218 Democratic cosponsors, Raskin, Cicilline, and Lieu submitted House Resolution 24 that contained just one article of impeachment against the president for engaging in "high Crimes and Misdemeanors by inciting violence against the Government of the United States." The text of the resolution cited some of Trump's rhetoric just prior to the riot such as "if you don't fight like hell, you're not going to have a country anymore."[178] On January 13, with all 222 Democrats and ten Republicans in favor, the House Resolution passed by a vote of 232 to 197. It was now up to the Senate to convict Trump.

Six more days were left in Trump's term and, if the Senate had proceeded and convicted him, Trump would have been removed and barred from holding office again. Under Senate rules, the trial is supposed to start the day after the article of impeachment is presented to the Senate. But the Senate was not scheduled to resume business until January 19, the day before Biden's inauguration. Pelosi sent the article of impeachment to the Senate on January 25, and Schumer, who had been hidden away with her at Fort McNair in the overnight hours of January 6–7, announced the trial would begin on February 9. Only fifty-seven senators, ten short of the required two-thirds majority, voted to find him guilty. Trump was acquitted. McConnell, who could have controlled the timing of the trial by receiving the article of impeachment prior to Biden's inauguration, was not one of the seven Republican senators that voted to convict Trump. Had he done so, rank-and-file Republicans likely would have followed suit, and the necessary two-thirds majority would have been obtained. Instead, McConnell delivered a scathing rebuke of the president on the Senate floor after the acquittal, using words like "terrorism," "looming catastrophe," and "dereliction of duty."[179] In the end, they were just words, and Trump, the only president in history to be impeached twice, was free to run for office again.

On Inauguration Day, the passing of power from Trump to Biden occurred without incident. As a result of the coronavirus, Cabinet members stayed home, and no designated survivor was chosen. Trump did not participate in the formality of attending his successor's swearing-in ceremony. He was the first president not to attend since Andrew Johnson in 1869, and only the fifth in US history. The chaos on January 6 had caused Americans to desire a return to some semblance of normalcy and America's opponents were also wary. Biden would need to work toward lowering the temperature on international tensions that seemed at the brink of boiling over.

Turning his attention to Russia, Biden attempted to lower tensions and prevent a war involving America's Cold War opponent. Beginning in November 2021, Biden took the uncharacteristic step of sharing classified US intelligence reports bilaterally with Ukraine and collectively with twenty-nine NATO allies.[180] The reports revealed evidence of Russian military preparations to attack Ukraine despite Russian President Vladimir Putin's denial. Russia had amassed 175,000 troops along Ukraine's border, including in the puppet-state of Belarus, and was planning to invade.[181] This intelligence sharing was prompted by "initial reluctance" by some European allies to treat US claims of a pending Russian invasion as credible.[182] Not only would this allow Ukraine and its allies to be more prepared, but Biden also hoped that, like the United States, NATO allies would put sanctions on Russia that would deter the nuclear power from starting a war. Putin was undeterred. With a goal of being the only nuclear successor state to the Soviet Union, Russia had annexed the Crimea Peninsula in late winter 2014.[183] In an expansion of that war, almost eight years to the day, Russia invaded Ukraine on February 24, 2022. On that day, a Russian deserter from a top-secret nuclear base later revealed that the nuclear weapons base he was serving at was put on full combat alert and stayed at that alert level for weeks.[184] Compounding the danger of nuclear warfare was the fact that nuclear plants were in the line of fire. On March 4, Russia took control of the Zaporizhzhia Nuclear Power Plant, the largest power plant in Europe and among the ten largest in the world, and Ukrainian officials warned that Russia planned to blow it up.[185] Russian troops stationed in Belarus also moved through the Chernobyl exclusion zone, a region highly contaminated by a 1986 meltdown and explosion at the Chernobyl nuclear plant, which had caused radioactive fallout throughout Western Europe.[186] On August 1, the UN chief warned that "humanity is just one misunderstanding, one miscalculation away from nuclear annihilation," citing not just the war in Ukraine, but other nuclear threats in the Middle East and Asia.[187] The peril of WWIII loomed larger than any time since the Cold War.

* * *

As Russian troops were building up along Ukraine's border, for only the fourth time in history, Biden invoked the Twenty-Fifth Amendment, turning the powers and duties of the presidency over to Vice President Kamala Harris for eighty-five minutes when he underwent a colonoscopy on November 19, 2021, a day before his seventy-ninth birthday.[188] The transfer of power was uneventful, but it ensured continuity and was the first time a woman had been acting president. After Biden's physical in February 2023, in which he had a cancerous skin lesion removed from his chest, Dr. Kevin O'Connor, his primary care physician, said that he "remained a healthy, vigorous eighty-year-old male."[189] The doctor also noted that although the president had contracted COVID-19 the previous summer, he showed no signs of long COVID, an infection-associated, chronic illness that is known to cause, among other symptoms, problems with memory or "brain fog."[190] Only his stiff gait and high cholesterol had worsened.[191] The following February, in what was to be his last physical before the 2024 election, the doctor stated, "President Biden is a healthy, active, robust eighty-one-year-old male, who remains fit to successfully execute the duties of the presidency, to include those as chief executive, head of state and commander-in-chief."[192] The doctor remarked that the only new health development was that the president had begun using a Positive Airway Pressure (PAP) for sleep apnea.[193] He was pronounced "fit for duty," for another four years by Dr. O'Connor.

Although Biden's physician certified that he was mentally and physically able, one other development that same month seriously called that prognosis into question. Special Counsel Robert K. Hur had been appointed by US Attorney General Merrick Garland to investigate Biden's handling of classified documents and questioned Biden for hours over the course of two days. Although Hur was not a doctor, Hur's report claimed Biden suffered from "diminished faculties and faulty memory," so much so that he could not remember the year his son Beau Biden had died.[194] Such an emotional topic that had nothing to do with the investigation at hand could have easily addled the president, who tried to make up for the error by detailing a long list of legislative achievements. But then he accidentally referred to Egypt's Abdel Fattah el-Sisi as the president of Mexico, answered questions on Afghanistan troop withdrawals incorrectly, and could not seem to remember what year his term as vice president had concluded.[195] Hur claimed that he did not pursue criminal charges for mishandling the classified documents for two reasons: Biden's history of public service and the fact that his obvious memory lapses would make it difficult for a jury to convict him.[196] The special counsel said that Biden came across as a "sympathetic, well-meaning, elderly man with a poor memory."[197] In a letter, the White House rebutted the report's detrimental findings on the president's memory lapses, stating that it is common for witnesses not to clearly remember events that happened five or more years in the past.[198] But the damage was done. It was a legal victory for Biden, but a political defeat.[199]

Biden's opponents had a field day with the report's release because they had been using questions of declining mental acuity and physical ability, as well as his advancing age, as reasons why he should not be reelected. After Hur's report, Republican presidential candidate Nikki Haley called for the president to take a "mental competency test," because "millions of Americans watch President Biden and believe he exhibits cognitive decline.... Sadly, he often seems disoriented and confused."[200] Biden Press Secretary Karine Jean-Pierre dismissed the need for the test outright saying O'Connor believed such a test was not warranted "because of just who [Biden] is as president of the United States and everything that he has to deal with."[201] Jean-Pierre was implying that the amount of information that the president had to process should speak for itself as far as his abilities were concerned. But it is precisely that reason—the ability to accurately and rapidly handle new material in a balanced manner under extreme pressure—that warranted looking more closely at Biden's abilities. This is especially true when one wrong decision during the nuclear age could lead to the destruction of humanity.

The messaging combined with Biden's blunders were disconcerting to voters who were beginning to agree with Haley's sentiments. The month of the Hur report and Biden's physical exam, 64% of Americans polled believed that Biden no longer had the "mental fitness to serve a second presidential term."[202] Almost the same percentage, 62%, also believed he was not physically fit enough to serve a second term.[203] This indicates that Americans were slightly more concerned about Biden's mental acuity than his physical fitness, but both were concerning. These same public opinion polls revealed the extent to which the public believed that Biden, at eighty-one, was simply too old for the job. A full two-thirds (67%) of Americans polled by Quinnipiac University believed him to be "too old to effectively serve another four years as president."[204] An *ABC News/ Ipsos* poll, also taken in February, was even worse for Biden, showing that most Americans—86% of the public—felt that Biden was too old, 27% more than the 59% that thought the same of former President Trump, the Republican frontrunner.[205] Since less than a four-year age difference exists between the two, this was essentially a vote of no confidence as to whether Biden would be of sound mind and body to serve and pointed to the fact that voters were upset about more than his numerical age.

The 27% gap correlated with the image each candidate projected as well as who controlled the messaging in the media. Trump carefully curated his image. He had engineered publicity stunts designed to make him look healthy and vigorous when he contracted COVID and took care to cover up a colonoscopy rather than follow the precedent set by his predecessors to invoke Section 3. Trump was known for long, rambling speeches that went off on tangents, often about the latest right-wing conspiracy theories or about someone that he wished to malign in the press. But this had been ongoing since at least 2015, so with no obvious change over time, observers saw this as part of his persona, rather than as a descent into senility.[206] By contrast, Biden, who had made gaffes throughout his political career, was in the news more than Trump during the period from 2021 to 2024, and every stumble—both literally on Air Force One's stairs and figuratively—was caught on camera.[207] Some individuals, including members of his own party, questioned his mental acuity and age privately.[208] According to a new book by authors Jonathan Allen and Amie Parnes, Democratic officials "gamed out Biden withdrawal scenarios" as early as 2023.[209] Another recently released book, *Original Sin: President Biden's Decline, Its Cover-up, and His Disastrous Choice to Run Again*, argues that Biden's inner circle quietly kept him away from his Cabinet so that Cabinet members would not discover his mental faculties had declined.[210] But these hushed doubts were not shaping public opinion. For some time, Biden's opponents had been controlling messaging in conservative media outlets like *Fox News*, ensuring these issues stayed front and center. David Folkenflik, media correspondent for the liberal-leaning *NPR*, gave an example of this phenomenon dating back to the previous November (2023) when *Fox* Correspondent Lucas Tomlinson traveled with the president in Martha's Vineyard. Tomlinson said that the questions surrounding Biden's mental acuity and age were inescapable, then asked "Mr. President, are you too old to be running for office?" without revealing that he was the one posing the question.[211] In other words, "Fox was essentially saying, this is an inescapable question for the president because we keep posing it to him. But we're not going to tell you that we're the ones doing that."[212] Questions of inability were plaguing the president and threatening his reelection chances.

The tipping point came in June. During a bilateral meeting with Ukraine President Volodymyr Zelenskyy in France, Biden's voice was so soft at first that it was nearly impossible to hear him, and he misspoke about a new $225 million tranche of funding.[213] At a Juneteenth concert, he appeared to freeze briefly while everyone else around him was dancing.[214] Then, at the end of June came the fateful first televised presidential debate in Atlanta, Georgia, between the two nominees. A book published nearly a year after the debate states that it was clear to Biden's former Chief of Staff Ron Klain that Biden was mentally and physically "out of it" during the debate preparations.[215] As the debate itself progressed, Trump delivered misleading statements and falsehoods, while Biden attempted to go into more substantive details about his policies and positions.[216] But what stood out was the stark difference in presentation.[217] Trump was confidently on the attack, at one point saying "I really don't know what [Biden] said at the end of that sentence. I don't think he knows what he said either."[218] By contrast, Biden spent much of the debate in profile to the camera, at times with his mouth hanging open, gaping at Trump. At the beginning, his voice was raspy and barely audible, like during his meeting with Zelenskyy earlier in the month. At times, he lost his train of thought. By the end, he had only succeeded in exacerbating fears that his mental abilities were failing.

After Biden's dismal debate performance, calls came for him to bow out of the presidential race, but he initially resisted pressure to do so. A one-on-one interview with *ABC News'* George Stephanopoulos failed to ease voters' qualms or even those within his own party.[219] A July *Harvard CAPS-Harris* survey found that the percentage of Americans that believed that Biden was not fit to serve again, and was too old, had increased since their last survey in May. Sixty-one percent of those surveyed agreed that "electing a president who raises questions about age, failing memory, or lapsed concentration" is "dangerous for the country."[220] Thirteen Democratic congressmembers, all close to former Speaker Pelosi, suggested he exit the campaign on July 19, the most in one day, bringing the number to thirty-five, or 10% of the combined House and Senate Democratic caucuses.[221] Failing to project an image of health and ability, on July 21, 2024, Biden announced he would no longer be seeking a second term and endorsed Harris.[222]

Americans thought that if Biden did not keel over suddenly due to natural causes, he could miscalculate or freeze when a quick decision might be required to avert Armageddon. The day after Biden pulled out of the race, Biden's Republican opponents in Congress called for Harris to invoke Section 4 of the Twenty-Fifth Amendment and expressed concern that he could authorize a nuclear strike. House Speaker Mike Johnson said, "He has the nuclear codes, he has major decisions to make every single hour of every single day.... He does not have the faculties to do that right now."[223] Along similar lines, Representative Nancy Mace of South Carolina stated, "If Joe Biden does not have the cognitive ability to seek reelection, he does not have the cognitive ability to serve the remainder of his term,"[224] and introduced a resolution calling on Harris to invoke the Twenty-Fifth Amendment.[225] The resolution was mostly political theater. Harris, whose power depended on the president and who needed to project an image of competency and vitality during the campaign, was not going to invoke the Twenty-Fifth Amendment and open herself up to the question of why she had not done so sooner.

Combining the Twenty-Fifth Amendment with impeachment, Trump boasted about his own mental abilities repeatedly, suggested Biden take a cognitive test, argued for Biden's removal from office, and that of Harris. In January 2018, Trump took a test called the Montreal Cognitive Assessment (MoCA), which is used to detect mild cognitive impairment and Alzheimer's disease. He took another cognitive test in summer 2020, boasting about his results in the memory section.[226] In June 2024, he renewed his suggestion that Biden should submit to a cognitive test. However, when making that suggestion, he misstated the name of his own White House physician, calling Dr. Ronny Jackson, who had been elected to Congress in Texas, "Dr. Ronny Johnson."[227] In September, Trump, repeating his claim that Harris helped hide the state of Biden's health, argued that the Twenty-Fifth Amendment should be changed to impeach a vice president. As reported in *Politico*, Trump stated:

> I will support modifying the 25th Amendment to make clear that if a vice president lies or engages in a conspiracy to cover-up the incapacity of the president of the United States—if you do that with a cover-up of the president of the United States, its grounds for impeachment immediately and removal from office....

A *Politico* reporter correctly wrote that Trump's suggested change to a constitutional amendment was unlikely to occur. (While only twenty-seven amendments have been made to the Constitution, according to an estimate by the Senate historian, approximately 11,985 measures have been proposed to amend the Constitution from 1789 through January 3, 2025.[228]) Yet the reporter made no mention of the how far removed the idea of punishing the vice president, on whom the mechanisms of the amendment depend, was from the intentions of its framers. And unless the president did not recover from the inability, the Twenty-Fifth Amendment was not intended as a tool to remove the president, never mind the vice president. This, too, was political theater and completely divorced from the framers' intentions.

However, by this point, the tables had turned, and the Democrats now had the younger candidate in the race. Rather than Biden's age, mental acuity, and physical fitness, Trump's now became the focus. If elected, by the end of his term, he would be the oldest person to ever serve in the Oval Office. Like Biden, Trump too, had confused names, and, "[h]e float[ed] from one subject to another seemingly at random, often baffling listeners looking for a main point, a pattern that experts call tangentiality that increases with age," *New York Times* reporter Peter Baker wrote just prior to the Harris/Trump debate on September 10.[229] During the debate, Harris argued, "[Trump's] former national security advisor has said he is dangerous and unfit."[230] A week after the debate, Trump claimed the audience was rooting for him, but there had not been an audience. This confusion about a very recent event that should have been memorable for Trump, prompted *The New York Times* to publish an article entitled "Trump's Speeches, Increasingly Angry and Rambling, Reignite the Question of Age."[231]

Yet another *New York Times* article pointed out that although Trump promised in August to release his medical records if Biden dropped out of the race, he had not. It also noted that he had a history of being secretive about his health; the public learned long after the fact how dire Trump's condition had been when he contracted COVID in 2020, for example. And, in July, when speaking at a rally at the Butler Farm Show grounds in the suburbs of Pittsburgh, Pennsylvania, and Thomas Matthew Crooks, a disgruntled twenty-year-old, took shots at the Republican presidential nominee and his ear was grazed by a bullet, his campaign did not allow doctors to provide a briefing.[232] On October 12, Harris released her medical records showing that she was "in excellent health" according to her physician, US Army Colonel Joshua R. Simmons, and that "[s]he possesses the physical and mental resiliency required to successfully execute the duties of the Presidency."[233] The healthy fifty-nine-year-old who came across as sharp as a tack during the debate then challenged Trump, almost an octogenarian, to release his records.[234] Joining in that call, 230 psychiatrists and mental health professions wrote a letter—published as a paid advertisement in *The New York Times* at the end of October—claiming Trump had severe, untreatable narcissism that rendered him "deceitful, destructive, deluded, and dangerous."[235] In addition, the letter stated that he was exhibiting symptoms of cognitive decline including: "a dramatic decrease in verbal fluency, tangential thinking, diminished vocabulary, overuse of superlatives and filler words … confusing people (not just names), as well as exhibiting deteriorating judgment, impulse control, and motor functioning (including a wide-based gait)."[236] It concluded that the Republican candidate was "grossly unfit for leadership."[237]

If Trump's rambling and sometimes incoherent speeches did not signal the beginning of Alzheimer's disease that his father, Fred, had suffered from for six years, or his lack of exercise and diet of cheeseburgers did not cause a heart attack, the former president's life was still threatened by the possibility of an Iranian assassination attempt. A newly published book, *Revenge: The Inside Story of Trump's Return to Power*, by Axios' senior political reporter Alex Isenstadt, details fears that Iran had positioned surface-to-air missiles inside the United States to shoot down Air Force One and the extraordinary precautions the Trump campaign employed, including a decoy plane at one point, to preserve his life.[238] The animus that Iran harbored toward the United States had continued to grow since the killing of Soleimani and an earlier, foiled assassination attempt. On October 14, Biden was forced to warn Iran that killing Trump would be an act of war.[239]

In addition to threatening to assassinate Trump, Iran was an antagonist in the Israel-Hamas War in which America was providing support to Israel. October 2024 had marked a year since the war in Gaza erupted when Hamas launched an attack by air, land, and sea during Rosh Hashanah. On the Jewish New Year holiday, October 7, 2023, Hamas and other militants killed more than 1,200 people, including forty-three Americans, and took another 251 men, women, and children as hostages.[240] Within days, Israel launched a siege on Gaza, and, after ordering an evacuation, began a full-scale invasion.[241] The war escalated, and, as the one-year anniversary of the war approached, Israel killed Hassan Nasrallah, the longtime political leader of Iran-backed Hezbollah, in an airstrike in Beirut. In retaliation, on October 1, 2024, in a major offensive, Iran launched approximately 180 ballistic missiles at Israel.[242] Israel's Iron Dome missile defense shields blocked most of the missiles, and the United States aided in Israel's defense. No Israeli casualties occurred because of the ballistic missile strikes, but a year after Hamas initiated the war, 720 Israeli soldiers had been killed, forty-one thousand Palestinians had died, and over ninety-six thousand Palestinians had been injured,[243] Israel, with support from the United States, was fighting against seven enemies in a regional war that threatened to become a larger one.

The United States was also helping to fund Ukraine's effort to fend off Russia, and this effort resulted in an uptick in saber rattling by both Russia and the United States that underscored the tension that had been building for many years. In 2019, Trump took a similarly aggressive posture against Putin as he had with Kim. That year, the United States formally withdrew from the Intermediate Nuclear Forces Treaty with Russia, blaming repeated Russian violations, and resumed testing missiles that had been banned under that treaty.[244] In May 2020, Trump considered testing a nuclear explosion, something presidents had not done since Operation JULIN, seven tests that1991–1992 spanned , at the culmination of the Cold War.[245] On January 22, 2021, two days after Biden assumed the presidency, the U.N. Treaty for the Prohibition of Nuclear Weapons, entered into force, but was ignored by most nuclear powers—a signal that tensions would continue to rise.[246]

Putin became particularly bellicose toward the United States after invading Ukraine, resenting US and NATO activity in an area he considered within Russia's sphere of influence, and he threatened that certain actions would trigger nuclear war. Like during the Cuban Missile crisis, when Khrushchev believed the United States had missiles "pointing at his dacha," Putin felt that having NATO members backed by the United States on the Russian border was an existential threat, and Ukraine was clamoring to join NATO. In early 2022, Russia moved some of its nuclear weapons into neighboring Belarus.[247] By October 2022, Putin's speeches indicated that he was considering using these weapons in the war.[248] After a year of war, Russia suspended its participation in a US–Russian treaty that limited the countries' deployed long-range nuclear forces and then revoked its ratification of the Comprehensive Nuclear-Test Ban Treaty (CTBT).[249] In November 2023, the US Congressional Commission on the Strategic Posture of the United States suggested the United States invest in nuclear modernization and innovation, because, citing both Russia and China, "for the first time since the dawn of the atomic era, the United States must deter two nuclear peer adversaries simultaneously."[250] Also given as reasons for a nuclear build-up were North Korea's growing and increasingly sophisticated nuclear program and Iran having obtained enough uranium to develop nuclear bombs. International tensions had reached a crescendo.

Tensions took another turn for the worse with Russia when, on February 14, 2024, chair of the House Intelligence Committee, Representative Michael R. Turner of Ohio, called on Biden to release all classified information on a "serious security threat."[251] Those privy to the classified briefing believed evidence existed that Russia had made advances in space-based nuclear weaponry and might directly violate the 1967 Outer Space Treaty by placing nuclear weapons in space.[252] When signing this treaty in the East Room of the White House on January 27, 1967, just a few weeks before he signed the Twenty-Fifth Amendment, President Johnson stated that although humanity had not succeeded in freeing our planet from the implements of war, it could "keep the virus from spreading," and "keep the ugly and wasteful weapons of mass destruction from contaminating space," because of the treaty, "orbiting man-made satellites will remain free of nuclear weapons."[253] Yet it now seemed that no frontier would be free from the weapons of the apocalypse.

Then, World War III beckoned when, on August 6, 2024, Ukraine advanced into Russia's Kursk region, the greatest incursion into Russian territory since World War II. The United States and its NATO allies considered allowing Ukraine to use western missiles to strike further into Russia.[254] In response, Putin cautioned that World War III would not be limited to Europe.[255] He altered his country's official nuclear doctrine, warning that Russia could use nuclear weapons if it is struck by long-range missiles the West provided to Ukraine.[256] Russia could launch if it comes under "massive attack" from conventional missiles by a non-nuclear state but "with the participation or support of a nuclear state."[257] This was an alarming change from the 2020 doctrine that dictated nuclear weapons could be deployed if Russia faced an attack using nuclear or other weapons of mass destruction or conventional weapons only "when the very existence of the state is put under threat."[258]

By the November 2024 election, Russia's nuclear arsenal contained approximately 4380 operational nuclear warheads, but only 1700 were "deployed" or ready for use.[259] Similarly, the United States maintained a stockpile of approximately 3708 warheads, with only about 1,770 warheads deployed (meaning approximately 1,938 are held in reserve).[260] To put this in perspective, there are 12,121 nuclear warheads across the globe, about 9,585 of which are in military stockpiles for potential use. Russia and the United States control 88% of that total.[261] With the increase in threats and the new nuclear doctrine, concerns deepened that, at the very least, Putin might deploy smaller, tactical nuclear weapons.[262] Although these weapons would not cause widespread fallout, this would still be an extreme escalation in a war that would soon enter its third year. Additional escalations using more powerful nuclear weapons could come quickly on their heels. By avoiding direct confrontation with Russia, the United States thought that it might be able to avoid Armageddon.[263] This was no longer the case.

* * *

With international tensions at a height not reached since the Cold War, Biden promised a peaceful presidential transition, yet it would not come with a sense of stability. Trump had established patterns during his first term that left many Americans uneasy. He did not follow precedents regarding affairs of state, foreign affairs, nor the Twenty-Fifth Amendment. He crossed the DMZ into North Korea, did not invoke Section 3 of the amendment when planning to be anesthetized for a colonoscopy, and did not attend Biden's inauguration. And in contrast to Obama, who in 2009, had "a backup to the backup"—Undersecretary of Intelligence James Clapper hid in the Raven Rock bunker, backing up Defense Secretary Robert Gates—no designated survivor was chosen during Trump's Second Inauguration, setting the stage for the term to come.[264]

Throughout Trump's first term, talk of invoking the Twenty-Fifth Amendment came from all quarters: the media, the Hill, and the highest echelons of the White House. Trump's abrupt and seemingly spur-of-the-moment actions led many to believe he was non compos mentis. But it was his tweets that threatened nuclear war that resulted in a cacophony of voices calling for his removal through invocation of the Twenty-Fifth Amendment. Scholars weighed in and a few corrected the record, underscoring the point that the amendment would not lead to removal, unless the inability was permanent. The way to remove the president was to vote him out of office, which Americans did in November 2020. Trump initially refused to leave office, undermining the democratic process. Instead, he encouraged his supporters to ransack the Capitol so that the Electoral College votes would not be certified. After January 6, calls for the president's "removal" via the Twenty-Fifth Amendment or via impeachment reached a fever pitch. The amendment was not invoked, and while he was impeached for a second time, he was not removed, nor barred from holding office again.

In fact, one of the biggest proponents of the misinformation surrounding the amendment was the president himself. Trump demonstrated a pattern of using the amendment as a rhetorical tool for political theater, rather than a legal guiding document. He was obsessed with projecting an image of strength, which would often inflame tensions. He did not take measured steps to handle COVID before it worsened, and when he contracted COVID, it was only the thought that not being able to walk to Marine One on the way to Walter Reed Hospital would be "bad imagery" that convinced him to be admitted. He then came up with a preposterous idea to rip open a button-down shirt to reveal a Superman t-shirt underneath, a photo op better suited to *DC Comics* than Washington, DC. Most saliently, when he was scheduled to undergo the colonoscopy, he did not transparently share with the public that a plan was in place, the Twenty-Fifth Amendment, that would ensure the continuity of the presidency while he was put under. It was a subtle sign that he would flout the Constitution when it suited him.

Connected to this pattern of failing to use the amendment as a guiding document was his insistence that his Cabinet and staff prove loyal to him rather than to the Constitution. Trump's demand for loyalty also led to a sense of destabilization. Sudden firings by tweet, like that of Defense Secretary Esper, gave the public no assurance that a sane president was at the helm constantly surrounded by aides that could wisely advise him in times of trouble. The infusion of loyalists during the transition bolstered the rhetoric that encouraged his supporters to march on the Capitol and would set a pattern of Trump's: surrounding himself by Cabinet members that would bend to his will for his second term.

Not only had Trump apparently avoided invoking Section 3 when it should have been invoked, but, as Americans began to question Biden's mental acuity, physical frailty, and old age, Trump's voice was the loudest, even though he, too, was known for confusing names and discursive campaign speeches. When Biden withdrew from the campaign trail, cognizant of poor polling numbers and convinced by members of his own party, Trump demanded that Harris invoke Section 4 to "remove" Biden from office, and, when she did not, Trump suggested a "double Twenty-Fifth Amendment," that would allow for the "removal" of both. He demonstrated no knowledge of the tenets of the amendment, nor who was next in line of succession.

The renewed focus on the Twenty-Fifth Amendment paralleled a resurgence in nuclear anxiety. In 2024, in addition to the United States, Russia, China, France, the United Kingdom, Pakistan, India, Israel, and North Korea all had nuclear warheads, and that number was increasing with Iran about to join the list any day. Iran, a known backer of terrorists, had threatened "vengeance" and sought to assassinate Trump. By the time Trump took office for a second time, major conflicts existed in every corner of the globe, with America's Cold War enemy threatening a third world war. Soon after Trump's taunting tweet to North Korean leader Kim about how the United States had a working nuclear button, due to a false alert, Hawaiians thought a missile was incoming and the end of days had truly come. With the next world war brewing and Trump's finger again on the nuclear trigger, it seemed the next alert, due to accident, miscalculation, or madness, could be the last.

Notes

1. Sarah, Vowell, "Presidential Incapacity: A Holiday Gift Guide," *The New York Times*. December 21, 2027, https://www.nytimes.com/2017/12/21/opinion/trump-holiday-gift-guide.html. See Joel K. Goldstein, "Talking Trump and the Twenty-fifth Amendment: Correcting the Record on Section 4," 21 U. Pa. J. Const. L. 73 (2018), 85, https://scholarship.law.upenn.edu/jcl/vol21/iss1/4.

2. Stephen, Eldridge, "Oppenheimer," *Britannica*, Updated March 14, 2025, https://www.britannica.com/topic/Oppenheimer-film.
3. Bob Woodward, *Fear: Trump in the White House* (New York: Simon & Schuster, 2018).
4. "President Bush Outlines Iraqi Threat," *The White House: President George W. Bush Archives*. October 7, 2002, https://georgewbush-whitehouse.archives.gov/news/releases/2002/10/20021007-8.html.
5. Michael, Nelson. Barack Obama: Foreign Affairs. Miller Center, University of Virginia, https://millercenter.org/president/obama/foreign-affairs.
6. "President Bush Outlines Iraqi Threat."
7. Tanya, Somanader, *"President Obama: 'We've Reached Havana',"* *The White House: President Barack Obama*. March 21, 2016, https://obamawhitehouse.archives.gov/blog/2016/03/21/president-obama-weve-reached-havana.
8. See, for example: Nabil Rahmatullah, "The World Must Secure Pakistan's Nuclear Weapons," *The New York Times* (April 20, 2017). See also: Adrian Levy and Catherine Scott-Clark, *Deception: Pakistan, the United States, and the Global Nuclear Weapons Conspiracy* (New York: Atlantic Books, 2007).
9. Robert Burns, "Mattis: North Korea a 'Clear and Present Danger' to World," *AP Newswire* (June 1, 2017).
10. Brad Lendon, "US Slams North Korea Missile Test as Kim Claims "Whole US Mainland" in Reach," (July 30, 2017). *CNN*, http://www.cnn.com/2017/07/29/asia/north-korea-intercontinental-ballistic-missile-test/index.html.
11. Because of his middle-of-the-night rants via social media site *Twitter*, Clinton repeated "A man you can bait with a tweet is not a man we can trust with nuclear weapons." See @HillaryClinton, *Twitter.com* (July 28, 2017). https://twitter.com/hillaryclinton/status/758864218439286784?lang=en.
12. The American Psychiatric Association established a "Goldwater Rule" when *Fact* magazine published the findings of a survey of 12,356 psychiatrists: out of 2417 respondents, 1189 believed that Goldwater was unfit to assume the presidency. The act of commenting on a candidate's mental health from afar can be viewed as compromising to the integrity of the psychiatry

profession. The Association believes this may have affected the results of the 1964 election. Offering an opposing viewpoint, family therapist and University of Minnesota psychology professor Bill Doherty's online manifesto "Citizen Therapists Against Trumpism," was the focus of a *WNYC* "On the Media" segment. Doherty insisted that, for the public good, he must violate the Goldwater Rule by condemning Trump's fear-mongering and questioning his mental health. Nuclear Launch Officers: Carol Morello, "Former Nuclear Launch Officers Sign Letter: 'Trump Should Not Have His Finger on the Button,'" *The Washington Post* (October 13, 2016). Compromising to the profession: Maria A. Oquendo, "The Goldwater Rule: Why Breaking It is Unethical and Irresponsible," *American Psychiatric Association* (August 3, 2016), https://www.psychiatry.org/news-room/apa-blogs/apa-blog/2016/08/the-goldwater-rule. Doherty: "Therapists Against Trumpism," *On the Media*, WNYC (August 26, 2016), https://www.wnycstudios.org/podcasts/otm/segments/therapists-against-trumpism.

13. During both the 1964 and 2016 presidential elections, the Republican nominee made statements implying that he would not hesitate to launch nuclear missiles; their extreme language led some Americans to believe they were mentally off-balance. See Chapter 3.
14. Maya Rhodan, "Hillary Clinton Uses 'Daisy Girl' in Ad Criticizing Trump," *Time* (October 31, 2016), http://time.com/4551744/hillary-clinton-daisy-girl-donald-trump-ad/.
15. Drew Desilver. "Why Electoral College Wins are Bigger Than Popular Vote Ones," *Pew Research Center,* December 20, 2016, https://www.pewresearch.org/short-reads/2016/12/20/why-electoral-college-landslides-are-easier-to-win-than-popular-vote-ones/. See also: Michael Crowley, "Clinton, Trump Go Nuclear," *Politico.* October 27, 2016, https://www.politico.com/story/2016/10/hillary-clinton-donald-trump-nuclear-war-230418.
16. "Trump Tells Reuters He Wants to Expand Nuclear Arsenal to Make Us Top of the Pack," *CNBC*, February 23, 2017, http://www.cnbc.com/2017/02/23/trump-tells-reuters-he-wants-to-expand-nuclear-arsenal-make-us-top-of-the-pack.html.

17. Mikhail Gorbachev, "It All Looks as if the World is Preparing for War," *Time*, January 26, 2017, http://time.com/4645442/gorbachev-putin-trump/.
18. Matthew Rosenberg and Eric Schmitt, "Trump Revealed Highly Classified Intelligence to Russia, in Break with Ally, Officials Say," *The New York Times*, May 15, 2017, https://www.nytimes.com/2017/05/15/us/politics/trump-russia-classified-information-isis.html.
19. "Trump Revealed Highly Classified Intelligence to Russia, in Break with Ally, Officials Say."
20. Adam Goldman and Michael S. Schmidt, "Rod Rosenstein Suggested Secretly Recording Trump and Discussed 25th Amendment," *The New York Times*. September 21, 2018, https://www.nytimes.com/2018/09/21/us/politics/rod-rosenstein-wear-wire-25th-amendment.html.
21. Stephanie, Grisham, *I'll Take Your Questions Now: What I Saw at the Trump White House* (New York: HarperCollinsPublishers, 2021), 210–211.
22. "Full Text: Trump's 2017 U.N. Speech Transcript," *Politico*, September 19, 2017, https://www.politico.com/story/2017/09/19/trump-un-speech-2017-full-text-transcript-242879.
23. "@realDonaldTrump status," *X.com*, https://x.com/realDonaldTrump/status/948355557022420992.
24. "Timeline of the Hawaii Missile Threat Shows How Drill Went Wrong," *CNN*, January 30, 2018, https://www.cnn.com/2018/01/30/us/hawaii-false-missile-alert-timeline/index.html.
25. "Timeline of the Hawaii Missile Threat Shows How Drill Went Wrong."
26. Cynthia Lazaroff, "Dawn of a New Armageddon," *Bulletin of the Atomic Scientist*, August 6, 2018, https://thebulletin.org/2018/08/dawn-of-a-new-armageddon/.
27. "Hawaii Missile Alert: False Alarm Warns Residents of 'Ballistic Missile Threat'," *CBS News*, January 13, 2018, https://www.cbsnews.com/news/hawaii-missile-alert-emergency-management-system-false-ballistic-missile-warning-2018-1-13/, See also: "Dawn of a New Armageddon."

28. "False Ballistic Missile Alarm Forces Hawaii into Panic Mode," *CBS News,* January 15, 2018, https://www.bing.com/videos/riverview/relatedvideo?q=missile+alert+Hawaii+January+2018&mid=3527ADC1CA6A50CF29A73527ADC1CA6A50CF29A7&FORM=VIRE.
29. The trailer pictured a small mushroom cloud rising from the vicinity of the Capitol, but did not reveal further detail. See "Designated Survivor," *Abc.com,* http://abc.go.com/shows/designated-survivor/video/most-recent/VDKA0_c9oq232r.
30. Mark T. Esper, *A Sacred Oath: Memoirs of a Secretary of Defense During Extraordinary Times* (New York: HarperCollins, 2022), 17–18.
31. Esper, *A Sacred Oath,* 19.
32. Ali Vitali, "Trumps 'Nuclear Button' Tweet Sparks Backlash," *NBC News,* January 3, 2018, https://www.nbcnews.com/politics/white-house/trump-s-nuclear-button-tweet-sparks-backlash-n834321.
33. "@RepStalwall status," *X.com,* January 2, 2018. https://x.com/RepSwalwell/status/948358670001344512?ref_src=twsrc%5Etfw%7Ctwcamp%5Etweetembed%7Ctwterm%5E948358670001344512%7Ctwgr%5Ef2d7e4b1e9962ed57dd69494ffee037ae0d4edcd%7Ctwcon%5Es1_&ref_url=https%3A%2F%2Fwwhouse%2Ftrump-s-nuclear-button-tweet-sparks-backlash-n834321.
34. Vitali, "Trump's 'Nuclear Button' Tweet Sparks Backlash."
35. Mike Pence, *So Help Me God.* (New York: Simon & Schuster, 2022), 308–309.
36. Bob Woodward, *Rage* (New York: Simon & Schuster, 2020), 171–172.
37. Woodward, *Rage,* 178.
38. Disastrous Deal: "Remarks by President Trump on the Joint Comprehensive Plan of Action," Trump White House Archives, May 8, 2018, https://trumpwhitehouse.archives.gov/briefings-statements/remarks-president-trump-joint-comprehensive-plan-action/. Pompeo to Pyongyang: Mark Landler, "Trump Abandons Iran Nuclear Deal He Long Scorned," *The New York Times,* May 8, 2018, https://www.nytimes.com/2018/05/08/world/middleeast/trump-iran-nuclear-deal.html?module=inline.

39. Landler, "Trump Abandons Iran Nuclear Deal He Long Scorned."
40. Baker, Peter and Michael Crowley. "Trump Steps Into North Korea and Agrees With Kim Jong-un to Resume Talks," *The New York Times*, June 30, 2019, https://www.nytimes.com/2019/06/30/world/asia/trump-north-korea-dmz.html.
41. As the potential for nuclear war looms ever closer, the possibility that Section 1 of the Twenty-Fifth Amendment will be invoked due to impeachment has been raised in Washington and in the media. Trump's refusal to distance himself from his business operations that deal with Russia, led Trump's critics to point to Article 1, Section 9, Clause 8 of the Constitution (forbidding US officeholders from accepting emoluments from foreign states) and call for his removal. On May 17, 2017, the Justice Department named Robert Mueller special counsel to oversee the department's investigation into the role of Russia in the 2016 presidential election. See: Tal Kopen, "Who is Robert Mueller?" *CNN* (May 18, 2017), http://edition.cnn.com/2017/05/17/politics/who-is-robert-mueller/index.html.
42. After introduction, the bill was referred to the House Judiciary Committee, then the House Rules Committee, and then made its way to the Subcommittee on the Constitution and Civil Justice. See Congress.gov. https://www.congress.gov/search?q={%22congress%22:%22115%22,%22source%22:%22legislation%22,%22search%22:%22\%22presidential%20capacity\%22%22}&searchResultViewType=expanded.
43. Another bill was introduced in April: H.R. 2093, entitled "Strengthening and Clarifying the Twenty-Fifth Amendment Act of 2017," was introduced by Democratic Representative Earl Blumenauer of Oregon and referred to the Subcommittee on the Constitution and Civil Justice. The bill is also designed to provide an alternative body to declare the president incapacitated. Blumenauer proposes that this body be composed of "every living president" and "every living vice president." https://www.congress.gov/bill/115th-congress/house-bill/2093?q=%7B%22search%22%3A%5B%22%5C%22presidential+incapacity%5C%22%22%5D%7D&r=1.
44. Mika Breziznski and Joe Scarborough are co-hosts of MSNBC's "Morning Joe" program. J. Freedem du Lac and Jenna Johnson,

"Mika Brezinski Explains What Trump's Tweets Reveal About Him," *The Washington Post* (June 30, 2017).

45. See, for example: Aaron Blake, "David Petraeus' Damning Nonresponse on Trump's Fitness to Serve," *The Washington Post* (July 5, 2017). Lisa Hagen and Ben Kamisar, "Pelosi: Is Trump Fit to Be President?" *TheHill.com* (May 16, 2017). https://thehill.com/homenews/house/333596-pelosi-is-trump-fit-to-be-%20president/. *Atlantic* is among those that have questioned the president's physical fitness, or lack thereof. See Stephanie Hayes, "The Unfit President," *The Atlantic* (April 3, 2017), https://www.theatlantic.com/health/archive/2017/04/trump-is-relatively-unfit-to-serve/521121/. Moreover, popular culture outlets such as *MAD Magazine* have satirized his mental abilities. See *MAD About Trump: A Brilliant Look at Our Brainless President.* (June 14, 2017). http://www.madmagazine.com/books/mad-about-trump.

46. Cease and desist letter: Christiano Lima. "Trump Lawyer Sends 'Cease and Desist' Letter to 'Fire and Fury' Author, Publisher," *Politico,* January 4, 2018, https://www.politico.com/story/2018/01/04/trump-cease-and-desist-michael-wolff-fire-and-fury-book-324023. Number one best-seller: Brian Stelter, "Michael Wolff's Trump Book Hits #1 on Amazon, Publisher Speeds Up Rollout Plan," *CNN,* January 4, 2018, https://money.cnn.com/2018/01/03/media/michael-wolff-fire-and-fury-book-interviews/index.html.

47. Michael Wolff, *Fire and Fury: Inside the Trump White House* (New York: Henry Holt & Co., 2018). "Like the world has never seen": Jeff Zeleny, Dan Merica, and Kevin Liptak, "Trump's 'Fire and Fury' Remark was Improvised but Familiar," *CNN,* August 9, 2017, https://www.cnn.com/2017/08/09/politics/trump-fire-fury-improvise-north-korea/index.html.

48. Annalisa Quinn. "Trump Expose Has Plenty of 'Fire and Fury,' Maybe a Little Less Substance," *NPR,* January 6, 2028, https://www.npr.org/2018/01/06/576026491/trump-expose-has-plenty-of-fire-and-fury-maybe-a-little-less-substance. See also Jonathan Martin, "From 'Fire and Fury' to Political Firestorm," *The New York Times,* January 8, 2018, https://www.nytimes.com/2018/01/08/books/review/michael-wolff-fire-and-fury-trump-white-house.html.

49. Peter Baker and Maggie Haberman, "Trump, Defending His Mental Fitness, Says He's a 'Very Stable Genius'," *The New York Times*, January 6, 2018, https://www.nytimes.com/2018/01/06/us/politics/trump-genius-mental-health.html.
50. "@realDonaldTrump status," *X.com*, January 6, 2018. https://x.com/realDonaldTrump/status/949618475877765120?ref_src=twsrc%5Etfw%7Ctwcamp%5Etweetembed%7Ctwterm%5E949618475877765120%7Ctwgr%5Ea16f2563126bd0dc71ecce28153d234f441886f5%7Ctwcon%5Es1_&ref_url=https%3A%2F%2Fwwway%2F2018%2F01%2F06%2F576204103%2Fa-very-stable-genius-trump-responds-to-renewed-criticism-of-his-mental-state And https://x.com/realDonaldTrump/status/949619270631256064?ref_src=twsrc%5Etfw%7Ctwcamp%5Etweetembed%7Ctwterm%5E949619270631256064%7Ctwgr%5Ea16f2563126bd0dc71ecce28153d234f441886f5%7Ctwcon%5Es1_&ref_url=https%3A%2F%2Fwwway%2F2018%2F01%2F06%2F576204103%2Fa-very-stable-genius-trump-responds-to-renewed-criticism-of-his-mental-state.
51. "A President's Temperament," *NPR*, January 6, 2018, https://www.npr.org/2018/01/06/576197759/a-presidents-temperament.
52. Robert Dallek, "Is Trump Unfit for Office? The Constitution Says Yes," *Newsweek*, December 16, 2017, https://www.newsweek.com/trump-25th-amendment-constitution-750157.
53. Dallek, "Is Trump Unfit for Office? The Constitution Says Yes."
54. "I Am Part of the Resistance Inside the Trump Administration," *The New York Times*, September 5, 2018, https://www.nytimes.com/2018/09/05/opinion/trump-white-house-anonymous-resistance.html.
55. David Greenberg and Rebecca Lubot, "Stop Talking About the 25th Amendment. It Won't Work on Trump. And It Might Just Set Off a Constitutional Crisis," *Politico Magazine*, September 8, 2018, https://www.politico.com/magazine/story/2018/09/08/trump-25th-amendment-constitutional-crisis-219739/.
56. Stephanie Grisham, *I'll take Your Questions Now: What I Saw at the Trump White House* (New York: HarperCollins Publishers, 2021), 284.
57. Grisham, *I'll take Your Questions Now*, 284.
58. Grisham, *I'll take Your Questions Now*, 284.

59. Jeff Mason, "Harris was Briefly First Woman to be Acting US President as Biden Underwent Colonoscopy," *Reuters*, November 19, 2021, https://www.reuters.com/world/us/biden-transfer-power-harris-during-colonoscopy-friday-white-house-2021-11-19/.
60. Jeremy Herb and Ashely Killough, "Democratic Lawmaker Introduces Articles of Impeachment Against Trump," *CNN*, July 16, 2019, https://www.cnn.com/2019/07/16/politics/al-green-articles-of-impeachment/index.html. See also Alex Swoyer, "Brad Sherman, California Democrat, to Introduce Articles of Impeachment Against Trump," *AP News*, January 3, 2019, https://apnews.com/article/california-impeachments-brad-sherman-f63cb4bf390f7181c2e55beb2b22af13.
61. Maggie Haberman, *Confidence Man: The Making of Donald Trump and the Breaking of America* (New York: Penguin Press, 2022), 386–387.
62. Brandon Carter, "Read: House Intel Committee Releases Whistleblower Complaint on Trump-Ukraine Call," *NPR*, https://www.npr.org/2019/09/26/764071379/read-house-intel-releases-whistleblower-complaint-on-trump-ukraine-call.
63. "Articles of Impeachment Against Donald John Trump," *House Resolution 755, One Hundred Sixteenth Congress, First Session*. December 18, 2019, https://www.congress.gov/116/bills/hres755/BILLS-116hres755enr.pdf.
64. The House vote on Article I was 230 in favor, 197 against, and 1 present, and on Article II, 229 in favor, 198 against, and 1 present. Michael D. Shear and Peter Baker, "Key Moments: The Day the House Impeached Trump," *The New York Times*, December 18, 2019, and updated December 31, 2019, https://www.nytimes.com/2019/12/18/us/politics/impeachment-vote.html.
65. Peter Baker, Michael Schmitt, and Eric Crowley, "An Abrupt Move That Stunned Aides: Inside Trump's Aborted Attack on Iran," *The New York Times*, September 21, 2019, https://www.nytimes.com/2019/09/21/us/politics/trump-iran-decision.html?unlocked_article_code=1.R04.uyT3.h9DnPMCvPm42&smid=nytcore-ios-share&referringSource=articleShare&tgrp=bth.
66. Carol Leonnig and Philip Rucker, *I Alone Can Fix It: Donald J. Trump's Catastrophic Final Year* (New York: Penguin Press,

2021), 16. In September 2014, the US and five Arab allies launched air strikes against the Islamic State in Aleppo and Raqqa. For a timeline of the Syrian crisis see: "Syria-Timeline", *BBC*, July 2017, http://www.bbc.com/news/world-middle-east-14703995.
67. Leonnig and Rucker, *I Alone Can Fix It*, 19.
68. "Buckley Air Force Base Played Key Role Warning US Troops in Iraq About Incoming Missiles," *CBS News*, March 10, 2021, https://www.cbsnews.com/colorado/news/warning-iraq-missile-colorado-aurora-buckley-air-force/.
69. Michael Stephens, "Iran's First Response to Soleimani's Death, and Tehran's Future, Moves," *Royal United Services Institute*, January 8, 2020, https://www.rusi.org/explore-our-research/publications/commentary/irans-first-response-soleimanis-death-and-tehrans-future-moves.
70. Esper, *A Sacred Oath*, 169.
71. Dareh Gregorian, "Trump Told Bob Woodward That He Knew in February That COVID-19 Was 'Deadly Stuff' But Wanted to 'Play It Down'," *NBC News*, September 9, 2020, See also Bob Woodward, *Rage* (New York: Simon & Schuster, 2020).
72. Jonathan Lemire and Zeke Miller, "Trump Took Shelter in White House as Protests Raged," *AP News*, May 31, 2020, https://apnews.com/article/donald-trump-ap-top-news-george-floyd-politics-a2326518da6b25b4509bef1ec85f5d7f.
73. Carol D. Leonnig, "Protesters' Breach of Temporary Fences Near White House Complex Prompted Secret Service to Move Trump to Secure Bunker," *The Washington Post*, June 3, 2020, https://www.washingtonpost.com/politics/secret-service-moved-trump-to-secure-bunker-friday-after-protesters-breached-temporary-fences-near-white-house-complex/2020/06/03/e4ae77c2-a5b9-11ea-b619-3f9133bbb482_story.html.
74. Baker, Peter and Maggie Haberman, "As Protests and Violence Spill Over, Trump Shrinks Back," *The New York Times*, May 31, 2020, https://www.nytimes.com/2020/05/31/us/politics/trump-protests-george-floyd.html. See also: Chris Cillizza, "Donald Trump's 'Bunker' Story Tells You Everything You Need to Know About Him," *CNN*, June 3, 2020, https://www.cnn.com/2020/06/03/politics/donald-trump-bunker-secret-service-protests/index.html.

75. "@realDonaldTrump status," *X.com*, October 2, 2020, https://x.com/realdonaldtrump/status/1311892190680014849.
76. Maggie Haberman, *Confidence Man: The Making of Donald Trump and the Breaking of America* (New York: Penguin Press, 2022), 457.
77. Olivia Nuzzi, "The Entire Presidency is a Superspreading Event: Down in the Polls, High on Steroids, and Clinging to Good Health While Endangering Everyone Else's," *NY Magazine*, October 9, 2020, https://nymag.com/intelligencer/2020/10/donald-trump-covid-19-white-house.html.
78. Nuzzi, "The Entire Presidency is a Superspreading Event."
79. Haberman. *Confidence Man*, 458.
80. Ahmad, Cisewski JA and Miniño A, Anderson RN, "Provisional Mortality Data—United States, 2020," *Centers for Disease Control and Prevention*, April 19, 2021, https://www.cdc.gov/mmwr/volumes/70/wr/mm7014e1.htm.
81. By October 3rd, his oxygen levels had decreased to 86% and could have trended lower, which was dangerous for individuals his age. Maggie Haberman and Noah Weiland, "Trump's Blood Oxygen Level in Covid Bout was Dangerously Low, Former Aide Says," *The New York Times*. December 6, 2020. https://www.nytimes.com/2021/12/06/us/politics/trump-covid-blood-oxygen.html.
82. Isaac Chotiner, "Trump's Illness and the History of Presidential Health," *The New Yorker*, October 6, 2020, https://www.newyorker.com/news/q-and-a/trumps-illness-and-the-history-of-presidential-health.
83. See Robert Dallek, *An Unfinished Life: John F. Kennedy 1917–1963* (New York: Little, Brown and Company, 2003).
84. Olivia Nuzzi, "The Entire Presidency is a Superspreading Event: Down in the Polls, High on Steroids, and Clinging to Good Health While Endangering Everyone Else's," *NY Magazine*, October 9, 2020, https://nymag.com/intelligencer/2020/10/donald-trump-covid-19-white-house.html.
85. "Read the Letter from White House Physician Dr. Sean Conley About Trump's COVID Diagnosis," *NBC News*, October 2, 2020, https://www.nbcnews.com/politics/donald-trump/read-letter-white-house-physician-dr-sean-conley-about-trump-n1241771.
86. Anita Kumar, Nancy Cook, Gabby Orr, and Meridith McGraw, "White House Triggers Questions and Confusion About Trump's

Coronavirus Case," *Politico,* October 3, 2020, https://www.yahoo.com/news/trump-doing-very-well-white-155018791.html?guccounter=1&guce_referrer=aHR0cHM6Ly93d3cuYmluZy5jb20v&guce_referrer_sig=AQAAAEKJx3ln4KL49Emq60ma6xfDqtITaRAzqFEH_oMd4vDaLNfYjpBjPSj97EZ1mS0fObO05Ox8mx92AKb6ERFHj_3SPPNNg3rpHHHiz085pwO6kKfLaveXJvuNDgafOISRcyozZkg2joIA9RgXHKFLmybiMmEXTp408dZHwwfwfx2c.

87. Kumar et al., "White House Triggers Questions and Confusion About Trump's Coronavirus Case."
88. Leonnig and Rucker, *I Alone Can Fix It,* 306–307.
89. Haberman, *Confidence Man,* 458.
90. Roy E. Brownell II, "Now is the Time to Address Presidential and Vice-Presidential Incapacity," *The Hill,* October 2, 2020, https://thehill.com/opinion/white-house/519352-now-is-the-time-to-address-presidential-and-vice-presidential-incapacity/.
91. "Press Release: Raskin Reintroduces 25th Amendment Legislation Establishing Independent Commission on Presidential Capacity," *Jamie Raskin, Serving Maryland's Eighth District.* October 9, 2020, https://raskin.house.gov/2020/10/raskin-reintroduces-25th-amendment-legislation-establishing-independent#:~:text=October%209,%202020.%20WASHINGTON,%20D.C.%20E2%80%93%20Congressman%20Jamie%20Raskin%20(MD-08).
92. "Press Release: Pelosi Remarks at Press Conference on Introduction of Legislation to Establish a Commission on Presidential Capacity," *Congresswoman Nancy Pelosi, California's 11th District,* October 9, 2020, https://pelosi.house.gov/news/press-releases/pelosi-remarks-at-press-conference-on-introduction-of-legislation-to-establish-a#:~:text=The%20legislation%20would%20create%20the%20Commission%20on%20Presidential%20Capacity%20to.
93. "Press Release: Pelosi Remarks at Press Conference on Introduction of Legislation to Establish a Commission on Presidential Capacity."
94. "Press Release: Pelosi Remarks at Press Conference on Introduction of Legislation to Establish a Commission on Presidential Capacity."

95. "Press Release: Pelosi Remarks at Press Conference on Introduction of Legislation to Establish a Commission on Presidential Capacity."
96. Leonnig and Rucker, *I Alone Can Fix It*, 306–307.
97. Haberman, *Confidence Man*, 459.
98. Haberman, *Confidence Man*, 459.
99. Haberman, *Confidence Man*, 460.
100. Nuzzi, "The Entire Presidency is a Superspreading Event."
101. Scott Neuman, "Doctor: Trump Dictated Letter Attesting to His 'Extraordinary' Health," *NPR*, May 2, 2018, https://www.npr.org/sections/thetwo-way/2018/05/02/607638733/doctor-trump-dictated-letter-attesting-to-his-extraordinary-health.
102. Soon thereafter, Trump gave White House Physician Ronny Jackson another star by promoting him to Navy rear admiral from Navy rear admiral (lower half). Elizabeth McLaughlin, "Trump Nominates His White House Physician to Rank of Rear Admiral," *ABC News*, March 23, 2018, https://abcnews.go.com/Politics/trump-nominates-personal-physician-rank-rear-admiral/story?id=53965556.
103. Compounding the unhealthiness of his fast-food diet, Trump did not workout because he believed that humans are born with a certain amount of energy that exercise depletes. Ryan Bort, "A History of Donald Trump's Confused Understanding of Diet Coke, His 'Garbage" Beverage of Choice," *Newsweek*, July 7, 2017, https://www.newsweek.com/donald-trump-drinking-diet-coke-history-633436. See also Julie Pace, "Trump At 100 Days: "It's a Different Kind of Presidency'," *Associated Press*, April 23, 2017, https://apnews.com/united-states-government-c9dd87102306491793296816d6c2c2d.
104. Bob Woodward, *Peril* (New York: Simon & Schuster: 2021), X.
105. "US Top General Secretly Called China Over Fears Trump Could Spark War—Report," *Reuters*, September 15, 2021, https://www.reuters.com/world/us/us-top-general-secretly-called-china-twice-trump-term-ended-report-2021-09-14/.
106. John Ratcliffe, "China is National Security Threat No. 1," *Wall Street Journal*, December 3, 2020, https://www.wsj.com/articles/china-is-national-security-threat-no-1-11607019599?msockid=31a957df733a64e63f05425e7279657a.

107. Nick Niedzwiadek, "The 9 Most Notable Comments Trump Has Made About Accepting the Election Results," *Politic,* September 24, 2020, https://www.politico.com/news/2020/09/24/trump-casts-doubt-2020-election-integrity-421280.
108. "Official 2020 Presidential Election Results: General Election Date: 11/03/2020," *Federal Elections Commission.* January 28, 2021, https://www.fec.gov/resources/cms-content/documents/2020presgeresults.pdf.
109. Kevin Freking, "Trump Tweets Words 'He Won'; Says 'Vote Rigged,' Not Conceding," *AP,* November 16, 2020, https://apnews.com/article/donald-trump-tweets-he-won-not-conceding-9ce22e9dc90577f7365d150c151a91c7.
110. Terminated: "@realDonaldTrump status," *X.com,* November 9, 2020. https://x.com/realDonaldTrump/status/1325859407620689922?ref_src=twsrc%5Etfw. "Not sufficiently loyal": Esper, *A Sacred Oath,* 654.
111. Helene Cooper, Eric Schmitt, and Maggie Haberman, "Trump Fires Mark Esper, Defense Secretary Who Opposed Use of Troops on US Streets," *The New York Times,* November 11, 2020, https://www.nytimes.com/2020/11/09/us/politics/esper-defense-secretary.html#:~:text=WASHINGTON%20%E2%80%94%20President%20Trump%20fired%20Defense%20Secretary%20Mark%20T.%20Esper.
112. "Reckless": Cooper, et al., "Trump Fires Mark Esper, Defense Secretary Who Opposed Use of Troops on US Streets." "Unstable Internationally": Robert Burns and Lolita C. Baldor, "Trump Fires Esper as Pentagon Chief After Election Defeat, *AP,* November 9, 2020, https://apnews.com/article/joe-biden-donald-trump-counterterrorism-christopher-miller-mark-esper-634cd9a8cc00690b7ec8993b8bd64719.
113. "Read the Statement from 100-Plus Former National Security Officials," *The Washington Post,* November 23, 2020, https://www.washingtonpost.com/context/read-the-statement-from-100-plus-former-national-security-officials/a559eb00-6e6c-4671-ab49-7bc9ccb967dc/.
114. "Infusion of Loyalists": Jonathan Swan and Zachary Basu, "Off the Rails: Episode 2: Barbarians at the Oval," *Axios,* January 17, 2021, https://www.axios.com/2021/01/17/trump-lawyers-biden-election-victory. Giuliani: "What You Need to Know

About Rudy Guiliani's 2020 Election Charges," *PBS,* August 17, 2023, https://www.pbs.org/newshour/politics/rudy-giulianis-2020-election-charges-explained.
115. Kevin Freking, "Trump Tweets Words 'He Won'; Says 'Vote Rigged,' Not Conceding," *AP.* November 16, 2020. https://apnews.com/article/donald-trump-tweets-he-won-not-conceding-9ce22e9dc90577f7365d150c151a91c7.
116. Aram Roston and Peter Eisler, "The Man Behind Trump World's Myth of Rigged Voting Machines," *Reuters,* December 20, 2022, https://www.reuters.com/investigates/special-report/usa-election-montgomery/. See also the "Off the Rails" series of investigative reporting: "Infusion of Loyalists": Jonathan Swan and Zachary Basu, "Off the Rails: Episode 2: Barbarians at the Oval," *Axios,* January 17, 2021, https://www.axios.com/2021/01/17/trump-lawyers-biden-election-victory.
117. Will Sommer, "Here's How Hugo Chavez, Dead Since 2013, Became Responsible for Trump's Election Loss," *The Daily Beast*, November 19, 2020, https://www.thedailybeast.com/heres-how-hugo-chavez-dead-since-2013-became-responsible-for-trumps-election-loss/.
118. "Infusion of Loyalists": Jonathan Swan and Zachary Basu, "Off the Rails: Episode 2: Barbarians at the Oval," *Axios,* January 17, 2021, https://www.axios.com/2021/01/17/trump-lawyers-biden-election-victory.
119. Leonnig and Rucker, *I Alone Can Fix It*, 435.
120. David Brennan, "Iran Vows Soleimani Revenge as First Anniversary of Assassination Looms," *Newsweek*, December 30, 2020, https://www.newsweek.com/iran-vows-soleimani-revenge-first-anniversary-assassination-looms-1557927.
121. Leonnig and Rucker, *I Alone Can Fix It*, 436.
122. Leonnig and Rucker, *I Alone Can Fix It*, 437.
123. Ashton Carter, Dick Cheney, William Cohen, Mark Esper, Robert Gates, Chuck Hagel, James Mattis, Leon Panetta, William Perry, and Donald Rumsfeld, "Opinion: All 10 Living Former Defense Secretaries: Involving the Military in Election Disputes Would Cross into Dangerous Territory," *The Washington Post*, January 3, 2021.

124. Leonnig and Rucker state that ten permits were acquired, and 15,000 protestors were expected. Leonnig and Rucker, *I Alone Can Fix It*, 435.
125. "2020 Electoral College Results," *National Archives*, April 16, 2021, https://www.archives.gov/electoral-college/2020.
126. Trump tweet: "@realDonaldTrump status," *X.com*, January 5, 2021. https://x.com/realDonaldTrump/status/1346488314157797389?s=20. Pence told Trump he lacks power: Maggie Haberman and Annie Karni, "Pence Said to Have Told Trump That He Lacks Power to Change Election Result," *The New York Times*. September 14, 2021, https://www.nytimes.com/2021/01/05/us/politics/pence-trump-election-results.html.
127. Gerhard Peters and John T. Woolley, "Mike Pence: The Vice President's Letter to Members of Congress on the Electoral Vote Count," *The American Presidency Project*, January 6, 2021, https://www.presidency.ucsb.edu/documents/the-vice-presidents-letter-members-congress-the-electoral-vote-count.
128. Maggie Haberman, "Trump Told Crowd 'You Will Never Take Back Our Country with Weakness," *The New York Times*, January 6, 2021, https://www.nytimes.com/2021/01/06/us/politics/trump-speech-capitol.html.
129. Haberman, "Trump Told Crowd 'You Will Never Take Back Our Country with Weakness."
130. Haberman, "Trump Told Crowd 'You Will Never Take Back Our Country with Weakness." See also: Katelyn Polantz. "Guiliani, Who Urged Trump Supporters to Have 'Trial By Combat,' Says He Wasn't Literally Calling for Insurrection," *CNN*, May 18, 2021, https://www.cnn.com/2021/05/18/politics/rudy-giuliani-january-6-insurrection-lawsuit/index.html.
131. Andrew Restuccia and Siobhan Hughes, "Trump's Tweet About Pence Seen as Critical Moment During Riot," *The Wall Street Journal*, July 21, 2022, https://www.wsj.com/livecoverage/jan-6-hearing-today-trump/card/trump-s-tweet-about-pence-seen-as-critical-moment-during-riot-fmPxoFkeoTKxi0NqPLCL?msockid=31a957df733a64e63f05425e7279657a.
132. Nancy Pelosi, *The Art of Power: My Story as America's First Woman Speaker of the House* (New York: Simon & Schuster, 2024), 257.

133. "Watch: Pence Made It to Secure Location on Jan. 6 'Barely Missing' The Rioters, House Committee Says" *PBS,* June 17, 2022, https://www.pbs.org/newshour/politics/watch-pence-made-it-to-secure-location-on-jan-6-barely-missing-the-rioters-house-committee-says. See also Jill Colvin, "What We Know About How Pence's Day Unfolded on Jan. 6," *PBS,* July 16, 2022, https://www.pbs.org/newshour/politics/as-jan-6-hearings-what-we-know-about-how-pences-day-unfolded-on-jan-6.
134. Barbara Starr and Caroline Kelly, "Military Officials Were Unaware of Potential Danger to Pence's 'Nuclear Football' During Capitol Riot," *CNN,* February 21, 2025, https://www.cnn.com/2021/02/11/politics/military-officials-were-unaware-pence-nuclear-football-riot/index.html.
135. Jill Colvin, "What We Know About How Pence's Day Unfolded on Jan. 6," *PBS,* July 16, 2022, https://www.pbs.org/newshour/politics/as-jan-6-hearings-what-we-know-about-how-pences-day-unfolded-on-jan-6.
136. "40 Months Since the Jan. 6 Attack on the Capitol," United States Attorney's Office, District of Colombia, May 6, 2024, https://www.justice.gov/usao-dc/39-months-since-the-jan-6-attack-on-the-capitol. Healy, Jack Healy, "These Are the People Who Died in the Capitol Riot," *The New York Times,* January 11, 2021, https://www.nytimes.com/2021/01/11/us/who-died-in-capitol-building-attack.html.
137. "Watch: Trump Lunged at Agent Who Said He Couldn't Go to Capitol Amid Jan. 6 Violence, Aide Says," *PBS News,* June 28, 2022, https://www.pbs.org/newshour/politics/watch-trump-lunged-at-agent-who-said-he-couldnt-go-to-capitol-amid-jan-6-violence-aide-says.
138. Haberman, *Confidence Man,* 483. See also Jeremy Stahl, "The Biggest Takeaway from the First Night of the Jan. 6 Hearings Was About Mike Pence," *Slate,* June 9, 2022, https://slate.com/news-and-politics/2022/06/jan-six-hearing-trump-wanted-hang-mike-pence.html.
139. Nancy Pelosi, *The Art of Power: My Story as America's First Woman Speaker of the House* (New York: Simon & Schuster, 2024), 260–261.
140. "2020 Electoral College Results," *National Archives,* April 16, 2021, https://www.archives.gov/electoral-college/2020.

141. Jeremy Stahl. "The Biggest Takeaways From the First Night of the Jan. 6 Hearings Was About Mike Pence," *Slate*. June 9, 2022. https://slate.com/news-and-politics/2022/06/jan-six-hearing-trump-wanted-hang-mike-pence.html.
142. Andy Craig, "Mike Pence Could Have (and Should Have) Invoked the 25th Amendment on Jan. 6," *Cato Institute*, June 16, 2022, https://www.cato.org/commentary/mike-pence-could-have-should-have-invoked-25th-amendment-jan-6.
143. Craig, "Mike Pence Could Have (and Should Have) Invoked the 25th Amendment on Jan. 6."
144. Tanya Snyder, "Chao Resigns From Transportation Department, Citing 'Traumatic,' and 'Avoidable' Capitol Riot, *Politic*,. January 7, 2025, https://www.politico.com/news/2021/01/07/elaine-chao-to-resign-as-transportation-secretary-455919.
145. "Betsy DeVos Resignation Letter," *The Washington Post*, January 7, 2021, https://www.washingtonpost.com/context/betsy-devos-resignation-letter/cfd93504-2353-4ac3-8e71-155446242dda/.
146. Haberman, *Confidence Man*, 484.
147. This is a quote from House Majority Whip Jim Clyburn. See Quint Forgey, "'They are Running Away,': Clyburn Blasts DeVos, Chao for Resigning Without Invoking 25th Amendment," *Politico*, January 8, 2021, https://www.politico.com/news/2021/01/08/clyburn-devos-chao-resigning-before-invoking-25th-amendment-456454.
148. Joseph Choi, "Warren Claps Back at DeVos Following Resignation Announcement: 'Good Riddance'," *The Hill*, January 7, 2021, https://thehill.com/homenews/senate/533284-warren-claps-back-at-devos-following-resignation-announcement-good-riddance/.
149. "@AOC status," *X.com*, January 7, 2021, https://x.com/AOC/status/1347251720393519105?s=20.
150. Jacob Jarvis, "Betsy DeVos, Elaine Chao Accused of Resigning to Dodge 25th Amendment Calls," *Newsweek*, January 8, 2021, https://www.newsweek.com/betsy-devos-elaine-chao-resigning-dodge-25th-amendment-1559911.

151. Quint Forgey, "'They are Running Away,': Clyburn Blasts DeVos, Chao for Resigning Without Invoking 25th Amendment," *Politico*, January 8, 2021, https://www.politico.com/news/2021/01/08/clyburn-devos-chao-resigning-before-invoking-25th-amendment-456454.
152. Michael Stratford, "DeVos Resigned After Believing 25th Amendment was Off the Table," *Politico*, January 8, 2021, https://www.politico.com/news/2021/01/08/devos-resignation-trump-rioters-456574. See also: Zachary Cohen and Kristen Holmes, "Betsy DeVos Acknowledges 25th Amendment Discussions with Mike Pence and Cabinet Members," *CNN*, June 9, 2022, https://www.cnn.com/2022/06/09/politics/betsy-devos-trump-january-6/index.html.
153. Leonnig and Rucker, *I Alone Can Fix It*, 486.
154. Jonathan Karl, *Betrayal: The Final Act of the Trump Show* (New York: Dutton, 2021), xv.
155. Karl, *Betrayal*, xv.
156. Haberman, *Confidence Man*, 484.
157. Julia Shapiro, "Jan. 6 Transcript: Mnuchin Briefly Discussed 25th Amendment Removal of Trump," *The Hill*, December 28, 2022, https://thehill.com/blogs/blog-briefing-room/3790713-jan-6-transcript-mnuchin-briefly-discussed-25th-amendment-removal-of-trump/.
158. "Here's Every Word from the Sixth Jan. 6 Committee Hearing on its Investigation," *NPR*, June 28, 2022, https://www.npr.org/2022/06/28/1108396692/jan-6-committee-hearing-transcript.
159. Nancy Pelosi and Chuck Schumer, "Joint Statement on Call to Vice President Pence on Invoking 25th Amendment," *Nancy Pelosi, Speaker of the House*, January 7, 2021, https://speakeremeritapelosi.house.gov/newsroom/1721-0.
160. Nancy Pelosi, *The Art of Power: My Story as America's First Woman Speaker of the House* (New York: Simon & Schuster, 2024), 277.
161. Pence, *So Help Me God*, 474–475.

162. "House Resolution Calling on Vice President Pence to Invoke 25th Amendment" Congressional Materials, 38, *House of Representatives, United States,* 2021, https://ir.lawnet.fordham.edu/cgi/viewcontent.cgi?article=1037&context=twentyfifth_amendment_congressional_materials.
163. "Letter to Speaker Nancy Pelosi on the Twenty-Fifth Amendment, January 12, 2021," As printed in: Pence, *So Help Me God,* 522.
164. "Letter to Speaker Nancy Pelosi on the Twenty-Fifth Amendment, January 12, 2021."
165. Pence, *So Help Me God,* 523.
166. Cynthia J. Arnson, Robert Daly, Daniel S. Hamilton Michael Kugelman, Monde Muyangwa, and Peter B. Zwack, "The World's Reaction to the Events of January 6th," *Wilson Center,* January 7, 2021, https://www.wilsoncenter.org/article/worlds-reaction-events-january-6th. James, Frater, Angela Dewan, Jessie Yeung, and Tara John, "World Leaders Condemn 'Horrifying' Riot at US Capitol Building," *CNN,* January 7, 2021, https://www.cnn.com/2021/01/06/world/world-reaction-us-capitol-riot-intl/index.html. See also Woodward, *Peril,* xvii. See also: "'Beautiful sight': What China, Russia and Iran Said on US Capitol Riots," *Times of India,* January 7, 2021, https://timesofindia.indiatimes.com/world/us/beautiful-sight-what-china-russia-and-iran-said-on-capitol-riots/articleshow/80156241.cms.
167. Woodward, *Peril,* xix.
168. Pelosi, *The Art of Power,* 277.
169. Woodward, *Peril,* xxiv.
170. William J. Perry and Tom Z. Collina, "Trump Still Has His Finger on the Nuclear Button. This Must Change," *Politico Magazine,* January 8, 2021, https://www.politico.com/news/magazine/2021/01/08/trump-still-has-his-finger-on-the-nuclear-button-this-must-change-456667.
171. Perry and Collina, "Trump Still Has His Finger on the Nuclear Button."

172. "Congressman Lieu, Senator Markey Introduce the Restricting First Use of Nuclear Weapons Act of 2017," *Ted Lieu, Congressman for California's 36th District,* January 24, 2017, https://lieu.house.gov/media-center/press-releases/congressman-lieu-senator-markey-introduce-restricting-first-use-0.
173. "Congressman Lieu, Senator Markey Introduce the Restricting First Use of Nuclear Weapons Act of 2017."
174. Charlie Savage, "Trump Had Power to Attack Syria Without Congress, Justice Dept. Says," *The New York Times,* June 1, 2018, https://www.nytimes.com/2018/06/01/us/politics/trump-war-powers-syria-congress.html.
175. Pelosi, *The Art of Power,* 277–278.
176. Terry Gross, "Republicans Suggested Invoking the 25th Amendment After Jan. 6—But Failed to Act," *NPR,* https://www.npr.org/2022/05/03/1096099918/republicans-suggested-invoking-the-25th-amendment-after-jan-6-but-failed-to-act.
177. Pelosi, *The Art of Power,* 276.
178. "Text: H.Res.24 –117th Congress (2021–2022)," *Congress.gov,* January 26, 2021, https://www.congress.gov/bill/117th-congress/house-resolution/24/text.
179. "Read McConnell's Remarks on the Senate Floor After Trump's Acquittal," *CNN,* February 13, 2021, https://www.cnn.com/2021/02/13/politics/mcconnell-remarks-trump-acquittal/index.html.
180. Henry Foy, "US Intelligence-Sharing Convinces Allies of Russian Threat to Ukraine," *Financial Times,* December 5, 2021, https://www.ft.com/content/b287f2e3-3b8b-4095-b704-c255a943c84c.
181. Foy, "US Intelligence-Sharing Convinces Allies of Russian Threat to Ukraine."
182. Foy, "US Intelligence-Sharing Convinces Allies of Russian Threat to Ukraine."
183. See Mariana Budjeryn, *Inheriting the Bomb: The Collapse of the USSR and the Nuclear Disarmament of Ukraine* (Johns Hopkins University Press, 2022).
184. Will Vernon, "Russian Deserter Reveals War Secrets of Guarding Nuclear Base," *BBC News,* November 25, 2025, https://www.bbc.com/news/articles/c9dl2pv0yj0o?utm_source=flipboard&utm_content=user/BBCNews.

185. Nadine El-Bawab, "What Could Happen if Russia Blows Up the Zaporizhzhia Nuclear Power Plant?" *ABC News*, July 8, 2023, https://abcnews.go.com/US/happen-russia-blows-zaporizhzhia-nuclear-power-plant/story?id=100846888.
186. Geoff Brumfiel, "Satellite Photo Shows Russian Troops Were Stationed in Chernobyl's Radioactive Zone," *NPR*, April 7, 2022, https://www.npr.org/2022/04/07/1091396292/satellite-photo-shows-russian-troops-were-stationed-in-chernobyls-radioactive-zo. See also: "Ukraine: Russia-Ukraine War and Nuclear Energy," *World Nuclear Association*, Updated February 25, 2025, https://world-nuclear.org/information-library/country-profiles/countries-t-z/ukraine-russia-war-and-nuclear-energy.
187. Edith M. Lederer, "UN Chief Warns World Is One Step From 'Nuclear Annihilation'," *AP News*, August 1, 2022, https://apnews.com/article/russia-ukraine-covid-health-antonio-guterres-2871563e530f9a676d7884b3e2d871c3.
188. Kate Sullivan, "Kamala Harris Becomes First Woman With Presidential Power While Biden was Under Anesthesia for Routine Colonoscopy," *CNN,* November 19, 2021, https://www.cnn.com/2021/11/19/politics/kamala-harris-presidential-power/index.html.
189. Brett Samuels and Alex Gangitano, "Biden's Physician Says He is 'Fit for Duty' at 80 Years Old," *The Hill*, February 16, 2023, https://thehill.com/homenews/administration/3862215-bidens-physician-says-he-is-fit-for-duty-at-80-years-old/.
190. "Long COVID: Lasting Effects of COVID-19," *Mayo Clinic,* April 23, 2024, https://www.mayoclinic.org/diseases-conditions/coronavirus/in-depth/coronavirus-long-term-effects/art-20490351.
191. Brett Samuels and Alex Gangitano, "Biden's Physician Says He is 'Fit for Duty' at 80 Years Old," *The Hill*, February 16, 2023, https://thehill.com/homenews/administration/3862215-bidens-physician-says-he-is-fit-for-duty-at-80-years-old/.
192. Samuels and Alex Gangitano, "Biden's Physician Says He is 'Fit for Duty' at 80 Years Old."
193. Justin Gomez, "Biden 'Fit for Duty' Physical 'Identified No New Concerns,' His Doctor Says," *ABC News.* February 28,

2025, https://abcnews.go.com/Politics/biden-undergo-annual-physical-ahead-november-election/story?id=107626969.
194. Alexander Panetta, "'Diminished Faculties,' 'Faulty Memory,' 'Significant Limitations': A Damning Report on Biden's Mental State," *CBS News,* February 8, 2024, https://www.cbc.ca/news/world/special-counsel-faculties-biden-analysis-1.7109811. Son Beau Biden had died: "6 Takeaways from the Special Counsel's Report on Biden's Classified Documents," *PBS,* February 8, 2024, https://www.pbs.org/newshour/nation/6-takeaways-from-the-special-counsels-report-on-bidens-classified-documents.
195. "Report from Special Counsel Robert K Hur February 2024," Special Counsel's Office, US Department of Justice, February 5, 2024, as reported in *CNN* and *Fox News.* See *CNN,* February 5, 2024, https://www.cnn.com/2024/02/08/politics/robert-hur-report-biden-classified-documents-read/index.html. See also: "Part 1 Report from Special Counsel Robert K Hur February 2024," *Fox News,* February 5, 2024, https://static.foxnews.com/foxnews.com/content/uploads/2024/02/PART-1-report-from-special-counsel-robert-k-hur-february-2024-_compressed.pdf.
196. Alexander Panetta, "'Diminished Faculties,' 'Faulty Memory,' 'Significant Limitations'."
197. Jeannie Suk Gersen, "Why Robert Hur Called Biden an "Elderly Man with a Poor Memory," *The New Yorker,* March 24, 2024, https://www.newyorker.com/news/daily-comment/the-impossible-role-of-robert-hur. See also David A. Graham, "The Special Counsel's Devastating Description of Joe Biden," *The Atlantic,* February 8, 2024, https://www.theatlantic.com/ideas/archive/2024/02/special-counsels-devastating-charge-against-biden/677396/.
198. Alexander Panetta, "'Diminished Faculties,' 'Faulty Memory,' 'Significant Limitations'." See also Evan Perez Homes Lybrand, Hannah Rabinowitz, Devan Cole, Jeremy Herb, Zachary Cohen, and Kaanita Iyer, "Special Counsel Report Concludes Biden Willfully Retained Classified Information But Will Not Face Charges," *CNN,* February 8, 2024, https://www.cnn.com/2024/02/08/politics/white-house-special-counsels-report-response/index.html.

199. The reverse—a political victory, and a legal defeat—would probably have been a better outcome for Biden's chances of reelection. Alexander Panetta, "'Diminished Faculties,' 'Faulty Memory,' 'Significant Limitations'."
200. Nikki Haley, "It's Time for a Competency Test for Politicians. Here's Why," *Fox News*, May 1, 2023, https://www.foxnews.com/opinion/time-competency-test-politicians-heres-why?msockid=31a957df733a64e63f05425e7279657a.
201. Justin Gomez, "Biden 'Fit for Duty' Physical 'Identified No New Concerns,' His Doctor Says," *ABC News*, February 28, 2025, https://abcnews.go.com/Politics/biden-undergo-annual-physical-ahead-november-election/story?id=107626969.
202. "2024 Election: Biden Holds on to Slight Lead Over Trump. Quinnipiac University National Poll Finds; Trump Gets Higher Marks on Age, Mental & Physical Fitness; Biden Does Better on Ethics, Empathy & Temperament," *Quinnipiac University Poll*, February 21, 2024, https://poll.qu.edu/images/polling/us/us02212024_upox75.pdf. Note that *ABC News* quotes the *Quinnipiac University* poll erroneously stating 62 % of Americans believe that Biden is not mentally fit, and 62 percent believe he is not physically fit. Quinnipiac lists their results as 64% and 62% respectively. This indicates that Americans were slightly more concerned about Biden's mental acuity. See also: Justin Gomez, "Biden 'Fit for Duty' Physical 'Identified No New Concerns,' His Doctor Says," *ABC News*, February 28, 2025, https://abcnews.go.com/Politics/biden-undergo-annual-physical-ahead-november-election/story?id=107626969.
203. "2024 Election: Biden Holds on to Slight Lead Over Trump. Quinnipiac University National Poll Finds."
204. "2024 Election: Biden Holds on to Slight Lead Over Trump. Quinnipiac University National Poll Finds." See also: Trump Gets Higher Marks on Age, Mental & Physical Fitness; Biden Does Better on Ethics, Empathy & Temperament," *Quinnipiac University Poll*, February 21, 2024, https://poll.qu.edu/images/polling/us/us02212024_upox75.pdf.
205. "Majority of Americans Think Both Biden and Trump Are Too Old To Serve Second Terms," *Ipsos*, February 11, 2024, https://www.ipsos.com/en-us/majority-americans-think-both-biden-and-trump-are-too-old-serve-second-terms.

206. Tamara Keith and David Folkenflik, "Is There a Double Standard on Age Between Trump and Biden?" *NPR*, February 13, 2024, https://www.npr.org/2024/02/13/1231221343/is-there-a-double-standard-on-age-between-trump-and-biden.

207. Ascending the tall stairs to Air Force One is an iconic image of the presidency, but the short stairs keep the president mostly out of sight of the media, which had caught him tripping and falling while climbing the tall stairs on more than one occasion. See Tamara Keith, "Why Biden is Now Routinely Taking the Short Stairs Up to Air Force One," *NPR*, August 31, 2023, https://www.npr.org/2023/08/31/1196803354/biden-air-force-one-short-stairs.

208. Individuals such as Representative Eric Swalwell, who ran against Biden in 2020, claimed that Biden did not recognize him at a congressional picnic in the summer of 2023. See Taegan Goddard, "Biden Didn't Recognize Eric Swalwell," *Political Wire*, March 22, 2025, https://politicalwire.com/2025/03/22/biden-didnt-recognize-eric-swalwell/.

209. Martin Pengelly, "Democrats Staged 'Hush-Hush Talks' in 2023 for Biden to Withdraw from the Race, Says Book," *The Guardian*, March 26, 2025, https://www.theguardian.com/books/2025/mar/26/democrats-biden-withdraw. See Jonathan Allen and Aimee Parnes. *Fight: Inside the Wildest Battle for the White House* (New York: HarperCollins Publishers, 2025).

210. In May 2025, four months into Trump's second term, the book *Original Sin: President Biden's Decline, Its Cover-up, and His Disastrous Choice to Run Again* was published. Based on about 200 interviews, authors Jake Tapper and Alex Thompson also argue that Biden's inner circle discussed having him use a wheelchair should he be elected to a second term. See Jake Tapper and Alex Thompson, *Original Sin: President Biden's Decline, Its Cover-up, and His Disastrous Choice to Run Again* (New York: Penguin Random House, 2025).

211. Keith and Folkenflik, "Is There a Double Standard on Age Between Trump and Biden?"

212. Keith and Folkenflik, "Is There a Double Standard on Age Between Trump and Biden?"

213. Annie Linskey, Lawrence Norman, and Drew Hinshaw, "The World Saw Biden Deteriorating. Democrats Ignored the Warnings," *The Wall Street Journal,* June 28, 2025, https://www.wsj.com/politics/elections/biden-age-concerns-world-leaders-democrats-6d753921?msockid=31a957df733a64e63f05425e7279657a.
214. Mataeo Smith, "President Biden 'Freezes' Mid-Dance in Bizarre Glitch at White House Concert," *MSN,* June 11, 2024, https://www.msn.com/en-us/news/politics/president-biden-freezes-mid-dance-in-bizarre-glitch-at-white-house-concert/ar-BB1nZzD1.
215. Taegan Goddard, "Biden Aide Describes an 'Out of It' President," *Political Wire,* https://politicalwire.com/2025/04/02/biden-aide-describes-an-out-of-it-president/. See: Chris Whipple, *Uncharted: How Trump Beat Biden, Harris, and the Odds to Win the Wildest Campaign in History* (New York: HarperCollins Publishers, 2025).
216. "Debate Fact Check: Biden and Trump on the Economy, Immigration and Foreign Policy, *The New York Times,* June 27, 2024, https://www.nytimes.com/live/2024/06/27/us/biden-trump-debate-fact-check.
217. Shane Goldmacher and Jonathan Swan, "Six Takeaways from the First Biden-Trump Presidential Debate," *The New York Times.* June 27, 2024, Updated July 22, 2024, https://www.nytimes.com/live/2024/06/27/us/biden-trump-debate.
218. "Read: Biden-Trump Debate Transcript," *CNN.* June 28, 2024, https://edition.cnn.com/2024/06/27/politics/read-biden-trump-debate-rush-transcript/index.html.
219. Rachel Looker and Courtney Subramanian, "Biden Interview Fails to Quell Democrat Fitness Concerns," *BBC News.* July 6, 2024, https://www.bbc.com/news/articles/c8971wl12r8o.
220. Julia Manchester, "Doubts Have Grown Over Biden's Mental Fitness: Poll," *The Hill,* July 1, 2024, https://thehill.com/homenews/campaign/4750357-doubts-have-grown-over-bidens-mental-fitness-poll/.

221. Scott Wong, Ali Vitali, and Rebecca Kaplan, "13 More Democrats Call for Biden to Withdraw from 2024 Race," *NBC News,* July 19, 2025, https://www.nbcnews.com/politics/joe-biden/eight-democrats-pelosi-allies-call-biden-exit-2024-election-rcna162726.
222. "Read Biden's Full Letter Announcing the End of His 2024 Reelection Bid," *PBS News.* July 21, 2024, https://www.pbs.org/newshour/politics/read-bidens-full-letter-announcing-the-end-of-his-2024-reelection-bid. See also: Arit John, "Harris Will Seek Democratic Nomination and Could Be the First Black Woman and Asian American to Lead a Majority Party Ticket," *CNN,* July 21, 2024, https://www.cnn.com/2024/07/21/politics/kamala-harris-biden-endorsement-democratic-nominee/index.html.
223. "Joe Biden Faces Calls for Removal Under Twenty-Fifth Amendment. Is It Likely He'll Be Forced from Office?" *NBC News,* July 22, 2024, https://www.nbcchicago.com/news/local/joe-biden-faces-calls-for-removal-under-25th-amendment-is-it-likely-hell-be-forced-from-office/3497496/.
224. "Joe Biden Faces Calls for Removal Under Twenty-Fifth Amendment."
225. "Press Release: Congresswoman Nancy Mace Calls on Vice President Harris to Invoke 25th Amendment," *Office of Congresswoman Nancy Mace,* July 22, 2024, https://mace.house.gov/media/press-releases/congresswoman-nancy-mace-calls-vice-president-harris-invoke-25th-amendment.
226. Christopher Brito, "'Person, Woman, Man, Camera, TV': Trump Describes Difficulty of Recent Cognitive Test," *CBS News,* July 23, 2020, https://www.cbsnews.com/news/trump-cognitive-test-difficulty-claim/.
227. Will Weissert, "Trump Challenges Biden to a Cognitive Test But Misstates the Name of the Doctor Who Tested Him," *Los Angeles Times,* June 15, 2024, https://www.latimes.com/world-nation/story/2024-06-15/trump-challenges-biden-to-a-cognitive-test-but-confuses-the-name-of-the-doctor-who-tested-him.
228. "US Senate: Measures Proposed to Amend the Constitution," *United States Senate,* https://www.senate.gov/legislative/MeasuresProposedToAmendTheConstitution.htm.

229. Peter, Baker, "As Debate Looms, Trump Is Now the One Facing Questions About Age and Capacity," *The New York Times,* September 9, 2024, Updated November 6, 2024, https://www.nytimes.com/2024/09/09/us/politics/debate-trump-capacity.html.
230. Riley Hoffman, "READ: Harris-Trump Presidential Debate Transcript," *ABC News,* September 10, 2024, https://abcnews.go.com/Politics/harris-trump-presidential-debate-transcript/story?id=113560542.
231. Peter Baker and Dylan Freedman, "Trump's Rambling Speeches Reinforce Question of Age," *The New York Times,* October 6, 2024, Updated November 6, 2024, https://www.nytimes.com/2024/10/06/us/politics/trump-speeches-age-cognitive-decline.html?smid=nytcore-ios-share&referringSource=articleShare.
232. Emily Baumgaertner and Maggie Haberman, "Trump Promised to Release His Medical Records. He Still won't Do It," *The New York Times,* October 3, 2024, https://www.nytimes.com/2024/10/03/health/trump-health-records.html.
233. Eric Bradner, "Vice President Harris is in 'Excellent Health' According to Detailed Letter From Her Physician," *CNN,* October 12, 2024, https://www.cnn.com/2024/10/12/politics/kamala-harris-health-records/index.html.
234. Moore, Elena and Miguel Macias. "Harris is Using Her Medical Report to Raise Questions About Trump," *NPR.* https://www.npr.org/2024/10/12/g-s1-28012/harris-releases-medical-report-drawing-another-contrast-with-trump.
235. Andrew Feinberg, "More than 230 Doctors Say Trump is Too Unstable to Be President in Open Letter," *The Independent,* October 24, 2024, https://www.independent.co.uk/news/world/americas/us-politics/trump-george-conway-anti-psychopath-election-b2634614.html.
236. Feinberg, "More than 230 Doctors Say Trump is Too Unstable to Be President in Open Letter."
237. Feinberg, "More than 230 Doctors Say Trump is Too Unstable to Be President in Open Letter."
238. Alex Isenstadt, *Revenge: The Inside Story of Trump's Return to Power* (New York: Grand Central Publishing, 2024).

239. Steve Holland, "US Warns Iran to Stop Plotting Against Trump, Says US Official," *Reuters,* October 15, 2024, https://www.reuters.com/world/us-warns-iran-stop-plotting-against-trump-says-us-official-2024-10-15/.
240. Layla Ferris and Emmet Lyons, "Israel and Hamas at War: A Timeline of Major Developments in the Year Since Oct. 7, 2023," *CBS News,* October 8, 2024, https://www.cbsnews.com/news/israel-hamas-war-timeline-major-events-since-october-7-2023/.
241. Aditi Bhandari, Prasanta Kumar Dutta, and Jonathan Saul, "What We Know About Israel's Invasion So Far," *Reuters,* October 30, 2023, https://www.reuters.com/graphics/ISRAEL-PALESTINIANS/MAPS/movajdladpa/#mapping-israels-ground-invasion-of-gaza.
242. Layla Ferris and Emmet Lyons, "Israel and Hamas at War: A Timeline of Major Developments in the Year Since Oct. 7, 2023," *CBS News,* October 8, 2024, https://www.cbsnews.com/news/israel-hamas-war-timeline-major-events-since-october-7-2023/.
243. "The Israel-Hamas War's Devastating Toll, By the Numbers," *The Associated Press,* October 7, 2024, https://apnews.com/article/israel-palestinians-hamas-war-anniversary-statistics-e61765035c725b3c8d4840e2bab565cd.
244. Todd Lopez, "US Withdraws from Intermediate-Range Nuclear Forces Treaty," *US Department of Defense,* August 2, 2019, https://www.defense.gov/News/News-Stories/Article/Article/1924779/us-withdraws-from-intermediate-range-nuclear-forces-treaty/.
245. "Completion Report: Operation Julin: Part 1, Fiscal Year 1992," National Technical Reports Library, US Department of Commerce, 1993, https://ntrl.ntis.gov/NTRL/dashboard/searchResults/titleDetail/DE93018382.xhtml.
246. "Guterres Hails Entry into Force of Treaty Banning Nuclear Weapons," *UN News,* January 22, 2021, https://news.un.org/en/story/2021/01/1082702.

247. "Bluffing or Not, Putin's Nuclear Weapons Deployment to Belarus Raises Tensions," *AP News*, July 27, 2023, https://apnews.com/article/russia-ukraine-war-belarus-putin-nuclear-3bc2aefef4ee6b4478c81ae76bebdd4e.
248. "Has Putin Threatened to Use Nuclear Weapons?" *Reuters*. October 27, 2022, https://www.reuters.com/world/europe/has-putin-threatened-use-nuclear-weapons-2022-10-27/.
249. Thomas Gualkin, Francois Diaz-Maurin, Jessica McKenzie, Sara Goudarzi, and Matt Field, "An Existential Timeline of the Trump/Pence and Biden/Harris Presidencies," *Bulletin of the Atomic Scientists*, October 23, 2024, https://thebulletin.org/2024/10/an-existential-timeline-of-the-trump-pence-and-biden-harris-presidencies/.
250. "Congressional Commission on the Strategic Posture of the United States," *Committee on Armed Services, House of Representatives*, November 15, 2023, (Washington: US Government Publishing Office, 2024), https://www.congress.gov/118/chrg/CHRG-118hhrg56378/CHRG-118hhrg56378.pdf.
251. "@HouseIntel status," *X.com*, February 14, 2014, https://x.com/HouseIntel/status/1757805804885823775.
252. Francois Diaz-Maurin, "US Intelligence Warns About Russia Wanting Nuclear Weapons in Space," *Bulletin of the Atomic Scientists*, February 15, 2024, https://thebulletin.org/2024/02/us-intelligence-warns-about-russia-wanting-nuclear-weapons-in-space/.
253. "Remarks at the Signing of the Treaty on Outer Space, January 27, 1967," *LBJ Presidential Library*, January 27, 1967, https://www.lbjlibrary.org/object/text/remarks-signing-treaty-outer-space-01-27-1967.
254. "NATO's Stoltenberg Says Each Country Must Decide if Ukraine Can Use Its Long-Range Missiles on Russia," *Reuters*, September 16, 2024, https://www.reuters.com/world/europe/natos-stoltenberg-says-each-country-must-decide-if-ukraine-can-use-its-long-2024-09-16/.
255. Guy Faulconbridge and Vladimir Soldatkin, "Russia Warns the United States of the Risks of World War Three," *Reuters*, August

27, 2024, https://www.reuters.com/world/russia-warns-united-states-risks-world-war-three-2024-08-27/.
256. Maia Davies, "Putin Approves Changes to Russia's Nuclear Doctrine," *BBC News*, November 19, 2024, https://www.bbc.com/news/articles/cj4v0rey0jzo.
257. Anna Chernova, Nathan Hodge, Christian Edwards, and Clare Sebastian, "Putin Fine-Tunes Russia's Nuclear Doctrine After Biden's Arms Decision on Ukraine, in Clear Signal to West," *CNN*, November 19, 2024, https://www.cnn.com/2024/11/19/europe/putin-russia-update-nuclear-doctrine-ukraine-intl/index.html.
258. Faulconbridge and Soldatkin. "Russia Warns the United States."
259. Will Vernon, "Russian Deserter Reveals War Secrets of Guarding Nuclear Base," *BBC News*, November 25, 2025, https://www.bbc.com/news/articles/c9dl2pv0yj0o?utm_source=flipboard&utm_content=user/BBCNews.
260. Hans M. Kristensen, Matt Korda, Eliana Johns, and Mackenzie Knight, "United States Nuclear Weapons, 2024," *Bulletin of the Atomic Scientists*, May 7, 2024. https://thebulletin.org/premium/2024-05/united-states-nuclear-weapons-2024/.
261. Guy Faulconbridge and Anton Kolodyazhnyy, "Putin Issues Warning to United States with New Nuclear Doctrine," *Reuters*, November 19, 2024, https://www.reuters.com/world/europe/putin-issues-warning-us-with-new-nuclear-doctrine-2024-11-19/.
262. "Putin Says "There Can Be No Winners in a Nuclear War and It Should Never Be Unleashed"," *NBC News*, August 1, 2022, https://www.nbcnews.com/news/world/putin-says-can-no-winners-nuclear-war-never-unleashed-rcna40964.
263. David E. Sanger, Eric Schmitt, Helene Cooper, and Julian E. Barnes, "US Makes Contingency Plans in Case Russia Uses Its Most Powerful Weapons," *The New York Times*, March 23, 2022, https://www.nytimes.com/2022/03/23/us/politics/biden-russia-nuclear-weapons.html.
264. Garrett M. Graff, "Who's In Charge of America After a Catastrophe? Who Knows?" *Politico Magazine*, September 21, 2016, https://www.politico.com/magazine/story/2016/09/designated-survivor-president-succession-doomsday-plans-214271/.

CHAPTER 7

Conclusion: The Next Stages—Nuclear Anxiety and the Amendment

After 179 years without a presidential succession and inability amendment to build on and clarify Article II, the framers of the Twenty-Fifth Amendment adjusted America's foundational document not as dictated by a momentary whim, but by the exigencies of the times.[1] With the Twenty-Fifth Amendment's ratification on February 10, 1967, the nuclear anxiety of the era became ingrained in the Constitution itself. And while President Kennedy's assassination highlighted the need for an amendment, the context of nuclear anxiety provides another important explanation for its incorporation. Yet the amendment's inscription of the various forms of nuclear anxiety into the Constitution has not relieved the stress over a nuclear apocalypse, nor has it solved all the issues pertaining to succession and inability. This study of the amendment in practice reveals some formative and unpredictable effects, including not only those stemming from gaps and vagaries in the amendment as "novel challenges, threats, and capabilities that did not exist at the time of the framing"[2] have arisen, but also from how presidents, already wielding the godlike power to push the button, have the power to avoid the intention of the law. Presidents, who in America's democratic republic govern thanks to the will of the people, have devised covert and extralegal COG plans to ensure their hold on power in events of disaster, especially nuclear devastation. Now, almost sixty years after the amendment's ratification, nuclear weapons have proliferated to other countries and could potentially proliferate to

© The Author(s), under exclusive license to Springer Nature Switzerland AG 2025
R. C. Lubot, *Keeping a Finger on the Button*, https://doi.org/10.1007/978-3-032-02478-7_7

non-state actors. Public concern over this fact as well as the temperament and mental ability of US presidents, who wield the sole power to order nuclear strikes, is approaching the high levels reached in the 1960s, 1980s, and after the attacks of September 11, 2001.

Understanding the constitutional revision as a product of nuclear anxiety broadens our thinking about the 1960s, the decade of the amendment's conception and ratification. Among the symbols of the decade, Americans recognized the circular peace sign divided into three triangles. But another well-known circular symbol also containing three triangles is the emblem designating a fallout shelter.[3] The hopeful attitude that came to be associated with the youth movement of the "hippies," was in part a reaction to the reality that the world could come to an end in an instant. Sociologist and former President of Students for a Democratic Society Todd Gitlin writes about the bomb as the "underside" of the positivity of the 1960s. According to Gitlin, if Americans believed "Everything might be possible.... So might annihilation [be possible]."[4] The bomb was "the shadow hanging over all human endeavor." Americans prepared their bomb shelters, talked about these shelters at P.T.A meetings, viewed countless depictions of nuclear anxiety in popular culture, and looked to their leaders for a sense of security from a sudden attack.[5] Yet lawmakers also needed to secure the line of succession in case of a strike and to ensure that a president of sound mind was in place to make and execute decisions that could affect billions. And yet another facet of this anxiety was the fear that a president could go crazy, Dr. Strangelove-style,[6] and launch nuclear weapons bringing about a retaliatory response. Through the amendment, these disparate strains of anxiety have become a permanent part of American law.

The Doomsday Clock stewards, which include sixteen Nobel Laureates, have asserted that the world is on the brink of nuclear apocalypse. They "believe the world is as close to total catastrophe today as it was at the worst point in the Cold War."[7] In 2016, the stewards announced the clock was set at three minutes to midnight, denoting a high probability of catastrophe. "The Clock ticks. Global danger looms. Wise leaders should act—immediately," they urged.[8] These Nobel Laureates are not alone in arguing that nuclear tensions have increased since Donald Trump won his first term.[9] Now in 2025, Trump has ushered in a new world order, disrupting the global economy, alienating America's traditional allies, all while vastly expanding executive power. Although outcomes are difficult to predict in this time of misinformation and volatility, certain historical patterns regarding the use of the Twenty-Fifth Amendment bear consideration. It is probable that Trump will continue to use the amendment as a rhetorical tool to battle his political enemies. The president, and those around him whose power is derived from his position, are highly likely to conceal any potential presidential inabilities to project an image of strength and competency. Possible succession scenarios suggest solutions for filling the gaps in the amendment by statute and for addressing the president's sole control of nuclear weapons, including an emergency use of the amendment in cases of "irreparable catastrophe." For now, decision-makers are frozen by loyalty to the president and fear of retribution and the gaps in the amendment are likely to remain unresolved. For all these reasons, this is a crucial time to study a constitutional amendment, especially as the Constitution itself is under attack by executive overreach.

"Why Should We Worry?" Gaps and Vagaries in the Amendment

The Twenty-Fifth Amendment can be seen as part of a broader movement, at the state, not just the federal level, to put in place bulwarks against a nuclear-related leadership crisis. Fear of nuclear attack convinced many states to reevaluate and expand their succession provisions by passing "disaster acts" in the 1960s.[10] All fifty state constitutions now designate an official who is next in line for gubernatorial succession. California, which became the tenth state to ratify the Twenty-Fifth Amendment on October 21, 1965, adopted Article V, Sect. 10 of its Constitution on November 8, 1966. It named the lieutenant governor as next in line to become governor, further clarifying succession law, and creating the Commission on Governorship to oversee the transitions. State legislatures have continued to revisit their succession plans. Decades later in New York, for example, The Nelson A. Rockefeller Institute of Government convened a forum to consider changes to the line of succession. New York Assemblyman Robin Schimminger suggested looking to the federal government's solution: the Twenty-Fifth Amendment. During the forum, Columbia Law School professor Richard Briffault posed a question: "Yes, it's the governor, but it's only the governor and he doesn't have nuclear weapons under his control. So, why should we worry?"[11] The professor is implying succession law was a matter of greatest import at the national level because the president holds the nuclear codes.

Questions about the gaps and vagaries arose during, and just after, the first uses of the amendment. During confirmation proceedings, members of Congress repeatedly questioned former Governor of New York Nelson Rockefeller, and afterward debated the proper extent of congressional inquiry into the president's nomination of a vice president under Sect. 2 versus that individual's right to privacy.[12] After the confirmation, experts on the amendment, including Senator Birch Bayh and the American Bar Association's John Feerick, agreed that a simple statute would fix some of the inadequacies. Members of Congress began to introduce legislation to that end.[13] The first invocations tested Sects. 1 and 2 of the amendment, and presidents starting with Reagan invoked Sect. 3 when they knew they would be under general anesthesia. But Sect. 3 and especially Sect. 4, both dealing with inability, raised additional questions.[14] Thus, while the amendment answered John Dickinson's question dating back to 1787—Who is to be the judge of inability?[15]—Congress would have to interpret the meaning and effect of the amendment's purposefully vague term of art, "inability." Now, in a crisis, a previously agreed-upon government "officer" would always be in charge, but Bayh admitted that putting the amendment into practice revealed challenges. He concluded: "It is easy to find fault with the amendment. It is much more difficult to envision an alternative solution which does not possess greater imperfections."[16] Bayh also acknowledged that the political process is polarized but asserted his belief that Congress will fix any gaps in succession and inability law for the good of the people in case of nuclear disaster.[17]

It is worth reiterating that Bayh stated that nuclear anxiety was "on the forefront, not back of, his mind"[18] at all times. A pragmatist, Bayh viewed the Constitution as a tool to address both predictable and unknown dangers. He understood that anxiety—an amorphous concept that ebbs and flows but is ever-present—might contribute to a concrete law that allowed for a clearer sense of presidential continuity. Here we see the politician who got the job done—the architect of multiple amendments to the Constitution who ushered the Twenty-Fifth through the ratification process from inception to completion—was convinced that because the succession and inability issue is of incredible importance, Congress would act.

The heightened nuclear anxiety that moved the ratification process forward in the mid-1960s did not disappear at the end of the Cold War, nor was it "replaced" by concern over terrorism. Instead, what is significant about the events of September 11 is that they compounded the existing fear. In addition to the nation-states that had the known capability to launch a nuclear Armageddon, non-state actors in the form of terrorists were attempting to acquire the materials to build small nuclear bombs, or dirty bombs. The proliferation of material unaccounted for (MUF), particularly in unsecured locations in the former Soviet Union, made their acquisition by terrorists a very real possibility.[19] Policymakers at the top echelons of the executive branch were forced to weigh even the minute possibility that terrorists might acquire weapons of mass destruction as a primary factor in decision-making.[20]

The terrorist attacks on September 11 resulted in an immediate focus on presidential continuity as the pre-rehearsed COG drills called for in President Ronald Reagan's top-secret directive were carried out. Reagan had issued this directive during another period of heightened nuclear anxiety in the 1980s. Circumventing Congress' input, Reagan had teams of advisors in place to direct whichever Cabinet member had survived a nuclear attack. The terrorist attacks of September 11, the largest in scale and scope on American soil during the nuclear age, generated a revival of interest in the presidential line of succession, and COG plans took on an added urgency.[21] COG exercises have been carried out and updated, at great expense to the taxpayer, and without transparency.[22]

When President Barack Obama took the reins of power from George W. Bush, he reiterated the hope that the proliferation of nuclear weapons, and therefore, the nuclear threat, would come to an end. Instead, some argue that the threat had increased during his administration, because smaller yet more numerous American bombs were created. General James E. Cartwright, a retired vice chairman of the Joint Chiefs of Staff and key advisor to Obama on nuclear weapons, stated: "what going smaller does… is to make the weapon more thinkable."[23] Significantly, the last time nuclear weapons became "more thinkable" was during the Reagan administration when senior officials suggested that Americans could survive a nuclear war. Three decades later, in 2016, diplomats, nuclear security experts, and missileers worried that Donald Trump did not possess the right temperament to have a finger on the nuclear trigger and might take the consideration to launch lightly thereby instigating an unsurvivable war. This fear grew when he antagonized North Korean leader Kim Jong-un with tweets threatening to use nuclear bombs. Some argued that it was part of the "madman strategy" that Nixon had employed decades earlier to convince the Soviets and North Vietnamese that if they did not bend to his will, he might be crazy enough to launch a nuclear strike.

This concept ran contrary to "mutually assured destruction," a game-based theory that rested on the premise that leaders would be "rational" enough not to begin a nuclear war that would end in the destruction of both countries. The difference between Nixon and Trump's threats was that while Nixon's aides knew that he was bluffing, at least when the thirty-seventh president was not under the influence of alcohol, no one was quite sure with Trump.

"A DOUBLE TWENTY-FIFTH AMENDMENT"? A RHETORICAL TOOL AND A BARRAGE OF MISINFORMATION

From the very start of his first term, calls quickly came to remove Trump from office due to his perceived unfitness to serve, and with these calls came a barrage of misinformation on the Twenty-Fifth Amendment. The amendment was not designed for removal, though, as a practical matter, it could result in the removal of the president's powers and duties for the remainder of his presidency if his inability proved to be permanent. But had Trump's first impeachment trial ended in a conviction and disqualification in February 2020, he could have been removed from office. After denying his election loss to Joseph Biden and instigating an insurrection on the Capitol complex on January 6, 2021, the vice president and Cabinet discussed invocation of Sect. 4. That possibility was swiftly dismissed by Vice President Mike Pence. The House impeached Trump again, but, because the Senate failed to convict him and subsequently disqualify him, he was free to run against President Biden in 2024.

Biden also faced calls for removal via the Twenty-Fifth Amendment, not due to issues with temperament, but worries around his mental acuity, physical fitness, and advanced age. These concerns grew until a dismal public debate performance led to Biden's withdrawal from the 2024 election race. Despite assassination attempts and criminal indictments against him, Trump emerged from the race victorious and claimed that he had won an "unprecedented and powerful" mandate even though he only beat Biden's last-minute successor, Vice President Kamala Harris, by a few hundred-thousand votes in key areas.[24] Throughout Biden's lame duck period, Trump argued that Harris should invoke Sect. 4 of the amendment, and then suggested a "double Twenty-Fifth Amendment" to "remove" both Biden and Harris. Trump proved to be a major spreader of misunderstanding and misinformation around the amendment. (A double Twenty-Fifth Amendment procedure does not exist, and the amendment does not involve removal of the president, only removal of his powers and duties and potentially only for a brief period.) In fact, throughout his first term and his 2024 election campaign, he used the amendment as a rhetorical tool for political gain rather than a legal guiding principle.

In reality, Bayh and the framers of the amendment designed Sect. 3 as a means to allow the president to willingly invoke the amendment when incapacitated and then take back powers when he felt the period of inability ended. However, presidents infrequently relinquish power willingly. The need for a finger on the button conflicted at times with political concerns, namely the president's desire to project an image of strength and competence.[25] The history of presidential disinclination to invoke Sect. 3 stretches back prior to the amendment's ratification. Those around the president, such as the White House physician, first lady, and presidential advisors "have been very invested in [concealing] their frailties, disabilities, and inabilities from public view." President Grover Cleveland hid his jaw surgeries—which were performed on a yacht in the middle of Buzzard's Bay, Massachusetts and his doctors were sworn to secrecy. And President Woodrow Wilson downplayed his condition after his stroke with the help of his friend, Dr. Cary Grayson and the first lady, Edith Bolling. These are examples from an age when presidents and those close to them had the luxury of time; while foreign policy decisions needed to be made, none needed to be made instantly. Although some decisions during that period might have caused great loss of life, none might have brought about the end of mankind. In the nuclear age, presidential decisions related to nuclear weapons have to be made in fifteen minutes or less.[26] The logical conclusion suggested by the amendment is that Sect. 4 would be invoked when a president is incapacitated if Sect. 3 has not been invoked, so that a sane president's finger is always on the nuclear button. Instead, the president's coterie has blocked access to the president in times of inability. And in the case of Nixon's advisors, aides have even decided to raise the Defense Condition (DEFCON) level during times of high nuclear tensions without authorization.[27]

In March 1981, after the assassination attempt, Reagan could have invoked Sect. 3, but he was probably more focused on whether he was going to die, and it was up to the vice president and Cabinet to invoke Sect. 4. Given Reagan's stagger into the hospital before collapsing and his reassuring quips such as "who is minding the store?" he was conscious of the image he was projecting prior to being anesthetized and operated on. Trump, focused on his age throughout his career, also was repelled by sickness and hospitals and apparently declined to invoke Sect. 3 when undergoing a colonoscopy. He staged photo ops designed to convince Americans of his superhuman strength when he contracted COVID. Presidents made the determination that the image of a strong and competent—though temporarily absent—president would be better for the nation. Yet by failing to follow through on the intention of Sect. 3 of the amendment, presidents have sometimes failed to put the safety of the nation over their personal desire to hold on to power.[28]

Section 4 provides a back-up plan if the president does not, or cannot, recognize his inability: The vice president and a majority of the Cabinet, or the vice president and "such other body as Congress may by law provide," can declare the president incapacitated. The choice is clear if the president is unconscious but becomes much murkier when he is not. The vice president and Cabinet have been reluctant to invoke Sect. 4, bowing to political pressures and fearing reprisal either before a letter is transmitted to the senate president pro tempore and the speaker of the house or after the president has recovered and reassumes his powers and duties. This fear of retaliation was warranted, particularly with Trump, who had fired aides for disloyalty and sought revenge against those who went against him. Vice President Pence, after refusing to block certification of the Electoral College votes, for example, became a persona non grata and was not asked by Trump to join his 2024 ticket.

"No Legal Certainty": Possible Solutions to Fill the Gaps in the Amendment

To bring clarity to Sect. 4 deliberations, scholars and policymakers have suggested that Congress design a body composed of experts to determine inability. This body could advise the vice president and Cabinet to act or could make the determination only under special circumstances. However, the vice president would have to agree with the medical body's decision or Sect. 4 would not be invoked, unless the Twenty-Fifth Amendment itself was amended. The suggestion to create such a body dates to a *New York Times* op-ed written by former President Truman in 1957, if not before. He proposed a seven-member commission composed of representatives of all three branches of government that would choose a panel of medical experts from top medical schools.[29] In 1993, the

Working Group on Presidential Disability recommended that the White House physician—who, it should be noted, is in the president's chain of command and is therefore conflicted—be overseen on final decisions regarding disability by an official consultation group. An impartial medical body would not owe their positions to the president, nor would it be concerned with image or retaliation. It would therefore be more likely than the vice president and Cabinet to invoke Sect. 4. If the amendment was invoked and Congress was still the source of appeal, a two-thirds vote in both Houses would have to affirm the medical body's determination, which is a high bar. Setting up a body, or bipartisan commission, was the purpose of Representative Raskin's legislation in 2017 and 2020, and this bill should be reintroduced in the current Congress.

One of the main reasons Raskin reintroduced the legislation in 2020, this time with House speaker Nancy Pelosi, was because of the rapidly spreading coronavirus that could quickly take the life of the president and those in the line of succession as well. Without an able vice president, the Twenty-Fifth Amendment's inability procedures cannot be invoked. In 1965, the lack of specifics around vice presidential inability during the nuclear age almost prevented the ratification of the amendment in Colorado; the new COVID threat added urgency to the need to fill the amendment's dual incapacity gap. It has recently come to light that White House counsels to Presidents Reagan, George H.W. Bush, and Clinton drafted vague executive contingency plans for use as guidance on dual incapacity, but even these plans stated that there was "no legal certainty" attached to them.[30] Yet Article II of the Constitution gives Congress the power to legislate procedures for handling cases of dual incapacity and a statute should be passed in which the means for determining dual incapacity would mirror the provisions already set forth for presidential inability in Sect. 4. A statute could give clear direction to the next presidential successor (the speaker under current law) and the Cabinet as to how and when to declare the two officeholders incapacitated. It could also provide clarity as to how both the president and the vice president would later regain their powers and duties. And inclusion of the president's Cabinet in a statutory dual incapacity process would give the speaker the much-needed political cover to act, especially if the latter were not a member of the president's party. Until such a law is enacted, Roy Brownell suggests that if a de facto dual incapacity scenario arises, the speaker should meet with the next officer in the line of succession (the Senate president pro tempore) and the Cabinet, and they should decide together whether the speaker should become acting president. They then should have Congress ratify the decision and provide a legislative path for the president and vice president to regain their powers and duties once their inabilities have ended.[31]

Yet another reform that, for now, could require similar real-time decision-making is one that Congressman Ted Lieu pointed to after the events of January 6. When the two Cabinet Secretaries, Elaine Chao and Betsy DeVos, resigned, he questioned by tweet whether the acting Cabinet secretaries replacing them would be "patriots" and invoke the amendment. While Lieu was asking whether they would "do the right thing," the real question is, would their votes count toward the majority needed to invoke Sect. 4? The Twenty-Fifth Amendment and the Presidential Succession Act, which delineates the line of succession after the vice president, are silent on this matter. Because of the possibilities that multiple Cabinet members could be killed by a nuclear bomb or felled by coronavirus or fired by the president to prevent invocation of Sect. 4—and then a majority could not be reached—Congress should enact a statute to expressly include acting secretaries. Congress would be free to put parameters around which acting secretaries count, such as including only those who served in the deputy post for a certain length of time and had been confirmed by the Senate. Congress also should add ambassadors at the end of the line of succession to ensure that a nuclear explosion in the nation's capital would not eliminate all potential acting presidents.[32]

Rather than mass catastrophe, the possibility of the presidency switching political parties if dual incapacity occurs is the destabilizing factor that has caused some constitutional law scholars to suggest reforming the Presidential Succession Act of 1947 to make Cabinet secretaries the immediate successors to the presidency after the vice president as the law required from 1886–1947.[33] President Truman pushed for the speaker to be second in line for the presidency because the speaker, after the president and vice president, is most representative of the people.[34] From a practical perspective, pleasing the house speaker and senate president pro tem in this way made it easier for the Presidential Succession Act to move through both houses of Congress and land on Truman's desk for signature. Bayh believed the opposite—that the line of succession should remain in the executive branch—but had to concede this point, in part for similar practical reasons: to keep the amendment moving through Congress.[35] In addition to reverting to the executive line of succession, Brownell and Fordham Law School Senior Fellow John Rogan also suggest reforming the 1947 Act to eliminate the "bumping provision" that would allow the speaker or senate pro tem to supplant the acting president later, and to remove the requirement that a successor resign from his or her underlying position.[36] The supplantation provision, also known as the "bumping provision," and mandatory resignation could lead to multiple presidential successors in a short period of time, potentially destabilizing the country.[37] While political parties are more fractious than during the Truman era and the speaker or Senate president pro tem would not necessarily carry out the incapacitated president's policies, these recommendations should be seriously considered because the country cannot afford this type of rapid turnover, especially during the current period of domestic turmoil and foreign uncertainties.

However, given the current political landscape, solutions to gaps in the Twenty-Fifth Amendment are not likely to happen right now. If Trump fully understood the mechanisms of the Twenty-Fifth Amendment, he would appreciate the fact that it was designed to empower the president and protect the officeholder from unwarranted efforts to declare him incapacitated. The amendment allows the president to give up and take back the powers and duties of the office. Only with Sect. 4 would the president not make the decision to relinquish his powers and duties, they would be taken from him because it would be assumed that he would be incapable or unwilling to give them up. Even then, once recovered from the inability, he can take action to attempt to have his powers and duties restored. After calls to invoke the amendment during his first term, Trump would not be likely to look favorably at any suggestion to raise the issue publicly, and, in his mind, conceivably lose some of the powers granted to him in the amendment. Congress has not passed any legislation for the president to consider and, knowing Trump would not sign any such reforms into law, is unlikely to do so at this time.

"Long Live the King": Additional Legislative Reforms Around Sole Control of the Nuclear Button

While Congress has not demonstrated strong interest in enacting statutes to fill in the gaps in the amendment, some legislators, at least since Trump's first term, have sought restrictions around the president's potential deployment of nuclear weapons. The president's sole control of the nuclear weapons dates to just days after the dropping of the atomic bombs on Hiroshima and Nagasaki, on August 10, 1945, when President Truman ordered that nuclear bombs could not be used without the president's express permission. He sought to prevent overly aggressive generals using nuclear bombs like war toys.[38] In 1948, the military requested that Truman issue an Executive Order to turn over custody of the atomic bomb to them.[39] But Truman believed that nuclear weapons were not like normal weapons such as "rifles and cannons and ordinary things like that." The president said, "You have got to understand that this isn't a military weapon ... It is used to wipe out women and children and unarmed people, and not for military uses."[40] Truman then followed up with a memo retaining civilian control over the bomb. Arguing that Congress would not have time to gather and declare war because of ICBMs thirty-minute travel time, Eisenhower solidified the precedent that the president's finger was the sole finger on the nuclear button.[41]

The concern that it was President Trump's finger on the nuclear trigger reawakened this debate. The genesis for Lieu's 2017 "Restricting First Use of Nuclear Weapons Act," which has been reintroduced in every Congress from the 116th to the current 119th, was the Democrats' belief that Trump's temperament meant he was unfit to make a rational decision around the use of weapons of mass destruction. Lieu's H.R. 669 reasons that the Constitution grants Congress the sole power to declare war, any nuclear strike by the president would be so calamitous that it would constitute a major act of war, and, therefore, any nuclear strike conducted in the absence of a declaration of war would violate the Constitution.[42] If the bill were to become law, it will limit the president's sole authority over nuclear weapons because Congress would weigh in on the matter first.

In addition to congressional oversight, it would make sense that the secretary of state, who has the best insight into international relations and whether a diplomatic solution can be found, and a military official such as the secretary of defense or the chair of the Joint Chiefs, should also join in the decision-making. Garrett Graff points out that every other step of the launch chain requires a "two-man" policy, so that no one individual must make the decision to launch alone.[43] According to a 2023 poll, a majority of Americans are uncomfortable with the president having sole authority over nuclear weapons and would most likely favor "no lone zone" legislation, meaning that no single leader should have ultimate control over the launch of nuclear bombs.[44] At the very least, the sole authority policy represents a departure from the system of checks and balances ingrained in the Constitution, dates back to the Cold War, and should be revisited as soon as passage of a statute is feasible.

Since Trump's inauguration in January 2025, the system of checks and balances are being stretched to their limit and policies dating to the beginning of the Cold War are being summarily discarded, as are the foundations of American democracy. Part of Trump's rhetorical strategy to rid himself of the constraints placed on the executive branch is to refer to himself as a king. Referencing the assassination attempts in his victory speech that recalled the Divine Right of Kings, Trump said, "Many people have told me that God spared my life for a reason. And that reason was to save our country and restore America to greatness."[45] Trump's idea of restoring America to greatness includes imperialist designs on the Panama Canal, Canada, and Greenland, none of which want to be annexed by the United States. Within a month of his second inauguration, he leaned into this monarchical imagery by punctuating a post claiming to have "saved," Manhattan and all of New York from congestion pricing with, "LONG LIVE THE KING." The White House retweeted the post, adding a picture of Trump with a crown made to look like the cover of *Time*.[46] In a constitutional democracy, the crown may be an empty symbol, yet as Graff eloquently writes, "the nuclear football is in some ways the only physical manifestation of our nation's head of state"[47] and control of it suggests a very real and specific kind of power that Trump seems to relish.

"Methods You Could Do It": The Possibility of a Third Term and a Constitutional Attack

In line with his admiration of autocrats and his authoritarian leanings, Trump has said repeatedly that he might serve a third term as president. However, the Twenty-Second Amendment forbids any president to be elected to the office more than twice. In this case, the first question for the Supreme Court is, does "elected" also mean any president who has served two terms cannot serve a third, as the framers of the amendment intended? To court favor, Tennessee Republican Representative Andy Ogles has introduced a House Joint Resolution to amend the Constitution to allow a president who has not served two consecutive terms to serve a third term.[48] In response to Trump's rhetoric, Democratic Representative Dan Goldman of New York has reintroduced a resolution calling for the House to reaffirm that the Twenty-Second Amendment refers to two terms in the aggregate and that it applies to Trump.[49]

At the end of March 2025, Trump's *NBC News' Meet the Press* interview revealed that Trump "was not joking" about a third term and that there were "methods you could do it."[50] When asked if he was suggesting that Vice President JD Vance would run for president and Trump would join him on the ticket as vice president, Trump agreed "that's one" way to circumvent the term limit.[51] However, the Twelfth Amendment states that anyone constitutionally ineligible to run for president cannot be elected vice president. The second question for the Supreme Court is whether, if Trump cannot be elected to a third term, does that make him ineligible to be vice president due to the Twelfth Amendment? If the Supreme Court's read is a strict one and the answer is yes, then Republicans' recourse is repealing or changing a constitutional amendment. This requires a two-thirds majority vote in both the House and the Senate and ratification by three-quarters of the states and is highly unlikely.

In a hypothetical scenario in which a president tries to extend his hold on power beyond the constitutionally mandated two terms, the Twenty-Fifth Amendment could play a role. One way is for a two-term president to run for vice president. However, the Twelfth Amendment eligibility problem remains. If that ticket is chosen by voters, the president could invoke Sect. 3 enabling the vice president to assume the powers and duties of the presidency as acting president until the end of that president's term. Alternatively, the president could resign triggering Sect. 1 of the amendment; the vice president would then assume the presidency. If the president decided not to resign, it is possible that the vice president with a majority of the Cabinet could invoke Sect. 4, although the Twenty-Fifth Amendment was not to be used in cases of policy or political disputes, only in cases of incapacity. It would take a two-thirds majority in both houses—seventy more House votes than impeachment—to allow the vice president to continue to serve as acting president when the president transmits a letter that he is able. The minority party probably would not vote in the vice president's favor and would have to hold less than a third of the seats in both houses for the vice president to continue as acting president. It is unlikely that such a large margin would agree that the president was unable to discharge his powers and duties if he was not actually incapacitated.

Another hypothetical scenario is the triggering of Sect. 2 of the Twenty-Fifth Amendment twice. In other words, a vice president would resign, and the two-term president would be appointed and confirmed by Congress to be vice president, like Gerald Ford in 1973, and Nelson Rockefeller in 1974. Then the president who appointed the vice president would resign, and the vice president would succeed to the presidency. If a president and vice president resign simultaneously, because Article I, Clause II, Sect. 5 of the Constitution states that "the House of Representatives shall choose their speaker," but does not specify that the speaker must be a member, it is possible that the two-term president could be picked by Congress to become speaker and then succeed to the presidency. To date, the House has never chosen a speaker that was not a member, although Republican Representative Matt Gaetz of Florida did cast a vote for Trump as speaker in January 2023.[52] However, the Succession Act requires successors to meet constitutional eligibility requirements.

Extralegal methods do exist to install Trump in the Oval Office again as well, including a coup d'etat, which Trump has proven he would entertain based on his actions on January 6. It is also possible that Trump could have his name put on the ballot for president, and even if the Supreme Court orders that his name be removed, he might flout the order.[53] Individual states could decide to put him on the ballot, but they would face lawsuits. It is likely, however, that the question of temperament and unfitness may arise again, never mind that, at eighty-two years of age, he will be the oldest president to ever serve by the time the 2028 election rolls around. Taken in June 2025, an Axios-Ipsos poll reveals nearly three-quarters of Americans believe that elected officials are dishonest with the American public about their health and that it should be a legal requirement for the president to share health records.[54] An even greater amount, 81 percent, feel that age limits should be put in place for all federally elected officials.[55] However, as the *Politico Magazine* op-ed "Stop Talking About the 25th Amendment. It Won't Work on Trump. And It Might Just Set Off a Constitutional Crisis" argues, temperament, unfitness, and age do not equate to incapacity, and should Trump or a slate that has promised to make him a three-time president appear on the ballot in 2028, the simplest answer may be not to vote him into office in the first place.[56]

If Trump does not seek a third term, he does not have to answer to voters again. This fact, coupled with the Supreme Court's 2024 ruling that a president is immune from prosecution over official acts has empowered him to exceed the powers of the presidency.[57] Thus it is not only

Trump's rhetoric about monarchy, but his actions during the early part of his second term in office that have caused both scholars and the media to suggest that not only has Trump greatly expanded presidential power, but that America is in the middle of a constitutional crisis. In fact, when it comes to Trump's actions and interactions with the judicial branch, the term "constitutional attack" is more appropriate. Facing indictments for attempting to overturn the results of the 2020 election and improperly handling classified documents as well as other crimes, Trump avoided prosecution in part by winning a second term. He then promised to exact retribution on the judicial branch for what he mistakenly believes was partisan "weaponization" of the law against him that had resulted in the indictments.[58] Trump called for the impeachment of judges whose opinion he did not agree with; issued executive orders targeting law firms and lawyers that represent clients he views as enemies; ignored judicial orders to unfreeze billions of dollars in federal grants and stonewalled other court orders.[59] In truth, while Trump may continue to resist compliance, it is not the president's choice as to whether to obey the law. During his first term, he appointed three Supreme Court justices and by the end of his second term, half of all federal judges may be Trump appointees, so judges may rule in his favor more often than not.[60] Henceforth the judicial branch will serve as a check, although an extremely weakened one, on the Trump administration.

Congress' powers vis-à-vis the executive branch have waned over the course of several decades and it is currently failing to serve as a check on the administration. For example, while a Democratic Representative issued seven articles of impeachment against Trump, including "tyrannical overreach," the vote was canceled immediately because it had no hope of success.[61] The days of Senators Birch Bayh and Everett Dirksen "going along to get along," a hallmark of the 1960s and 1970s, no longer exist. Bipartisan efforts to further the national interest deteriorated long before Trump took office, a reason Senator Birch Bayh's son Evan, a senator in his own right, cited for not running for reelection in 2010.[62] And although Trump claims to be undoing the policies of his predecessor Joe Biden, his executive orders targeting affirmative action, desegregation, education, the environment, health care, immigration, and voting rights are dismantling Johnson's Great Society.[63] In contrast to President Johnson's strong leadership, which shepherded the monumental Civil Rights Act of 1964 and Voting Rights Act of 1965 through Congress, Trump has intimidated members of his own party who, afraid of retribution, have acted against the national interest in approving his Cabinet appointees, most, if not all, of whom are Trump loyalists. These appointees lack the credentials for the job and would not go against Trump's wishes by invoking Sect. 4 should he become incapacitated. Beyond convincing Congress to bend the knee, Trump has encroached upon Congress' power of the purse by freezing appropriated funds. Brushing aside Congress' powers has made the United States less safe in numerous ways such as when he suspended aid to international nuclear inspectors, including those responsible for preventing Iran from developing nuclear weapons.[64]

If the number one priority of a country is the security of its citizens, Trump has further reneged on that responsibility by exercising the unitary executive theory and eviscerating executive departments. As soon as he assumed office for the second time, he quickly and significantly reduced the number of federal employees—after seventy-five thousand responded affirmatively to an offer letter to leave voluntarily with severance pay, the administration laid off an additional ten thousand within the first three weeks alone.[65] Trump's overzealous effort also led to the mistaken termination of more than three hundred National Nuclear Security Administration (NNSA) workers in the Department of Energy who oversaw the nation's stockpile of nuclear weapons.[66] The administration tried to rescind the termination letters of the NNSA staff the next morning but had difficulty finding them via personal emails.[67] In addition, Department of Government Efficiency members who had no experience in the handling of nuclear weapons nor in classified information have been given accounts on classified networks that hold highly classified information about the nation's nuclear secrets.[68] Not only has the president eroded the system of checks and balances, by taking away these checks on the nuclear stockpile and understaffing key nuclear security operations, he has undermined the country's security.

This decimation of the federal workforce—composed mostly of employees that could have made higher salaries in the private sector but were doing their civic duties by performing roles in government—has not only drained America of talent but has created opportunities for adversaries to recruit hundreds of rejected staffers with knowledge of classified information as spies. 2025's "Signalgate"—the group chat to which the editor-in-chief of *The Atlantic* was accidentally invited by Defense Secretary Peter Hegseth on Signal, an encrypted but unsecure app, to discuss sensitive military attack plans against Houthi rebels in

Yemen—further underscored the Trump administration's recklessness and America's untrustworthiness when it comes to intelligence sharing. It also revealed that behind closed doors, administration officials believe Europeans are "pathetic" "freeloaders."[69] As if that were not enough to make allies uneasy, Trump's historic tariffs on foes and friends alike caused fear of a global economic collapse and engendered vows of retaliation. Bill Ackman, a billionaire investor and strong Trump supporter, wrote on X that if Trump did not reconsider, America was headed for a "self-induced, economic nuclear winter."[70] Implementing the tariffs against the advice of economists also indicates that Trump has a "limitless potential for risk,"[71] which the world can only hope does not extend to nuclear warfare.

"An Acute and Growing Threat": Nuclear Proliferation in a New World Order

In many ways, the trans-Atlantic alliance, in place since the dawn of the Cold War, seems to have ended and, understanding that America can no longer be counted on as Europe's ultimate defender, NATO members are now looking to build up their own nuclear arsenals. Poland, citing the "profound change in American geopolitics," has stated explicitly that it is thinking of "building its own atomic weapon."[72] France is now considering "extending its country's small nuclear umbrella over Europe."[73] It has disseminated survival guides to its citizens describing how to prepare for imminent threats—guides that are reminiscent of the pamphlets sent out to Americans on how to construct, and what to store in, a bomb shelter in the 1960s.[74] The European Union has developed a defense preparedness plan to make the region more militarily independent. The *Joint White Paper for European Defense 2030* states that Europe is facing an "acute and growing threat" and that "the international order is undergoing changes of a magnitude not seen since 1945." As a result, although Europe has "benefitted immensely from both NATO and the European Union… it must do far more to restore credible deterrence…. It is time for Europe to re-arm."[75] Nuclear proliferation may be the defining characteristic of a dangerous new world order.

The impetus for rearming, according to the *Joint White Paper,* is threats common to America: the military superpowers Russia and China. In June 2024, Russia and North Korea signed a strategic partnership agreement with a mutual defense clause.[76] North Korea has supplied troops and munitions for Russia's war in Ukraine.[77] In exchange, Russia has helped to advance North Korea's nuclear technology and North Korea says it is building a nuclear-powered submarine to enhance its nuclear weapons capabilities.[78] Moving beyond land and sea, tensions among the major powers are increasingly reflected in competition for the final frontier.[79] In February 2024, the White House stated that Russia has developed anti-satellite capabilities, though they are not yet operational.[80] Although Russian President Vladimir Putin has denied it, the fear that Russia plans to place nuclear weapons in orbit in violation of the 1967 Outer Space Treaty is a threat to the entire globe.[81]

To defend against such threats and build out the Space Force, the branch of the military he created in December 2019, Trump signed Executive Order 14,186 to build a "Golden Dome."[82] A massive budget of $175 billion is to be earmarked for the Golden Dome's development in the Pentagon while drastic cuts are being made to the federal government.[83] No current public plans exist to bring this dome to fruition, making it impossible to estimate true costs.[84] Further, the United States has been down this road before with President Reagan's Strategic Defense Initiative announced in March 1983. While it may have contributed to the Soviet Union's eventual downfall by convincing the USSR that it needed to spend more money on defense in return, at the time, it cost American taxpayers billions of dollars before being scrapped due to insurmountable technical and logistical difficulties.[85] The same challenges exist four decades later. Trump wants the project to protect America from long-range nuclear missiles, but long-range missiles can re-enter the atmosphere anywhere, which would require the dome to cover the entirety of America's vast territory. Retired Rear Admiral Mark Montgomery suggests that a project protecting some government buildings and cities could be completed in about a decade.[86] Typically, this type of dome would defend against short-range ballistic missiles and, unless Trump enrages long-standing allies Canada and the United Kingdom enough for the United Kingdom to send Canada these weapons, no short-range threat exists that close to America's borders. John Tierney, a former Democratic congressman who held years of hearings on ballistic missile defense concluded that "strategically… technically… [and] economically, it doesn't make any sense."[87] Longtime national security and nuclear policy analyst Joe Cirincione put it more bluntly, calling the idea for national missile defense the "longest running scam in the history of the Department of Defense."[88]

The inspiration behind the Golden Dome is Israel's Iron Dome that, with the United States' aid, helped protect Israeli citizens from an Iranian drone attack in October 2024, and additional attacks in 2025. In June 2025, for the first time in twenty years, the International Atomic Energy Agency censured Iran for failing to comply with nuclear nonproliferation obligations.[89] Within hours, Israel began bombing Iran's nuclear and military facilities and Iran responded in kind with strikes hitting hospitals and apartment complexes. Only American-made "bunker busters," the Massive Ordnance Penetrator (MOP) bombs carried by American B-2 planes, have the power to destroy Iran's heavily fortified nuclear facilities located deep within mountains.[90] On June 22, the United States bombed Fordo, Natanz, and Isfahan. Trump claimed that "Operation Midnight Hammer" had "completely obliterated" Iran's nuclear capabilities—even comparing the dropping of the MOPs to the dropping of the atomic bombs on Hiroshima and Nagasaki.[91] A leaked US Defense Intelligence Agency report contradicted the president's claims, stating that Iran's nuclear program had only been set back by a few months.[92] US involvement could precipitate a much larger war.

Supposedly to counter the threats in the Middle East as well as perils from Russia, China, and North Korea, the United States is growing its nuclear weapons capabilities by "spending $75 billion annually—the equivalent of two Manhattan Projects every year ... until at least 2032. In total, the country is set to spend over $1.7 trillion on nuclear modernization over 30 years."[93] However, the United States' most recent military actions coupled with the plan to engineer a Golden Dome and the nuclear weapons build-up sends a signal to the other nuclear powers, not of deterrence and the desire to protect American lives, but that the United States is planning for World War III.

"A Potentially Mad President": Emergency Use of the Twenty-Fifth Amendment to Avert "Irreparable Catastrophe"

As Trump began his second term, the Bulletin of the Atomic Scientists moved the Doomsday Clock to eighty-nine seconds to midnight, the closest it has ever been to the apocalypse. The Clock no longer solely takes nuclear anxiety into account. Nuclear anxiety has become a part of wider anxieties also measured in the Nobel Laureates' assessment that include climate change and climate change-caused disasters like superstorms, floods, and fires; loss of control over artificial intelligence (AI); and cyberwarfare. AI and cyberwarfare are of particular concern in relation to nuclear warfare, and systems that incorporate artificial intelligence in military targeting have been incorporated already in Ukraine and the Middle East. The Bulletin's *2025 Doomsday Clock Announcement* highlighted the "array of other disruptive technologies advanced last year in ways that make the world more dangerous" and added that this raises "questions about the extent to which machines will be allowed to make military decisions—even decisions that could kill on a vast scale, including those related to the use of nuclear weapons."[94] With its rapidly rising popularity, perhaps the best that can be hoped for is an international agreement that no AI will be used in the nuclear decision-making process—that the nuclear launch system be air-gapped (physically and wirelessly isolated) from any system using AI in command and control.

The concerns that caused the Nobel Laureates to move the Doomsday Clock to mere seconds before midnight are all closely interwoven with nuclear anxiety. Connecting climate change and nuclear weapons, in December 2022, the US Department of Energy conducted the first controlled fusion experiment at its Lawrence Livermore National Laboratory's National Ignition Facility (NIF). The breakthrough was couched as a step toward the use of fusion energy to provide carbon-free electricity and fight climate change. While the use of fusion could produce carbon-free electricity at scale—and an announcement was made in December 2024 that the first nuclear fusion plan will be built in Chesterfield County, Virginia—development of this new energy source may take some time.[95] Like America's relationship with atomic energy since its advent, the reality is more complicated. Hope exists that "new nuclear" will be a force for good, lowering greenhouse gas emissions and slowing climate change. However, NIF primarily monitors the US nuclear weapons stockpile, and the clean energy breakthrough was also a weapons advancement.[96] Two UCLA professors of atmospheric and oceanic sciences compare climate change with nuclear war, both of which could lead to mankind's doom. They write:

> Global warming is approaching slowly like a tsunami wave on the horizon. Nuclear war waits in the shadows, a rattlesnake ready to strike.... Manmade

climate change represents the slow withering of humankind. Nuclear war represents its swift annihilation, a vision of Armageddon.[97]

Like the eerily horrified figure in Edvard Munch's *The Scream*, Americans are facing an existential crisis. And just as the figure responds with open mouthed distress yet with its hands covering both ears, the current administration denies the devastating effects of climate change.

In fact, the Trump administration not only refuses to acknowledge that the world may be on the brink of the apocalypse, it will not even admit that climate change is an issue. In the United States' *2025 Threat Assessment* all mention of climate change has been elided for the first time in eleven years.[98] When questioned in a Senate Intelligence Committee hearing, Trump's Director of National Intelligence Tulsi Gabbard replied that global climate change was no longer a direct threat to US national security.[99] Despite such glib dismissals, the threat has not been eliminated; the omission is simply disingenuous. The report does acknowledge military threats including that China is intent on "modernizing, diversifying, and expanding its posture."[100] It also warns of increased risk of nuclear war with Russia, which is cooperating with Iran and North Korea, and which has the "largest and most diverse nuclear weapons stockpile" that "could inflict catastrophic damage to the Homeland."[101] The last time the United States confronted such an "axis of aggressors" was the beginning of the Cold War, and America's foes were not acting in concert as they appear to be doing now.[102] By denying the serious threat of climate change, the administration is underscoring the United States' untrustworthiness, and by alienating its traditional allies, it is pushing them, as well as other countries, toward closer ties with these aggressors. The United States is rapidly relinquishing its superpower status and, at this rate, will face Armageddon alone.

A last hope for avoiding nuclear war might lie in the use of the Twenty-Fifth Amendment itself. House speaker Nancy Pelosi believed Trump was "deranged" and "crazy." In other words, that a real Dr. Strangelove had his finger on the nuclear button and Sect. 4 of the Twenty-Fifth Amendment should have been invoked. Yet it is clear that Sect. 4 was not intended to be invoked due to policy disagreements, a lack of presidential temperament, or even generally perceived unfitness to serve. Constitutional law scholar Brian Kalt warns that employing it for any of these reasons will lead to legitimacy issues for the vice president, who, in some cases, could be viewed as an usurper.[103] Invocation of the amendment for these reasons also could lead to dilution of the efficacy of the amendment itself. Nevertheless, the Constitution has proved to be a flexible document and perhaps a loose reading and an emergency use of the Twenty-Fifth is called for if the president is about to order a first strike and cross the nuclear Rubicon. In cases of "irreparable catastrophe," Kalt poses the possibility of Sect. 4 action against a "conscious, lucid, but potentially mad president" if it is the only way to prevent a nuclear Armageddon.[104] Although impeachment for the high crime and misdemeanor of instigating nuclear war by ordering an unprovoked nuclear strike without Congress' permission would be more appropriate, in the case of a Sect. 4 action, the taking away of presidential powers and duties would be almost immediate and only temporary. It would allow a hotheaded president to cool down and reconsider the nuclear strike order while an acting president's finger is on the button.[105] Scholar Lawrence Trautman wrote: "In an age when technology has enabled the destruction of the Earth and elimination of all living beings within a matter of minutes, the Twenty-Fifth Amendment may prove to be the last hope for peace."[106]

We still live, in President Kennedy's words, "under the nuclear sword of Damocles… capable of being cut at any moment by accident, or miscalculation, or by madness."[107] The historical patterns revealed by this study of the intersection of nuclear anxiety and presidential continuity indicate that as tensions rise, government activity around the search for solutions to succession and inability problems will intensify—though we are less likely to see Sects. 3 and 4 of the Twenty-Fifth Amendment invoked in cases of "madness." The "form of madness" of the present will more likely be, as *The Bulletin of the Atomic Scientists* contends, in "blindly continuing on the current path."[108] The Twenty-Fifth Amendment is fundamentally about securing the continuity of the institution of the presidency. And, as John Feerick urges, the "gaps that persist [in the Twenty-Fifth Amendment] are serious and must be addressed because mass [nuclear] catastrophe, illness, or some other happenstance can occur at any time."[109] The Bulletin of the Atomic Scientists reminds us: "the Clock ticks."

Notes

1. In *Explicit and Authentic Acts*, Kyvig discusses whether the Constitution continues to serve as the "sovereign will of the

people as to their governance" or if it is "unable to check the momentary whims and excess of transitory power." See David E. Kyvig, *Explicit and Authentic Acts: Amending the Constitution, 1776–1995* (Lawrence, Kansas: University Press of Kansas, 1996), xviii.
2. Rose McDermott, Extensions on the Twenty-Fifth Amendment: The Influence of Biological Factors on Assessments of Impairment, 79. Fordham Law Review, 881 (2011), 882. Note that some of the gaps and vagaries were intentional on the part of the framers.
3. The peace sign can be dated to 1958, and attributed to Gerald Holtom who created the sign for the British Campaign for Nuclear Disarmament. See Kathryn Wescott, "World's Best-Known Protest Symbol Turns Fifty," *BBC News*, March 20, 2008, http://news.bbc.co.uk/2/hi/uk_news/magazine/7292252.stm.
4. Gitlin was also a founder of Harvard University's nuclear disarmament student group, Tocsin, in the early 1960s. Todd Gitlin, *The Sixties: Years of Hope, Days of Rage* (New York: Bantam Books, 1987), 22–23.
5. Allan M. Winkler, *Life Under a Cloud: American Anxiety About the Atom* (New York: Oxford University Press, 1993), 9.
6. Stanley Kubrick's 1964 movie *Dr. Strangelove or How I Stopped Worrying and Learned to Love the Bomb* is the archetypal movie about a president who volunteers to launch a nuclear strike on New York after an insane US general launches one on Moscow, to avoid additional nuclear reprisals.
7. Charlotte Alter, "Doomsday Clock Puts Us at Three Minutes Away from Midnight," *Time*, January 23, 2015, http://time.com/3680932/doomsday-clock-three-minutes/.
8. The movement of the clock to three minutes to midnight was matched in 1984, during the Reagan years, and one other time, in 1949, when the Soviet Union detonated its first atomic bomb. *Bulletin of the Atomic Scientists*. http://thebulletin.org/timeline.
9. The media has regularly made these assertions accompanied by a similar clarion call to reduce tensions. For example, William J. Broad and David E. Sanger of *The New York Times* argue that nuclear war is more likely now than at any time since the Cold War. In an article entitled "Cold War 2.0: How Russia

and the West Reheated a Historic Struggle" in *The Guardian*, authors Patrick Wintour, Luke Harding, and Jullian Borger cite Russian President Vladimir Putin's assertion that Russia would open military bases in Cuba as proof of the coming of a second Cuban missile crisis. The authors conclude from the British vantage point that a new Cold War has begun. They quoted both the former head of M16 Sir John Sawers and the German foreign minister Frank-Walter Steinmeier stating that this new Cold War is more dangerous than the first. The article argued that "[t]he reasons for this anxiety are not hard to find." More likely: William J. Broad and David E. Sanger, "As US Modernizes Nuclear Weapons, 'Smaller' Leaves Some Uneasy," *The New York Times*, January 11, 2016. Russian in Cuba: Patrick Wintour, Luke Harding, and Jullian Borger, "Cold War 2.0: How Russia and the West Reheated a Historic Struggle," *The Guardian*, October 24, 2016, https://www.theguardian.com/world/2016/oct/24/cold-war-20-how-russia-and-the-west-reheated-a-historic-struggle.

10. Ariz. Laws 1964, ch. 56 as quoted in John Feerick, *From Failing Hands*, 284.
11. In May 2008, after the resignation of New York Governor Eliot Spitzer and the ascension to power of Lieutenant Governor David Paterson, legislators reopened the question of who should succeed the lieutenant governor. The goal of the Nelson A. Rockefeller Institute of Government's forum was to begin a discourse that would ensure that the executive branch positions of governor, lieutenant governor, as well as attorney general and comptroller, remained filled at all times. See "Gubernatorial Succession and the Powers of the Lieutenant Governor: A Public Policy Forum," *The Nelson A. Rockefeller Institute of Government*, May 28, 2008, http://www.rockinst.org/pdf/public_policy_forums/2008-05-29-public_policy_forum_gubernatorial_succession_and_the_powers_of_the_lieutenant_governor.pdf. Interest in this issue was revived in 2023, after Governor Kathy Huchel exercised unfettered discretion to appoint two consecutive lieutenant governors. See Report and Recommendations of the New York Bar Association Committee on the New York State Constitution," *New York State Bar Association*, January 2023,

final-Report-on-Gubernatorial-Succession-NYSBA-Committee-on the-NYS-Constitution-January-2023.pdf.
12. This line of congressional questions included Rockefeller's policies on nuclear weapons, as Chapter 5 reveals.
13. Pastore introduced very specific legislation (S.J. 26): should a repeat of vice presidential and presidential resignations in the same administration occur, the vice president would serve as president only until a president elected in a special election took the oath of office as president. Senator William Hathaway introduced legislation (S. 2678) calling for a general election, rather than allowing the vice president to fill the president's shoes for the remainder of the term of four years as the Twenty-Fifth prescribed. Both bills died in committee.
14. The text of the amendment can be found in Chapter 4.
15. According to the copious notes taken by James Madison, John Dickinson asked this question of the framers assembled at the Constitution Convention in 1787, referring to the succession clause in Article II of the Constitution. He failed to receive an answer.
16. US Government Printing Office. Hearing Before the Subcommittee on Constitutional Amendments of the Committee on the Judiciary United States Senate Ninety-Fourth Congress First Session on S.J. Res. 26 Proposing Modification of the Twenty-Fifth Amendment of the Constitution of the United States. Printed for the use of the Committee on the Judiciary, (Washington: US Government Printing Office, 1976), 18.
17. Today's Congress stands in stark contrast to the one that passed the Twenty-Fifth Amendment. Bayh, in videotaped interviews with his official biographer Bob Blaemire, a former staff member, reminisced about the recreational baseball games played between Democratic and Republican Senators at RFK Stadium in D.C in the mid-1960s. From 1961–1968, just beyond the temporal boundaries of the Twenty-Fifth Amendment's drafting, passage and ratification, RFK Stadium was known as the "District of Columbia" Stadium. Ira Shapiro, in *The Last Great Senate*, paints a similar picture of camaraderie and suggests that this was an era of compromise in the name of the institution of the Senate, which was larger than any one individual. Perhaps the grass now growing in the upper areas of the stadium seats is analogous

to the lack of bipartisan spirit in today's Congress. Members of Congress can't see the ball for the weeds. The author has confirmed the presence of a tree, grass, and weeds. The upper deck press box has deteriorated as well. Demolition on the stadium began in January 2025. Bayh's assertion that Congress will fix: "A Modern Father of Our Constitution: An Interview with Former Senator Birch Bayh," 79 *Fordham Law Review* 781 (2011), 814. Weeds: Garrett Quinn, "Brokedown Palace: RFK Stadium is a National Treasure Cracks and All," *Washington City Paper*, June 5, 2013, https://washingtoncitypaper.com/article/453751/brokedown-palace-rfk-stadium-is-a-national-treasure-cracks-and-all/. See also: Ira Shapiro, *The Last Great Senate* (New York: PublicAffairs, 2013).
18. Birch Bayh, Interview with author, November 11, 2014.
19. Nine states are now widely known to have nuclear capabilities: the United States, Russia, the United Kingdom, France, China, Israel, India, Pakistan, and North Korea. See Hans M. Kristensen and Robert S. Norris, "Nuclear Notebook: Nuclear Arsenals of the World," *Bulletin of the Atomic Scientists*, http://thebulletin.org/nuclear-notebook-multimedia.
20. Cheney: As quoted in David Greenberg. Review of John M. Schuessler, *Deceit on the Road to War: Presidents, Politics, and American Democracy*," H-Diplo, H-Net Reviews (July, 2016), http://www.h-net.org/reviews/showrev.php?id=46082.
21. This was particularly true of the "designated survivor," a Cabinet official in the line of succession who would remain in office through the inauguration of the new president on Inauguration Day and not attend the festivities celebrating the president's annual State of the Union Address. Gerhard Peters, a co-founder of the American Presidency Project, which tracks data including designated survivors, said of the designated survivor program: "it's sort of a Cold War relic from the fear of a nuclear attack." Devin Dwyer, "State of the Union 'Designated Survivor' Demystified," *ABC News*, January 27, 2014, http://abcnews.go.com/Politics/state-union-designated-survivor-demystified/story?id=21637341.
22. Valerie Jarrett, a senior adviser to President Barack Obama informed Bayh that in the case of sudden disaster, the president had "a very comprehensive contingency plan." This plan is

classified, although with nuclear and other catastrophic threats still lingering, the public has asked for more transparency and clarity around Continuity of Operations Plans (COOP). The line between transparency and security has been proven difficult to walk. See also Garrett M. Graff, *Raven Rock: The Story of the US Government's Secret Plan to Save Itself—While the Rest of Us Die* (New York: Simon & Schuster, 2017), 393.

23. William J. Broad and David E. Sanger, "As US Modernizes Nuclear Weapons, 'Smaller' Leaves Some Uneasy," *The New York Times*, January 11, 2016. At the conclusion of Obama's term, the American arsenal consisted of 5,000 nuclear warheads and new, multi-billion dollar plans to build a new generation of nuclear weapons were in the works. Graff, *Raven Rock*, 405.

24. Margin of victory: James FitzGerald, "Just How Big was Donald Trump's Election Victory?" *BBC News*, November 23, 2024, https://www.bbc.com/news/articles/cn5w9w160xdo. Indictments: Kaela Malig and Kristina Abovyan, "A Guide to the Criminal Cases Against Donald Trump," PBS Frontline, Updated January 21, 2025, https://www.pbs.org/wgbh/frontline/article/a-guide-to-the-criminal-cases-against-donald-trump/.

25. For a study on the history of an image, see: Greenberg, *Nixon's Shadow*.

26. W.J. Hennigan, "The President's Sole Authority Over Nuclear Weapons is Dangerous," *The New York Times*, March 7, 2024, https://www.nytimes.com/interactive/2024/03/07/opinion/nuclear-weapons-president.html.

27. Nixon's advisors raised the DEFCON level during the Yom Kippur war of October 1973. In 1981, as Soviet troops amassing on the Polish border suggested nuclear war might be imminent, President Reagan was seriously wounded in an assassination attempt, but, even as surgeons searched desperately inside the president's lung for the bullet, the vice president and Cabinet did not invoke the amendment. See Chapter 5.

28. When he underwent surgery later in his presidency, Reagan followed the procedures outlined in the Twenty-Fifth Amendment, by writing the speaker and president pro tem, but he specifically stated in these official letters that he was not invoking the Twenty-Fifth Amendment. He followed the procedures called for in Sect. 3 of the amendment but called into question the

section's premises. The entire world knew when the president would be operated on and, therefore, an absence in the top seat of government would occur, but he irresponsibly, some argue, put his image and related political concerns over the welfare of the people. See William Safire, "Taking the 25th: Why the Legalistic Flimflam?" *The New York Times* (July 15, 1985).
29. Harry S. Truman, "Truman Proposes Disability Panel, *The New York Times* (June 24, 1957).
30. Roy E. Brownell II, "Now is the Time to Address Presidential and Vice Presidential Incapacity," *The Hill*. October 2, 2020. https://thehill.com/opinion/white-house/519352-now-is-the-time-to-address-presidential-and-vice-presidential-incapacity/.
31. Roy E. Brownell II, "What to Do if Simultaneous Presidential and Vice Presidential Inability Struck Today," *Fordham Law Review*, Volume 86, 2017, https://ir.lawnet.fordham.edu/cgi/viewcontent.cgi?article=5455&context=flr.
32. Roy E. Brownell II and John Rogan, "An Anniversary Best Uncelebrated: The 75th Year of the Presidential Succession Act of 1947," *Fordham Law Voting Rights and Democracy Forum*, Volume 1, Issue 1, November 2022, https://ir.lawnet.fordham.edu/vrdf/vol1/iss1/5.
33. Brownell and Rogan, "An Anniversary Best Uncelebrated."
34. The speaker is elected to the House by voters in his or her district and then to the speakership by a majority of the members of the House. See House of Representatives, Report Number 79–289, 1–2.
35. See Chapter 4.
36. Brownell and Rogan, "An Anniversary Best Uncelebrated."
37. Brownell and Rogan, "An Anniversary Best Uncelebrated."
38. Hennigan, "The President's Sole Authority."
39. "'Meeting at the White House—Atomic Bomb Custody,' 21 July 1948," *National Security Archive*, https://nsarchive.gwu.edu/document/16061-document-01a-meeting-white-house-atomic.
40. "'Meeting at the White House—Atomic Bomb Custody,' 21 July 1948," See also: Public Policy Papers, Department of Rare Books and Special Collections, Princeton University Library, David Lilienthal Papers, box 197.
41. Graff, "The Madman and the Bomb."

42. "Congressman Lieu, Senator Markey Introduce the Restricting First Use of Nuclear Weapons Act of 2017," *Ted Lieu, Congressman for California's 36th District,* January 24, 2017, https://lieu.house.gov/media-center/press-releases/congressman-lieu-senator-markey-introduce-restricting-first-use-0.
43. Graff, "The Madman and the Bomb."
44. Lama El Baz, "Most Americans Are Uncomfortable with the Policy of Nuclear Sole Authority," *Chicago Council on Global Affairs,* August 16, 2023, https://globalaffairs.org/commentary-and-analysis/blogs/most-americans-are-uncomfortable-policy-nuclear-sole-authority.
45. Note the contrast to President Reagan after Reagan survived the attempt on his life in March 1981. Reagan thought God might have spared him so that he could reduce the possibility of a nuclear war. See Chapter 5. Greg Norman, "Faith Leaders Reach to Trump Re-Election: 'God Spared My Life For a Reason,'" *Fox News,* November 6, 2024, https://www.foxnews.com/us/faith-leaders-react-trump-re-election-god-spared-my-life-reason?msockid=31a957df733a64e63f05425e7279657a.
46. "@WhiteHouse status," *X.com,* February 19, 2025, https://x.com/WhiteHouse/status/1892295984928993698.
47. Graff, "The Madman and the Bomb."
48. "Rep. Ogles Proposes Amending the 22nd Amendment to Allow Trump to Serve a Third Term," *Congressman Andy Ogles, Tennessee's 5th Congressional District,* January 23, 2025, https://ogles.house.gov/media/press-releases/rep-ogles-proposes-amending-22nd-amendment-allow-trump-serve-third-term. See text of House Resolution: https://ogles.house.gov/sites/evo-subsites/ogles.house.gov/files/evo-media-document/PIH-OGLES_006%20%28Constitutional%20Amendment%29.pdf.
49. "Congressman Dan Goldman Reintroduces Resolution Reaffirming House Support for the 22nd Amendment and Its Clear Prohibition on Third Trump Term," *Congressman Daniel Goldman, 10th District of New York,* February 27, 2025, https://goldman.house.gov/media/press-releases/congressman-dan-goldman-reintroduces-resolution-reaffirming-house-support-22nd.
50. Erica L. Green, "Trump Says He's 'Not Joking' About Seeking a Third Term in Defiance of the Constitution," *The New York*

Times, March 30, 2025, https://www.nytimes.com/2025/03/30/us/politics/trump-third-term.html?utm_source=flipboard&utm_content=user/newyorktimes.

51. Green, "Trump Says He's 'Not Joking' About Seeking a Third Term in Defiance of the Constitution."
52. Nicholas Reimann, "Trump Gets One Vote For House Speaker In Apparent Hard-Right Stunt –And He's Technically Eligible For The Job," *Forbes*, January 5, 2023, https://www.forbes.com/sites/nicholasreimann/2023/01/05/trump-gets-one-vote-for-house-speaker-in-apparent-hard-right-stunt-and-hes-technically-eligible-for-the-job/.
53. According to a *YouGov* poll taken April 9, 2025, "Support for Third Trump Term: Oppose: 65%; Support: 18%; Neutral: 16%." @USA_Polling, *X.com*, April 14, 2025. https://x.com/usa_polling/status/1911908319989575924?s=43&t=HDwg54Bei4kwkNm4K3CpQ.
54. Adriel Bettelheim and Margaret Talev, "Axios-Ipsos Poll: Americans Want to Force Presidents to Share Health Records," *Axios*, June 20, 2025, https://www.axios.com/2025/06/20/axios-ipsos-poll-president-elected-officials-health.
55. Bettelheim and Talev, "Axios-Ipsos Poll: Americans Want to Force Presidents to Share Health Records."
56. Greenberg and Lubot, "Stop Talking About the 25th Amendment. It Won't Work on Trump." Note that while too early to predict, Trump's approval rating at one hundred days was lower than any president in at least seven decades, indicating that a third Trump term may be unlikely. See Jenifer Agiesta and Ariel Edwards-Levy, "Poll: Trump's Approval Rating at 100 Days in Office," *CNN*, April 27, 2025, https://www.cnn.com/2025/04/27/politics/approval-rating-trump-100-days/index.html.
57. David E. Sanger, "Trump's Tariffs Are Latest Sign of His Second-Term Appetite for Risk," *The New York Times*, April 3, 2025, https://www.nytimes.com/2025/04/03/us/politics/trumps-tariffs-risks-second-term.html?smid=nytcore-ios-share&referringSource=articleShare.
58. Caitlin Yilek and Kathryn Watson, "In Address About Vision for Justice Dept., Trump Airs Grievances about Prior Investigations into Him," *CBS News*, March 14, 2025, https://www.cbsnews.com/news/donald-trump-justice-department-remarks/.

59. J. Michael Luttig, "Opinion: Trump Won't Win a War Against the Courts," *The New York Times,* March 23, 2025, https://www.nytimes.com/2025/03/23/opinion/trump-judge-venezuela-deportation.html?utm_source=flipboard&utm_content=topic/politics. *The New York Times/Siena College Poll* published as Trump reached the one-hundred-day mark revealed that Americans believed he was overreaching. Shane Goldmacher, Ruth Igielnik, and Camille Baker, "Voters See Trump's Use of Power as Overreaching, Times/Siena Poll Finds," *The New York Times,* April 25, 2025. https://www.nytimes.com/2025/04/25/us/politics/trump-poll-approval.html?campaign_id=60&emc=edit_na_20250425&instance_id=153335&nl=breaking-news&regi_id=72367047&segment_id=196754&user_id=400f40c3b01e9281941f8ed8c22fc033.Shane
60. Sonam Sheth, "Half of All Federal Judges Could Be Trump Appointees by End of His Next Term," *Newsweek,* November 7, 2024, https://www.newsweek.com/donald-trump-federal-judges-appointments-judiciary-1982390.
61. Martha McHardy, "Donald Trump Issued Warning as Impeachment Vote Abruptly Cancelled," *Newsweek*, May 20, 2025, https://www.newsweek.com/donald-trump-impeachment-vote-canceled-2072567?utm_source=Flipboard&utm_medium=App&utm_campaign=Partnerships.
62. Shapiro, *The Last Great Senate*, ix.
63. Russel Contreras, "Trump's 2025 Moves Seeks to Reverse LBJ's 1965 Civil Rights Legacy," *Axios,* March 22, 2025, https://www.axios.com/2025/03/22/trump-2025-reverse-lbj-1965-civil-rights-poverty?utm_source=newsletter&utm_medium=email&utm_campaign=newsletter_axiosam&stream=top.
64. Wiliam J. Broad, "Trump's Foreign Aid Freeze Affects Iran's Nuclear Inspectors," *The New York Times,* March 8, 2025, https://www.nytimes.com/2025/03/08/science/trump-nuclear-inspectors-aid-freeze.html?smid=nytcore-ios-share&referringSource=articleShare.

65. Garrett Haake and Megan Lebowitz, "White House Says about 75 K Federal Workers Accepted 'Deferred Resignation' Offer," *NBC News,* February 12, 2025, https://www.nbcnews.com/politics/white-house/white-house-says-75000-accepted-federal-buyout-trump-rcna191971.
66. Antoinette Radford, "The Latest on Donald Trump's Presidency," *CNN,* February 16, 2025, https://www.cnn.com/politics/live-news/trump-administration-news-02-16-25/index.html.
67. Brandon Drenon, "US Government Struggles to Rehire Nuclear Safety Staff It Laid Off Days Ago," *BBC News,* February 15, 2025, https://www.bbc.com/news/articles/c4g3nrx1dq5o?utm_source=flipboard&utm_content=user/BBCNews.
68. Geoff Brumfiel and Jenna McLaughlin, "DOGE Employees Gain Accounts on Classified Networks Holding Nuclear Secrets, *NPR,* April 28, 2025, https://www.npr.org/2025/04/28/nx-s1-5378684/doge-energy-department-nuclear-secrets-access?utm_source=flipboard&utm_content=topic/politics.
69. Jeanna Smialek and Steven Erlanger, "Trump's Team Calls Europe 'Pathetic' in Leaked Signal Group Chat Messages," *The New York Times,* March 25, 2025, https://www.nytimes.com/2025/03/25/world/europe/signal-jeffrey-goldberg-message-hegseth.html?unlocked_article_code=1.604.cPCw.I7jRR3dVPszC&smid=url-share&utm_source=newsletter&utm_medium=email&utm_campaign=newsletter_axiosam&stream=top.
70. "@BillAckman status," *X.com,* April 6, 2025, https://x.com/BillAckman/status/1908992002366292286.
71. David E. Sanger, "Trump's Tariffs Are Latest Sign of His Second-Term Appetite for Risk," *The New York Times,* April 3, 2025, https://www.nytimes.com/2025/04/03/us/politics/trumps-tariffs-risks-second-term.html?smid=nytcore-ios-share&referringSource=articleShare.
72. "Europe Thinks the Unthinkable on a Nuclear Bomb," *The Economist,* March 12, 2026, https://www.economist.com/international/2025/03/12/europe-thinks-the-unthinkable-on-a-nuclear-bomb.

73. Daniel Michaels, Noemie Bisserbe, and Michael R. Gordon, "Trump Prompts European Calls for a Homegrown Nuclear Umbrella," *The Wall Street Journal,* March 24, 2025, https://www.wsj.com/world/europe/europe-nuclear-umbrella-france-britain-nato-10c78d15.
74. Lisa Klaassen, "France to Distribute 'Survival Manual' to Prepare Households for Emergencies—Including Armed Conflict," *CNN,* March 19, 2025, https://www.cnn.com/2025/03/19/europe/france-survival-manual-scli-intl/index.html?utm_source=cnn_Evening+Newsletter+-+Wednesday%2C+March+19%2C+2025&utm_medium=email&bt_ee=SSKAc%2FXtAJCitrwr5 1oA8PqJJpdSCsjuHIE9OTxTVC6EoKS8ZGHA7c7%2BzhNM9k9H&bt_ts=1742421220481. Heightened international tensions have prompted one-third of Americans to prepare shelters and escape tunnels today. See Coralie Kraft, "The 'Panic Industry' Boom," *The New York Times Magazine,* April 10, 2025, https://www.nytimes.com/interactive/2025/04/10/magazine/bunkers-prepping.html.
75. Joint White Paper for European Defense Readiness 2030, *High Representative of the Union for Foreign Affairs and Security Policy* (Brussels: *European Commission,* March 2025), https://defence-industry-space.ec.europa.eu/document/download/30b50d2c-49aa-4250-9ca6-27a0347cf009_en?filename=White%20Paper.pdf&utm_source=newsletter&utm_medium=email&utm_campaign=newsletter_axiosam&stream=top.
76. Hyonhee Shin, "Key Points of North Korea, Russia Landmark Strategic Partnership," *Reuters,* June 20, 2024, https://www.reuters.com/world/asia-pacific/key-points-north-korea-russia-landmark-strategic-partnership-treaty-2024-06-20/.
77. "Unlawful Military Cooperation including Arms Transfers between North Korea and Russia," *Multilateral Sanctions Monitoring Team,* May 29, 2025, https://msmt.info/view/save/2025/05/29/1085cade-a4b1-4405-94c0-7c980c24fd21-Unlawful_Military_Cooperation_including_Arms_Transfers_between_North_Korea_and_Russia_(MSMT_2025_1).pdf.
78. Choi Sang-hun, "North Korea Says It's Building a Nuclear-Powered Submarine," *The New York Times,* March 8, 2025,

https://www.nytimes.com/2025/03/08/world/asia/north-korea-nuclear-powered-submarine.html?smid=nytcore-ios-share&referringSource=articleShare.

79. John Mecklin, "2025 Doomsday Clock Statement," *Bulletin of the Atomic Scientists,* January 28, 2025, https://thebulletin.org/doomsday-clock/2025-statement/.
80. Aamer Madhani and Zeke Miller, "Russia Has Obtained 'Troubling' Emerging Anti-Satellite Weapon, US Says," *AP News,* February 15, 2024, https://apnews.com/article/russia-anti-satellite-weapon-threat-technology-2880f9c55122dcafe87188bc92dd6cde.
81. Madhani and Miller, "Russia Has Obtained 'Troubling' Emerging Anti-Satellite Weapon, US Says." See also: Mecklin, "2025 Doomsday Clock Statement."
82. "The Iron Dome for America," *President Donald J. Trump, The White House*, January 27, 2025, https://www.whitehouse.gov/presidential-actions/2025/01/the-iron-dome-for-america/.
83. Colin Demarest, "Beltway Bloat Could Doom Trump's Golden Dome, *Axios,* May 28, 2025, https://www.axios.com/2025/05/28/trump-golden-dome-challenges-cost.
84. Zachary Cohen and Owen Liebermann, "Trump Wants a 'Golden Dome' Capable of Defending Entire US: 'Strategically, It Doesn't Make Any Sense'," *CNN*, March 22, 2025, https://www.cnn.com/2025/03/22/politics/pentagon-golden-dome-scramble/index.html. According to *CNN*, the Congressional Budget Office has estimated the US could have to spend more than $500 billion – over the course of 20 years – to develop a viable Golden Dome. See Zachary Cohen, Katie Bo Lillis, and Natasha Bertrand, "Trump's 'Golden Dome' Missile Shield Could Cost Hundreds of Billions," *CNN*, May 19, 2025, https://www.cnn.com/2025/05/19/politics/golden-dome-missile-shield-price-billions?utm_source=flipboard&utm_content=topic/unitedstates.
85. Reagan had the foresight to include NATO in Strategic Defense Initiative developments whereas Trump has been alienating allies, taking an isolationist stance that had died out with the bombing of Pearl Habor. For an international history of SDI see: Aaron Bateman, *Weapons in Space: Technology, Politics, and the Rise and Fall of the Strategic Defense Initiative* (MIT Press, 2024).
86. Cohen and Liebermann, "Trump Wants a 'Golden Dome'."

87. Cohen and Liebermann, "Trump Wants a 'Golden Dome'."
88. John Mecklin, "The 15-Minute Interview: Joe Cirincione on Golden Dome and the Long-Running US Missile Defense Debacle," *Bulletin of the Atomic Scientists*, May 22, 2025, https://thebulletin.org/2025/05/the-15-minute-interview-joe-cirincione-on-golden-dome-and-the-long-running-us-missile-defense-debacle/?utm_source=ActiveCampaign&utm_medium=email&utm_content=Is%20Trump%20s%20Golden%20Dome%20a%20bad%20idea%3F&utm_campaign=20250526%20Monday%20Newsletter.
89. Stephanie Liechtenstein, Jon Gambrell, and Aamer Madhani, "Iran Announces a New Nuclear Enrichment Site After UN Watchdog Censure," *AP News*, June 12, 2025, https://apnews.com/article/iran-nuclear-iaea-sanctions-728b811da537abe942682e13a82ff8bd.
90. Barak Ravid and Marc Caputo, "Trump Presses Aides on Whether Bunker-Buster Plan to Bomb Iran Will Work," *Axios*, June 18, 2025, https://www.axios.com/2025/06/18/trump-bunker-buster-bomb-iran-nuclear-program?utm_source=newsletter&utm_medium=email&utm_campaign=newsletter_axiosam&stream=top.
91. Jeff Mason and Gram Slattery, "Comparing US Iran Strike to Hiroshima, Trump Plays Down Intelligence Report, *Reuters*, June 25, 2025, https://www.reuters.com/world/middle-east/trump-says-intelligence-iran-was-inconclusive-suggests-severe-damage-2025-06-25/.
92. Although the centrifuges at Fordo were most likely destroyed (because centrifuges, by nature, are sensitive to intense vibrations like those caused by the bombings), it is likely that Iran moved the uranium they had already enriched to safer locations and that other nuclear facilities still exist within the country. See: Aurelien Breeden, "Centrifuges at Fordo 'No Longer Operational' UN Nuclear Watchdog Head Says," *The New York Times*, June 26, 2025, https://www.nytimes.com/2025/06/26/world/middleeast/centrifuges-fordo-damage-iran.html?smid=nytcore-ios-share&referringSource=articleShare. See also: Julian E. Barnes and David E. Sanger, "Fate of Iran's Enriched Uranium Is a

Mystery," *The New York Times*, June 26, 2025, https://www.nytimes.com/2025/06/26/us/politics/iran-nuclear-program-uranium.html?smid=nytcore-ios-share&referringSource=articleShare. Set back by a few months: Gram Slattery, Alexander Cornwell, and Parisa Hafezi, "US Strikes Failed to Destroy Iran's Nuclear Sites, Intelligence Report Says," *Reuters*, June 24, 2025, https://www.reuters.com/world/middle-east/trump-announces-israel-iran-ceasefire-2025-06-23/.

93. Lucas Ruiz and Geoff Wilson, "What Trump Got Right About Nuclear Weapons—And How to Step Back from the Brink," *Bulletin of the Atomic Scientists*, February 24, 2025, https://thebulletin.org/2025/02/what-trump-got-right-about-nuclear-weapons-and-how-to-step-back-from-the-brink/. Note that North Korea has made significant strides in its nuclear weapons program since Trump's first term. As Trump reached the one-hundred-day-mark of his second term, *Axios* suggests he is looking to reengage with Kim. See: Barak Ravid and Dave Lawler, "Scoop: Trump Admin Game-Planning for North Korea Talks," *Axios*, April 27, 2025, https://www.axios.com/2025/04/27/north-korea-talks-kim-jong-un-trump?utm_source=newsletter&utm_medium=email&utm_campaign=newsletter_axiosam&stream=top.
94. Mecklin, "2025 Doomsday Clock Statement."
95. "Governor Glenn Youngkin Announces World's First Commercial Fusion Power Plant," *Governor of Virginia Glenn Youngkin*, December 17, 2024, https://www.governor.virginia.gov/newsroom/news-releases/2024/december/name-1037752-en.html.
96. Thomas Gualkin, Francois Diaz-Maurin, Jessica McKenzie, Sara Goudarzi, and Matt Field, "An Existential Timeline of the Trump/Pence and Biden/Harris Presidencies," *Bulletin of the Atomic Scientists* October 23, 2024, https://thebulletin.org/2024/10/an-existential-timeline-of-the-trump-pence-and-biden-harris-presidencies/.
97. Richard P. Turco and Owen Brian Toon, "The Fires of Hiroshima and Los Angeles: Apocalypse Redux," *Bulletin of*

the Atomic Scientists, February 12, 2025, https://thebulletin.org/2025/02/hiroshima-and-los-angeles-compared-apocalypse-redux/?utm_source=ActiveCampaign&utm_medium=email&utm_content=The%20end%20of%20American%20scientific%20dominance%3F&utm_campaign=20250213%20Thursday%20Newsletter.

98. *2025 Annual Threat Assessment of the US Intelligence Community* (Office of the Director of US National Intelligence, March 2025), https://www.intelligence.senate.gov/sites/default/files/2025%20Annual%20Threat%20Assessment%20of%20the%20U.S.%20Intelligence%20Community.pdf.
99. Jessica McKenzie, "Maine Senator Grills Intelligence Director Gabbard on Omission of Climate Change from Annual Threat Report," *Bulletin of the Atomic Scientists,* March 25, 2025, https://thebulletin.org/2025/03/maine-senator-grills-intelligence-director-gabbard-on-omission-of-climate-change-from-annual-threat-report/.
100. *2025 Annual Threat Assessment of the US Intelligence Community.* (Office of the Director of US National Intelligence, March 2025), 15, https://www.intelligence.senate.gov/sites/default/files/2025%20Annual%20Threat%20Assessment%20of%20the%20U.S.%20Intelligence%20Community.pdf.
101. McKenzie, "Maine Senator Grills Intelligence Director Gabbard on Omission of Climate Change from Annual Threat Report," 22.
102. Frederick Kempe, "Trump is Inheriting a More Dangerous World," *The Atlantic Council,* November 13, 2024, https://www.atlanticcouncil.org/content-series/inflection-points/trump-is-inheriting-a-more-dangerous-world/.
103. Brian C. Kalt, *Unable: The Law, Politics, and Limits of Sect. 4 of the Twenty-Fifth Amendment* (New York: Oxford University Press, 2019), 160.
104. Kalt, *Unable,* 87.
105. Kalt, *Unable,* 123.
106. Trautman wrote the statement in relation to Congress providing a body of highly regarded physicians to determine inability, but it is applicable to allowing the amendment to be invoked in the case of irrevocable catastrophe. Lawrence Trautman, *The Twenty-Fifth*

Amendment, Cleveland State Law Review Vol.67:373. 2019, 425.
107. "Address by President John F. Kennedy to the UN General Assembly," *John F. Kennedy Presidential Library and Museum*, September 25, 1961, https://www.jfklibrary.org/learn/about-jfk/historic-speeches/address-to-the-united-nations-general-assembly.
108. Mecklin, "2025 Doomsday Clock Statement."
109. "Report: Ensuring the Stability of Presidential Succession in the Modern Era," Volume 81, Number 1, *Fordham Law Review*, October 2012, 25.

Index

A
ABC News' George Stephanopoulos interview, 229
Acheson, Dean, 43
Ackman, Bill, 286
1886 Act, 23, 31
acting president, 3, 103, 112, 113, 158, 165, 167, 170, 172, 175, 220, 226, 278, 279, 282, 291
  Bush, 165
  Cheney, 170
  Harris, 226
  Quayle, 167
  Tyler, 18
Adams, John, 36
Adams, John Quincy, 18
Afghanistan, 156, 201, 227
  Biden, 227
  Bush, 201
  Obama, 201
  Soviet, 156
Agnew, Spiro T., 150
  resignation, 150
"A Hard Rain's a-Gonna Fall", 51

Bob Dylan, 51
Air Force I, 66, 168, 170, 228, 232, 261
Air Force II, 158
Albert, Carl, 180
Allen, Jonathan, 261
Allen, Richard, 86, 138, 142, 143, 160, 171, 228
Al Qaeda
  bin Laden, Osama, 171
Amazing Colossal Man, The, 51
amendment, 2, 5–9, 12, 15, 18, 22, 27, 3234, 45, 49, 63, 66, 91, 92, 9497, 99, 100, 102, 104–107, 109–120, 125, 126, 130–136, 138–141, 144, 145, 148, 151–153, 155, 159, 160, 164–167, 170–172, 174, 178, 179, 183, 194, 196, 199, 205, 206, 209, 214, 220, 221, 231, 236, 237, 240, 269, 271, 274–279, 281, 282, 290, 294, 296, 306

310 INDEX

invoke, 8, 147, 148, 151, 165, 170, 172, 200, 203, 209, 220, 236, 275, 278, 279
language, 2, 5, 6, 118, 119
twelfth, 17, 282
twentieth, 27
twenty-fifth, 2, 3, 6–9, 15, 48, 49, 60, 62, 70, 91, 95, 101, 112, 113, 116–118, 120, 147–156, 159, 160, 162, 164–174, 203, 204, 207–209, 213, 214, 217, 220–224, 226, 230, 231, 234–237, 269, 271, 274–279, 282, 288, 290, 291
twenty-second, 281, 282
American Bar Association (ABA), 5, 12, 95, 108, 110, 113–117, 119, 124, 127, 128, 138–146
  Tooley, Dale, 95
  Channell, Donald E., 95
  Feerick, 95
  Kirby, Jim, 95
  Junior Bar Association, 95
  Lewis Powell, 110
  Powell, Lewis, 95
  Beck, Lowell, 95
  Taylor, Martin, 95
  Spence, Michael, 117
An American Life, 157
Andropov, Yuri, 191
Apocalypse Game, The, 163
Arkansas, 107, 114, 115, 119, 130
  Cottrell, 115
  Faubus, 115
arms race, 34, 35, 53–55, 61, 157
Arthur, Chester A., 10, 20–22, 38, 39, 77, 80, 81, 116, 140
  stalwart, 20
Artificial Intelligence (AI), 289
Asia, 226
  China, 172, 201, 204, 210, 215, 222, 237, 290
  North Korea, 172, 201, 204–207, 216, 235, 286, 290
  South Korea, 205
Asimov, Isaac, 4, 50
Assassination, 5, 9, 16, 20, 21, 38, 45, 48, 49, 64–66, 85, 96, 120, 123, 124, 158, 160, 161, 165, 166, 185–188, 206, 210, 232, 274, 275, 281, 296
  Kennedy, 70
  Lincoln, 19, 20
  Reagan, 158, 161, 165, 166, 275
  Roosevelt, 24
  Trump, 206, 210, 232, 274, 281
atomic
  age, 33–35, 96, 115
  attack, 33, 99, 101, 109, 118
  bomb(fission bomb), 28, 47, 54, 61, 75, 117, 169, 203, 280, 288
  cocktail, 49
  Hiroshima, 49, 204, 280, 288
  holocaust, 6, 101, 111, 117, 118
  Manhattan Project, 28, 288
  Nagasaki, 49, 280, 288
  warfare, 55
1946 Atomic Energy Act, 13, 47
Atoms for Peace speech, 55
Atzerodt, George, 19
Axis of aggressors, 290
Axios, 232

B

B-52 bombers, 1, 75, 149
Baghdadi, Abu Bakr al-, 210
Baker, Howard, 166
Baker III, James A., 159
Baker, Peter, 231
Bayard, Thomas F., 21
Bayh, Birch, 1, 2, 4–6, 9–13, 36, 45, 49, 60, 66, 68, 70, 80, 89, 91,

92, 94–97, 99–111, 113–116, 119–147, 155, 164–166, 174, 180, 189–192, 198, 272, 275, 278, 284, 294, 295
  the freshman senator, 2
  Indiana, 1, 94
  Keefe, 94, 95, 103
  National Governors' Conference, 115
  One Heartbeat Away: Presidential Inability and Succession, 5, 11, 12, 95, 121, 123–127, 129, 130, 132, 134–136, 138, 139, 141, 142, 144–146
  Subcommittee on Constitutional Amendments, 2, 34, 92–94, 155
Bayh-Celler Plan. *See* Twenty-Fifth Amendment
Bayh, Evan, 126, 285
Bay of Pigs, 58, 77, 176
Beck, Lowell, 95
Bedford Incident, The, 51
Beginning or the End, The, 50
Belarus, 225, 266
Bermingham, John R., 12, 114, 117, 118, 128, 139, 143, 144
Bethesda Medical Center, 70
Betrayal: The Final Act of the Trump Show, 221
Biden, Beau, 226, 259
Biden, Joseph, 9, 192, 200, 209, 215, 216, 218, 224–235, 237, 245, 258–263, 266, 267, 274, 284, 305
  acuity, 9, 200, 226–231, 237, 262, 274
  Afghanistan, 227
  age, 9, 200, 227–229, 231, 237, 274
  Beau, 226
  cancerous skin lesion, 226
  cognitive test, 230
  colonoscopy, 209, 226
  debate, 229, 274
  fitness, 200, 226–229, 231, 260, 262, 274
  gaffes, 227, 228
  George Stephanopoulos interview, 229
  Hur, 226, 227
  Jean-Pierre, 227
  Klain, 229
  PAP, 226
  Trump, 231, 232, 237, 284
  vice president, 209
Black Lives Matter, 211
  Floyd, 211
  Secret Service alert, 211
Blaine, James A., 21
Blount, William, 43
Bolton, John R., 171, 206
bomb, 2, 5, 7, 11, 13, 28, 32, 34, 47–54, 56–59, 61, 64, 70, 72, 73, 75, 77, 78, 105, 107, 110, 111, 117, 132, 147, 163, 168, 169, 172, 173, 175, 177, 200, 203, 234, 270, 273, 278, 280, 286, 288, 292
Brady, James, 158
Breathitt, Edward, 115
Brezhnev, Leonid, 156, 161, 187, 191
Briffault, Richard, 271
Brown, Edmund, 99
Brownell, Herbert, 32, 62
  "Presidential Disability: The Need for a Constitutional Amendment", 34, 45
  proposal, 32–35
Brownell II, Roy E., 213
Brown, George S., 154
Buchanan, James, 39
Buchen, Philip W., 153

Bulletin of the Atomic Scientists, 47, 56, 61, 71, 76, 80, 266, 267, 288, 291, 292, 295, 303–306
   Doomsday Clock, 47, 288
   Lapp, Ralph E., 60
Burr, Aaron, 17, 77, 175
Bush, George H.W., 158, 167, 168, 189, 277
   Eagleburger, Lawrence, 150
   Quayle, 167
   Reagan, 8
   vice president, 159, 164
Bush, George W., 8, 169, 189, 200, 201, 205, 209, 212, 273
   Afghanistan, 201
   Barksdale Air Force Base, 170
   colonoscopies, 170, 209
   Iraq, 201
   september 11, 169, 273
Byrd, Robert, 170, 196
Byrnes, James F., 29, 43
By the Dawn's Early Light, 168

C
Cabinet, 3, 5, 11, 18, 19, 21, 22, 24, 25, 29, 31–34, 37, 39, 64, 74, 76, 83, 96, 99, 100, 135–137, 139, 151, 159, 162, 165, 166, 169, 172, 173, 189, 190, 199, 200, 203, 213, 220, 221, 225, 228, 236, 255, 273–278, 282, 285, 295, 296
   on plane, 5, 63
   secretaries, 29, 96, 278
   United States, 11
California, 52, 97, 99, 106, 172, 205, 216, 220, 223, 271
Camp David, 150, 163, 170
campaign, 1, 2, 10, 32, 52, 57, 58, 69, 95, 102, 113, 114, 128, 146, 156, 202, 223, 230, 232, 237, 275

1964, 68
Bayh, 2, 102
1964 campaign
   1964 Democratic National Convention, 68
   1964 Democratic platform pamphlet, 68
   Cow Palace, 69
   Daisy ad, 202
   Khrushchev, 5, 59, 61, 65, 69
Canada, 281, 287
Capehart, Homer E., 1, 2, 60
Carter, Jimmy, 41, 156, 167, 173, 178, 183, 184, 194, 196, 245, 251
   SALT II, 156
Cartwright, James E., 273
Cass, Lewis, 39
CASTLE BRAVO, 55
Cato Institute, 220, 254
Celler, Emanuel, 33, 102, 105, 108, 110, 116, 132, 135, 142
   H.J. Res. 1, 102
Central Intelligence Agency (CIA), 5, 11, 58, 64, 65, 83–85, 189, 195, 217
Cermak, Anton, 27
Chance for Peace speech, 54
Channell, Donald E., 95
Chao, Elaine, 220, 278
Chase, Salmon P., 19, 38
Chavez, Hugo, 10, 217, 251
Checks and balances, 281, 285
   Trump, 281
Cheney, Dick, 77, 162, 169–171, 189, 194–196, 251, 295
   hyperkalemia, 169
   In My Time, 170
   resignation letter, 169
   September 11, 169
   vice president, 169, 171
Chernenko, Konstantin, 191

Chief justice, 17
China, 172, 201, 204, 210, 215, 216, 222, 234, 237, 286, 288, 290
China is National Security Threat No. 1, 215
China Syndrome, The, 156
Churchill, Winston, 29
Cicilline, David, 224
Cirincione, Joe, 287, 304
Civil defense, 49, 56, 61, 70, 76, 81, 128, 188, 270
  1956 Federal Highway Act, 56
  Continuity of Government Planning, 7, 157
  Continuity of Operations Planning, 56, 163
  Director of Office of Emergency Planning, 62
  duck and cover, 56
  fallout shelter, 50, 61
  Family Fallout Shelter, 61
  National Defense Executive Reserve, 57
  Operation Alert Eisenhower, 56
  The Minuteman, 61
Clapper, James, 235
Clark, Ramsey, 102
Cleveland, Grover, 15, 16, 22–24, 39, 170, 176, 275, 307
  Buzzard's Bay, 23
  jaw, 23, 275
  Sherman Anti-Trust Act, 24
  Sherman Silver Purchase Act of 1890, 23
Climate change, 203, 289, 290
Clinton, Hillary, 202
  Daisy ad, 202
  Democratic nominee, 202
Clinton, William Jefferson, 168, 277
Cold War, 6, 9, 35, 48, 59, 73, 77, 79, 96, 147, 170, 188, 191, 200, 201, 226, 233, 270, 272, 281, 286, 292, 295
  anxiety, 6, 9
  culture, 6
  Operation JULIN, 233
Colorado, 12, 31, 92, 106, 114–119, 128, 130, 139, 141–144, 210, 277
  Bermingham, 117, 118
  Love, 116
  Rocky Mountain News, 117
  The Denver Post, 116
Committee for Economic Development, 97, 126
Comprehensive Nuclear-Test Ban Treaty (CTBT), 234
CONELRAD (Control of Electromagnetic Radiation), 50
Conference Committee, 92, 106, 109, 135, 136
Congress, 3–6, 8, 10, 12, 16–24, 26–31, 33–35, 37, 39, 41–45, 47, 49, 52, 57, 61, 66, 68, 74, 77, 86, 87, 92–98, 100–104, 106–110, 112, 114–116, 118, 121, 124–132, 134, 136–138, 140, 143, 145, 149, 150, 152–155, 162–164, 167, 169, 173, 174, 179, 182, 183, 186, 189, 198, 201, 205, 206, 209, 213, 214, 218, 222–224, 230, 235, 242, 245, 252, 257, 272, 273, 276–280, 283, 284, 291, 294, 306
The Hill, 66
congressional
  succession, 33, 96
Congressional Quarterly, 86, 101
Conley, Sean P., 211, 212
Constitution, 3, 4, 6, 8, 12, 15–17, 24, 31, 36, 40, 48, 62, 64, 68, 72, 95, 96, 110, 113, 117–120,

125, 132, 136–139, 142, 145, 148, 159, 162, 163, 175, 182, 183, 190, 191, 194, 198, 200, 207, 208, 216, 218, 223, 231, 236, 242, 244, 263, 269, 271, 272, 277, 280, 281, 283, 291, 293–295, 298, 299
  Article I, 16, 36, 283
  Article II, 4, 15–17, 31, 62, 116, 118, 269, 277, 294
continuity, 2, 4, 7, 24, 54, 56, 57, 66, 67, 70, 73, 92, 102, 106, 118, 148, 161, 184, 200, 204, 213, 214, 226, 236, 272, 273, 291
Continuity of Government (COG), 7, 10, 56, 70, 157, 162, 173, 174, 184, 269, 273
  Greenbrier Hotel, 163
  Mount Weather, 163
  (PS3), 162
  TREETOP, 162
Continuity of Government Commission, 10, 173, 174
Continuity of Operations Planning (COOP), 49, 56, 163
  Reagan, 56, 163
Coolidge, Calvin, 26, 27
  Fall, 27
  Teapot Dome scandal, 27
Cooper, John Milton, 24–26
Cornyn, John, 173, 174, 207
Cottrell, J.H., 115
COVID-19, 200, 210, 211, 213–215, 226, 228, 231, 236, 246, 247, 258, 276, 277
  influenza pandemic, 210
Cranston, Alan, 153
Crimson Tide, 168
Crooks, Thomas Matthew, 232
Cuba, 1, 9, 58, 60, 62, 78–80, 201, 293

Bay of Pigs, 58
Calvin Coolidge, 201
Guantanamo, 1
Havana, 64
Kennedy, 1, 58, 60, 62, 70
missile crisis, 2, 3, 10, 60, 61, 80, 176, 233, 293
Obama, 201
quarantine, 1, 60
Cuban missile crisis, 2, 3, 60, 61, 65, 70, 88, 233
  Gronzy, 60
  The Cuban Missile Crisis in American Memory, 60
  Warsaw Pact, 60
Cuban Missile Crisis in American Memory, The, 60
  Stern, Sheldon M., 60
Culture, 4, 7, 9, 48, 49, 70, 91, 168, 175, 182, 199, 200, 243, 270
Cyberwarfare attack, 217
  Hammer, 217
  Scorecard, 217
Czechoslovakia, 67, 188

D

Daisy ad
  1964 campaign, 202
  2016 campaign, 223
  Doyle, Dane, and Bernbach, 69
  Luiz, Monique Corzilius, 202
Dallek, Robert, 78, 121, 122, 151, 176, 178, 208, 244, 247
  LBJ, 208
  Nixon and Kissinger: Partners in Power, 151
  Trump, 208
  Harding, Warren, 15
Darman, Richard, 159, 160, 186, 187
Davis, David, 21
Day After, The, 163

INDEX   315

DC Comics, 236
Deaver, Michael K., 159
DEFCON (Defense Condition), 275
Demilitarized Zone (DMZ), 206, 235
Democracy, 9, 28, 30, 107, 215, 217, 222, 269, 281
Democrat, 19, 21, 26, 33, 75, 107, 114, 128, 131, 132, 134, 137, 179, 245, 262
1964 Democratic National Convention, 68
1964 Democratic platform pamphlet, 68
Democratic-Republican, 18
Denver Post, The, 116, 143
Department of Energy, 285, 289
Department of Government Efficiency, 285
Department of Homeland Security's Federal Protective Service, 219
Designated Survivor, 204
DeVos, Betsy, 220, 221, 254, 255, 278
Dickinson, John, 272
Director of the Office of Emergency Planning (OEP), 62
Dirksen, Everett McKinley, 95, 104, 105, 107, 109, 131, 132, 284
Divine Right of Kings, 281
4-D Man, 51
Dodd, Thomas J., 39, 95, 121, 130
Donaldson, Sam, 161
Doomsday Clock, 47, 54, 270, 289
  2025 announcement, 289
  Nobel Laureates, 270, 289
dual incapacity, 277, 278. *See also* incapacitated
duck and cover, 56, 172, 204

E
Eagleburger, Lawrence, 150
Early, Steve, 28
Eastland, James O., 94, 95
Eisenhower/Nixon letter (letter agreements), 7
Eisenhower, Dwight D., 7, 10, 15, 29, 31, 32, 34, 35, 44, 47, 49, 52–58, 62, 63, 66, 74–77, 82, 86, 88, 91–93, 97, 106, 107, 109, 126–128, 184, 280
  Atoms for Peace, 55
  Chance for Peace, 54
  heart attack, 32, 107
  illness, 7, 54
  supreme commander of Allied forces, 29
Election, 1, 4, 16, 17, 19, 23, 32, 37, 41, 44, 52, 53, 57, 60, 68, 69, 102, 135, 145, 155, 163, 182, 183, 200, 202, 215–218, 226, 239, 242, 262, 274, 275, 283, 284, 294
  1956, 52
  1962, 60
  1964, 4
  2016, 202
  2024, 226, 235, 275
  2028, 283
Electoral College, 17, 107, 129, 135, 202, 219, 236, 239, 252, 253, 276
  Trump, 218
Enemy Within, The, 168
  Seven Days in May, 168
Ervin, Sam, 6, 107, 108, 110, 111, 149
  Select Committee, 149
  S.J. Res. 1, 107
Esper, Army Mark, 205, 210, 216, 221, 236
  South Korea, 205
Europe, 29, 79, 226, 286, 301
  European Union, 286, 287
  Joint White Paper, 287

NATO, 225, 234, 286, 287
US, 225

F
Fail-Safe, 4, 51, 52, 175
Fall, Albert, 27
"Family Fallout Shelter, The", 61
Faubus, Orval, 115, 141, 142
Federal Emergency Management Agency (FEMA), 157
1956 Federal Highway Act, 56
Federalists, 18, 22, 37
Feerick, John D., 10, 18, 38, 40, 44, 45, 95, 114, 116, 117, 124, 130, 136, 137, 139–146, 179, 193, 272, 291, 293
  American Bar Association, 5, 18, 93, 95, 103, 108, 113, 272
  South Carolina Law Review, 115
  The Twenty-Fifth Amendment: Its Complete History and Earliest Applications, 18
Fielding, Fred, 159, 166
Fillmore, Millard, 19
Fire and Fury: Inside the Trump White House, 207
First Congress, 17
first lady, 167, 184, 275
Fitzwater, Marlin, 193
Floyd, George, 211
  Black Lives Matter, 211
Folkenflik, David, 228, 261
Fong, Hiram L., 95
Ford, Gerald R., 152, 283
Fordham Law Review, 124, 174, 189, 292, 295, 297, 307
Fort McNair, 218, 224
founders, 16
Fourth K, The, 168, 194
Fox News, 228

framers, 2, 7, 9, 31, 120, 155, 159, 167, 174, 181, 199, 205, 214, 231, 269, 275, 281, 292, 294
  amendment, 9, 159, 174, 199, 275, 281
Constitution, 2

G
Gabbard, Tulsi, 290
Gaetz, Matt, 283
Garfield, James, 15, 20, 21, 23, 24, 38, 48, 68
  Guiteau, Charles J., 20
  shooting, 20
Garland, Merrick, 226
Gates, Robert, 235
Gelfand, Eugene, 114, 115
Geneva, Switzerland, 165
George Washington University Hospital, 159
Georgia, 19, 27, 119, 130, 146, 198, 216, 229
Germany, 42, 58, 188
  Berlin, 58–60, 62, 65
  East Germany, 58
Gergen, David, 181
Giordanno, Joseph, 159
Gitlin, Todd, 50, 51, 270
Giuliani, Rudolph, 250
Godzilla: King of the Monsters!, 51
Golden Dome, 287, 288, 303, 304
  Iron Dome, 288
  Montgomery, 115, 287
  scam, 288
  Strategic Defense Initiative, 287
  Trump, 287, 288
Goldman, Dan, 281
Goldwater, Barry, 69, 70, 73, 87, 88, 238, 239
  quoted, 69
  The Conscience of a Conservative, 69

Goodwin, Doris Kearns, 38, 208
Gorbachev, Mikhail, 165, 202
   Geneva, 165
   Reagan, 165
Gore, Al, 110, 111, 130, 137, 168
Goshko, John M., 59, 79
Governor, 16, 17, 127, 129, 154, 271, 293
Graff, Garrett M., 74, 75, 77, 78, 162, 175, 180, 184, 185, 189, 267, 280, 281, 296–298
   no lone zone, 280
   nuclear football, 281
   Raven Rock, 162
   sole authority, 280
Grayson, Cary T., 25, 26, 64, 192, 275
Great Depression, 27
Great Society, 119, 131, 146
   Civil Rights Act of 1964, 284
   Twenty-Fifth Amendment, 119, 120, 284
   Voting Rights Act of 1965, 284
Greenbrier Hotel, 163
Greenland, 281
Grisham, Stephanie, 203, 209, 240, 244
Guiliani, Rudolph, 216
Guiteau, Charles J., 20

H
Haberman, Maggie, 211, 218, 244–250, 252–255, 264
Haig, Alexander, 150, 151, 154, 157–161, 186, 187
   chief of staff, 150
   National Security Decision Directive 1, 157
   secretary of State, 157
Haimbaugh, George D., 115, 116, 142
   South Carolina Law Review, 115
Haley, Nikki, 227, 260
Halloran, Richard, 162, 188
Hamas, 232, 265
   Gaza, 232
   Israel, 232, 233
Hamilton, Alexander, 16, 98
   British Plan, 16
Hamilton, Laurens, 98
Hansen, Richard H., 140
   The Year We Had No President, 35
Harding, Warren, 15, 26, 27, 43, 208, 293
   heart trouble, 26
Harrington, Michael J., 153
Harris, Kamala, 226, 230, 274
   acting president, 226
   debate, 231
   Democratic presidential nominee, 232
   medical records, 232
   Simmons, 232
   vice president, 209
Harrison, William Henry, 15, 18, 44, 74, 75
   pneumonia, 18
Hastert, Dennis, 170, 196
Hathaway, William, 155, 179, 182, 294
Hawaii, 237
   Hawaii Missile Threat, 240
Hayden, Carl, 66, 95, 119
Heath, Edward, 150
Hegseth, Peter
   Signalgate, 286
Hendricks, Thomas, 22
Hersey, John, 49, 72
   Hiroshima, 49, 72
   Life, 49
   The New Yorker, 49, 72
Hinckley, John W., 158, 161
Hiroshima, 49, 56, 204, 280, 288

H.J. Res. 1, 102, 105, 106
  Celler, 102
Hoar, George Frisbie, 22, 23, 39
Hobart, Garrett, 24
House Judiciary Special Subcommittee on the Study of Presidential Inability, 33
houses of Congress, 8, 16, 31, 33, 62, 154, 213
  Greenbrier Hotel, 163
H.R. 1987, 206
  Oversight Commissionon Presidential Capacity, 206
  Pelosi, 206
H.R. 2749, 173
H.R. 3587, 30
H.R. 669/S. 200, 223
  Markey, 223
  Lieu, Ted, 223
Humphrey, Hubert, 70, 101, 119
Hunt for Red October, The, 163
Hur, Robert K., 226, 227
Hussein, Saddam, 201
Hutchinson, Cassidy, 221
Hutschnecker, Arnold A., 148, 175
hydrogen bomb, 32, 53

I
Iceland, 166
Impeachment, 19, 20, 43, 108, 150, 152, 153, 166, 168, 169, 200, 209, 210, 224, 225, 230, 231, 236, 242, 274, 282, 284, 291
  Clinton, 168, 210
  Jackson, 210, 230
  Trump, 200, 210, 224, 274, 284
inability, 3–8, 12, 15–18, 21–26, 30–35, 40, 44, 45, 48, 53, 62–64, 68, 70, 91–99, 101–112, 114, 116, 117, 120, 122, 124, 129, 132, 133, 135, 137, 142–144, 147–151, 155, 159, 161, 166, 167, 169, 171, 173, 174, 177, 193, 196, 207, 208, 221, 222, 229, 231, 236, 269, 272, 274–277, 279, 291, 306
  definition, 3, 112
  madness, 291
  mental, 22, 149
  physical, 22
  temperament, 208
  unfitness, 9
Inauguration Day, 156, 225, 295
incapacitated, 3, 5, 15, 16, 18, 25, 33, 34, 53, 61–64, 68, 70, 93, 103, 106, 108, 109, 112, 113, 117, 135, 147, 150, 151, 159, 165, 166, 169, 172, 175, 179, 186, 199, 206, 208, 209, 213, 220, 221, 231, 242, 275–277, 279, 282, 283, 285, 292
  anesthesia, 165
  unconscious, 276
India, 201, 237, 256, 295
In My Time, 170
Inouye, Daniel, 166
Insurrection Act of 1807, 217
Intermediate Range Nuclear Forces Treaty, 166, 233
International Atomic Energy Agency, 288
Iran, 288
Iran, 172, 192, 201, 206, 210, 216, 217, 222, 232–234, 237, 241, 242, 245, 246, 251, 256, 265, 285, 288, 290, 300, 304
  drones, 201
  International Atomic Energy Agency, 288
  Iran-Contra, 166
Israel, 233, 288
Joint Comprehensive Plan of Action (JCPOA), 201
missiles, 166, 232

Obama, 201
Reagan, 166
Rouhani, 217
uranium, 201, 234
Iran-Contra investigations, 166
   Tower Commission, 166
Iraq, 201, 210
Iron Dome
   Golden Dome, 288
   Israel, 233, 288
   Trump, 232
Isenstadt, Alex, 232
Islamic State plot, 202
Israel, 150, 177, 178, 232, 237, 265, 288, 295
   Gaza, 232, 233
   Hamas, 233
   Hezbollah, 233
   Iran, 232, 233, 288
   Iron Dome, 233, 288
   Middle East, 150
   Palestinians, 233
   Trump, 232
Italy (Italian), 67, 68

J
Jackson, Andrew, 39
Jackson, Ronny, 215, 230
January 6, 2021, 200, 218, 274, 278, 283
   Capitol, 236, 274
   Ellipse, 218
   Homeland Security, 219
   January 6 Committee, 221
   Metropolitan police, 219
   National Guard, 149, 219
   nuclear football, 165, 219, 281
   Oath Keepers, 218
   Pelosi, 224
   Pence, 221, 222
   Proud Boys, 218

   Trump, 200, 218, 283
Javits, Jacob K., 98, 127
Jean-Pierre, Karine, 227
Jefferson, Thomas, 17, 18, 22, 37
Jennings, Scott, 212
Johnson, Andrew, 19, 20, 29, 107, 108, 168, 225
   Atzerodt, George, 19
Johnson, Lyndon B., 6, 10, 44, 48, 49, 51, 52, 63, 64, 66–70, 72, 78, 83–88, 91, 95, 98, 101, 102, 104, 108, 109, 119–121, 128, 130, 133, 134, 139, 146, 208, 211, 234, 242, 284
   1967 Outer Space Treaty, 234
   Bethesda Medical Center, 70
   Stoughton, Cecil, 68
   Great Society, 119, 284
   heart attack, 64
   joint session of Congress, 66, 67
   November 27 address, 95
   oath of office, 66, 68
   Parkland Hospital, 64
   state of the union, 102
   tracheitis, 70
Johnson, Mike, 230
Joint Chiefs of Staff (JCS), 149
   Readiness Test, 273, 280
Joint Comprehensive Plan of Action (JCPOA), 201
   uranium, 201
Joint White Paper for European Defense 2030 (*Joint White Paper*), 286
Jones, Thomas K.(T.K.), 161
Junior Bar Conference Committee on Presidential Inability and Vice Presidential Vacancy, 95
   Feerick, 95

K
Kalt, Brian, 290, 291

irreparable catastrophe, 291
Katzenbach, Nicholas deB., 101
Keating, Kenneth, 33, 34, 91, 93, 95, 96, 100, 101, 104, 130, 132, 139, 178
Keefe, Bob, 94, 95, 103, 122–124, 130
Kefauver, Estes, 34, 35, 91–95, 99, 101
  heart attack, 2, 94
  Senate Judiciary Subcommittee on Constitutional Amendments, 34
S.J. Res. 28, 92
Keifer, Warren, 21
Kennedy/Johnson letter agreement, 49, 64, 91, 98. *See also* letter agreements
Kennedy assassination, 2, 3, 5, 8, 16, 49, 63, 70, 91, 95, 100, 160, 169, 269
  DEFCON, 65, 296
  Roberts, Emory, 64, 83
  Richelson, Jeffrey T., 11, 65, 83, 84
  Oswald, Lee Harvey, 63, 64
  Parkland Hospital, 63, 64
  Kellerman, Roy, 64, 83
Kennedy, Edward, 111
Kennedy, Jacqueline, 176
Kennedy, John F., 1–3, 5, 7–10, 12, 15, 16, 36, 45, 48, 49, 51, 57–67, 70, 72, 74, 77–85, 88, 91, 94, 95, 98–100, 105, 114, 120, 122, 124, 131, 132, 139, 140, 146, 160, 169, 176, 184, 212, 247, 269, 291, 307
  Addison's disease, 212
  American University commencement, 61
  assassination, 3, 5, 8, 16, 48, 49, 63, 70, 91, 95, 99, 100, 160, 169
  Bay of Pigs, 58, 77
  Cuban missile crisis, 60, 61
  Kennedy's Cabinet, 63
  sudden death, 7, 49, 94, 114
  Sword of Damocles speech, 59, 291
Kenneth O'Donnell, 62, 64, 83
Kennedy, Robert, 58, 59, 62–64, 83, 105, 111, 123, 131, 132, 139
Meet the Press, 59
Kent State University, 38, 149
Kentucky, 115, 141
  Breathitt, 115
  Waterfield, 115
Keynes, John Maynard, 25, 39
Khrushchev, Nikita, 2, 5, 58, 59, 61, 65, 69, 164, 233
Kim, Jong-un, 201, 203–206, 233, 237, 273
  bomb, 203
  Rocket Man, 204
  Trump, 201, 204, 206
Kinzinger, Adam, 222
Kirby, Jim, 95
Kislyak, Sergey I., 202
Kissinger, Henry, 149–151, 154, 178, 179
Klain, Ron, 229
Knott, Lawson, 119
Kubrick, Stanley, 4, 52, 292
  Dr. Strangelove or How I Stopped Worrying and Learned to Love the Bomb, 4, 24, 29, 52, 147, 270, 290, 292
Kushner, Jared, 211
Kyvig, David, 6, 48
  Explicit and Authentic Acts: Amending the US Constitution, 1776–1995, 6

L

Lansing, Robert, 25

Lausche, Frank J., 110, 111, 137
Lavrov, Sergey V., 202
Lawrence Livermore National Laboratory's National Ignition Facility (NIF), 289
League of Nations, 25, 26
Lee, Sheila Jackson, 207
Lemnitzer, Lyman, 57
Leonnig, Carol, 213, 245, 246, 248, 249, 251, 252, 255
Lerner, Max, 53
   New York Post, 53
letter agreements, 34, 35, 63, 96, 97. *See also* Eisenhower/Nixon letter (letter agreements);Kennedy/Johnson letter (letter agreements
Levittowns, 50
Lieu, Ted, 220, 224, 278
Lincoln, Abraham, 15, 19, 20, 29, 37, 38, 45, 48, 108, 149, 176, 179
   assassination, 19, 108
   Lincoln, Robert Todd, 20
   sectionalism, 19
Link, Arthur S., 167
Lippmann, Walter, 97
Li, Zuocheng, 215
Lott, Trent, 173
Lou Grant, 163
Love, John Arthur, 116

M

Mace, Nancy, 230, 263
MacGregor, Douglas W., 31, 43
Madman theory, 148, 273
   Nixon, 148
   Trump, 148
Mahon, George H., 152
Manhattan Project, 28, 200, 288
   Oppenheimer, 200
   Roosevelt, 28
   Truman, 28

Man in the Grey Flannel Suit, 50
Marine One, 101, 212, 236
   Bayh, 101
   Trump, 212
Markey, Edward J., 223, 257, 298
Marshall, George C., 43
Marshall, Thomas R., 25
Martin, Joseph W., 31
Mattis, James, 201
McCarthy, Eugene, 111, 137, 138
McCarthy, Kevin, 224
McCarthy, Tim, 185
McClellan, John Little, 107
McConnell, Mitch, 212, 213, 219, 220, 224, 257
McCormack, John, 28, 29, 44, 66, 67, 95, 100, 101, 119
McCulloch, William M., 109, 110
McKinley, William, 15, 24, 48
   Buffalo, 24
   gangrene, 24
   Hobart, Garrett, 24
   Roosevelt, Theodore, 24
McKinney, Robert, 32, 44
McNamara, Robert, 80, 105
Meadows, Mark, 212, 214, 216, 221
Meese III, Edwin, 159, 186
Meet the Press, 59, 282
Meir, Golda, 150
Merzagora, Cesare, 68
Middle East, 150, 226, 288, 289
   Beirut, 233
   Gaza, 232, 233
   Hamas, 233
   Hezbollah, 233
   Iran, 288
   Iraq, 201, 210
   Israel, 150
   Palestinians, 233
   Yemen, 286
Mexico, 227

Miller Center Commission, 166, 167, 193, 194
Miller, Christopher C., 219
Milley, Mark, 215, 217, 222, 223
Miner, Ruth, 99, 128, 153
Minnesota, 111, 119, 239
missile, 1, 2, 9, 10, 55–58, 60, 61, 65, 69, 73, 80, 149, 157, 161, 163, 166, 168, 174, 201, 204, 210, 223, 232–235, 237, 287, 293
Missile gap, 57
Missile warning systems, 210
  Cheyenne Mountain, 210
  Colorado Buckley Air Force Base, 210
Mnuchin, Steven, 221
Monarch, 284
  British, 16
  Trump, Donald, 273
  King, 281
Mondale, Walter, 110, 111, 137, 138
Montgomery, Mark, 287
Montreal Cognitive Assessment (MoCA), 230. *See also* Trump, Donald J.
Moses, George H., 26
Mount Weather, 163
Moyers, Bill, 12, 52, 62, 65, 82, 102, 131
Multer, Abraham J., 106
Muratti, Jose, 160
Mutually Assured Destruction (MAD), 56, 274

N
Nagasaki, 49, 280, 288
Nasrallah, Hassan, 233
  Hezbollah, 233
  Israel, 233
National Aeronautics and Space Administration (NASA), 96
  vice president as member of, 96
National Defense Executive Reserve, 57
National Nuclear Security Administration (NNSA), 285
National Program Office called the Presidential Successor Support System (PS3), 162
National Review, 163
National Security Council (NSC), 41, 56, 66, 96
  1955 National Security Council study, 56
  vice president as member of, 96
National Security Decision Document 13 (NSDD 13), 162
naval, 1, 51, 65, 139, 149
  warships, 1
Nelson A. Rockefeller Institute of Government, 271
Nevada, 119
Nevins, Allan, 23, 39
New Jersey, 130
New Republic, 163
New York Review of Books, 163
New York Times, The, 4, 10, 20, 21, 25, 26, 29, 33, 38–40, 42, 44, 45, 59, 60, 66, 74, 75, 79, 85, 86, 88, 100, 119, 123, 124, 129, 133, 140, 146, 160, 162, 168, 171, 180, 187, 189–191, 194, 197, 211, 216, 231, 232, 237, 238, 240–247, 250, 252, 253, 257, 262, 264, 267, 292, 296, 297, 299–302, 304
  resistance op-ed, 208
  Reston, 4, 59, 65, 165
Nixon, Richard M., 7, 8, 31, 32, 34, 36, 49, 53, 58, 62, 63, 74, 78, 82, 91–93, 98, 99, 107, 122, 128, 129, 148–154, 157, 165,

175–181, 208, 224, 274, 275, 296
  Lincoln Memorial, 149, 176, 179
  madman theory, 148
  resignation, 150, 154
  Saturday Evening Post, 100
  Six Crises, 107
  Vice president, 53, 63, 93, 99
  Watergate, 151, 153, 224
Nobel Laureates, 270, 289
  Doomsday Clock, 270, 289
Nobel Peace Prize, 24
  Obama, 24
No lone zone, 280
North Atlantic Treaty Organization (NATO), 87, 190, 233, 234, 266, 286, 303
  Europe, 225, 234, 286
  France, 286
  Poland, 286
  Russia, 225, 233, 234
  trans-Atlantic alliance, 286
  US, 225, 233
North Dakota, 119
North Korea, 172, 201, 203–207, 216, 234, 235, 237, 238, 242, 286, 288, 290, 295, 302, 305
  China, 172, 204, 216, 237
  DMZ, 206, 235
  Kim, Jong-Un, 201, 273
  Mattis, 201
  Russia, 172, 216, 286
  Trump, 203, 204, 206, 207, 237
National Public Radio (NPR), 228
nuclear
  accident, 156, 172
  age, 2, 4, 15, 16, 27, 35, 52, 53, 62–64, 68, 92, 97, 98, 101, 105–107, 109, 110, 113, 116, 117, 148, 149, 152, 167, 205, 214, 227, 273, 275, 277
  American Strategic Forces, 162

annihilation, 160, 226
anxiety, 2, 4, 7–10, 35, 47, 49, 50, 59, 70, 91, 92, 99, 102, 105, 107, 113, 120, 139, 148, 151, 157, 160, 163, 168, 171, 174, 175, 200, 202, 206, 237, 269, 270, 272, 273, 288, 289, 291
apocalypse, 51, 58–60, 156, 169, 205, 223, 269, 270
Armageddon, 4, 7, 273, 291
attack, 5, 7, 48, 56, 57, 62, 65, 66, 69, 92, 99, 105–107, 109, 111, 113–118, 120, 148, 153, 155, 160, 162, 169, 171–174, 201, 204, 271, 273
bomb, 5, 52, 56, 58, 70, 78, 87, 105, 107, 110, 168, 172, 173, 200, 234, 273, 278, 280
bunker, 235, 288
catastrophe, 60, 78, 117, 147, 151, 155, 156
crisis, 2, 48, 114, 115, 117, 150
detonation, 200
disaster, 52, 58, 104, 161, 272
energy, 55, 172
explosions, 4, 52
fallout, 51
material unaccounted for (MUF), 273
missiles, 1, 4, 5, 201, 239, 287
proliferation, 286
shelter, 50, 70, 163, 286
strike, 4, 52, 172, 203, 219, 222, 230, 270, 273, 280, 291
trigger, 5, 52, 97, 108, 148, 157, 162, 200, 223, 237, 273, 280
war, 2, 4–6, 32, 51, 53–57, 59–61, 65, 67, 69, 94, 98, 106, 107, 109, 111, 155, 156, 161–163, 168, 188, 189, 201–205, 222, 233, 236, 242, 273, 274, 289–292, 296, 298

weapon, 3, 6, 7, 9, 13, 47, 57, 59, 60, 63, 67–69, 87, 88, 99, 111, 154, 157, 162, 168, 173, 177, 188, 191, 200–202, 205, 222, 223, 225, 234, 235, 238, 269–271, 273, 275, 279, 280, 285, 287–290, 294, 296, 305
weaponry, 3, 234
winter, 286
nuclear button (nuclear trigger), 5, 6, 32, 48, 52, 93, 97, 99, 102, 108, 122, 148, 156, 157, 162, 200, 202, 204, 207, 215, 223, 237, 271, 273, 275
    finger on the, 5, 52, 107, 199, 200, 223, 273, 280, 290
nuclear war, 286, 289

O

Obama, Barack, 77, 199–201, 235, 238, 273, 295, 296
    Afghanistan, 201
    Cuba, 201
    Iraq, 201
O'Brien, Tim, 4, 11, 50
    The Things They Carried, 4, 11
Ocasio-Cortez, Alexandria, 220
O'Connor, Kevin (Dr.), 226
O'Donnell, Kenny, 62
Ogles, Andy, 281, 298
O'Leary, Dennis, 159, 186
O'Neill, Tip, 159, 164
On the Beach, 51
    Shute, Nevil, 51
Operation Alert Eisenhower, 56
Operation JULIN, 233
Oppenheimer, Robert J., 200
    Nolan, Christopher, 200
    Manhattan Project, 200
    Oppenheimer, 200
Original Sin: President Biden's Decline, Its Cover-up, and His Disastrous Choice to Run Again, 228
Ornato, Anthony M., 213
Oswald, Lee Harvey, 63–65, 67
1967 Outer Space Treaty, 234, 287

P

Painter, Richard, 205
Pakistan, 201, 237, 238, 295
Panama Canal, 281
Pancoast, G. Sieber, 114
Paris Peace Talks, 148
    Vietnam, 148
Parnes, Amie, 228
Party
    Democratic, 152
    Republican, 20, 53, 205
Pastore, John, 134, 155, 294
Peacemaker, The, 168
Pearson, James B., 12, 81, 98, 127
Pelosi, Nancy, 196, 213, 214, 218, 219, 222–224, 230, 243, 248, 249, 252, 253, 255–257, 277, 290
    Raskin, 213, 277
Pence, Michael R., 209, 213, 218–222, 276
Pennsylvania, 77, 114, 115, 119, 130, 141, 156, 216, 232
    Gelfand, 114, 115
    Pancoast, 115
Pentagon, 77, 148, 154, 162, 169, 180, 188, 205, 217, 250, 287
Pepper, Claude, 29, 123
Perry, William J., 223, 251, 256
Pinckney, Charles, 17
    Pinckney Plan, 17
Poland, 69, 161, 188
    submarines, 161
Poll, 228, 237, 260, 280, 283, 299
    ABCNews/Ipsos, 228

INDEX 325

Axios-Ipsos, 283
Gallup, 54, 59
Harvard CAPS-Harris, 229
New York Times/Siena, 300
Quinnipiac University, 228
YouGov, 299
Pompeo, Michael R., 206, 221
pop culture, 204, 206
  in cultural representation, 5
Post-apocalyptic, 51
Potsdam Conference, 29
Powell, Lewis, 95, 110
Prague, Czechoslovakia, 67
President, 27, 53, 68, 97, 117, 158, 165, 223, 226
presidential
  deaths, 15, 16
  disability, 21, 24, 35, 48, 94, 96, 167, 277
  inability, 4, 15, 23, 26, 32, 33, 53, 62–64, 95, 104, 117, 147, 159, 161, 166, 169, 277
  powers, 3, 34, 53, 164, 168, 170, 173, 209, 291
  vacancy, 3, 68, 93, 96, 107, 151
"Presidential Disability: The Need for a Constitutional Amendment", 35
Presidential Emergency Operations Center (PEOC), 211
Presidential Succession Act of 1947, 278
1947 Presidential Succession Act, 7, 31, 67, 96, 97, 99, 100, 112, 118, 158, 162, 171, 278
Progressive Era, 24
PTL Club, The, 156
  Bakker, Jim, 156
  Reagan, 156
Putin, Vladimir, 170, 203, 225, 233–235, 266, 267, 293
  Belarus, 234

Comprehensive Nuclear-Test Ban Treaty, 234
NATO, 225, 233, 234
Trump, 203, 233
Ukraine, 225, 233, 234

Q
Quandt, William, 151, 177, 178

R
Radical Republican, 20
Randolph, Edmund, 17
  Virginia Plan, 17
Raskin, Jamie, 206, 213, 214, 222, 224, 248, 277
  H.R. 1987, 206
  Pelosi, 213
Ratcliffe, John, 215, 249
Rauh, Jr.Joseph L., 152
Raven Rock: The Story of the US. Government's Secret Plan to Save Itself—While the Rest of Us Die
  Graff, 162
Rayburn, Sam, 28, 30, 33
Reagan, Nancy, 192, 193
Reagan, Ronald, 8, 156–166, 169, 183–193, 198, 206, 215, 272, 273, 275, 277, 287, 292, 296, 298, 303
  Alzheimer's, 166
  An American Life, 157
  assassination attempt, 158, 161, 165, 166, 275
  Baker, 166
  Bethesda Hospital, 164
  Bush, 8
  Deaver, 159
  First Lady Nancy, 161, 165
  George Washington University Hospital, 158
  Giordanno, 159

Haig, 157
Iran-Contra, 166
Meese, 159
NSDD 13, 162
polyps, 164
The PTL Club, 156
Regan, 166
Reconstruction, 20
"99 Red Balloons", 164
Regan, Donald T., 158, 166, 185, 192
Reiner, Jonathan, 169, 195
Republican, 1, 10, 18, 20, 21, 26, 31, 33, 53, 69, 87, 93, 98, 99, 110, 114, 128, 131, 152, 156, 171, 173, 181, 188, 202, 205, 209, 210, 216, 222, 224, 227, 228, 230, 232, 239, 281, 283, 294
  Half Breed, 20
  Stalwart, 20
Reston, James, 4, 59, 65, 79, 85, 94, 123, 165, 191
Revenge: The Inside Story of Trump's Return to Power, 232
Reykjavik, Iceland, 166
Rice, Condoleezza, 170
Robison, Howard W., 106
Rockefeller, Nelson A., 99, 128, 154, 179, 181, 271, 272, 283, 293, 294
  Governor, 99, 272
  Nelson A. Rockefeller Institute of Government, 271
  Republican nominee, 202
  Vice President, 154, 283
Rogan, John, 278, 297
Rogers, Byron G., 106, 134, 135
Rolling Stone, 172
Roosevelt, Eleanor, 28
  Truman, 28
Roosevelt, Franklin D., 7, 15, 29, 40–42, 68, 70
  cerebral hemorrhage, 27, 68
  Cermak, 27
  Roosevelt, Eleanor, 28
  Yalta, 40
Roosevelt, Theodore
  Cooper, John Milton Jr., 24
  Nobel Peace Prize, 24
  Progressive Era, 24
  Russo-Japanese war, 24
  Taft, William Howard, 24
Rosenstein, Rod J., 203
  Twenty-Fifth Amendment, 203
Rouhani, Hassan, 217
Roybal, Edward R., 106, 110
Rucker, Phil, 213, 245, 246, 248, 249, 251, 252, 255
Ruge, Daniel, 160
Rules and Administration Committee, 152
Rumsfeld, Donald, 162, 170, 189, 251
Russia, 202, 204, 222, 225, 233–235, 237, 240, 242, 256, 258, 266, 267, 286, 288, 290, 292, 295, 302, 303
  Intermediate Nuclear Forces Treaty, 233
  Kursk, 234
  NATO, 225, 233, 234
  North Korea, 204, 287
  nuclear doctrine, 234, 235
  Putin, 170, 203, 225, 234, 287
  Trump, 202–204, 233
  Ukraine, 225, 233, 234, 287
Russians, 164
  Oppenheimer, 164
  Sting, 164
Russo-Japanese war, 24

S
S. 2073, 173

S. 2678, 155, 182, 294
  Hathaway, William, 155
Salinger, Pierre, 66
Salisbury, Harrison E., 32
San Francisco's Cow Palace, 69
Scalia, Gene, 221
Scheer, Robert, 161, 188–190
Schimminger, Robin, 271
Schlesinger, James R., 10, 80, 153, 180
Schumer, Chuck, 219, 222, 224
scientific development, 4
Scream, The, 290
Second Congress, 17
secretary of Defense (SecDef), 97, 158, 161, 170, 201, 210, 216, 220, 223, 280
secretary of State, 17, 18, 26, 30, 39, 43, 96, 97, 99, 100, 129, 146, 150, 158, 221, 280
  in line of succession, 20, 28, 29, 173, 218, 219, 237
Secret Service, 28, 66, 77, 86, 149, 169, 185, 195, 211, 219, 246
Section 1, 3, 103, 112, 149, 154, 168, 169, 282
Section 2, 3, 103, 112, 150, 152, 153, 155, 172, 272, 282
Section 3, 3, 8, 103, 112, 147, 151, 159, 164, 167, 168, 170–172, 200, 209, 213, 228, 235, 237, 272, 275, 276, 282
Section 4, 3, 8, 9, 103, 112, 115, 151, 153, 159, 160, 165, 167–169, 171–173, 199, 208, 221, 230, 237, 272, 274–279, 282, 285, 290, 291
Segni, Antonio, 67, 68
Select Committee on Presidential Campaign Activities, 149
Senate, 17

Senate Judiciary Committee, 94, 101, 105, 106
  Eastland, 94
  subcommittee, 93, 101
Senate president pro tempore, 3, 17, 20–23, 30, 31, 39, 66, 86, 96, 97, 107, 112, 113, 135, 159, 164, 170, 196, 276–279, 296
Senate Rules Committee, 152
September 11, 2001, 169–171, 198, 211, 270, 272, 273
  World Trade Center, 169
Serling, Rod, 51
Seven Days in May, 51, 168, 180
  Charles W. Bailey II, 51
  Fletcher Knebel, 51
  The Enemy Within, 168
Seward, William Henry, 19, 38
Signalgate, 285
  Hegseth, 285
Simmons, Joshua R., 232
Sisi, Abdel Fattah el-, 227
Sixties: Years of Hope, Days of Rage, The, 50
  Gitlin, Todd, 50
S.J. Res. 1, 62, 102–108, 111, 131, 132, 136–138
  Ervin, 107
  McClellan, 107
  Thurmond, 107
S.J. 26, 155, 294
  Pastore, John, 155
S.J. Res. 28, 92
S.J. Res. 35, 91, 93, 100, 104, 121, 132, 139, 178
  American Bar Association, 93
  Keating, 93, 104
  Kefauver, 93
S.J.Res 139, 97, 100–102, 104, 125, 126, 139
Smith, Adam, 216
Snyder, Lawrence H., 32

328 INDEX

Soleimani, Qassim, 210, 217, 232
Sorensen, Ted, 62, 81, 85
South Carolina Law Review (S.C. Law Review), 115
Soviet leader, 2, 5, 69, 202
  Brezhnev, Leonid, 156
  Gorbachev, Mikhail, 165, 202
  Khrushchev, Nikita, 2, 5, 58
Soviet Union (USSR), 51, 57, 58, 61, 69, 75, 88, 168, 192, 225, 257, 273, 287, 292
  Afghanistan, 156
  Cold War, 202
  Gronzy, 60
  Kremlin, 69
  Moscow, 4, 52, 61, 64, 67, 99, 165
  NATO, 225, 233
  nuclear, 1
  premier, 4, 52, 156, 165
  satellite, 67
  sphere, 233
  Sputnik, 55
  Tsar Bomba, 59
Sparkman, John J., 33, 34
speaker of the House, 3, 17, 21, 22, 30, 31, 96, 97, 112, 132, 135, 159, 163, 213, 277, 278, 283
Speakes, Larry, 158, 164
Special Message to Congress on Succession to the Presidency, 30
Spence, Michael, 12, 117, 118, 140, 144
Sputnik, 47, 55, 76, 92
S. Res. 419, 173
Star Wars. *See* Strategic Defense Initiative
State legislator, 6, 8, 114, 139
State of the Union Address, 87, 102, 119, 139, 204, 295
  attack, 173
  Johnson, 119
Stavridis, Jim, 216

Stettinius, Edward, 28, 29, 42, 43
Stevenson, Adlai, 32, 53, 67
  speech, 67
Stimson, Henry Lewis, 28, 41
"Stop Talking About the 25th Amendment. It Won't Work on Trump. And It Might Just Set Off a Constitutional Crisis", 208, 209, 283
Strategic Defense Initiative, 163, 191, 287, 303
Subcommittee on Constitutional Amendments, 2, 34, 92–94, 104, 122–125, 127, 155, 294
  Bayh, 2, 155
  Kefauver, 2, 34, 92
Subcommittee on the Constitution and Civil Justice, 207
succession, 2–8, 12, 15–23, 26–31, 35, 37, 38, 43, 45, 47–49, 57, 62, 64, 67, 68, 70, 91–96, 98–102, 104, 105, 107, 110–112, 114–120, 124, 127, 129, 140, 144, 147, 148, 155, 157, 158, 162, 163, 169–174, 179, 180, 195, 204, 207, 218, 237, 269–273, 277, 278, 291, 294, 295
  Act, 7, 21, 30, 31, 67, 99, 100, 112, 118, 158, 162, 171, 278, 283, 297
  ambassadors, 278
  cabinet, 16, 20
  executive branch line of, 99, 100
  law, 6, 16, 22, 96, 97, 118, 173, 271
  plans, 271
Summit in Hanoi, Vietnam, 206
Summit in Singapore, 205
Superpowers, 2, 7, 35, 47, 49, 54, 59, 61, 151, 157, 161
  Soviet Union, 2

United States, 215, 286, 290
"Supplantation provision ("Bumping provision")", 279
Supreme Court, 17, 18, 26, 34, 43, 77, 82, 84, 136, 153, 172, 281–283
  chief justice, 17
  Lamar v. US, 43
Swalwell, Eric, 205
Swan, Jonathan, 217, 250, 251, 262
Switzerland, 165
Sword of Damocles speech, 59, 291
  Kennedy, 59, 291
Syria, 223

T
Taft, William Howard, 24
Taylor, Martin, 95
Taylor, Zachary, 15, 19, 95
Temporary transfer of power, 15, 64
Terrorism, 171, 224, 272
Terrorist, 168, 169, 171–173, 195–199, 201, 211, 216, 219, 223, 237, 273
  Al Qaeda, 171
  nuclear, 171
  September 11, 169, 171, 211, 273
Test-ban treaty, 61
Texas, 2, 19, 44, 63, 123, 130, 131, 145, 158, 174, 230
  Johnson, 19
  Kennedy, 2, 63
thermonuclear bomb (fusion bomb), 54
  Titan II, 56
  Tsar Bomba, 59
Third term, 281–283
Threads, 163
2025 Threat Assessment, 290
Three Mile Island, 156
Thurmond, Strom, 107, 159, 164

Tierney, John, 287
Time, 281
Titan II, 56
Tomlinson, Lucas, 229
Tooley, Dale, 95, 116, 117
  Denver Post, The, 116
Tower Commission, 166
  Inouye, Daniel, 166
Tower, John, 111
Trans-Atlantic alliance, 286
transitions, 3, 8, 15, 33, 109, 147, 156, 183, 213, 216, 222, 271
  presidential, 6, 7, 27, 32, 68, 108, 137, 156, 205, 235
  vice presidential, 3
Trautman, Lawrence, 291
Treaty of Versailles, 25
TREETOP, 162
Troy, Gil, 160, 187
Truman, Harry S., 7, 27–31, 33, 35, 40–45, 50, 52, 56, 57, 66, 67, 77, 100, 276, 278–280, 297
  Byrnes, 29
  Early, 28
  Manhattan Project, 28
  McCormack, 28, 29
  Memoirs, 27, 28
  Potsdam, 29
  Rayburn, 28, 30
  Special Message to Congress, 30
  Stettinius, 28, 29
  Beginning or the End, The, 50
  United Nations, 28
  vice president, 28, 33, 278
  Yalta, 27
Truman Little White House, 32
Trump, Donald J., 9, 199, 200, 202–225, 228–233, 235–253, 255–257, 260–266, 270, 271, 274, 276, 279–288, 290, 296, 298–306
  2015 Iran nuclear deal, 206

INDEX

acuity, 9, 228, 230–232, 237, 263
age, 212, 231, 276, 283
Alzheimer's, 232
Apprentice, The, 206
Art of the Deal, The, 206
assassination attempt, 232, 274, 281
Bolton, 206
Butler, 232
colonoscopy, 200, 209, 213, 228, 235, 236, 276
Conley, 211, 212
COVID, 200, 211, 228
diet, 215
DMZ, 206
Esper, 205, 216, 221
inauguration, 202
Insurrection Act of 1807, 217
2015 Iran nuclear deal, 206
Brown, James, 214
January 6, 200, 218, 283
Kim Jong-Un, 201, 273
Mar-a-Lago, 217
Meadows, 212, 216, 221
mental stability, 202, 203, 205–207, 217, 221, 236
Brezinski, Mika, 207
Milley, 217, 222
Montreal Cognitive Assessment, 230
Nuclear Button, 204, 207, 280
Pence, 209, 213, 218, 219, 221
physical, 231
political theater, 230, 231, 236
Pompeo, 206, 221
Putin, 233
remove, 210, 224, 237, 274
Republican nominee, 202
Second Inauguration, 235
Soleimani, 210, 217, 232
Superman, 214
temperament, 202, 207, 208, 273, 280, 283
third term, 281–283
unfitness, 9, 208, 213, 214, 274, 283
United Nations General Assembly Address, 204
very stable genius, 207, 208
Reed, Walter, 209, 212
Trump, Melania, 211
Tsar Bomba, 59
Tumulty, Joseph, 25, 26
Turkey, 2
Turner, Michael R., 234
24, 171, 172, 204
TV Guide, 172
Twenty-Fifth Amendment, 2, 3, 6–10, 15, 17, 38, 45, 48, 49, 60, 62, 70, 91, 95, 101, 112, 113, 115–120, 127, 130, 134, 136, 138, 139, 143, 145, 147–156, 159, 160, 162, 164–175, 179–183, 186, 189, 191, 193, 194, 196–198, 203–209, 213, 214, 217, 220–224, 226, 230, 231, 234–237, 242, 256, 263, 269–272, 274–279, 282, 288, 290–292, 294, 296, 306
aftereffects, 9
creation, 9
drafting, 8, 294
invocation, 8, 159, 168, 169, 204, 224, 236
irreparable catastrophe, 271, 288, 291
mechanism, 173, 213, 279
passage, 294
ratification, 3, 7, 15, 49, 214, 269, 294
Section 1, 3, 149, 154, 168
Section 2, 150, 152, 153, 155, 282
Section 3, 151, 164

Section 4, 151, 153, 159, 167, 230, 278, 282, 290
Section 5, 103, 283
Tyler, John, 18, 19, 39, 73
  acting president, 18
  Tyler Precedent, 19

U
U-2, 55
  Gary Powers, 55
  Soviet capture, 55
Ukraine, 209, 225, 226, 229, 233, 245, 257, 258, 266, 267, 289
  Chernobyl, 225, 226
  Kursk, 234
  Russia, 225, 233, 234, 287
  Trump, 233
  whistleblower, 209
  Zaporizhzhia Nuclear Power Plant, 225
  Zelenskyy, 209, 229
United Auto Workers, 101
United Information Agency Research and Reference Service's Daily Report Supplement, 67
United Kingdom (U.K.), 237, 287, 295
United Nations, 43, 55, 59, 163, 178, 204, 226
  Kennedy, 59
  Security Council, 205
  Special Session on Disarmament, 163
  Treaty for the Prohibition of Nuclear Weapons, 233
Truman, 28
United States, 1, 4–6, 11, 12, 15, 18, 19, 24, 25, 29, 30, 34, 36, 37, 39, 40, 43–45, 47, 49, 51, 52, 54–63, 65, 68–70, 72–78, 80, 81, 83–85, 87, 88, 92, 94, 96, 98, 99, 104, 107, 108, 111, 120–122, 125–128, 136, 137, 139, 140, 145, 146, 148–154, 157, 161–163, 166–168, 170–172, 175–185, 187–191, 193–195, 198, 201–207, 210, 212, 215–217, 219, 223–227, 231–235, 237, 238, 242, 245–247, 249, 250, 252, 253, 255–257, 259, 263, 265–267, 269, 270, 281, 284–290, 292–296, 301, 303–306
  Cold War, 201, 203, 225, 235, 237, 290
  Dallas, 2, 63, 64
  Hawaii, 95, 166, 204
  Intermediate Nuclear Forces Treaty, 233
  NATO, 157, 225, 233
  New Jersey, 21, 61, 68
  New York, 4, 24, 29, 33, 52, 91, 98, 106, 154, 220, 271
  2025 Threat Assessment, 290
  Washington, 18, 20, 21, 24, 27, 32, 59, 107, 110, 116, 117, 149, 153, 161, 165, 173, 174, 200, 202, 204, 207, 209, 218, 236
United States House of Representatives, 16, 17, 19, 101, 102, 112, 113, 222, 283
  Judiciary Committee, 105, 106
United States Senate
  president pro tem, 17, 21, 23, 30, 31, 164, 278
US Congressional Commission on the Strategic Posture of the United States, 234
US Cybersecurity and Infrastructure Security Agency, 217
US Senate, 21
US Senate Historical Office, 30
US Space Force, 210, 287
US Strategic Air Command (SAC), 56

V

Vance, J.D., 282
Very stable genius, 207. *See also* Trump, Donald J.
vice president, 3, 5, 15–18, 20–24, 26–34, 36, 37, 41, 44, 48, 53, 63, 64, 66, 70, 82, 93, 96–99, 101, 103, 106, 107, 109, 112, 117, 129, 134–136, 150–155, 158–160, 162, 164–166, 168, 169, 171–173, 175, 177, 179, 183, 186, 187, 195, 199, 208, 213, 214, 218, 219, 221, 222, 224, 227, 230, 231, 242, 272, 274–278, 282, 290, 294, 296
  inability, 17, 23, 31, 63, 64, 95, 117, 169, 276
  qualifications, 3
  transition, 3, 66
Vienna conference, 122
Vietnam, 4, 50, 79, 80, 148, 149, 175, 206, 211
  madman theory, 148
  North Vietnamese, 148, 273
  Paris Peace Talks, 148
  The Things They Carried, 50
Vowell, Sarah, 199, 237
Voyage to the Bottom of the Sea, 51

W

Wade, Ben, 107
Wade, Benjamin J., 20
Wagner, Robert F., 29
Wall Street Journal, The, 29, 41, 80, 215, 252, 261, 302
Wallace, George, 144
Walter Reed National Military Medical Center, 209, 211
War Games, 163
Warren, Elizabeth, 220
Washington Post, The, 27, 40, 42, 59, 61, 79, 81, 84, 88, 94, 123, 126, 129, 177, 185, 187, 189, 217, 243, 246, 250, 251, 254
Waterfield, Harvey Lee, 115
Watergate, 149, 150, 176, 179
Watson, W. Marvin, 62
Weart, Spencer, 55
Weinberger, Casper, 158, 159, 161, 162
West Wing, The, 171, 197
Whitehead, Clay T., 153
White House, 10, 20, 25, 26, 28, 32, 37, 50, 56, 60, 62, 63, 65, 66, 80, 82, 83, 86, 87, 94, 120, 122, 127, 133, 149, 151, 153, 156–161, 164–167, 169, 170, 174, 176–178, 180, 184, 186, 192–194, 196, 201, 202, 204, 205, 211, 212, 214–218, 221, 227, 230, 234, 236, 238, 240, 241, 243, 244, 246–249, 261, 262, 275, 277, 281, 287, 297, 301, 303
  bunker, 169
  Cabinet Room, 28
  Pennsylvania, 28
White House Military Office, 157, 160
White House physician, 167, 275, 277
White House Situation Room, 158
Wills, Garry, 6, 13, 80
  Bomb Power: The Modern Presidency and The National Security State, 6, 13
Wilson, Edith Bolling, 25, 64, 161, 165, 192, 275
  presidentress, 25
Wilson, Woodrow, 4, 15, 24, 25, 64, 68, 150, 275
  First World War, 4
  foreign policy, 4
  Grayson, 25, 64

inability, 4, 26, 151, 161
Lansing, 25
League of Nations, 25, 26
Marshall, 25
stroke, 4, 25, 26
Treaty of Versailles, 25
Tumulty, 25, 26
Wilson, Edith, 25, 64, 161, 165
Wisconsin, 216
Witnesses– testimony, 8
Wolff, Michael. *See also Fire and Fury: Inside the Trump White House*
Woodward, Bob, 200, 210
Working Group on Presidential Disability, 167, 206, 277
   Carter, 167
   Link, 167
   White House physician, 167
World War III, 9, 54, 57, 65, 226, 234, 237, 288
Wyman, Louis C., 98, 127

X
Xi, Jingping, 215

Y
Yalta Conference, 27
Year We Had No President, The, 35
Yemen, 286
   Houthi rebels, 285
Yom Kippur War, 150, 151, 177

Z
Zelenskyy, Volodymyr, 209, 229

GPSR Compliance

The European Union's (EU) General Product Safety Regulation (GPSR) is a set of rules that requires consumer products to be safe and our obligations to ensure this.

If you have any concerns about our products, you can contact us on

ProductSafety@springernature.com

In case Publisher is established outside the EU, the EU authorized representative is:

Springer Nature Customer Service Center GmbH
Europaplatz 3
69115 Heidelberg, Germany

www.ingramcontent.com/pod-product-compliance
Ingram Content Group UK Ltd.
Pitfield, Milton Keynes, MK11 3LW, UK
UKHW021951210126
467150UK00010B/309